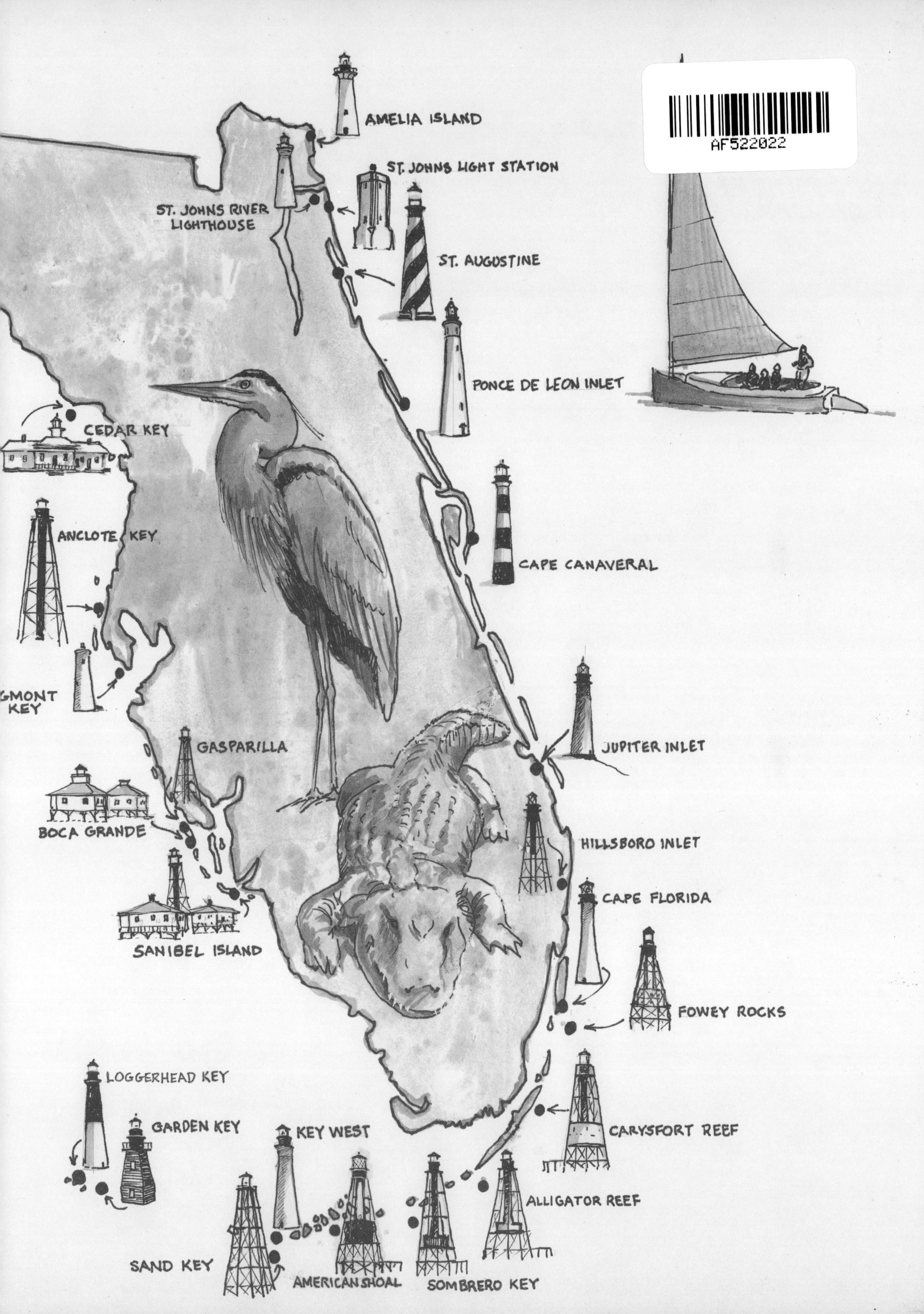
AMELIA ISLAND
ST. JOHNS LIGHT STATION
ST. JOHNS RIVER LIGHTHOUSE
ST. AUGUSTINE
PONCE DE LEON INLET
CEDAR KEY
ANCLOTE KEY
CAPE CANAVERAL
GMONT KEY
GASPARILLA
JUPITER INLET
BOCA GRANDE
HILLSBORO INLET
CAPE FLORIDA
SANIBEL ISLAND
FOWEY ROCKS
LOGGERHEAD KEY
GARDEN KEY
KEY WEST
CARYSFORT REEF
ALLIGATOR REEF
SAND KEY
AMERICAN SHOAL
SOMBRERO KEY

Bansemer's
Book of
Florida Lighthouses

Bansemer's
Book of
Florida Lighthouses

Roger Bansemer

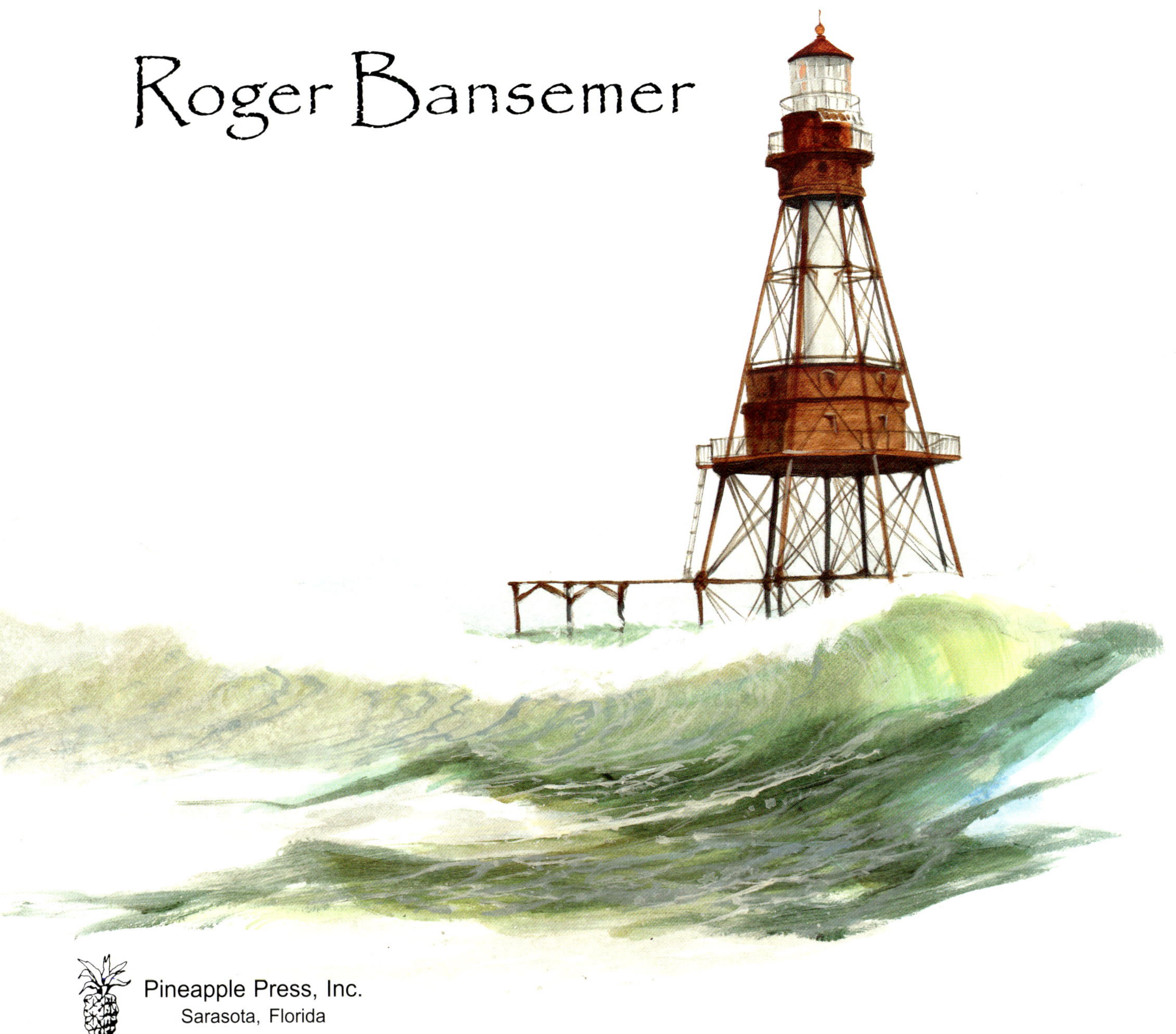

Pineapple Press, Inc.
Sarasota, Florida

Acknowledgments

Many thanks to Jim Dunlap, curator of exhibits at the Ponce de Leon Inlet Lighthouse, and Lieutenant Commander Neil Hurley, United States Coast Guard, for their help with my research. Thanks also to the Florida Park Service and especially to my wife, Sarah, who is my constant inspiration and guide.

Inquiries should be addressed to:
Pineapple Press, Inc.
P.O. Box 3899
Sarasota, Florida 34230

Library of Congress Cataloging in Publication Data

Bansemer, Roger.
Bansemer's book of Florida lighthouses / Roger Bansemer. — 1st ed.
p. cm.
Includes index.
ISBN 1-56164-172-3 (hc. : alk. paper)
1. Lighthouses—Florida. 2. Lighthouse keepers—Florida. I. Title.
VK1024.F6B36 1998
387.1'55'09759—dc21
98-42532 CIP

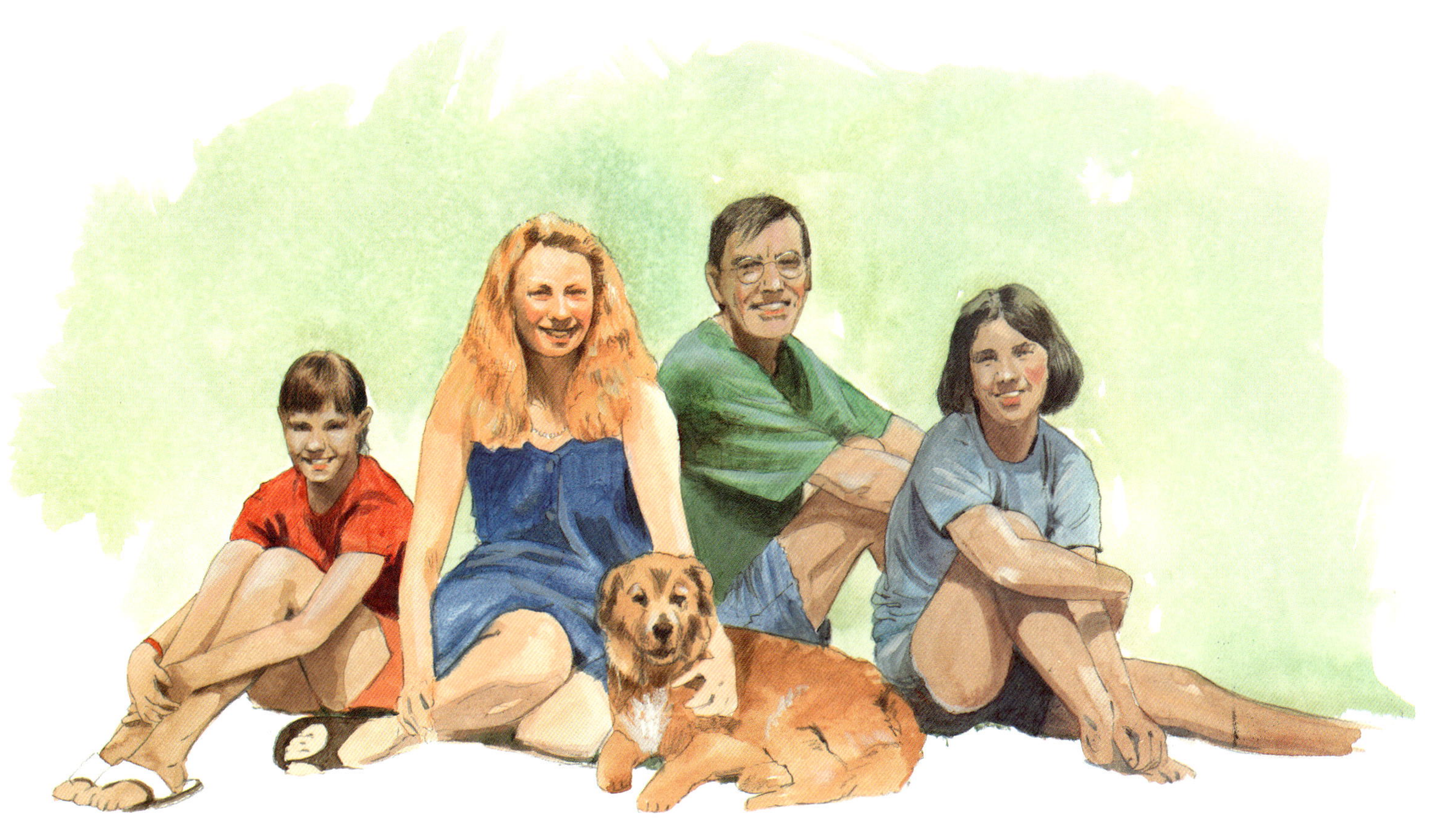

Dedicated to my loving and gentle wife Sarah and my precious children, Lauren and Rachael.

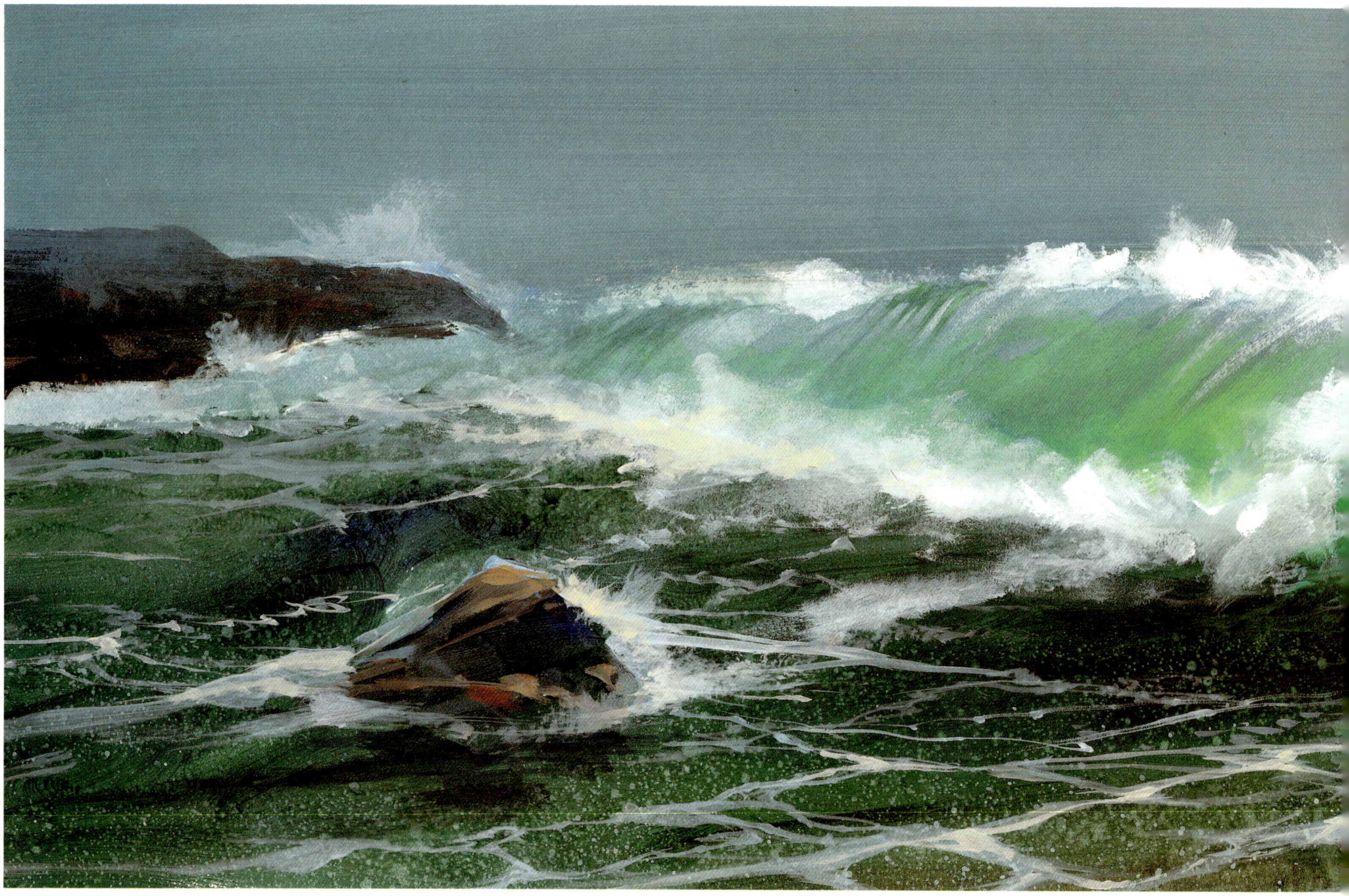

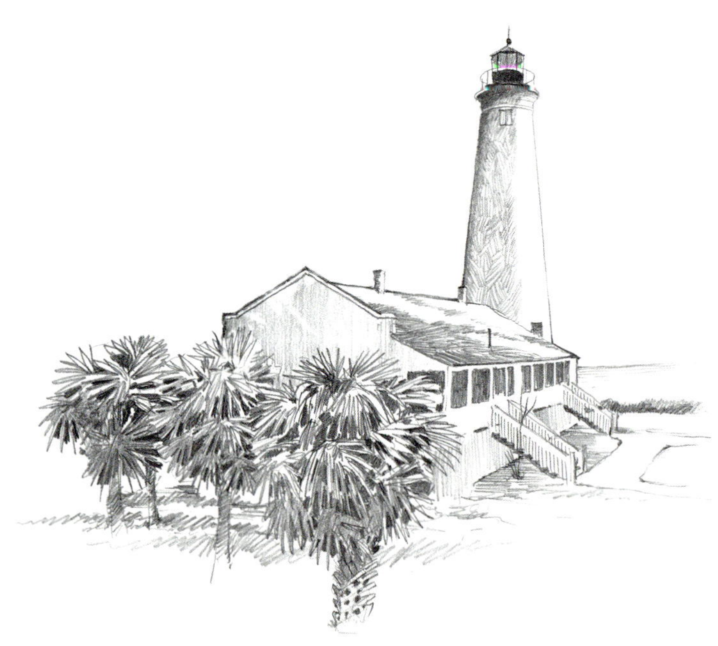

Contents

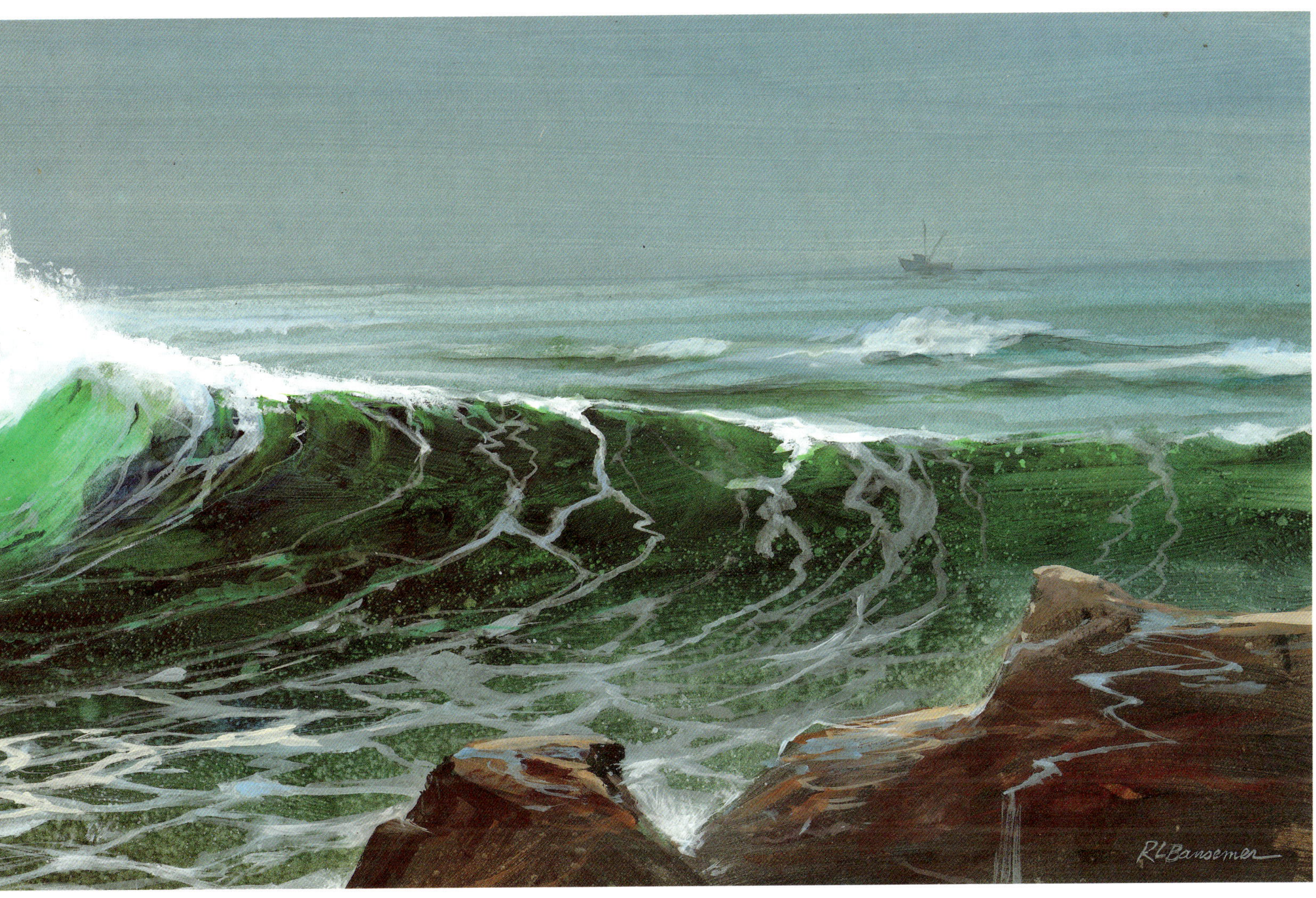

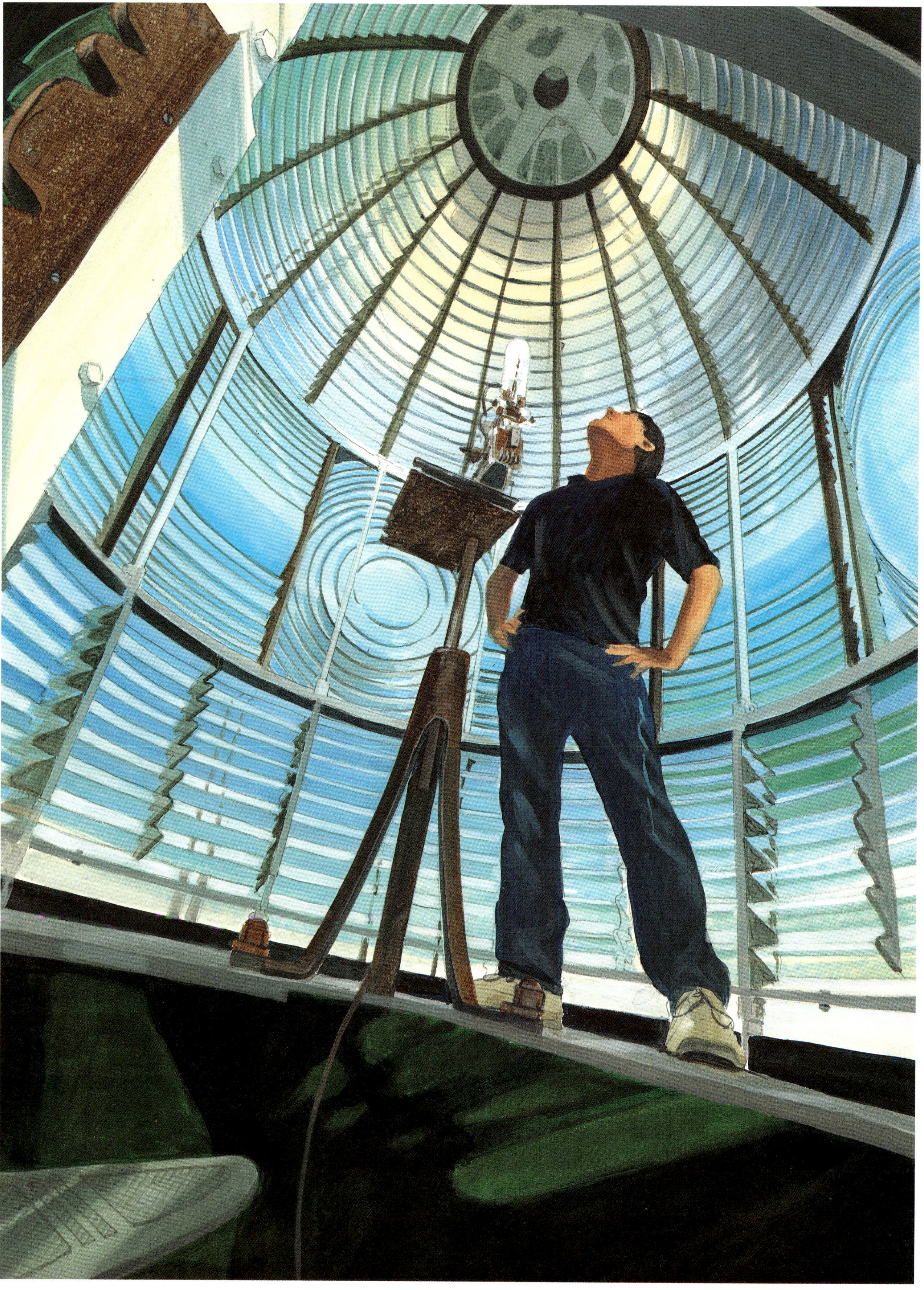

The Lights

The very first lighthouse in the United States was built in Boston Harbor in 1716. At the height of lighthouse construction, over six hundred lighthouses dotted the shores of our country. These structures—which have fascinated us since their creation—have saved the lives of countless sailors, helped establish commerce and trade, and in many ways made our country what it is today. Dedicated men and women spent their entire lives or gave their lives in order to keep the lights burning.

Lighthouses are among the oldest buildings that exist in the United States. Many still function, but many more have fallen because of storms, erosion, and neglect. As I visited each Florida lighthouse, I tried to accurately portray each one as it exists now rather than illustrate it as it might have appeared in the past.

The lighthouse's primary purpose is to be seen far out to sea, so there were a few major considerations for lighthouse builders. Most importantly, a light must be powerful enough and high enough to shine a long distance, particularly through haze and rain. For instance, if a lighthouse is one hundred feet tall, its light can be seen for about seventeen miles out to sea from a small boat before the curvature of the earth cuts off the beam. A large ship with a lookout sixty feet high can see the same lighthouse from twenty-four miles away.

When fog sets in, there is little advantage in having a lighthouse at all. On one of our foggy lighthouse expeditions, we were no more than one hundred yards from a powerful lighthouse in our small boat before we saw the flash. If we had been in a large boat, without a doubt we would have hit the island before we could have stopped. Fog horns were used when conditions like these existed but were more common in the Northern states and Great Lakes.

Standing inside the first-order Fresnel lens at the St. Augustine Lighthouse.

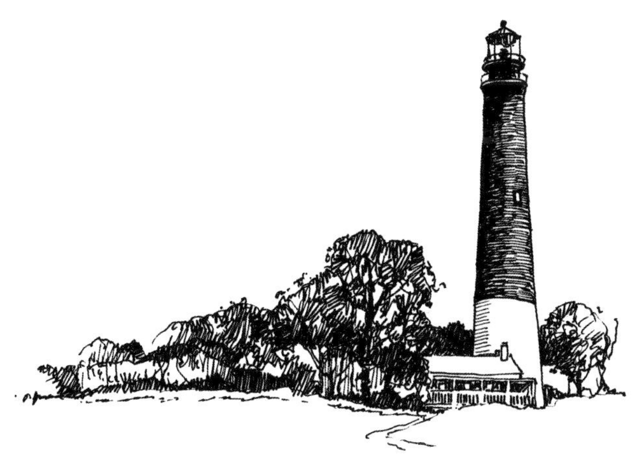

Here's a little history to start with that will explain how the lights and lenses evolved.

Candles 1700s

The early lighthouses in the United States used candles made from tallow, or beef fat. Although candles were more effective than the wood or coal stoves used previously to provide light, candles were smoky and burned quickly. Some lighthouse keepers used chandeliers to hold many candles, and the addition of a reflector behind the candles improved their intensity. Still, this was not very effective. To give you an idea of how weak these lights must have been, you can read a book if you're one foot from a candle. Move ten feet away, and the light is diminished one hundred times.

Oil Lamps 1790

Improvements were slow in coming and were not very significant. This was called the Spider lamp and replaced candles but made lots of smoke and soot. Its large wicks protruded up from a reservoir of refined oil made from the blubber of a sperm whale. The Boston Harbor lighthouse was the first in the United States to use it.

Wicks

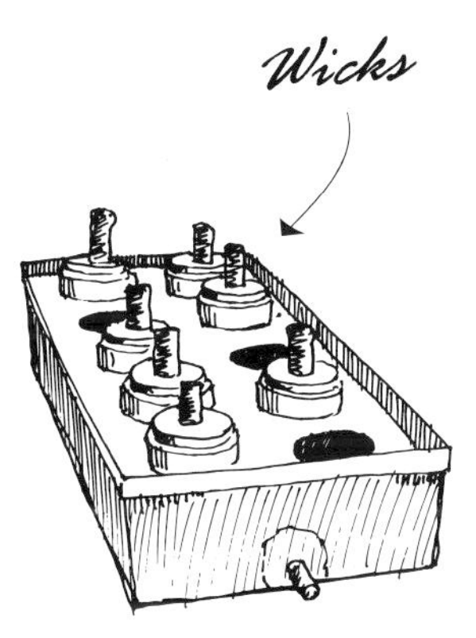

Argand Lamp 1812

Actually invented in 1781, the United States didn't put the Argand lamp into use until 1812. Named for the Swiss physicist who invented it, this design used a hollow circular wick. This allowed for more oxygen to pass along the inside and outside of the wick, creating a brighter flame and less soot buildup. One Argand lamp produced the light of seven candles. The development of the glass chimney was a significant improvement because it allowed for controlled ventilation of the flame, which produced a brighter and cleaner-burning light.

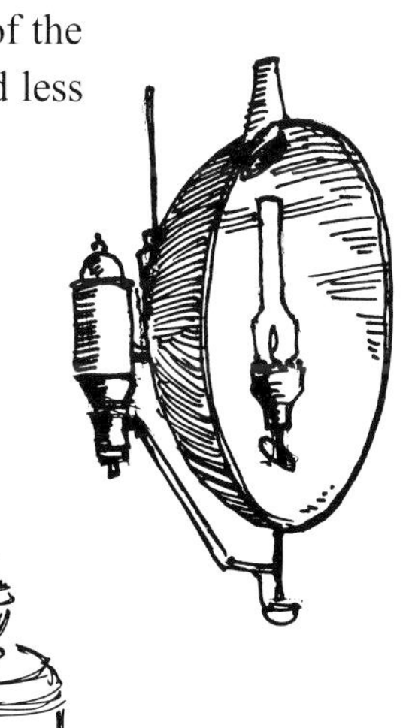

Lewis Lamp 1812

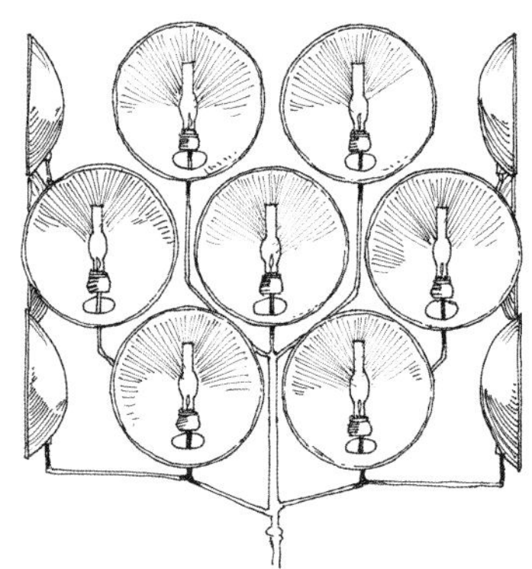

The Lewis lamp was adapted from the Argand lamp and put in use at the same time. It was a sort of chandelier grouping of Argand lamps with reflectors on the back of each lamp and a lens in front. Some of the chandeliers revolved, providing a flashing characteristic. By 1815, all of the lighthouses in the United States had been outfitted with Lewis lamps. Unfortunately, they weren't constructed very well: the flimsy reflector soon became misshapened and its silver coating quickly wore off, and, worst of all, the greenish glass bulls-eye lens actually absorbed so much light from the lamps that it dimmed rather than magnified the lamps' intensity. Politics had a lot to do with the Lewis lamp's staying in use as long as it did; some were still being used up until the Civil War. Although there isn't very much reference material available about these lamps, they looked something like this.

Fresnel Lens 1822

Invented in 1822, the Fresnel (pronounced *freh-NEL)* lens was not put into serious use in the United States until 1852. It proved to be the single most important advancement in lighthouse technology and made the Lewis lamp obsolete. A single Argand lamp in conjunction with the Fresnel lens outshone the chandelier arrangement of multiple lights from the Lewis lamp. An Argand lamp that shone the equivalent of one hundred and fifty candles could, with the aid of a Fresnel lens, magnify that light to over thirty-three thousand candlepower. The Fresnel lens was really the answer to the problem of shining lights far out to sea.

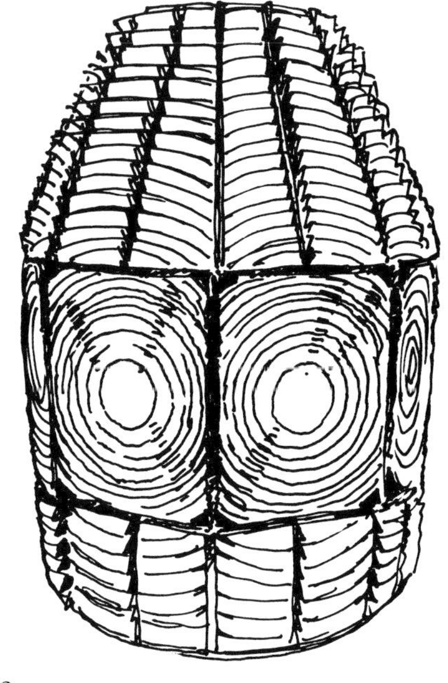

Frenchman Augustin Fresnel perfected the lens that bears his name and to this day remains the standard of excellence in lighthouse lenses. Early in life, Fresnel was frail and ill; he was also a poor student and found it difficult to master even his native language. However, he excelled in geometry and mathematics. His Fresnel lens was so perfectly made that today, with all our technology, it cannot be duplicated. The precise formula for the pure and highly polished Fresnel glass was kept secret and unfortunately destroyed in France during World War II. Despite his handicaps, Augustin Fresnel, who died at the age of thirty-nine, is known around the world for his accomplishment.

Fresnel lenses came in several sizes. The first-order Fresnel lens was the largest, weighing several thousand pounds and standing twelve feet high not including the base. It was so large, you could walk inside it. The lenses got consecutively smaller down to the sixth-order lens, which stands only eighteen inches tall. Variations were also developed, such as the huge clamshell lens used at the Hillsboro Inlet and Cape San Blas Lighthouses, and a smaller lens called the third-and-a-half-order lens.

The earliest Fresnel lenses were fixed and didn't rotate. Later, however, it was necessary for the lights to revolve to produce a flash so mariners could distinguish lighthouses from lights in the growing cities. In addition, lighthouses needed different flash characteristics so they wouldn't be confused for one another.

The Fresnel lens was turned by a clockwork mechanism attached to a heavy weight that hung down into the lighthouse tower below. Every two to four hours, or even more frequently, it had to be cranked back up in order for the light to keep turning. The principle of the Fresnel lens is used in many items today such as headlights, taillights, traffic lights, and even those flat magnifiers you see on the back of motor homes to give the driver a wide view.

New Lamps 1850s

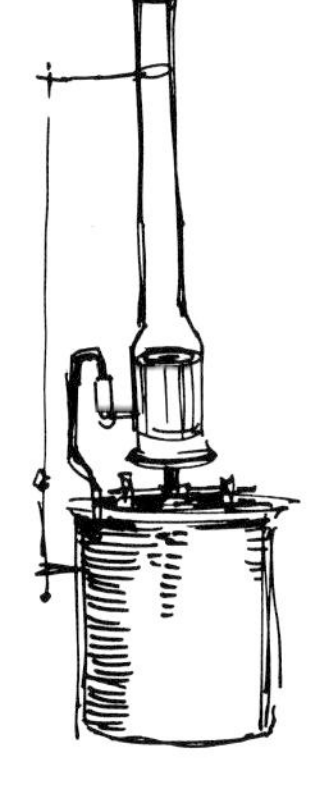

The Argand lamp saw improvements during this period. New versions used several circular-shaped wicks, one inside the other, making the light much brighter. Many different lamp fuels came into use at this time as whale oil became more expensive and harder to get. Coal and olive, fish, shark, seal, and even porpoise oils were tried but with poor results. Colza oil, made from wild cabbage, was used for a while, and farmers were encouraged to grow the plant, but it didn't catch on. Lard oil was finally adopted as the standard because it was both cheap and efficient.

Kerosene Lamps 1878

A new fuel called mineral oil, commonly known to us as kerosene, was adopted as the best fuel to burn in lighthouse lanterns. It burned brighter and cleaner than any previous fuel.

I.O.V. Lamps 1910

Oil wick lamps that used kerosene started to become obsolete around 1910, when many lighthouses began to switch over to the incandescent oil vapor system, called the I.O.V lamp. This type of lamp still used kerosene but instead of a simple wick, kerosene was forced under pressure into a hot chamber and was vaporized. Then it was driven through small holes where the fuel was ignited. It was very much like today's campers' lantern. A clean, white-hot flame and a light much stronger than anything before it were the result. This innovation also made trimming the wick every couple of hours unnecessary and soot was less of a problem that it had been previously.

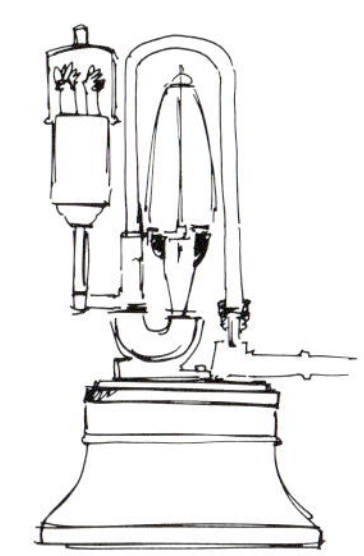

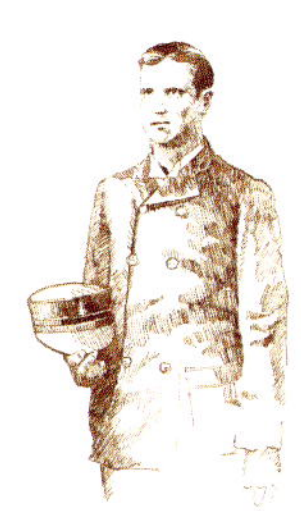

Lighthouse keepers still had to clean the lenses even though the lamps burned cleaner. It was part of the keepers' daily chores. To clean the glass, they used spirits of wine—known to us as vinegar, which, by the way, still makes a great glass cleaner if you can stand the smell. As often as once a week, the glass prisms of the Fresnel lens would be buffed with rouge. Since a Fresnel lens was so expensive—costing from five to ten thousand dollars back in the mid 1800s—keepers were required to wear linen aprons to prevent their rough woolen uniforms and metal buttons from scratching the precious lens glass.

Hot and heavy wool doesn't seem to be a very practical material to wear in the South, but it was the common material of the day. It was rugged and long-wearing, and also shed water to some degree, so it provided some protection from the rain. More than that, it was readily available. Soldiers in the Civil War wore it for the same reasons.

Electricity 1920s

Acetylene lights were used for a time and were very reliable for unmanned operation and had such automatic features as a sun valve to turn the light on at dusk and off at dawn. Acetylene gave way to the advent of electricity and the automatic lamp changer, which essentially made lighthouse keepers obsolete. Most automatic lamp changers used two thousand-watt lamps; when one lamp burned out, a spring automatically swiveled the second one into place. By the 1920s and 1930s, most lighthouses had been converted to electricity. The electric light needed little attention since it burned no oil and gave off no smoke to dirty the lens. If a timer was used to turn on the light at night, the keeper's job was reduced to a bare minimum. Only weekly or quarterly visits were then necessary.

Most lighthouses in the United States became automated in the late sixties, and all have been maintained by the United States Coast Guard since 1939. The days of the lighthouse keeper—who had once had such a huge part in establishing commerce in our country—finally became a thing of the past.

Aero-marine Beacons 1960s

Today, rather uninteresting-looking aero-marine beacons have replaced many of the traditional Fresnel lenses. These beacons use the automatic lamp changer and come in a variety of sizes and shapes. Some have a clear glass front and a large polished reflector in back, while others use a thin, plastic Fresnel lens in the front. The intensity of these lights can reach into the millions of candlepower, a far cry from the dim lights of the past.

Aero-Marine Beacon

Lighthouses had a hard time keeping up with the electronic age as well. As early as the 1940s, radio beacons that transmitted a short Morse code signal were placed in lighthouses. Ships equipped with a special radio direction finder could hone in on the signal and locate their position.

Marine Beacon

Global Positioning System 1990s

The massive lighthouse structure, with all its support equipment and personnel, has in many ways been reduced to a inexpensive gadget small enough to fit in the palm of your hand. Developed by the military and known as the Global Positioning System, or GPS, it works by picking up three or four signals from various satellites and gives mariners, drivers of automobiles, and even hikers precise information about their position within a few yards, as well as their direction, speed, and even altitude. In addition, ships' radar can show rain quite clearly, and weather information is always available over the radio via the National Weather Service.

Even with all these sophisticated and readily available marvels, the mariners I've talked to still find it comforting when they're sailing the seas to see that flashing beacon or tall tower. Hopefully, the lighthouses that still exist will continue to be an aid and comfort not only to mariners, but also to all of us who treasure the beauty and rich heritage of our lighthouses.

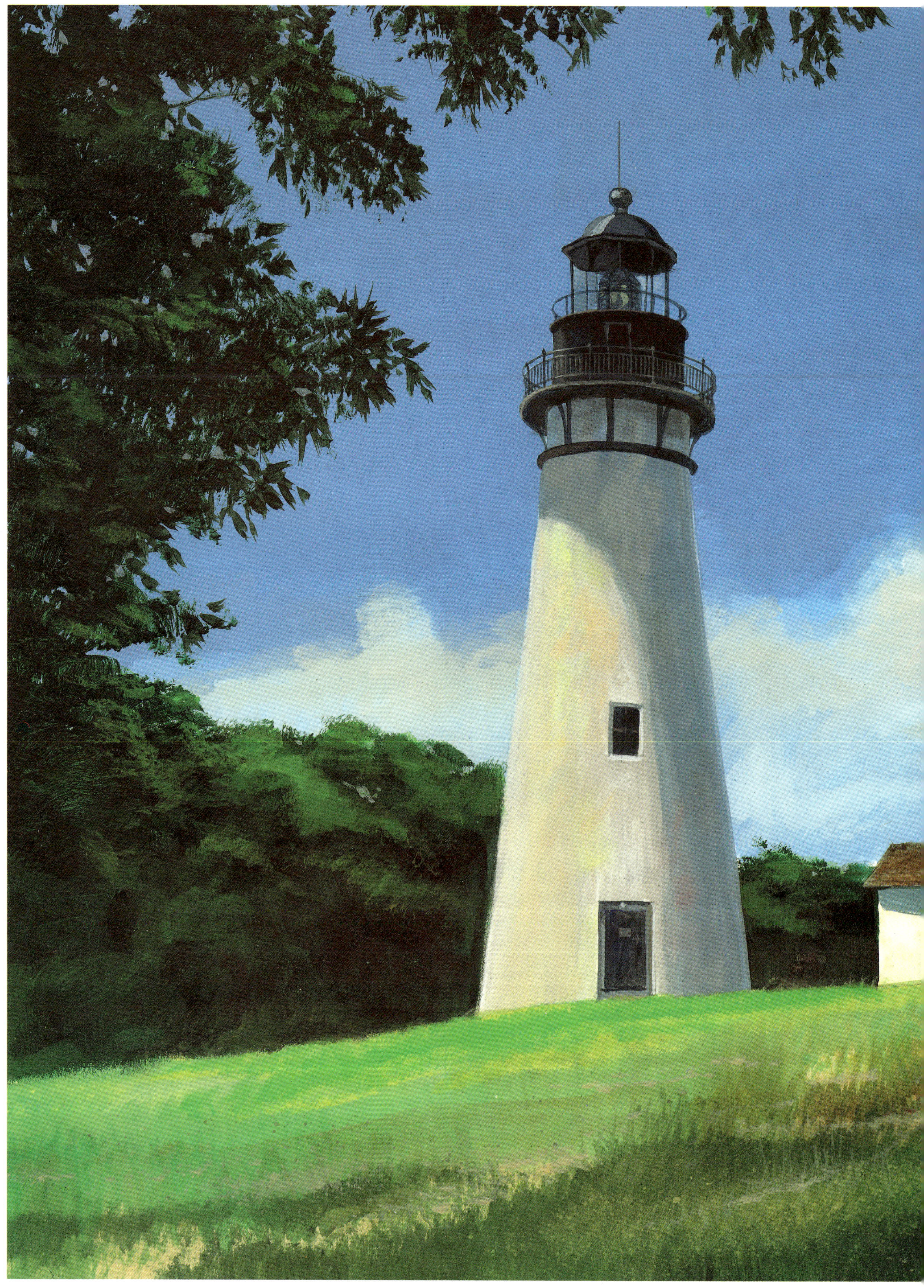

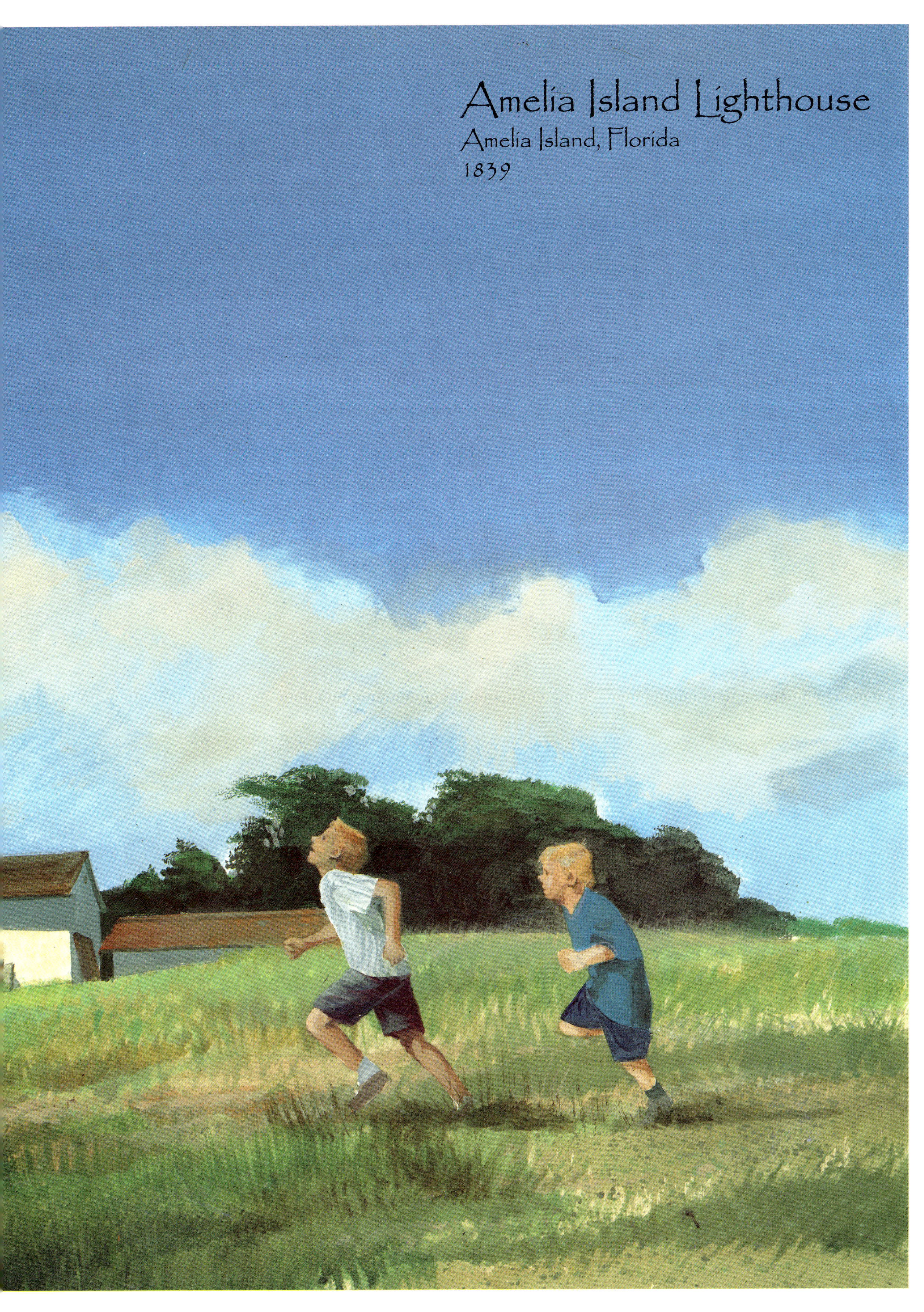

Amelia Island Lighthouse

Amelia Island, Florida

1839

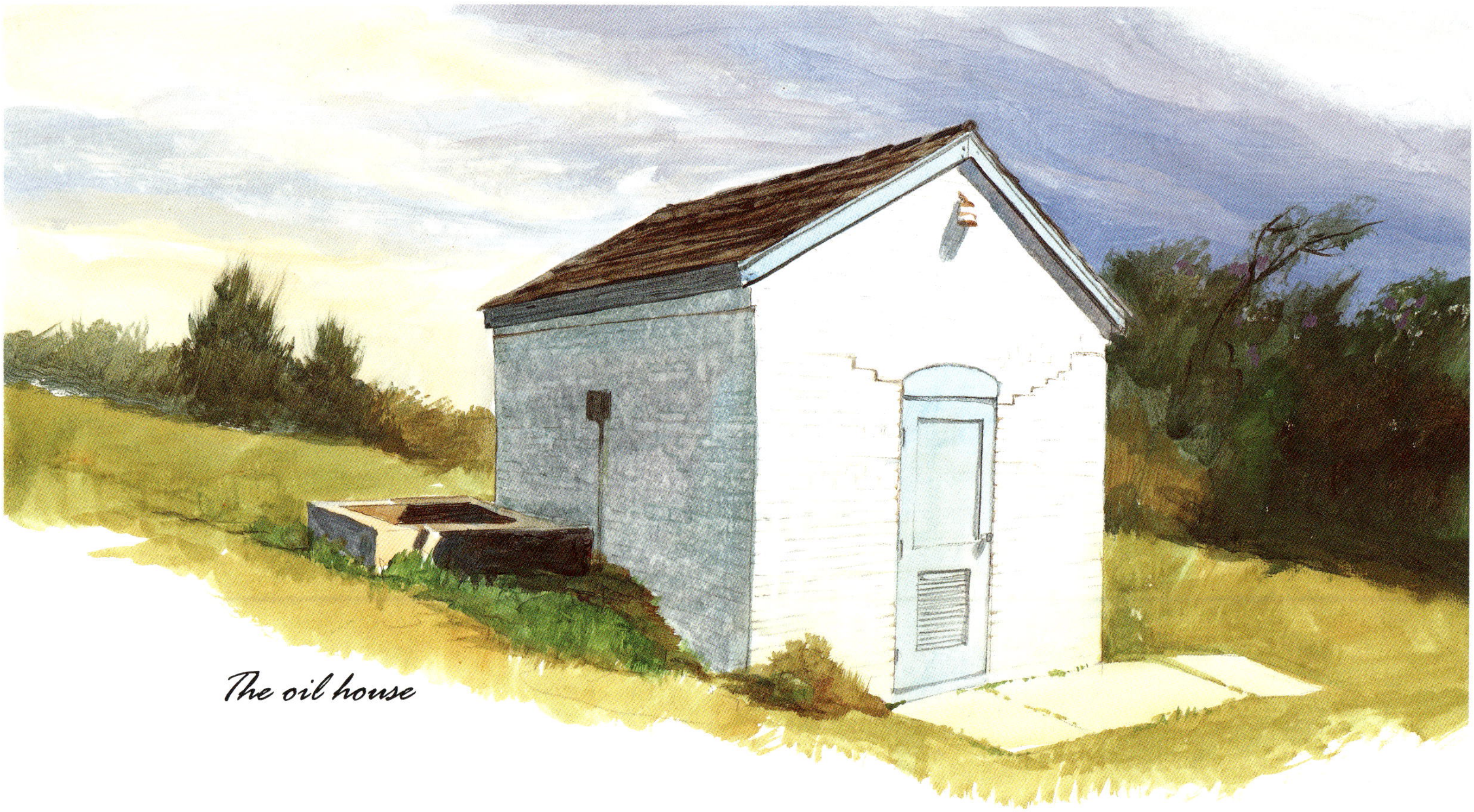

The oil house

Amelia Island marks the mouth of the St. Marys River, which is surrounded by thousands of acres of peaceful marshland. But during the early 1800s, slave trading, piracy, and smuggling were common in this area of Florida. The Victorian lighthouse built on this island was used to guide not only legitimate ships down the Atlantic coast, but also many slave ships into this area for their illegal trade. As many as one hundred fifty slaves were crowded into a single schooner with unspeakable conditions. Some history books say that one thousand slaves were brought in a year, but the real numbers are hard to know for sure. Rumors of Indian attacks were widely spread by traders at that time in order to keep people away from areas where slaves were brought in.

As the smugglers' trade fell off, it was replaced with other commerce such as lumber, fishing, shrimping, phosphate, and military supplies. Then, in the 1850s, the very first cross-state railway was built connecting Amelia Island and San Fernandina on the east coast of Florida with Cedar Key on the west coast, allowing the area to prosper. Jacksonville overshadowed this region with its larger port, however, and the area never developed as was hoped.

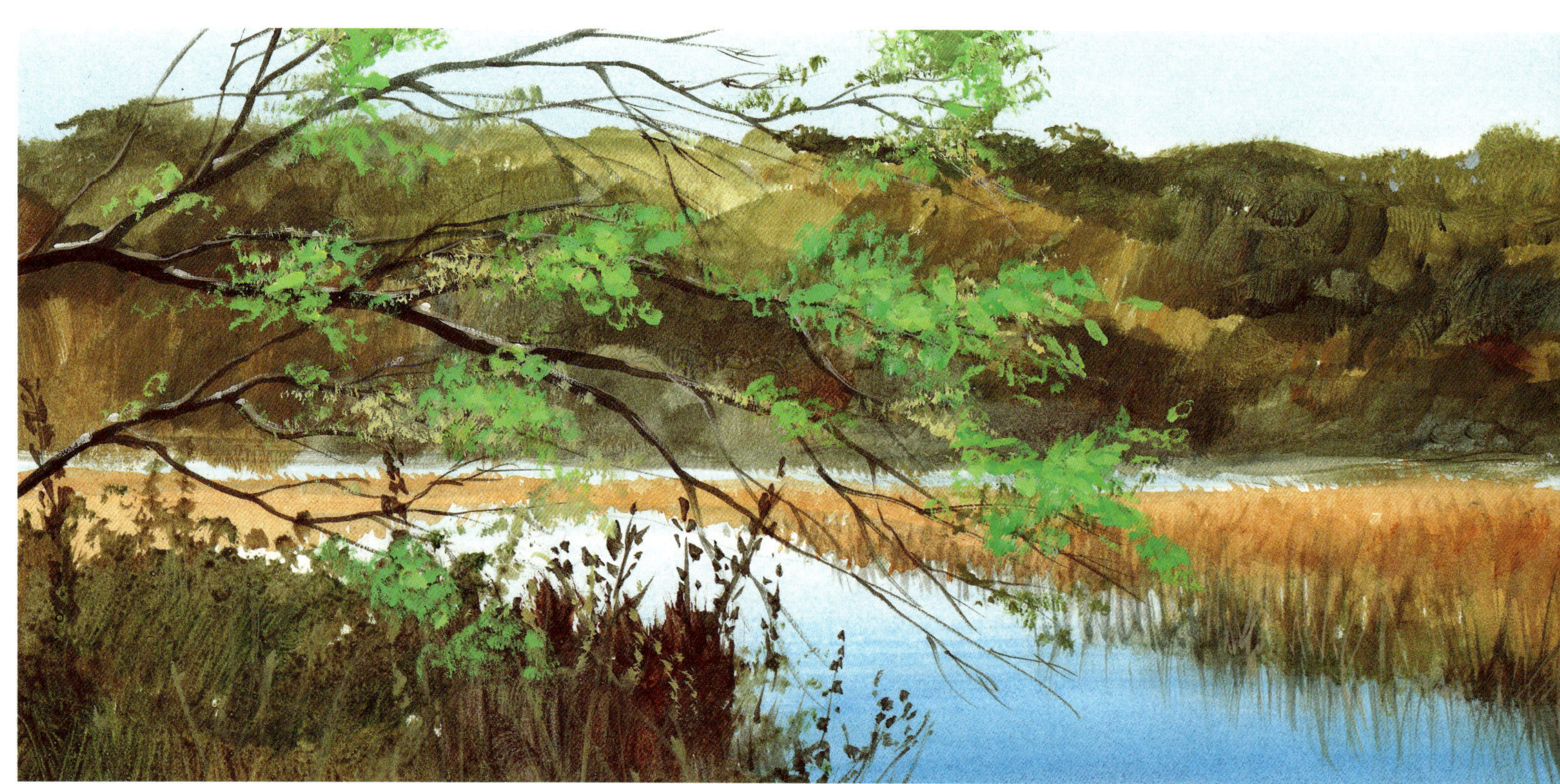

The sixty-four-foot lighthouse is well inland as lighthouses go and sits atop a fifty-foot hill. All the bricks used in the construction of the Amelia Island Lighthouse were taken from the one at Cumberland Island built in 1820. Concrete wasn't very good back then so chipping it off the bricks was easier than it would be today, especially with cheap labor.

The lighthouse is in a residential area and not open to the public, but you can get a good look at it from the edge of the property. There are no fences surrounding the lighthouse, and the customary "No Trespassing" sign is the only thing preventing anyone from walking onto the grounds. You can also get a nice view of the lighthouse from Atlantic Avenue. A few miles away is the town of Fernandina Beach. It's a lovely place to spend an afternoon, with its working shrimp boats, quaint shops, and restaurants.

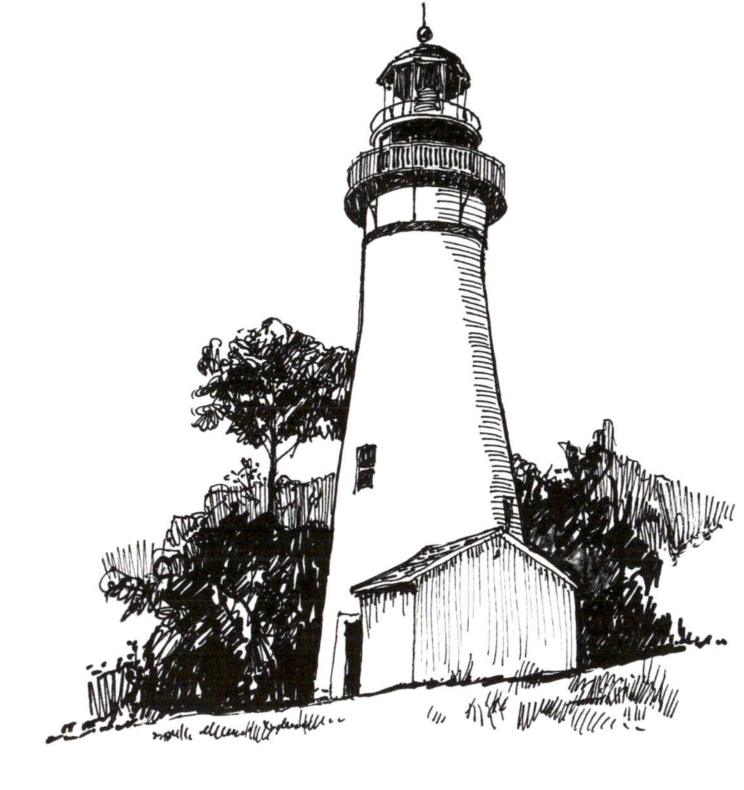

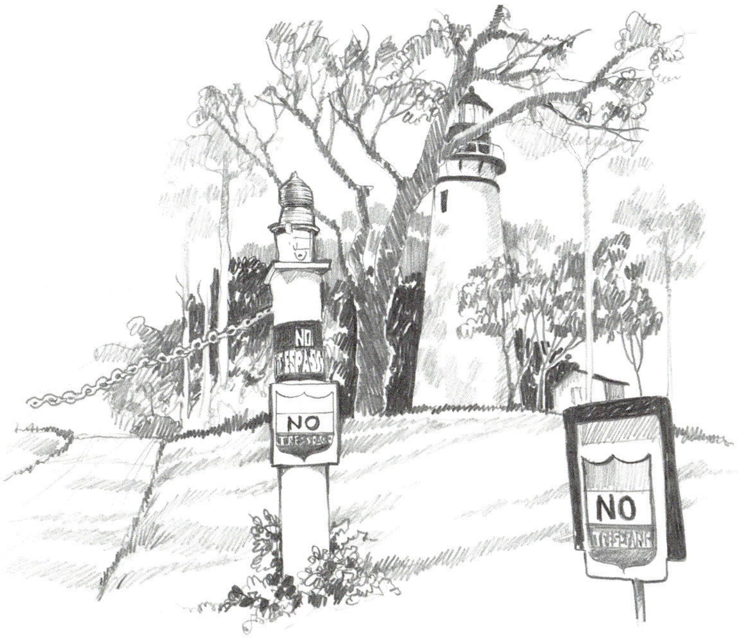

Only three lighthouses in Florida have granite stairs inside: Amelia Island, St. Johns River, and Loggerhead Key.

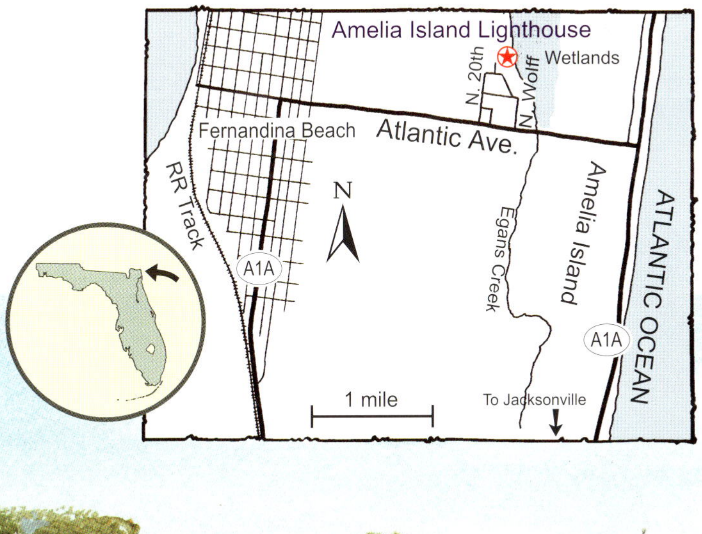

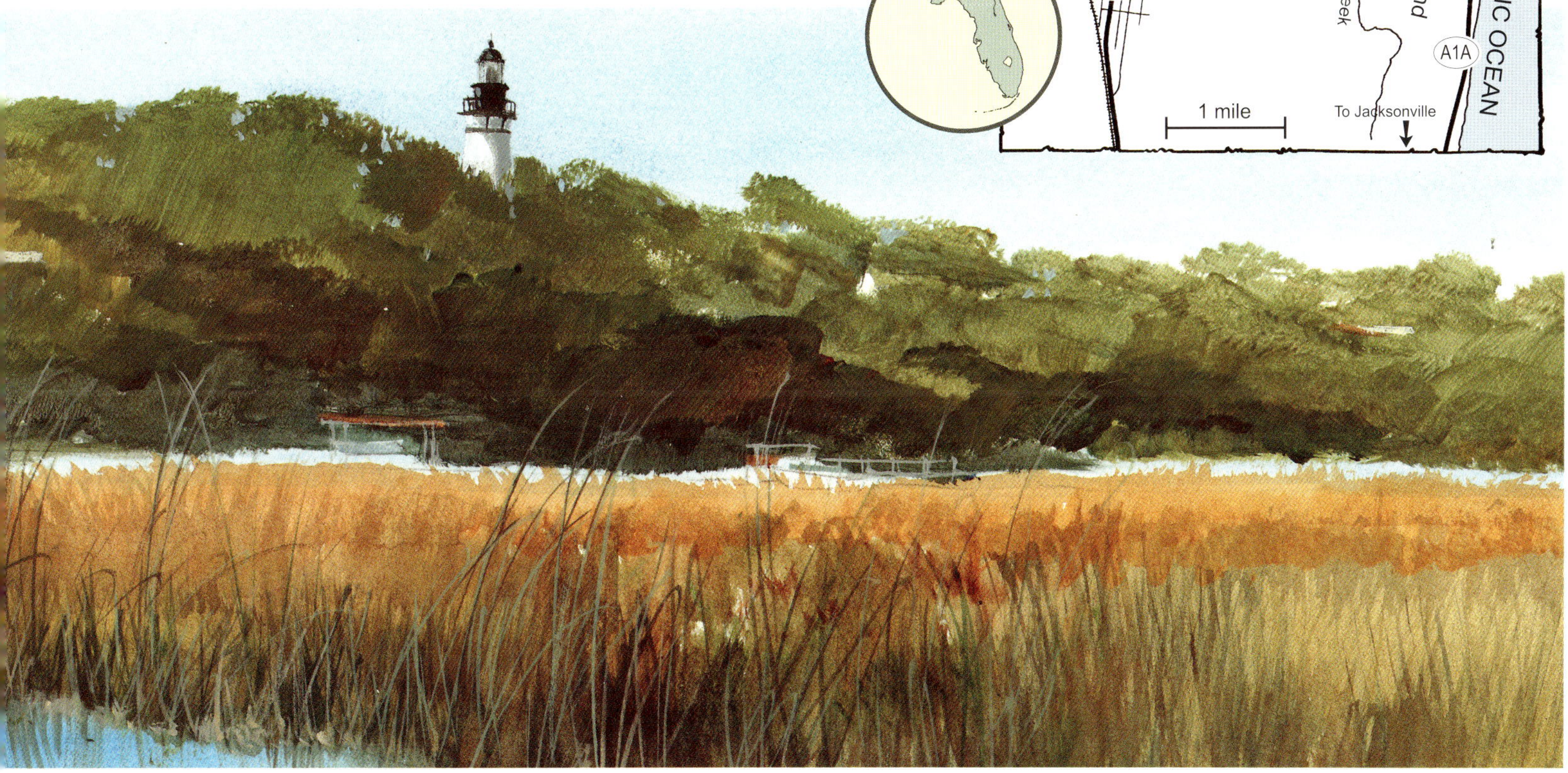

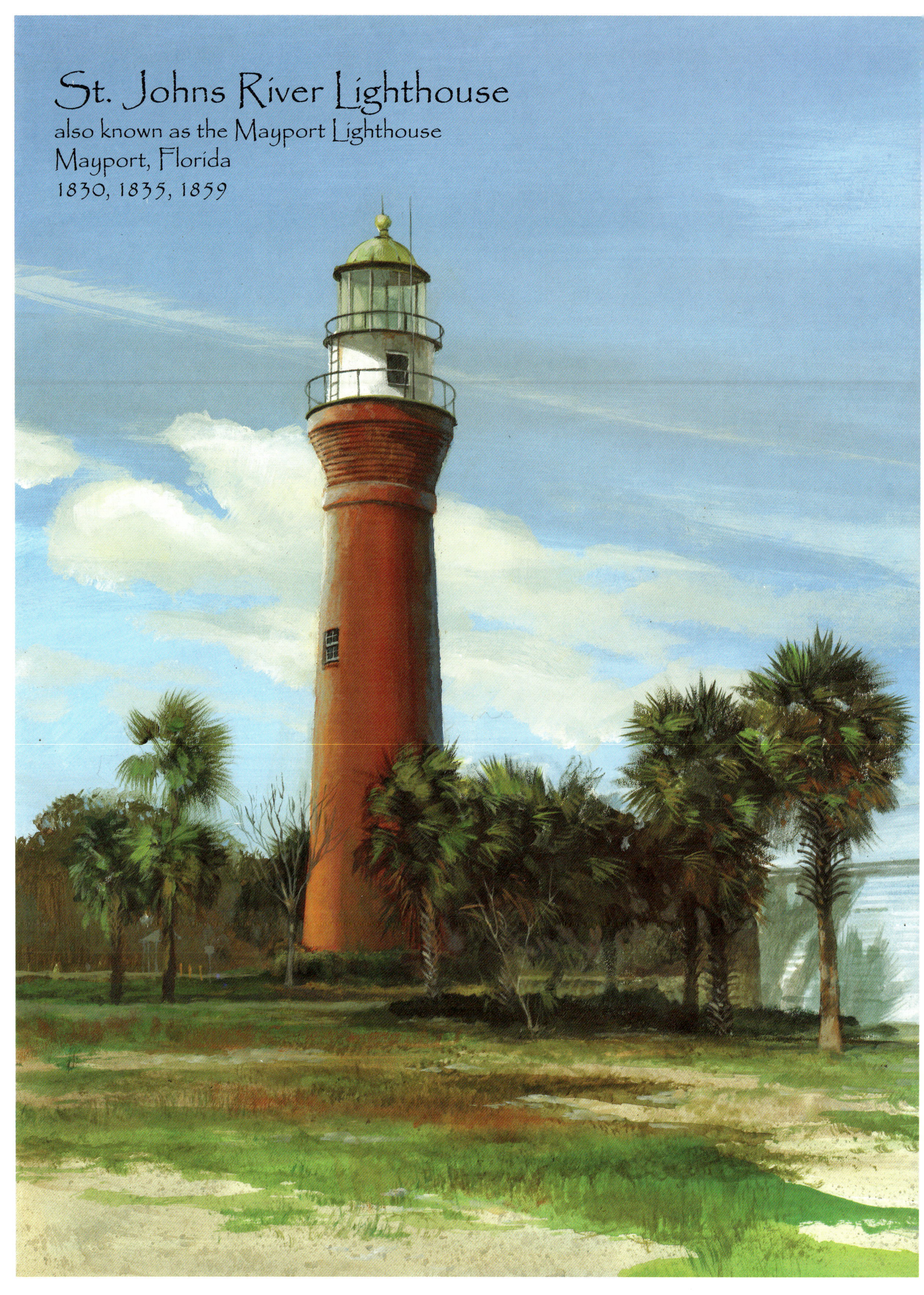

St. Johns River Lighthouse
also known as the Mayport Lighthouse
Mayport, Florida
1830, 1835, 1859

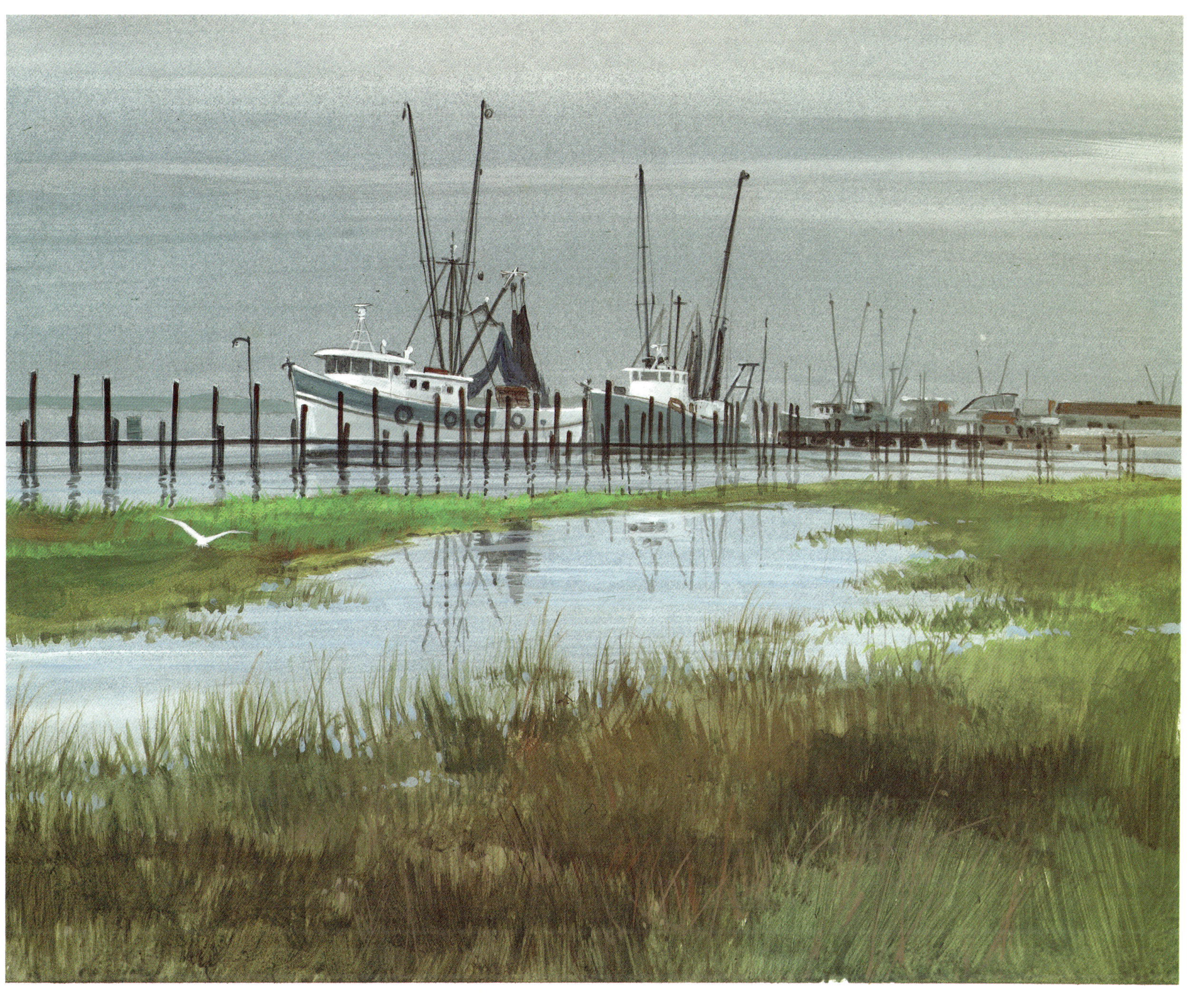

Near the lighthouse, these shrimp boats make the small town of Mayport an interesting place to visit and an even better place to have some lunch with seafood fresh from the boat.

Back when I was a young man in the early seventies, I was stationed in Mayport onboard the aircraft carrier USS *Franklin D. Roosevelt.* Living on an aircraft carrier was not what I remember as the highlight of my life, but I considered myself fortunate to be heading to the Mediterranean instead of to Vietnam. I was just a number and lost among the four thousand other men onboard the carrier. I served my time, painting and sketching when I could, and I remember casually looking at the lighthouse here on the naval base while in port, occasionally making a sketch or two. The lighthouse was insignificant to a sailor like me back then at the age of twenty, but to the many early mariners whose job it was to guide their ships safely into port, these lighthouses were a vital and important part of seafaring. To me, they were simply romantic images and remain so today.

The scenery around the lighthouse has changed completely since the St. Johns River Lighthouse was built in the 1800s when the area was quite desolate, but I could see little difference from a couple of decades ago when I served there. The correct name for the lighthouse is the St. Johns River Lighthouse but everyone in the area knows it as the Mayport Lighthouse. It remains proud but insignificant, lost among the powerful jet fighters, aircraft carriers, and destroyers—a forgotten relic of the past that stands only because of our concern for its history.

The original door to the lighthouse can't be seen. It sits below the current level of the landscape. This came about when the Navy graded and raised the area for the nearby runway, burying the lower 15 feet of the lighthouse. You can still see the ghostly outline of where a building was attached to the tower.

The St. Johns River is interesting as rivers go, and it goes north. Very few rivers in the Northern Hemisphere flow in that direction. It empties out into the Atlantic at the Mayport Naval Station not far from Jacksonville. There were several lighthouses built here in Mayport long before the naval base. The first one was built in 1830, fifteen years before Florida even became a state. An encroaching ocean required that it be torn down, and another one was built in 1835. It too was undermined and destroyed by the sea. Then in 1859 this lighthouse was built.

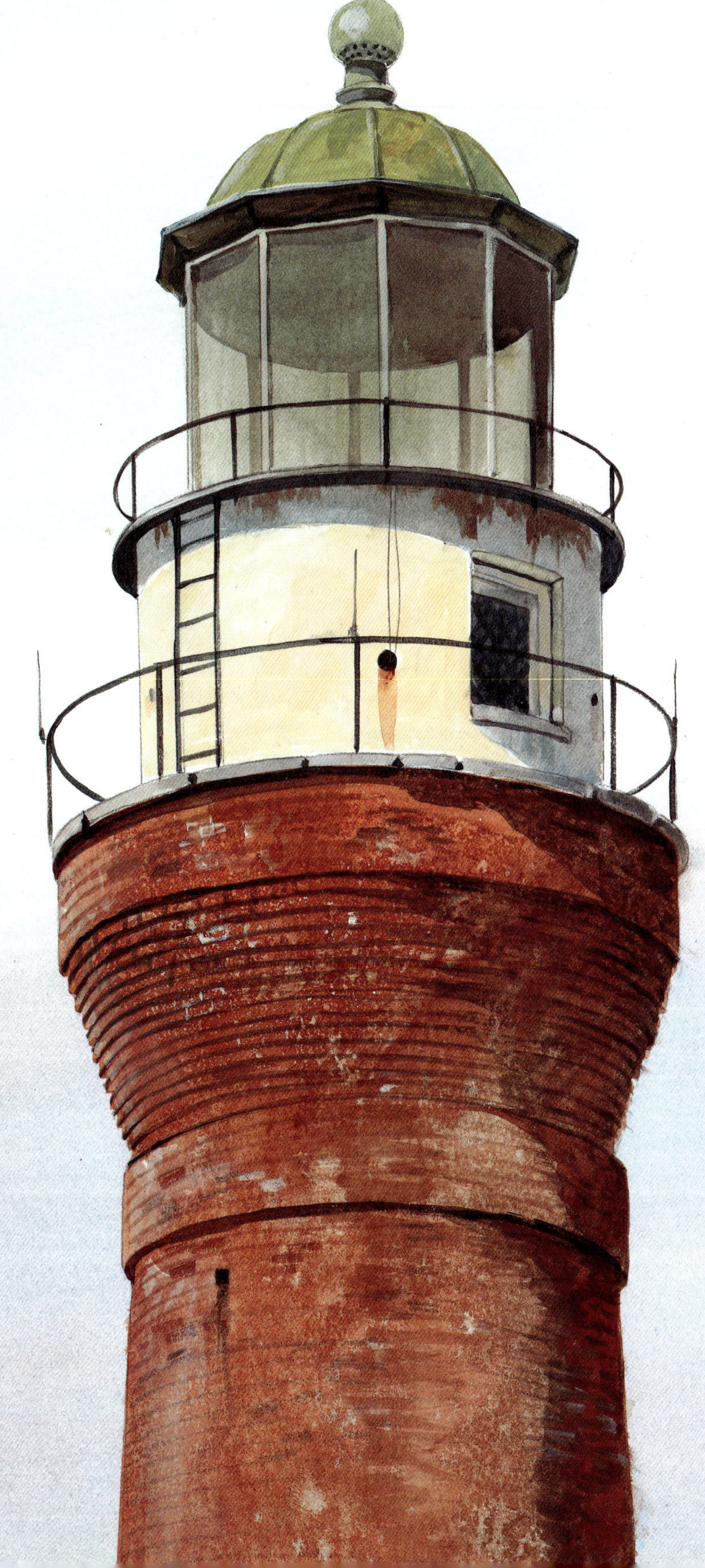

Once a remote location for a lighthouse keeper, the lighthouse is now rimmed by military jet runways, large naval ships, and of course those practical and most attractive military-style gray buildings. From here you can look right over at the runway where modern fighter jets take off and land and at the docks where large aircraft carriers and destroyers are tied up. It makes an interesting contrast.

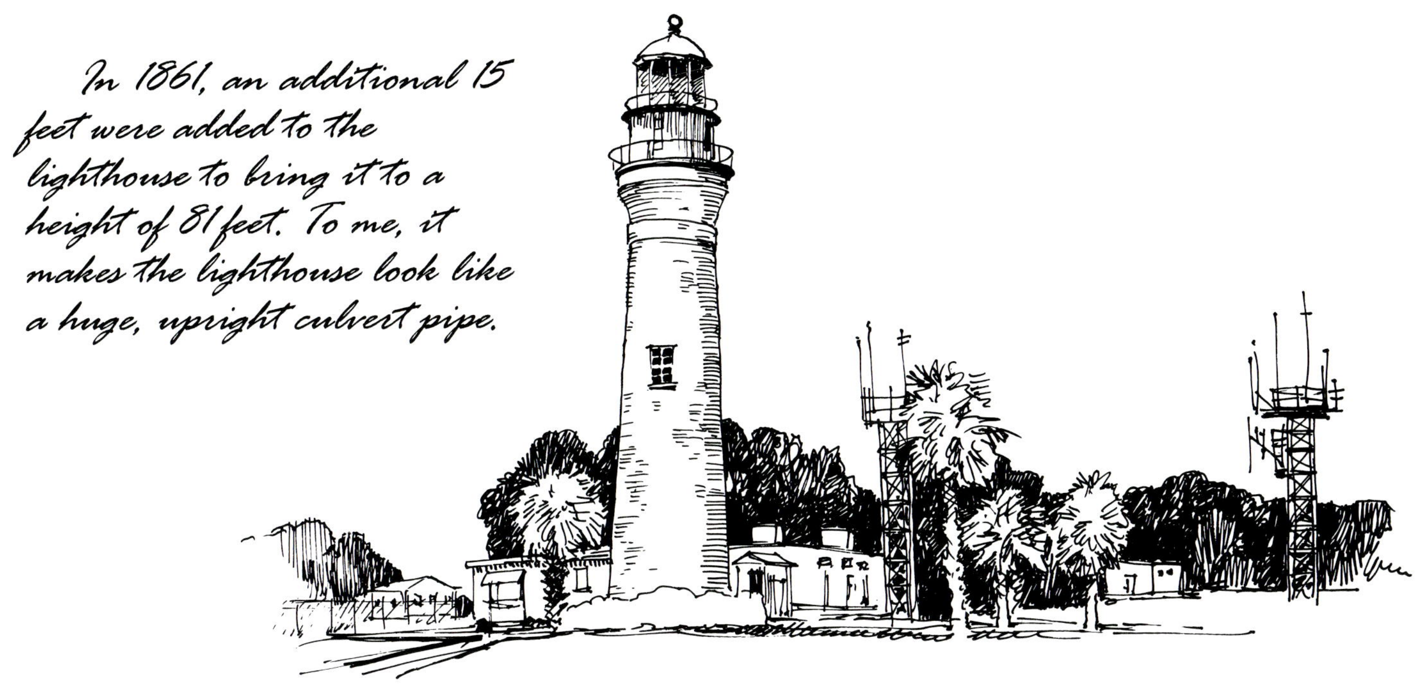

In 1861, an additional 15 feet were added to the lighthouse to bring it to a height of 81 feet. To me, it makes the lighthouse look like a huge, upright culvert pipe.

In 1929, a lightship seven miles offshore from the mouth of the St. Johns River replaced the usefulness of the Mayport light, and in 1954 a new lighthouse was built on another part of the Mayport Naval Station to replace the lightship. The old lighthouse no longer functions except as a day marker and as a reminder of the past for the many ships heading into the port of Jacksonville, as well as for the yachts and shrimp boats that make Mayport their home.

You might think it would be difficult to get onto the naval base to see the lighthouse, but when I was there to do the painting, the guard just waved me through. (Of course that can change at the discretion of the base at any time.) Drive to where the aircraft carriers are docked and make a left around the end of the paved runway onto what looks like a service road. The area around the lighthouse is far enough away from all the ships and military buildings that you still feel a sense of the past. The lighthouse is currently not open to the public, but the grounds around it are. In the meantime, the Mayport Lighthouse Association, with the help of the Navy, is working on plans to open the lighthouse to the public and to rebuild the keepers quarters.

If you can't get onto the Mayport Naval Station, you can still get quite close to the lighthouse by going to the delightful small village of Mayport with its picturesque shrimp boats and popular seafood restaurants. From there you can see the lighthouse through the chain-link fence of the naval base only a hundred yards away. From Mayport you can take a ferryboat ride across the St. Johns River, then drive along the sand dunes to the Amelia Island Lighthouse and Fernandina Beach.

This was the aircraft carrier I was stationed on back in the early '70s.

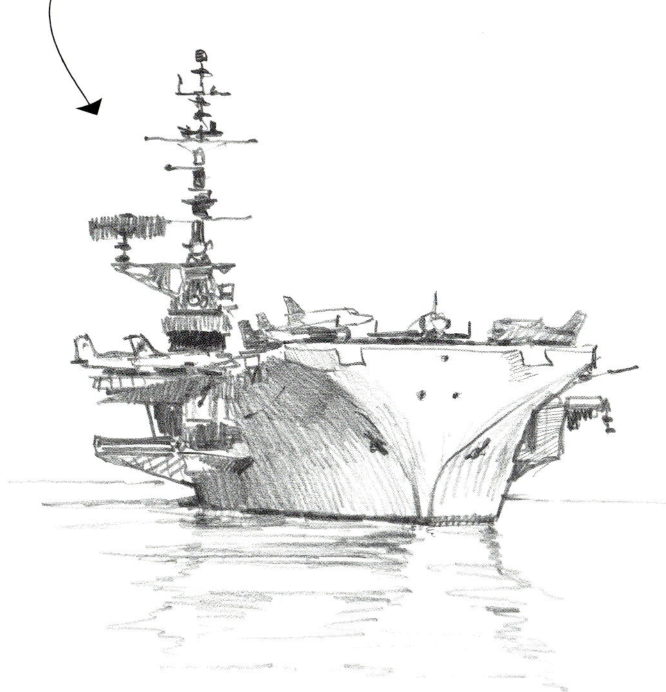

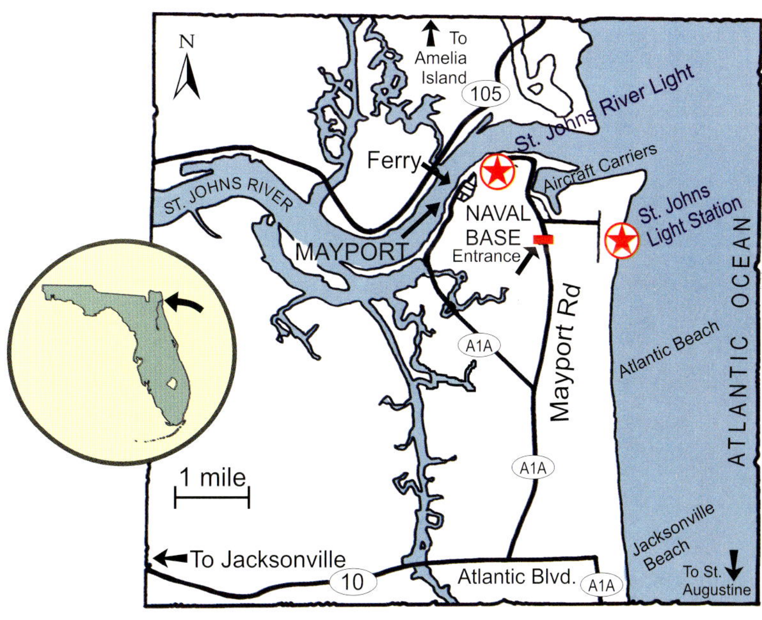

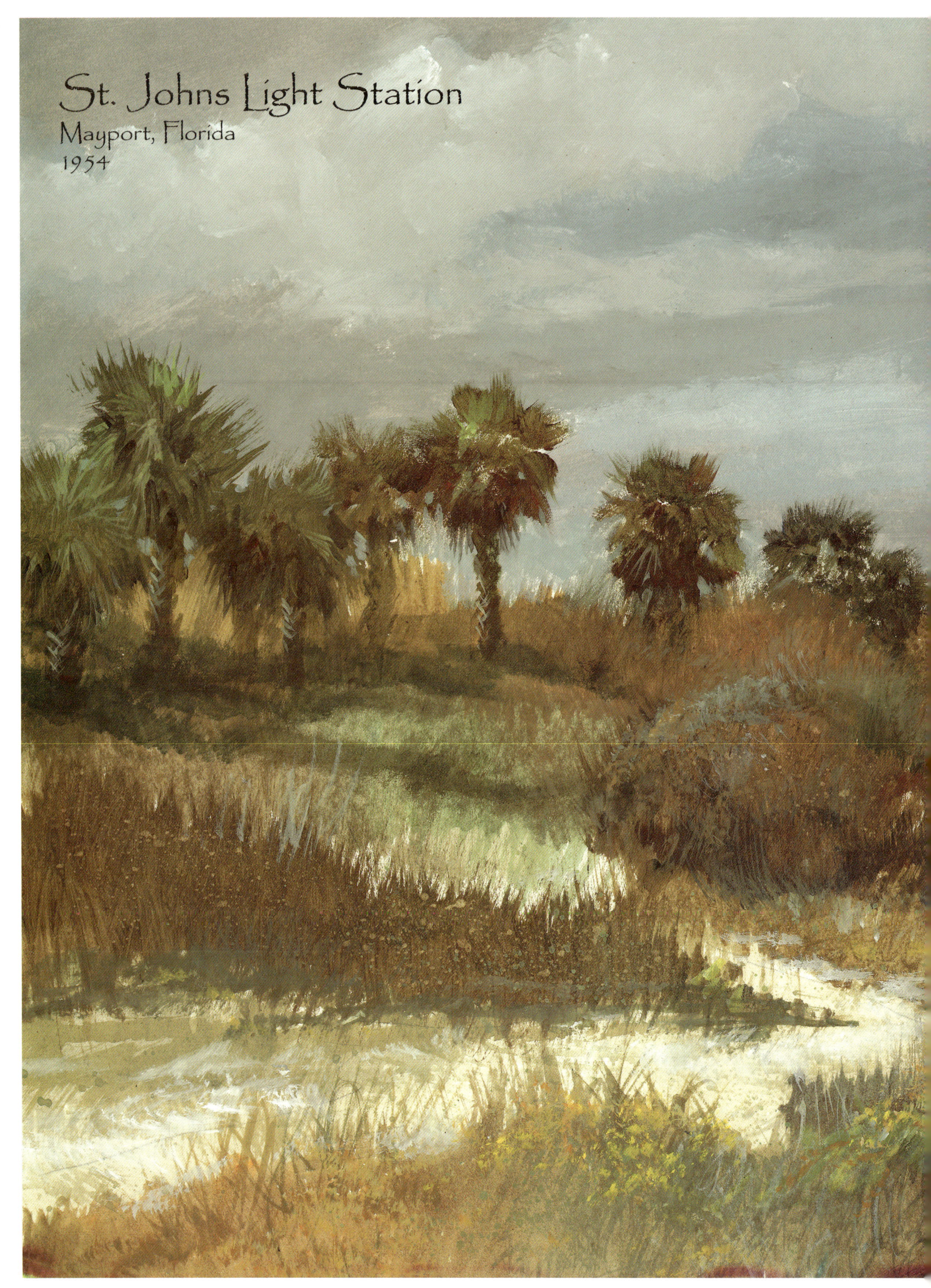

St. Johns Light Station
Mayport, Florida
1954

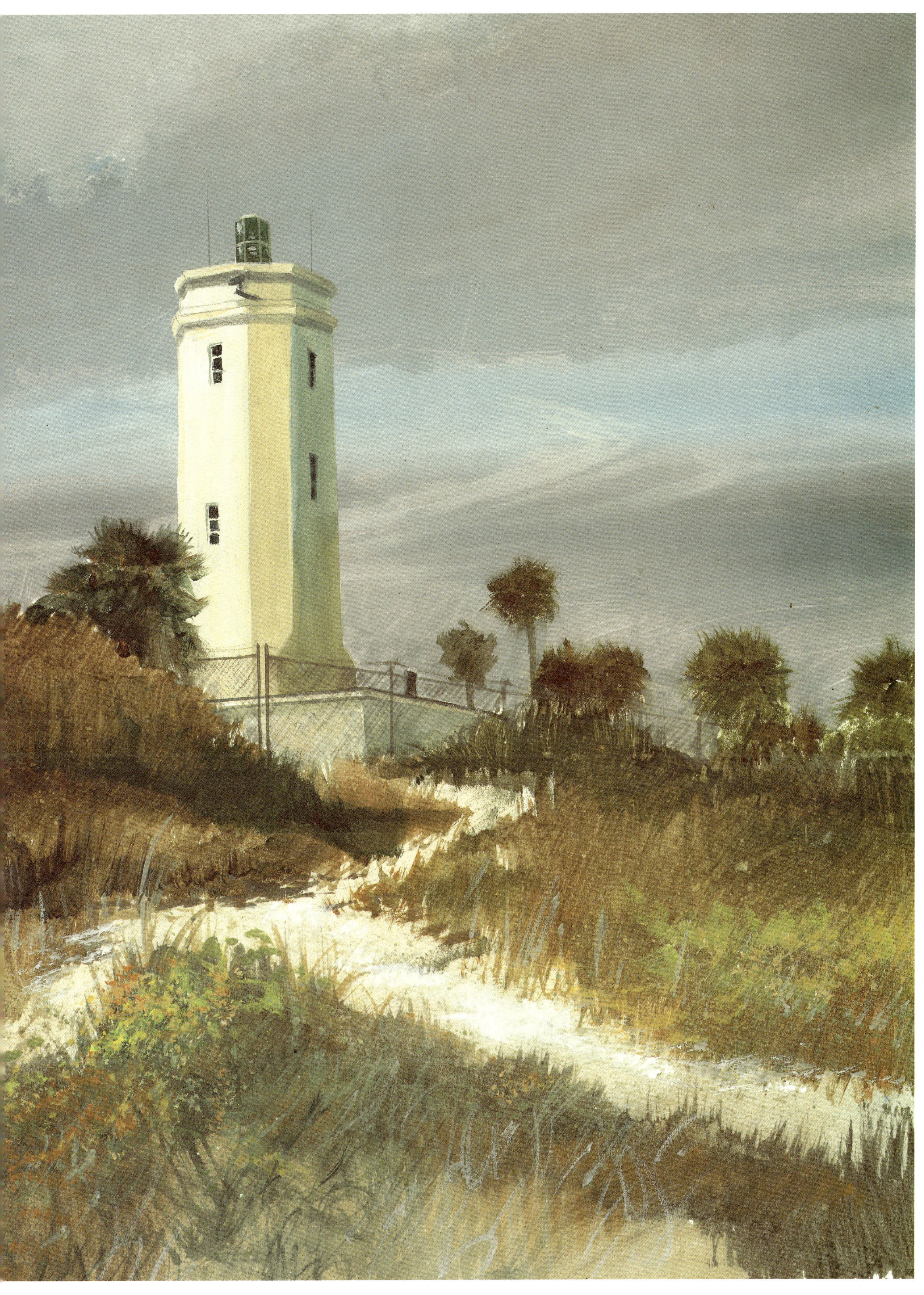

Only a mile from the old Mayport Light (St. Johns River Lighthouse) and directly overlooking the Atlantic Ocean is this nontraditional-looking lighthouse. The beacon doesn't fit our conventional idea of what a lighthouse should look like. The lantern room is so small it can hardly be called a room at all. There's barely enough space to walk around inside. In order for the lenses to be fully inspected or repaired, they have to be lowered with a set of pulleys and chains to the room below.

Today there are many beacons that are taking the role of traditional lighthouses—unrecognizable to us as we drive by them—that actually sit on top of condominiums and high rise buildings but fill the same role. Even with the satellite guidance systems that almost every boat owner uses to pinpoint his location within a few feet, the sailors I know still feel a sense of security when they see that reassuring flashing light.

This lighthouse was equipped with a radio beacon that mariners used to get a bearing on their location in bad weather. Radio beacons were widely used, especially by pleasure boats, into the 1980s because they were much cheaper than radar or loran. Radio beacons worked by sending out a Morse code signal that could be read by a passing ship equipped with a direction finder to determine its exact location. Today the GPS (Global Positioning System) is small, inexpensive, and more accurate than anything that has come before, so radio beacons are, for the most part, a thing of the past.

Situated on the Mayport Naval Station just north of Jacksonville Beach, the lighthouse is not open to the public, but after you get onto the base, you are free to park and walk on the beach and dunes close to the light. The base may or may not be open to the public, depending on military situations. It was open the day I visited, and the guard at the entrance just waved me through without question.

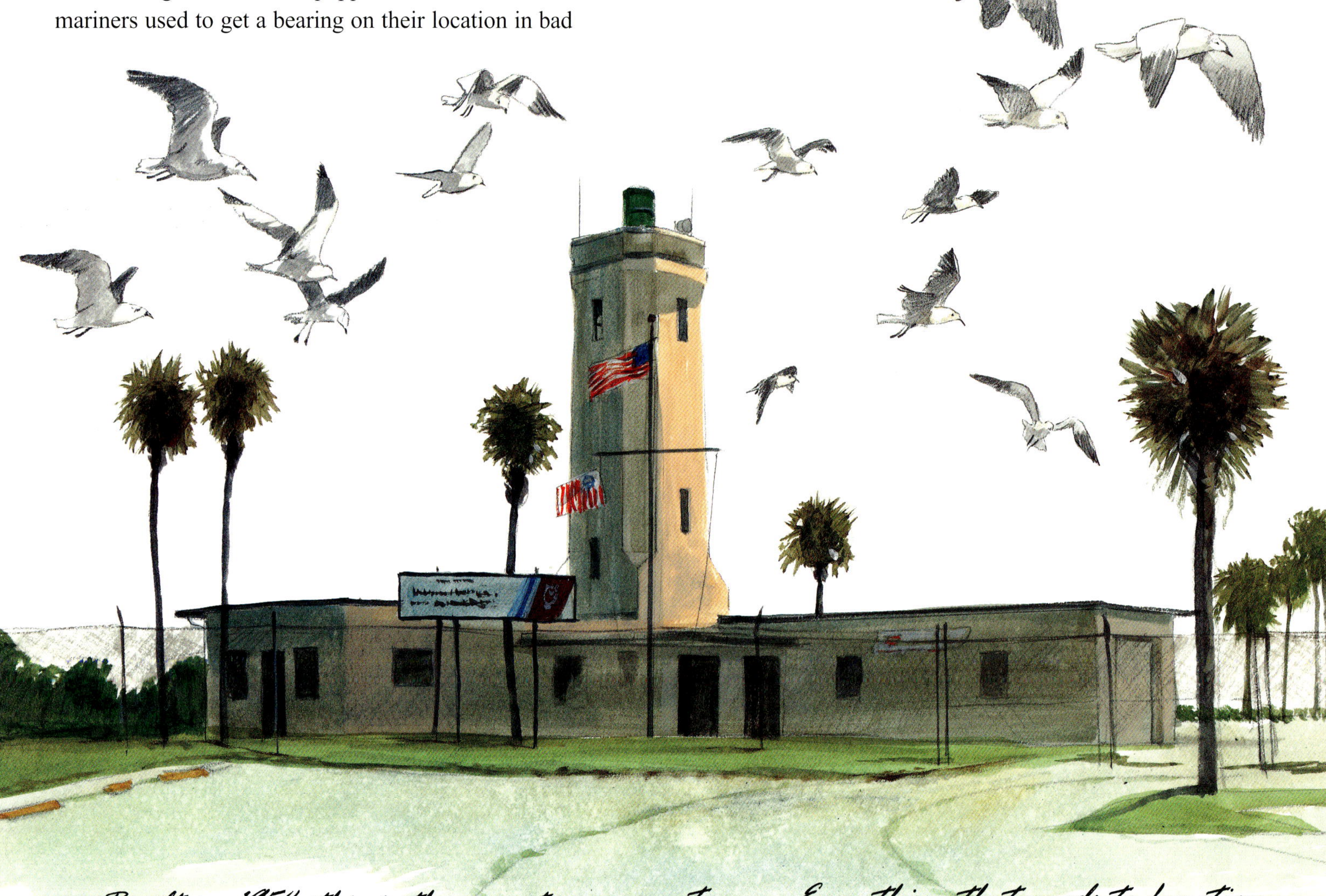

Built in 1954, this is the newest lighthouse in Florida. It has that typical military look and was once used to monitor the weather and maintain the radio beacon. Now it has been fenced off, and the lower part is used mainly for storage. Everything that needs to function inside—like the beacon—is automated. Even though the lighthouse is on the Mayport Naval Station, the Coast Guard is in charge of this and all other marine navigation lights in the United States.

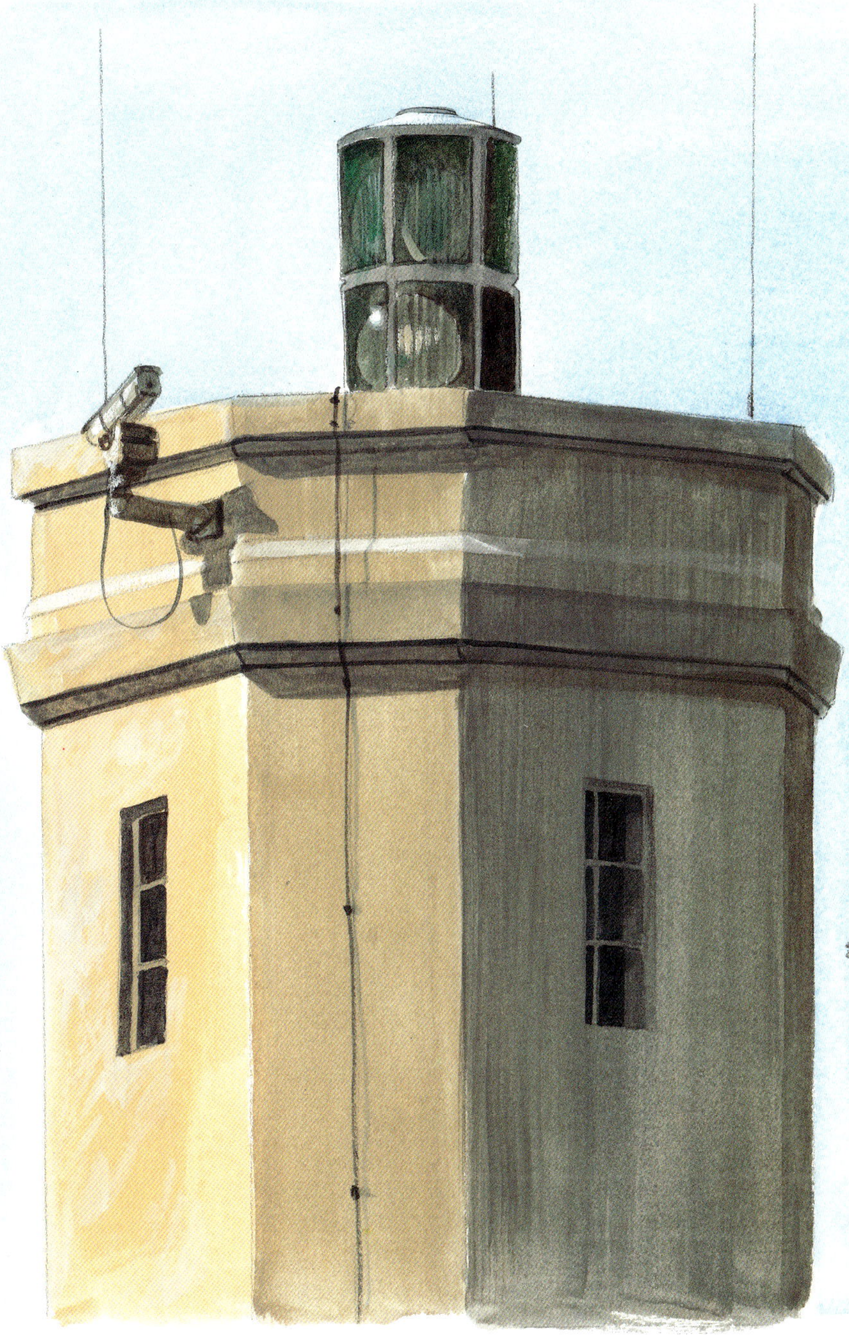

These rotating aero-marine beacons eliminate the need for the traditional lantern room. An impersonal surveillance camera mounted on the side has replaced a lighthouse keeper to watch the grounds. Even with this cold technology, the lighthouse is still stately in its own way.

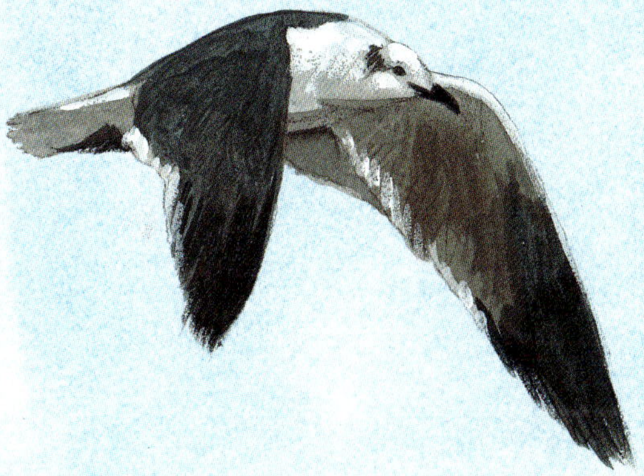

The St. Johns Light Station replaced both the Mayport Lighthouse and the St. Johns Lightship, which was in service some seven miles out in the Atlantic. In 1920, there were forty-nine such lightships around the country, but by 1985 there were none left operating. When the lightship was taken out of service at St. Johns River, this new lighthouse served as a replacement.

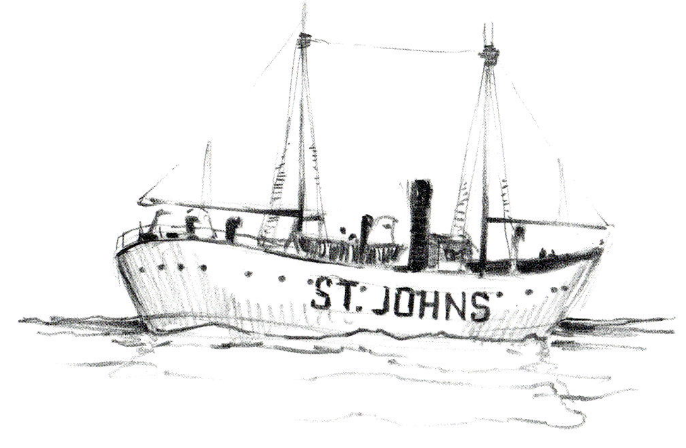

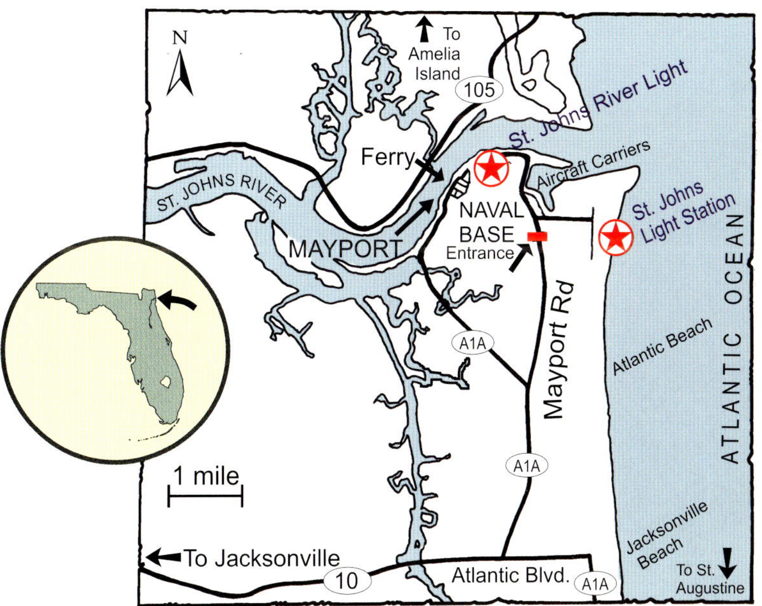

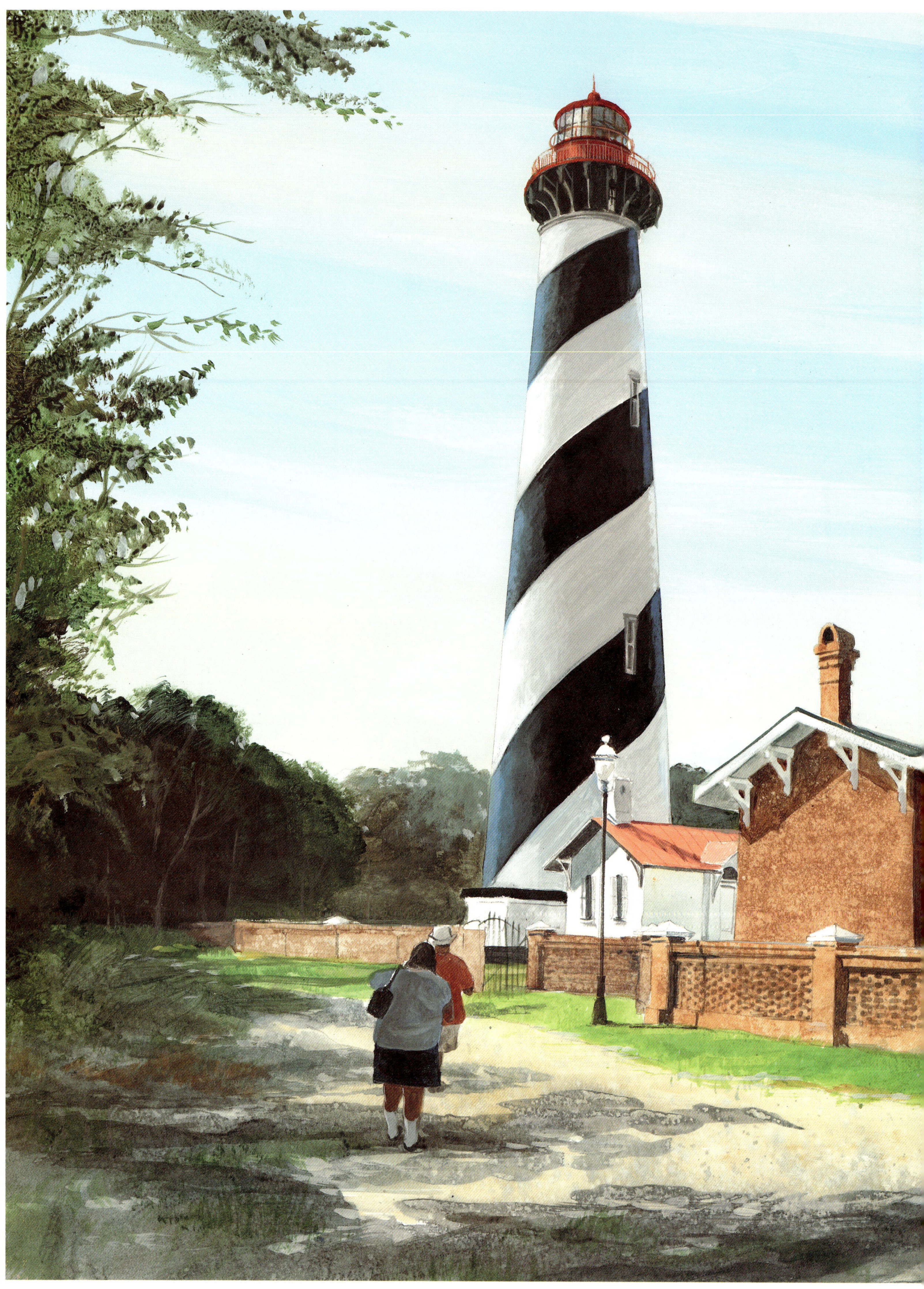

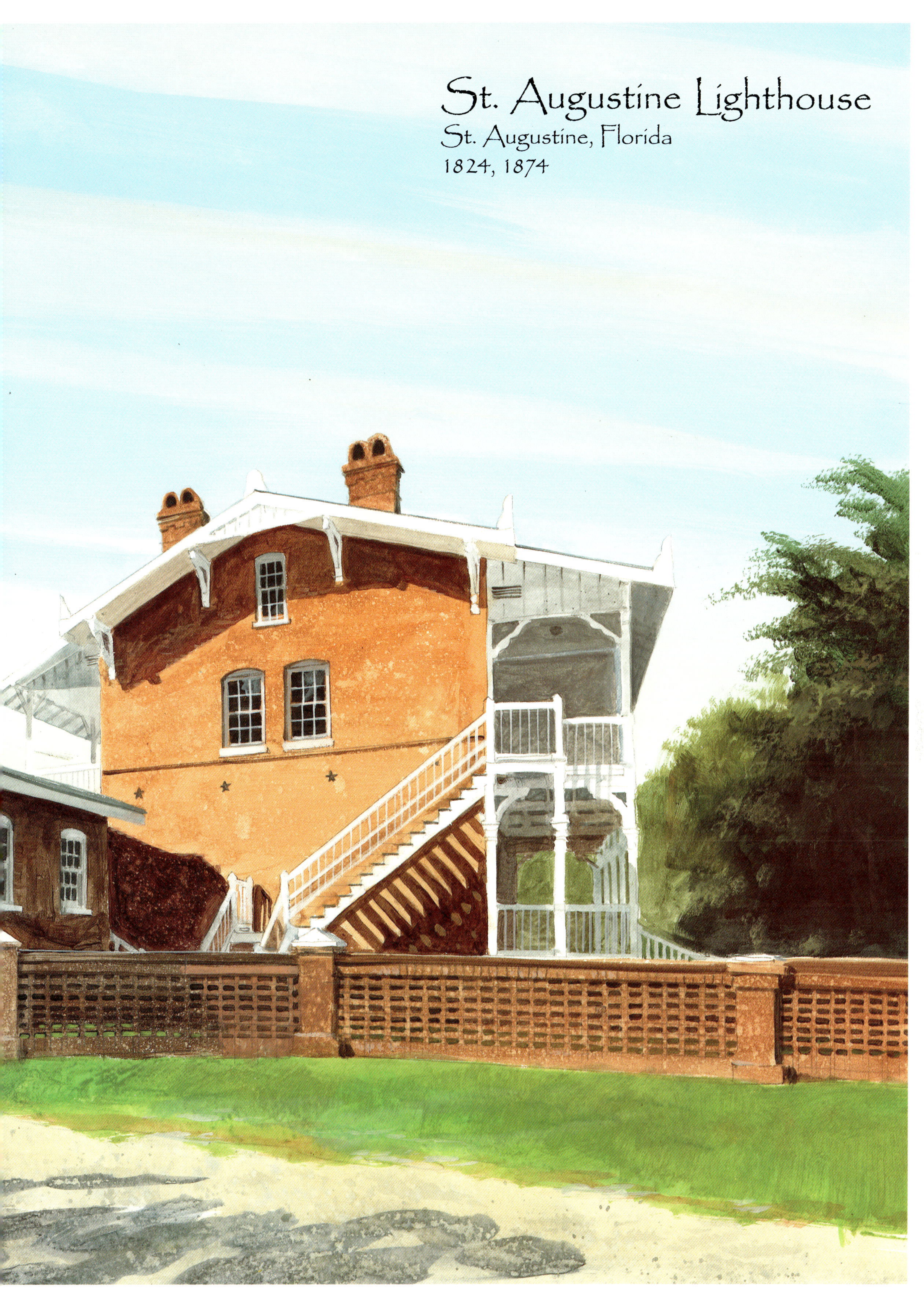

St. Augustine Lighthouse

St. Augustine, Florida

1824, 1874

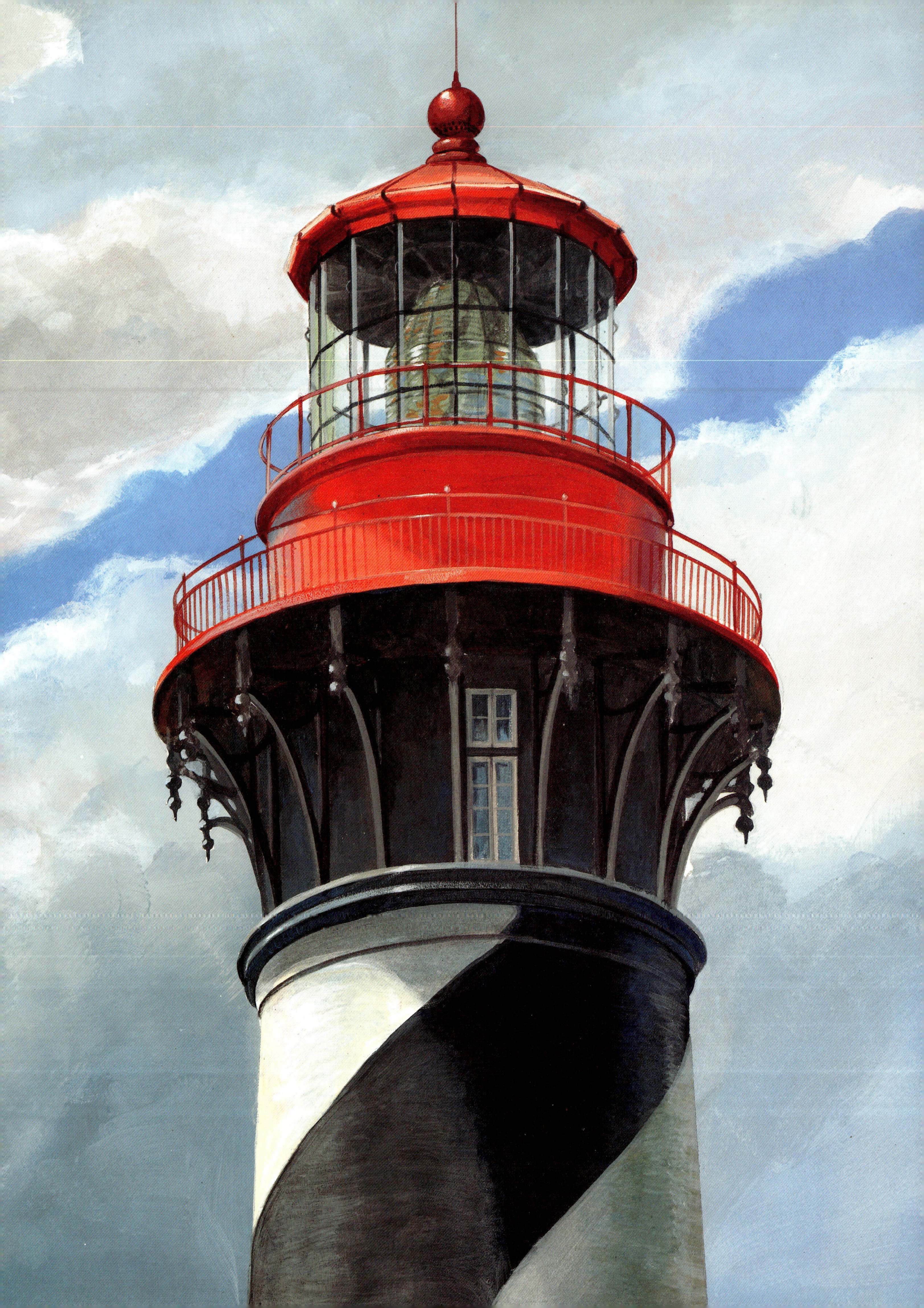

St. Augustine is our nation's oldest city and one of the most interesting places in all of Florida. Castillo de San Marcos, better known as the St. Augustine Fort, is over three centuries old and was built primarily of coquina, a locally mined stone composed of coquina shells in a limestone base. The Lightner Museum, one of my favorite places, houses a variety of curiosities and antiques. You can walk in the old section of town, dotted with fun shops and historical buildings, including the oldest wooden schoolhouse in the United States, dating back over two hundred years. A couple of miles south of St. Augustine is Anastasia Island, the site of Florida's most visited lighthouse.

In the mid 1500s, Spanish settlers built a wooden watchtower so an early warning could be sounded in case of enemy attack. In 1586, English explorer Sir Francis Drake saw the tower, investigated, discovered the town, and burned St. Augustine to the ground. However, the city remained in the hands of the Spanish until 1763, when England gained control for about twenty years. At that time the English erected a tower built of coquina rock, resembling what looked much like a fort on the same spot the Spanish had used for their tower. They also added a cannon on top in order to warn the town of approaching ships. Spain gained control of the area again for a final time in 1784 until it became a territory of the United States in 1821. The tower site was the logical place to construct the first lighthouse in St. Augustine. Placed on the existing tower and standing only 30 feet high, the light was completed and lit in 1824. Twice during the following years it was raised until it reached a height of 52 feet. Although it stood almost half a mile from the sea when it was built, mother nature had her eye on reclaiming the area as beachfront property. A jetty was built to try to stop the erosion but the lighthouse was eventually undermined and fell into the sea. The decision was made to build a new, 165-foot lighthouse at a new location, resulting in the present lighthouse that so far has never been threatened by beach erosion.

Children living at the lighthouse had to be inventive to fill their free time. One lighthouse keeper's oldest son, nicknamed Cracker, built model airplanes, and the lighthouse made an ideal launch pad. His younger sister Wilma had her own ideas about flight, namely, jumping off the roof with her newly purchased umbrella to see if it would also function as a parachute. That ended with a broken, inside-out umbrella but no broken bones. Cracker, older and more mature than Wilma, turned his sister's inspiring efforts from model aviation to model parachute experimentation. After several fairly successful attempts and modifications, Wilma's cat, Smoky, happened into the picture. Cracker attached the unsuspecting animal to his final prototype and launched the unwilling test pilot off the top of the lighthouse. Paws clawed the air frantically as the cat descended the 165 feet, hit the ground running, and dragged his parachute off behind him.

Strangely enough, Smoky didn't bother to show up for dinner that evening. Wilma searched the neighborhood, calling "Here Smoky, here kitty-kitty!," but there was no sign of Smoky. Of course Cracker knew absolutely nothing about where the cat was when asked at suppertime.

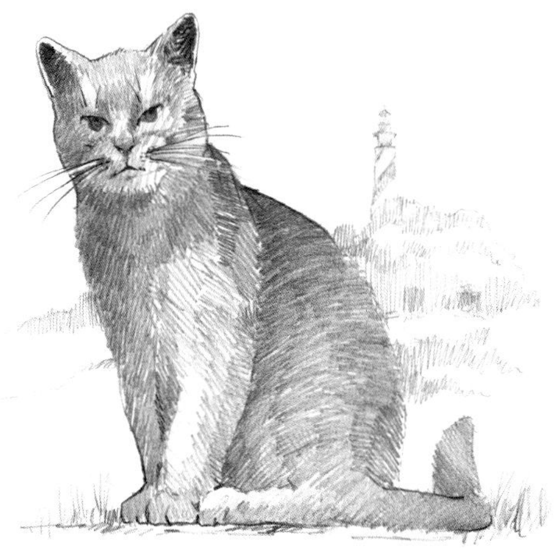

The cat eventually returned about a month later. The family concluded that Smoky must have jumped into a car of tourists visiting the lighthouse, and they praised the gallant feline for finding his way home from perhaps as far away as New Jersey or who knows where. It wasn't until fifty years later that Cardell "Cracker" Daniels let the cat out of the bag and told his sister about her pet's challenging experience.

For eighty years, lighthouse keepers and their families lived here. There were sometimes as many as fifteen adults and children occupying the house at one time, but in 1955 the light was automated and a keeper was no longer needed. The once-pristine grounds that had been regularly inspected for so many years began to deteriorate, and in 1970 the keepers' house was set ablaze by arsonists or vandals. The Junior Service League of St. Augustine spent fourteen years lovingly rebuilding and restoring the lighthouse and keepers' house to their original Victorian splendor. The league continues to improve the displays and buildings for the 110,000 people who visit each year.

The first-order Fresnel lens is still in operation as an active aid to navigation and stands twelve feet tall (eighteen feet counting its pedestal) and six feet wide. In 1986, a fourteen-year-old boy thought it might be a good idea to shoot out the lens with a high-powered rifle, and he did a fair job of damaging the lens. The Coast Guard was going to remove the lens, but the Junior Service League raised the half million dollars needed to replace the shattered prisms and to install bulletproof glass on the outside. I've been lucky enough to stand inside this lens. It is like standing in a huge jewel with its 370 hand-cut prisms slowly turning. There's an illustration on page 8 showing what it looks like.

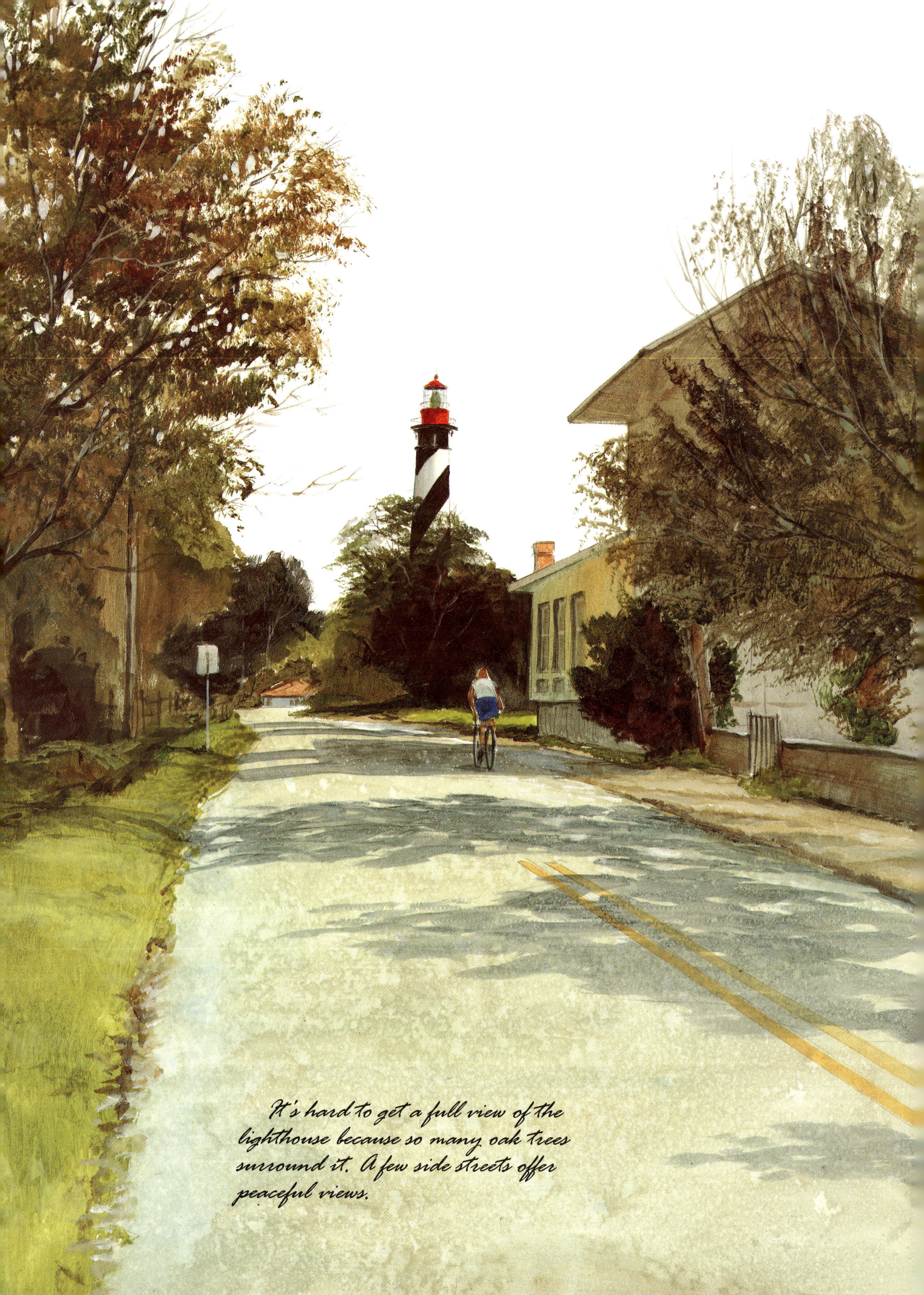

It's hard to get a full view of the lighthouse because so many oak trees surround it. A few side streets offer peaceful views.

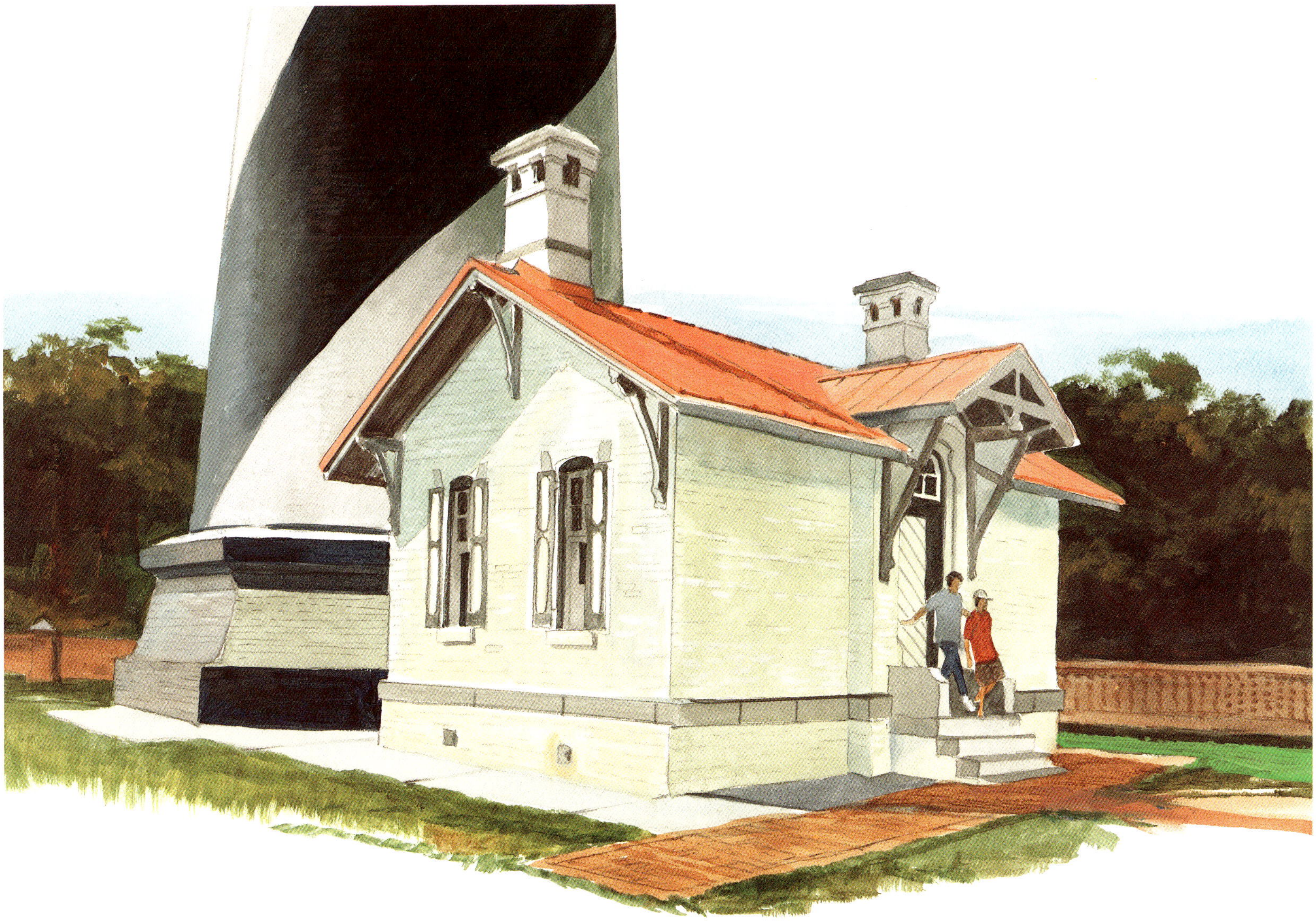

The oil house is attached to the base of the lighthouse. One room inside it served as a tool shed and as an office for the lighthouse keeper.

Not your everyday household tool, a wrench like this was used to bolt together the upper sections of the ironwork at the top of the lighthouse.

The lighthouse is open to the public every day. The keepers' house is a gift shop and museum, and you can climb the 219 steps to the top of the lighthouse for a nice view of the area. Sightseeing activities around St. Augustine are almost endless, and it's easy to spend a few days visiting the sites. Many attractions are educational, some are just for fun, but all are worth considering for a memorable visit to Florida's first city.

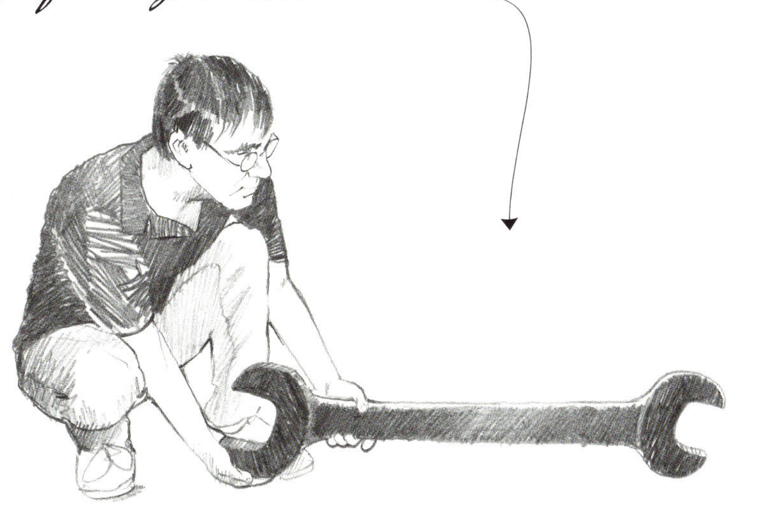

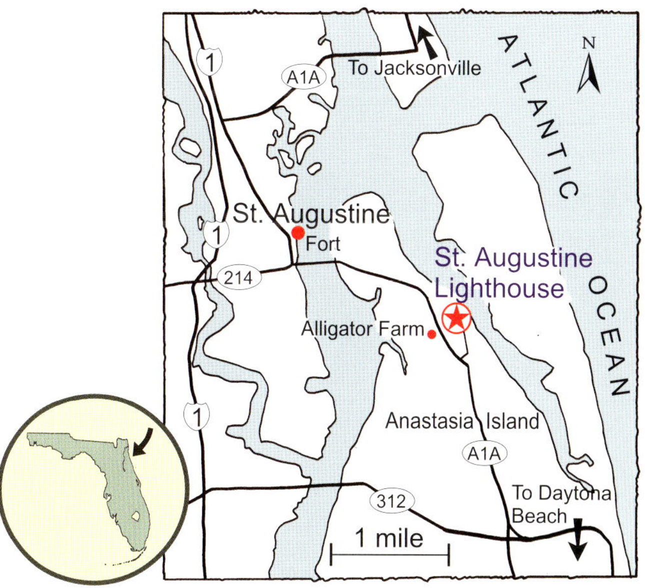

Ponce de Leon Inlet Lighthouse

Ponce Inlet, Florida

1834, 1887

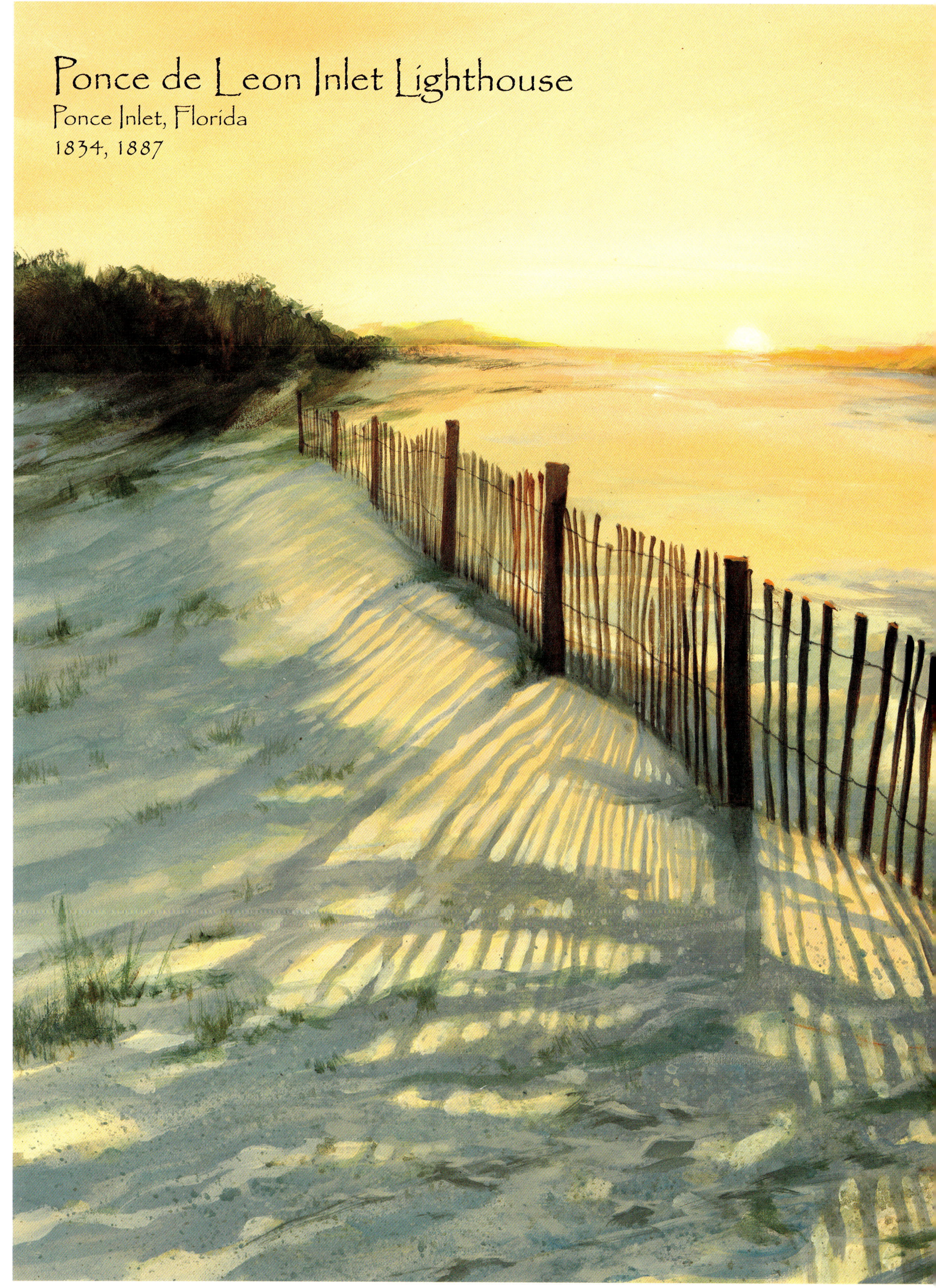

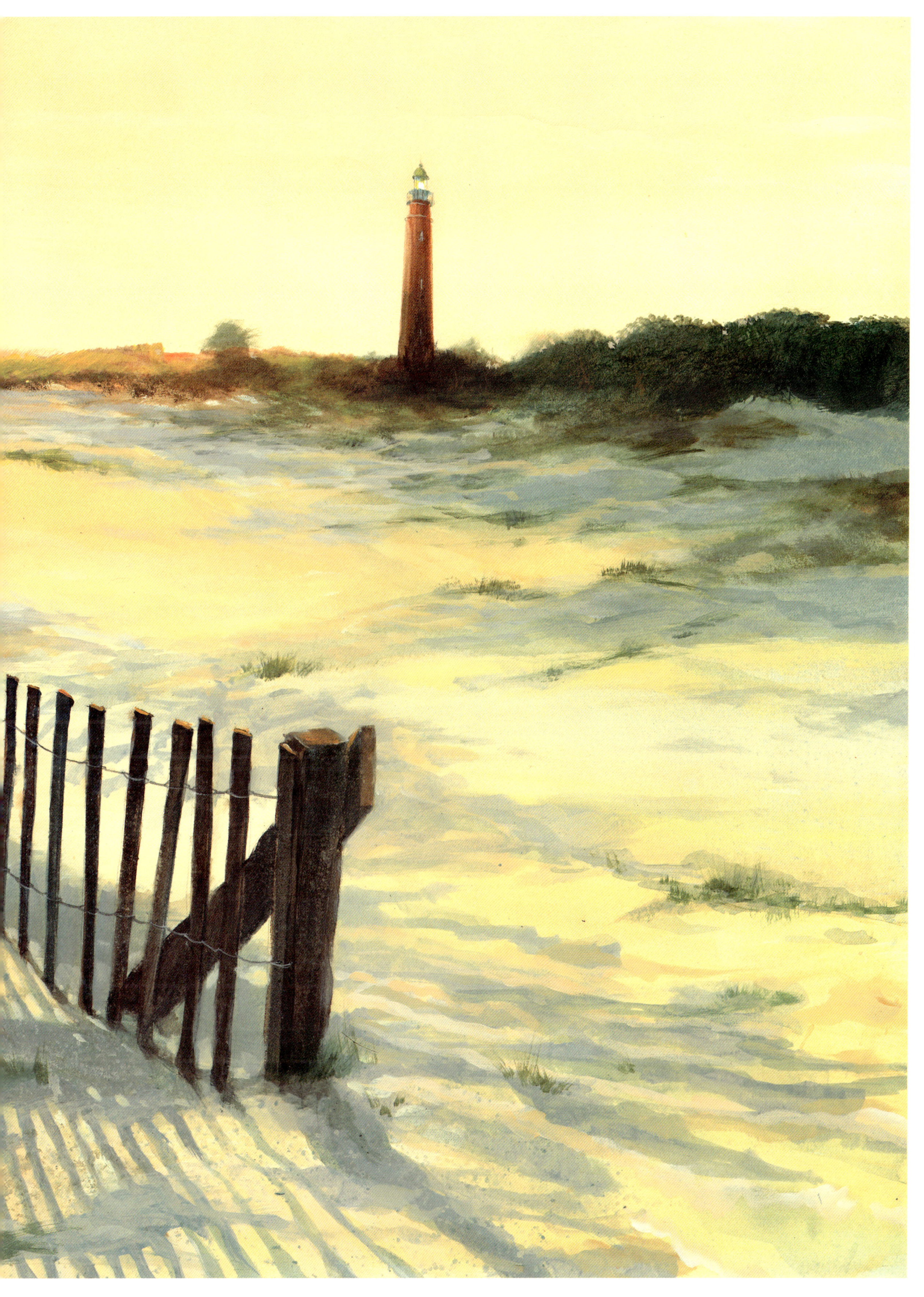

This area didn't always have the romantic name Ponce de Leon Inlet. Originally it was called Mosquito Inlet, and the village nearby the lighthouse was called Pons Park. Most historians now say that Ponce de León probably never visited here, even though he explored nearby parts of Florida in 1513. The name Mosquito Inlet was less than successful when it came to attracting tourists from the north who began to discover and flock to Florida, so in 1926 the name Mosquito Inlet was changed to Ponce de Leon Inlet. This more palatable name helped real estate developers sell mosquito-infested lots and at the same time honored the famous explorer and pillager.

There have been two lighthouses here. The first was built in 1834, but it never received any oil to light the lanterns (a bureaucratic oversight, I'm sure). Within a year, a storm undermined the lighthouse. It leaned over and finally collapsed, but not before the keeper dismantled the lanterns and stored them in his house. Seminole Indians had other ideas about what should be done about the entire situation and decided to burn all the homes and plantations in the area, so they ravaged the keeper's houses and what was left of the lighthouse. Chief Coacoochee wore one of the lighthouse's lantern room reflectors as a headdress during the Battle of Dunlawton three weeks later. So ended the first lighthouse.

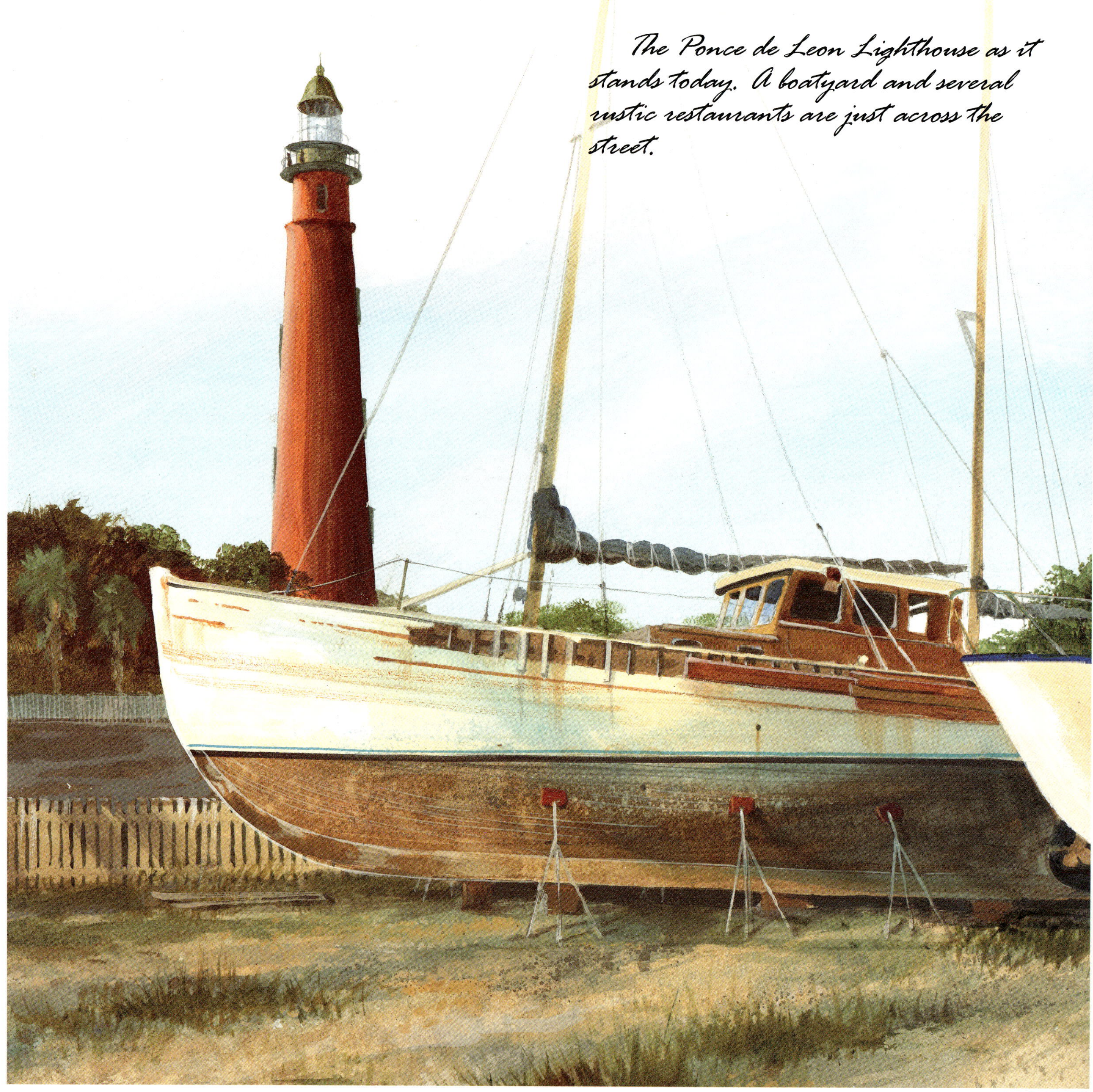

The Ponce de Leon Lighthouse as it stands today. A boatyard and several rustic restaurants are just across the street.

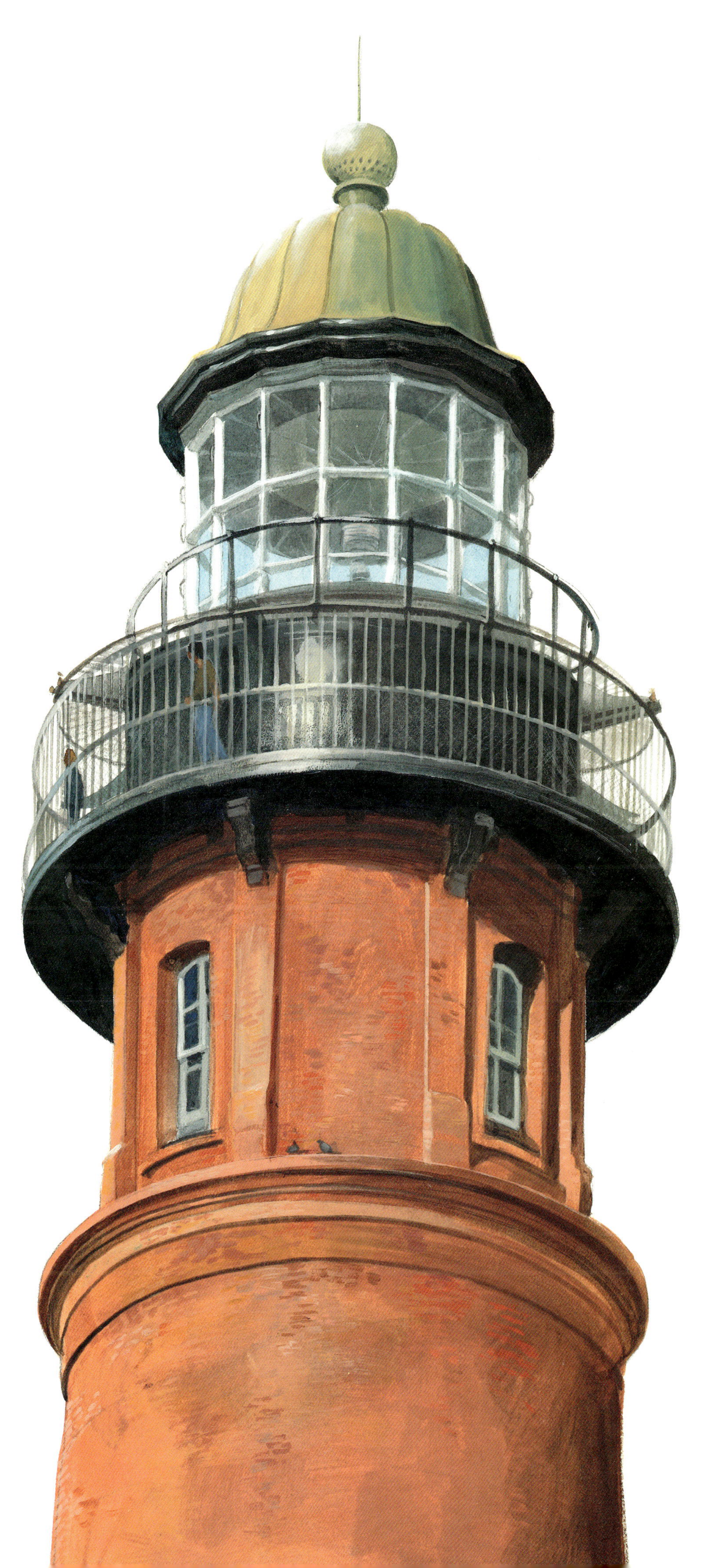

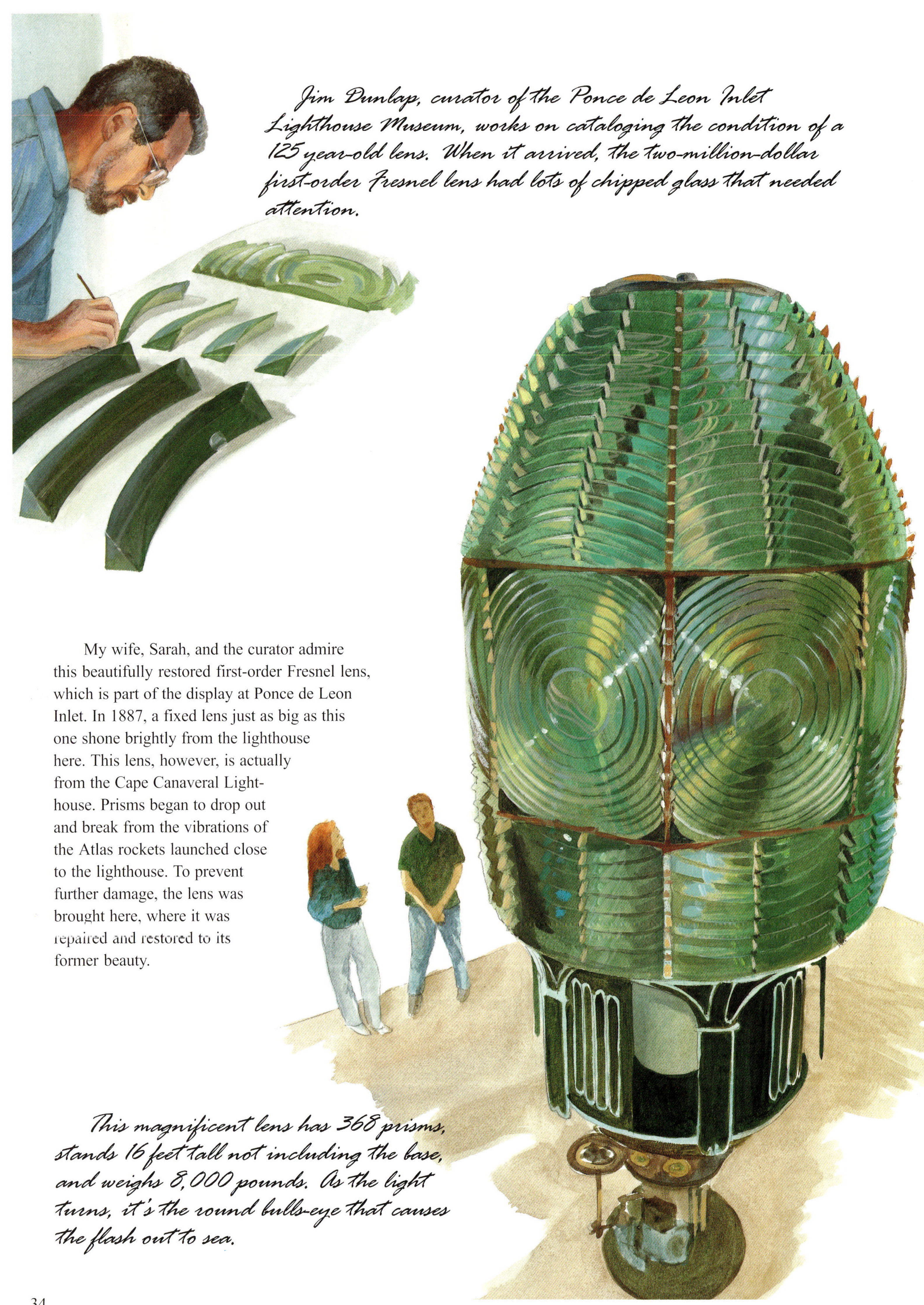

Jim Dunlap, curator of the Ponce de Leon Inlet Lighthouse Museum, works on cataloging the condition of a 125 year-old lens. When it arrived, the two-million-dollar first-order Fresnel lens had lots of chipped glass that needed attention.

My wife, Sarah, and the curator admire this beautifully restored first-order Fresnel lens, which is part of the display at Ponce de Leon Inlet. In 1887, a fixed lens just as big as this one shone brightly from the lighthouse here. This lens, however, is actually from the Cape Canaveral Lighthouse. Prisms began to drop out and break from the vibrations of the Atlas rockets launched close to the lighthouse. To prevent further damage, the lens was brought here, where it was repaired and restored to its former beauty.

This magnificent lens has 368 prisms, stands 16 feet tall not including the base, and weighs 8,000 pounds. As the light turns, it's the round bulls-eye that causes the flash out to sea.

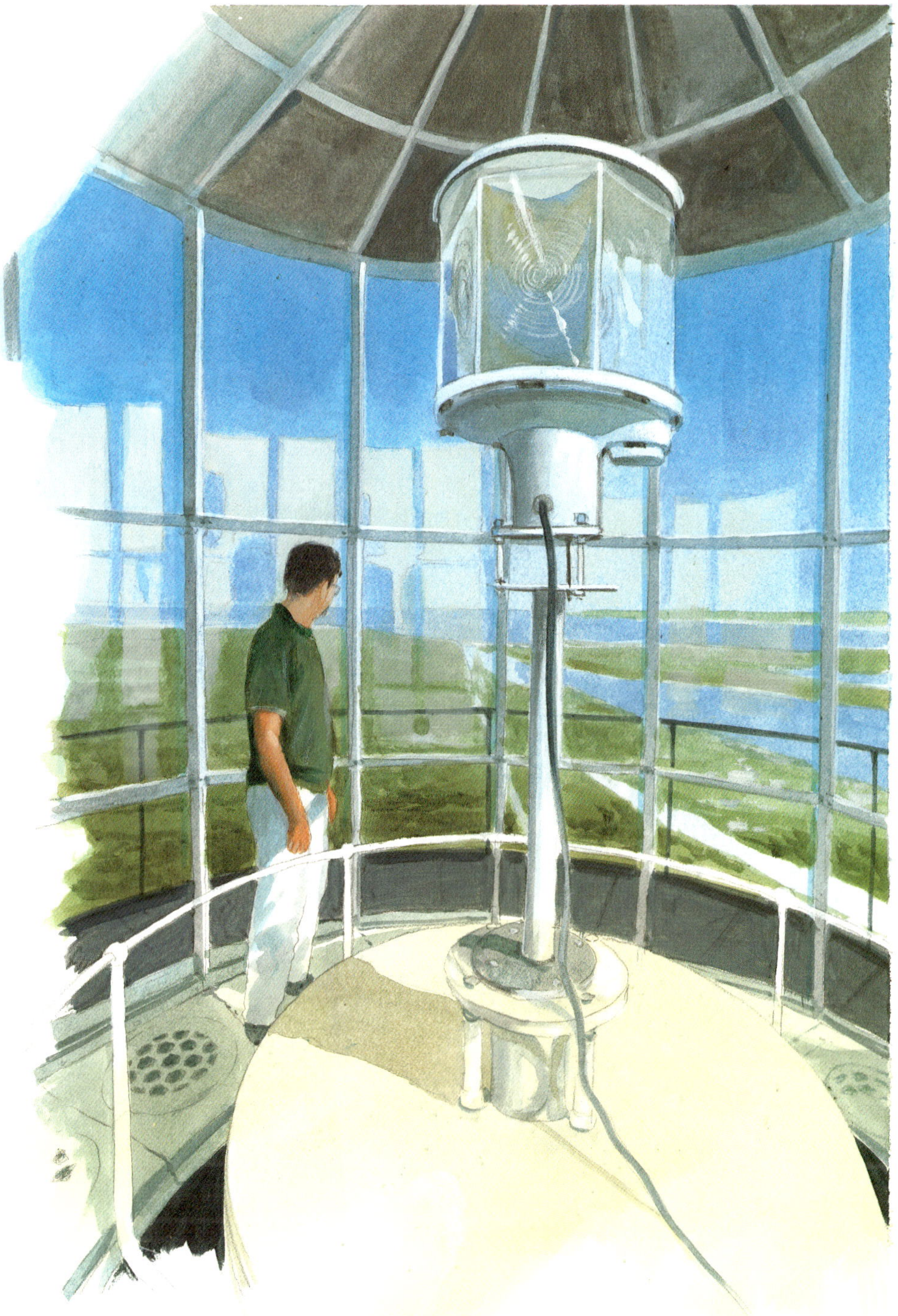

The lens that now sits atop the Ponce de Leon Inlet Lighthouse is this marine beacon. The small but powerful light was installed in 1995 and uses plastic prisms instead of glass.

The temperature inside the lantern room the day I was there was 155 degrees: a great view but not a great place to hang out. It can get a lot hotter if the windows in the room below aren't open for ventilation. It's much better to stand outside on the watch room observation deck where there's always a breeze.

Tom Cat, better known as TC around the lighthouse, relaxes in typical cat fashion just outside one of the keepers' houses, waiting for someone to come along and pet him. Cats were the favored pet of the children at most lighthouses. They only needed what attention you wanted to give them, didn't eat as much as a dog, and pretty much took care of themselves and the local mouse population as well.

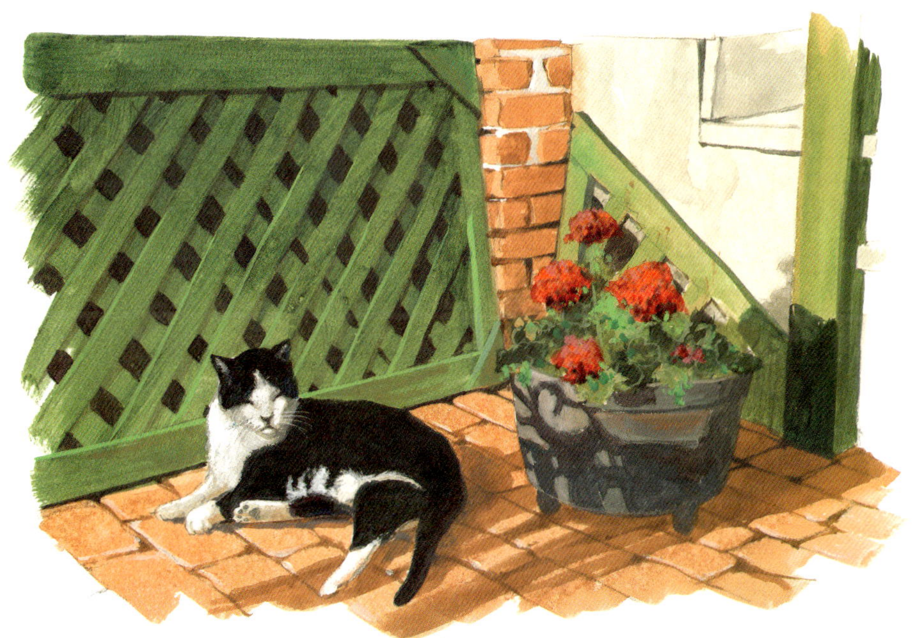

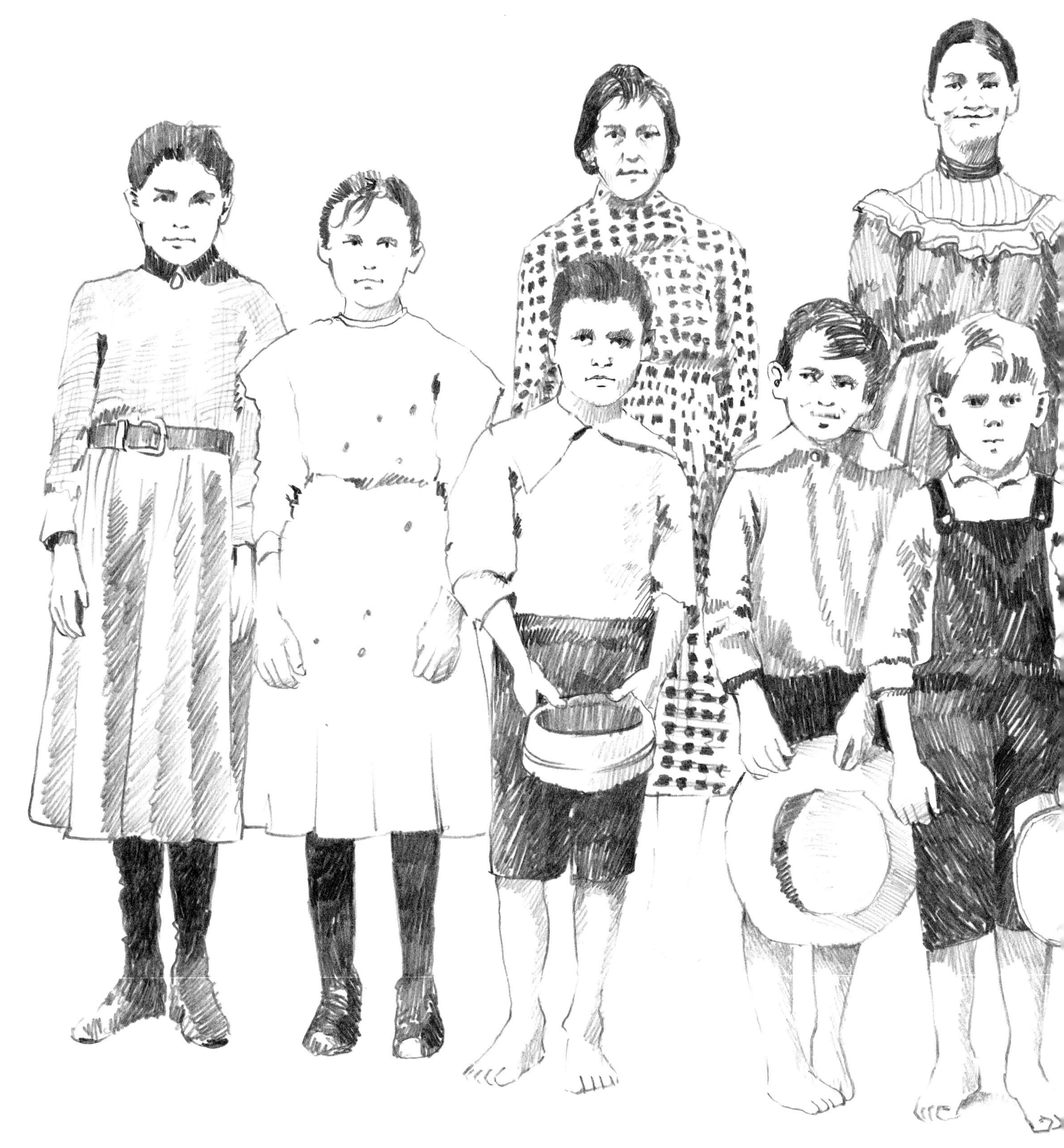

Thomas O'Hagan was a lighthouse keeper at Ponce de Leon Inlet. In many ways life at a lighthouse was remote and lonely. In other ways not so much. Eight of these twelve school children were his.

Families tended to be larger than they are today and very large families were not unusual. They led a life of having to make do with all but the necessities. At Mosquito Inlet, now Ponce de Leon Inlet, the children went to school by boat until a road and bridge were built. Horse-drawn buggy and later a school bus transported them, but the journey took between two and three hours each way.

In 1876, the Light House Service distributed a library of about forty books to each lighthouse keeper and his family. The book selections were changed about four times a year, but things like books were considered a luxury.

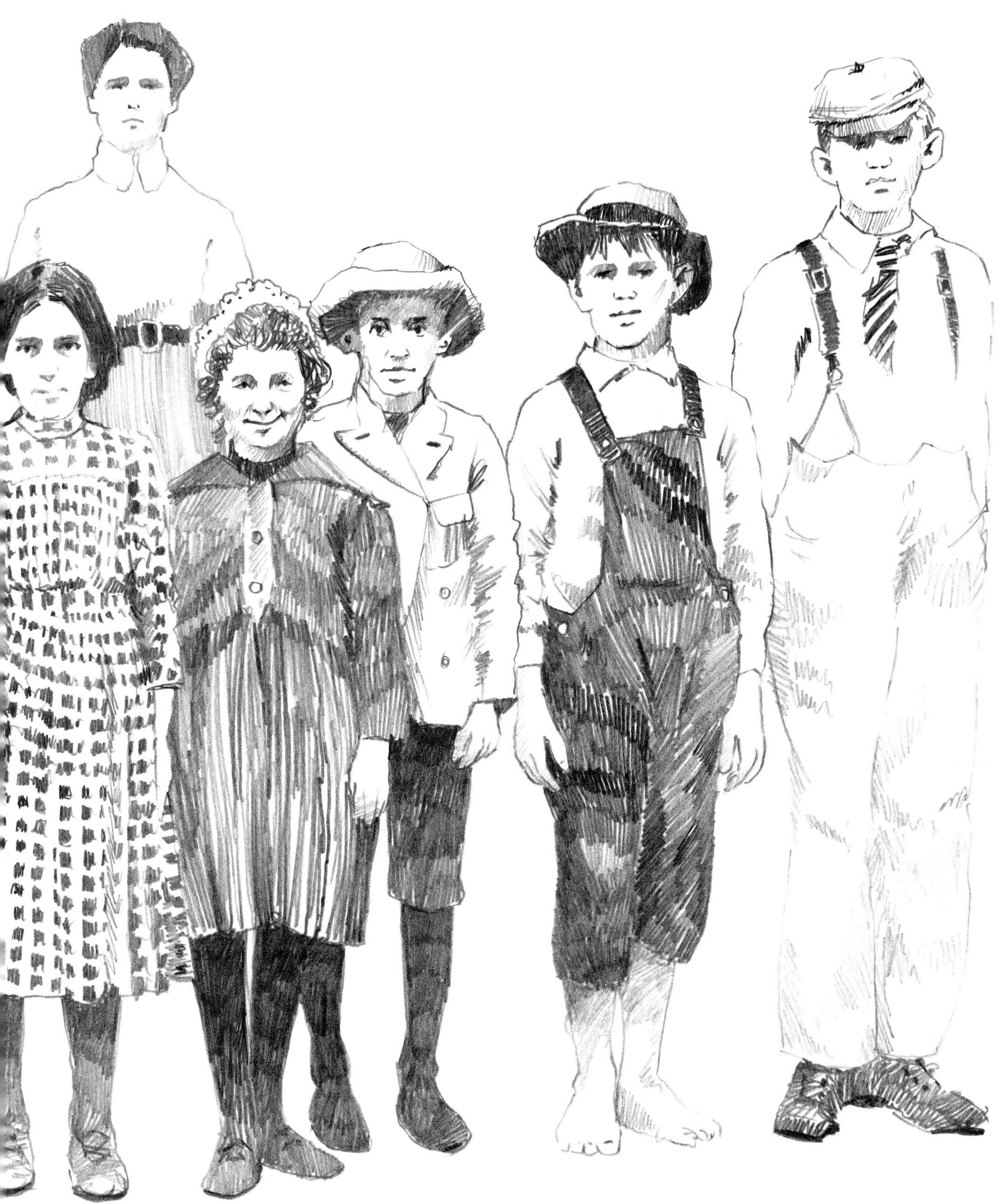

Lighthouse keepers and their families made do with very small salaries and little more than basic necessities. In 1887, the annual salary for a head keeper was $600; it was increased to $720 later that year. This also included an allowance of food: one hundred pounds of flour, forty pounds of salt pork, fifty-two pounds of salt beef, eighty pounds of biscuit (also known as hardtack), eleven pounds of brown sugar, six pounds of coffee, five pounds of rice, and two gallons of beans or peas. Some families tried to raise their own food as well, but sandy soil and salt spray made growing vegetables quite difficult. A few years later, the food rations were stopped and forty dollars was added to the salary. That still wasn't much of a salary—even back then—so lighthouse keepers sometimes supplemented their income by serving as pilots for incoming ships, taking odd jobs, and even selling small souvenirs that visitors to a lighthouse might like to buy after their free tour. The Light House Service did not look favorably upon keepers' taking on outside jobs, but it was done quite regularly.

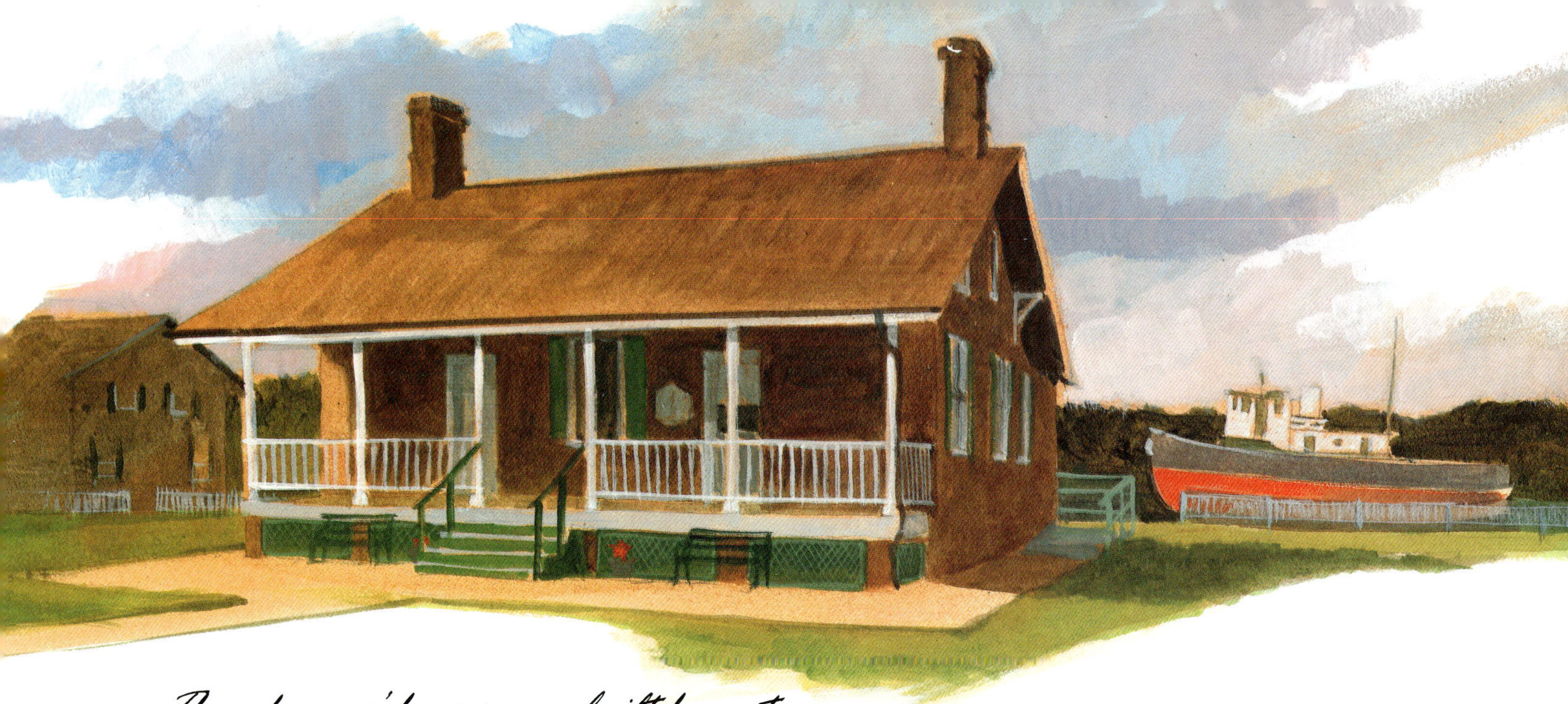

Three keepers' houses were built here at the Ponce de Leon Inlet Lighthouse. When the St. Augustine Lighthouse was built a decade earlier, it had one house for the keeper, his assistant, and their families. Quarters were just too close, so here it was decided to build smaller, separate houses—one for each assistant and a larger house for the keeper.

The present lighthouse at Ponce de Leon Inlet was built back in 1887 and is Florida's finest and tallest. Standing at 175 feet tall, over 1,300,000 bricks were used in its construction. The lighthouse rests on a brick foundation forty-five feet in diameter and extends twelve feet into the ground. The walls at its base are eight feet thick. Two hundred thirteen steps lead to the top—a long way to carry a five-gallon bucket of oil to light the lantern. The light was fully automated in 1952, so the houses were no longer needed for the keepers. The structure began to fall into decay, like so many other lighthouses, but the Preservation Society stepped forward in 1972 and by 1981 had carefully restored the entire complex to its original beauty. Each of the seven buildings on the property houses many interesting displays dating back to when the light was first built. The keepers' houses, with their artifacts and period furnishings, give you a sense of what life might have been like as a lighthouse keeper.

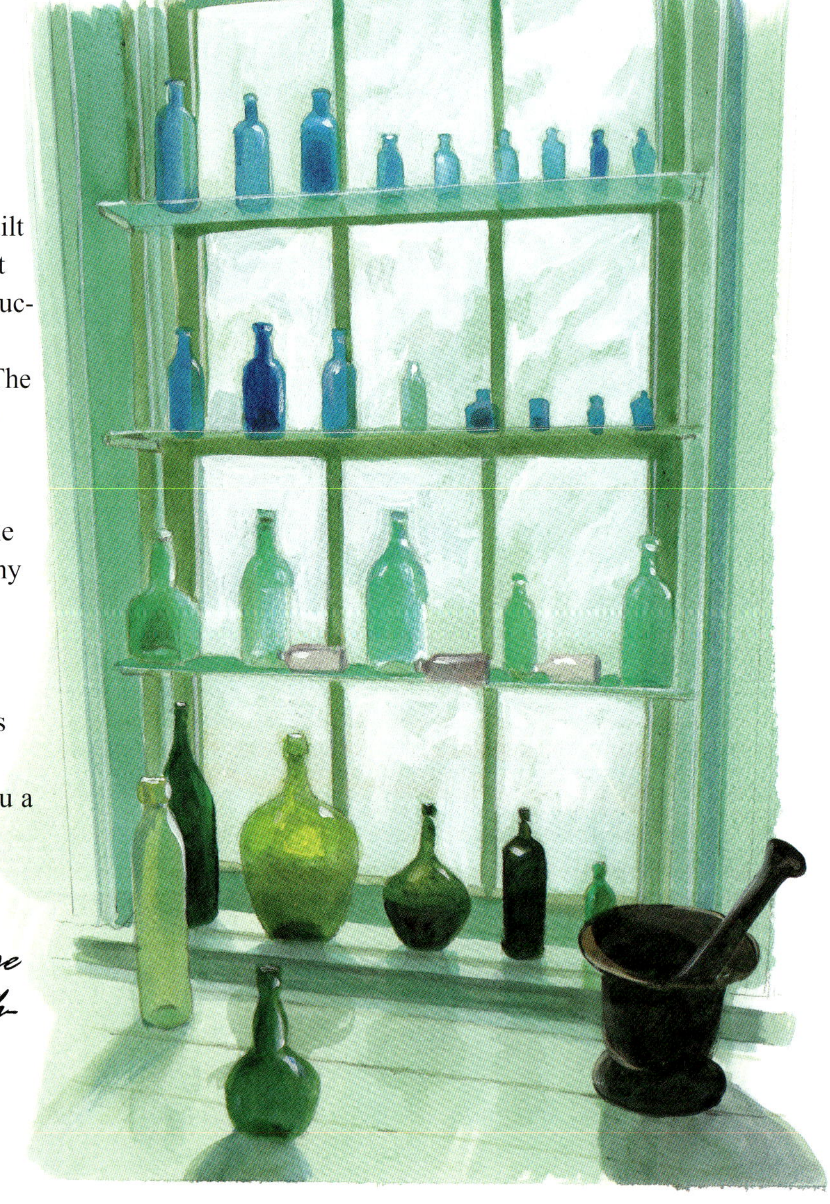

The family of one of the last lighthouse keepers collected all these early twentieth-century bottles. Old bottles actually increase in color and darkness the more they are exposed to the sun.

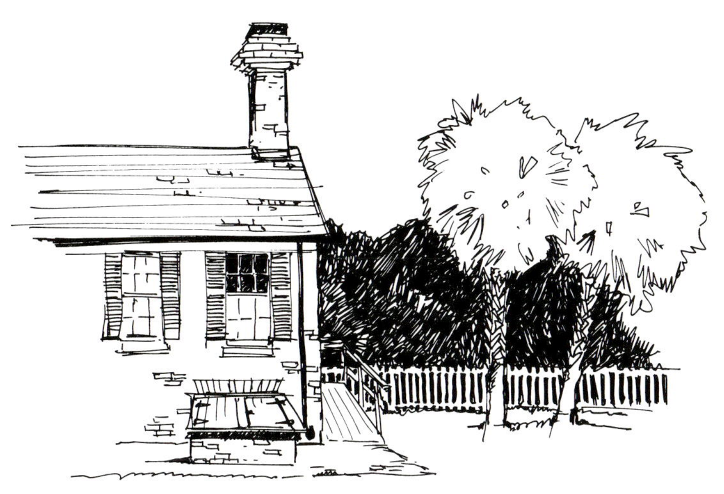

One of the buildings at the lighthouse museum features antiques such as this ice box, stove, and washing machine.

The family who lived here in 1926 enjoyed the advancements of the times, including the luxury of running water, indoor plumbing, and generator-produced electricity. The water tank was even filled by an electric pump from the sulfur-water well below. However, water used for cooking and drinking was still collected from the roof into a cistern. Before electricity, a windmill was used to bring water to the surface, and a hand pump used in the kitchen is still on display in one of the houses.

When indoor plumbing was installed, the original brick outhouse was transformed into a play-actors' dressing room by the lighthouse keeper's children. From there they emerged as heroic and grand actors performing their original dramas. Their make-up consisted of burnt matches, which proved handy as black face paint—but not for long. Matches were significant possessions for someone whose job it was to fire up a lighthouse every night. Needless to say, face paint was removed from theater activities shortly, and dad handed out the punishment of "sitting in the chair."

It wasn't all fun and games at the lighthouse, especially for the grown-ups. Ponce de Leon Inlet is quite treacherous. The lighthouse keeper would have to rescue many sailors whose ships ran aground and wrecked. Often the family would share their lodging, give them dry clothes, and the keeper's wife would serve up a hot meal for the unfortunate mariners.

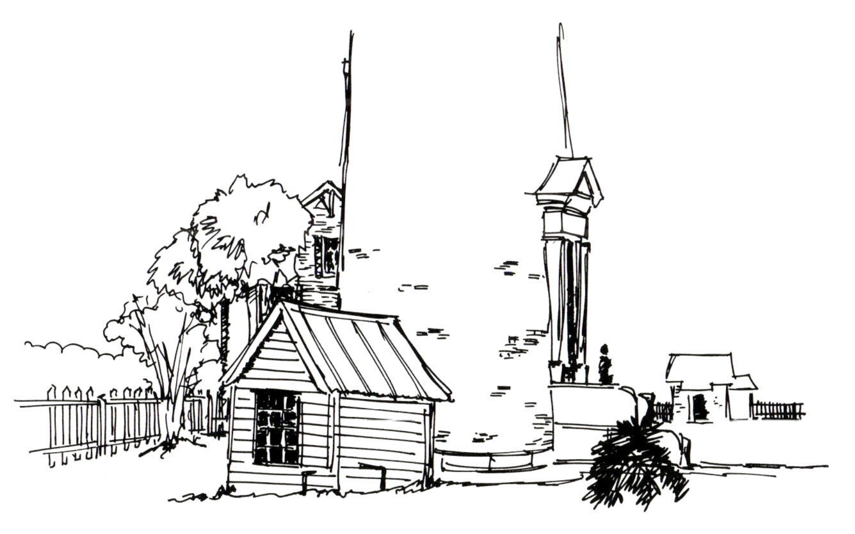

There are many great stories and displays at the Ponce de Leon Inlet Lighthouse, and, of the thirty lighthouses in Florida, this one will give you the best lighthouse experience of them all. It is one you should not miss seeing. The museum, gift shop, keepers' houses and displays are open daily. Best of all, you can climb to the top of the lighthouse.

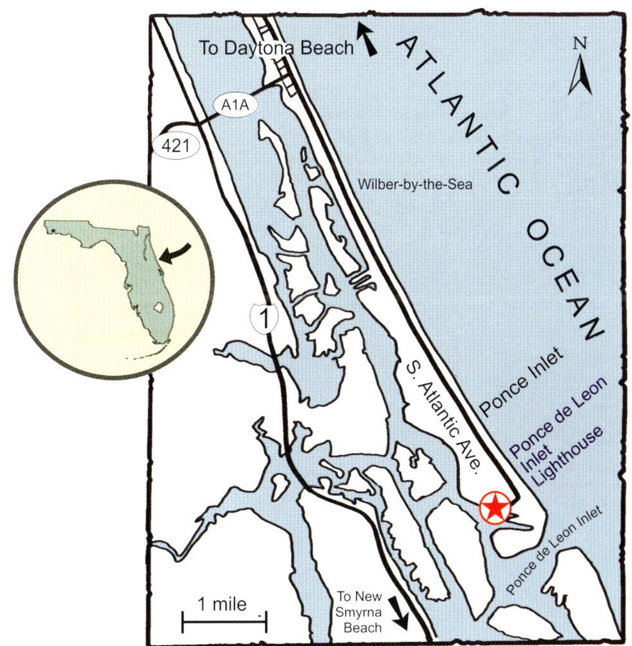

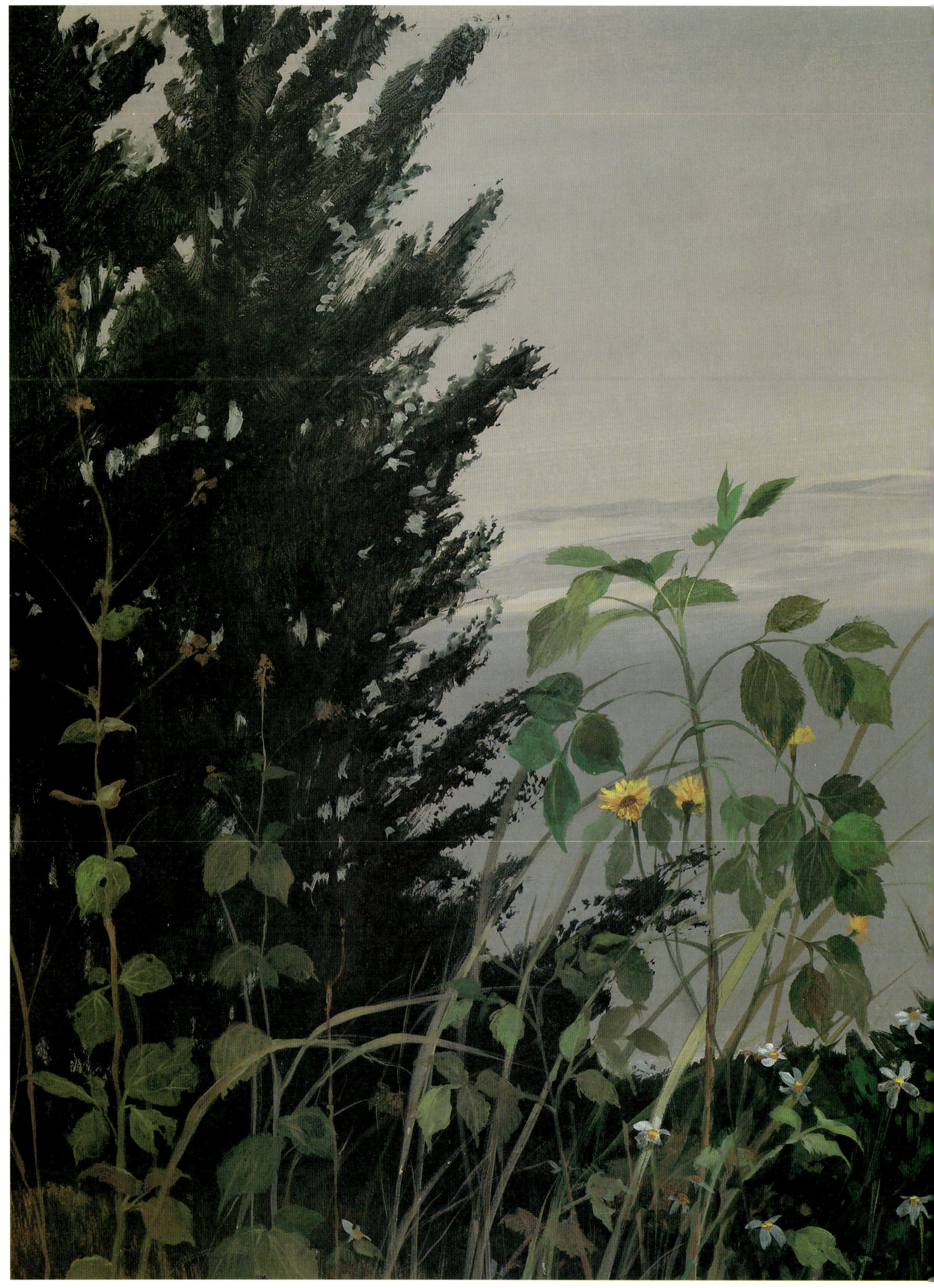

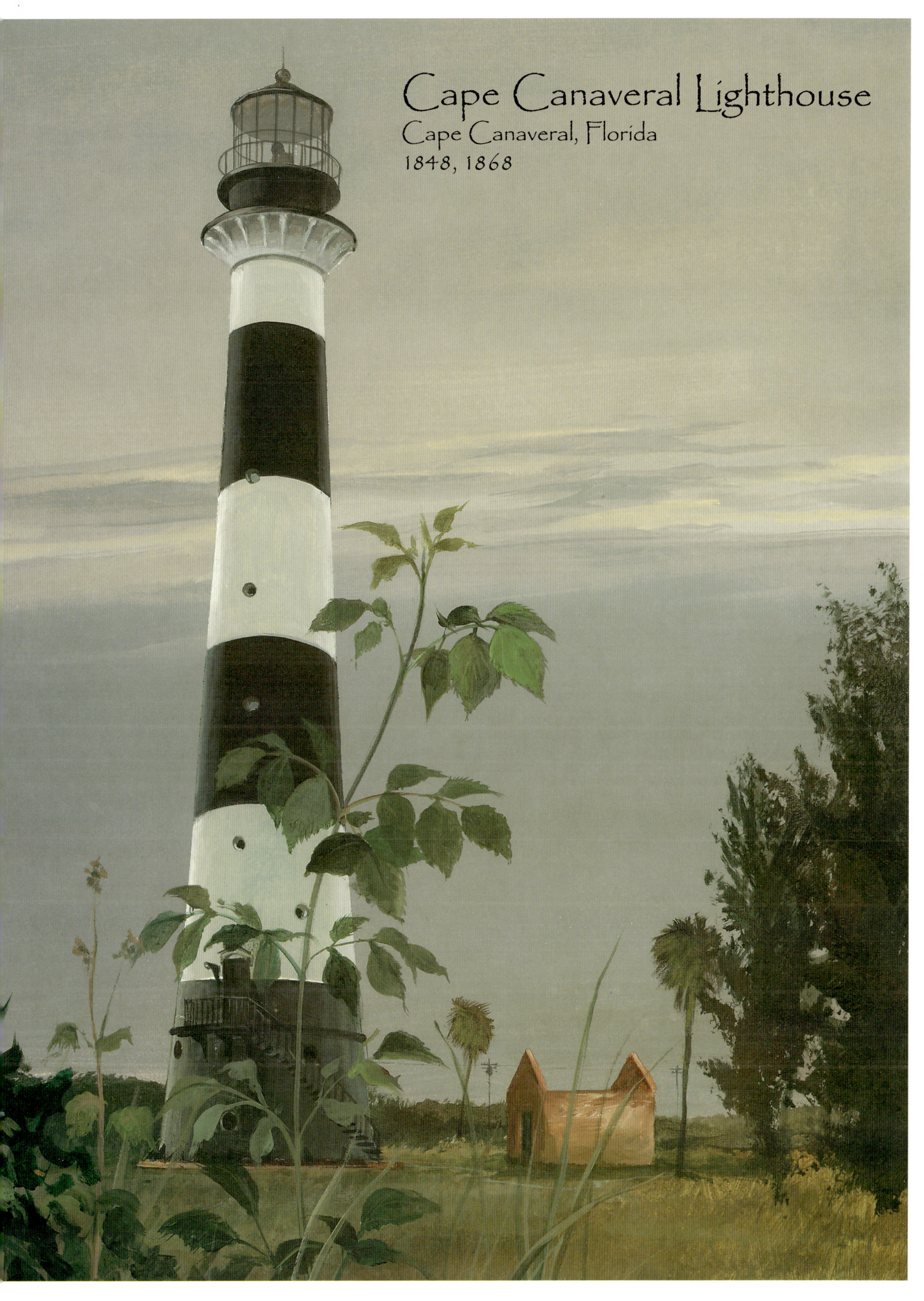
Cape Canaveral Lighthouse
Cape Canaveral, Florida
1848, 1868

The Cape Canaveral Lighthouse was guiding ships along the Atlantic long before anyone dreamed of ships in space. It still shines its guiding light off the east coast of Florida only a few thousand feet from where the first men left Earth to visit the moon. Dr. Wernher von Braun, a pioneer of the space effort, used the lighthouse as a platform to observe early rocket launches. Later, the military used the lighthouse to house and monitor electronic equipment. Being so close to the launch pads has posed a threat to the light in several ways. The huge first-order Fresnel lens began to crack from the severe vibrations caused by the nearby launch of rockets, and in 1997, an Atlas rocket exploded on liftoff and debris narrowly missed the lighthouse.

Before this lighthouse, another one stood at Cape Canaveral. It was built in 1848 but was inadequate: It stood only sixty-five feet tall and had a dim light. Ships that got close enough to see the light were in danger of hitting the reef they were trying to avoid.

Just before the Civil War started, construction on the present lighthouse began, but it was put on hold until the war ended. The light was completed in 1868 and stood 139 feet above sea level. Unfortunately, erosion threatened the lighthouse a mere ten years latert. Jetties were constructed to hold back the sea, but as people are still learning today, not much can be done when the power of waves begins to move a beach. Eventually, the entire structure was moved about a mile inland.

A Coast Guardsman showed me around the top of the Cape Canaveral Lighthouse. From here, it was easy to see the Delta rocket launch pads.

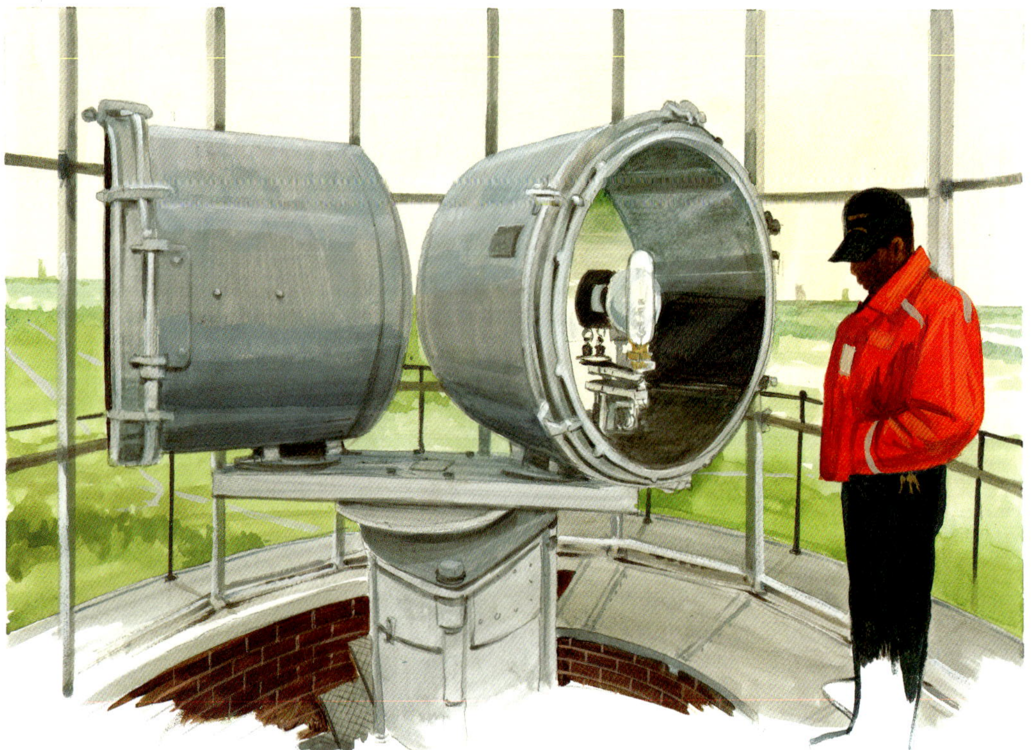

The lighthouse was designed in huge sections of cast iron, bolted together and entirely lined with bricks for added strength. Although this made disassembling the structure possible, it must have been a monumental undertaking and no record remains of how they actually accomplished it. Tens of thousands of bricks first had to be chipped away from the concrete, removed, and then the cast iron sections each weighing tons were unbolted, lowered to the ground and moved.

The first two floors of the lighthouse were surprisingly large living quarters, with a spiral staircase through the center of the interior rather than around the outside walls. The original cabinets were built to fit the curve of the walls.

Whale oil was used to light the beacon from the time it was built until 1885, when kerosene was put into use. Large barrels of whale oil would sometimes be unloaded from a cargo ship, floated ashore in the shallow surf, and then loaded onto a wagon and hauled to the brick oil house. Events like this were exciting for the lighthouse keeper's children, who seldom saw much outside activity. Trips to Titusville for supplies were made only once a month, so living at the lighthouse was quite spartan and solitary. The only regular callers were the mosquitoes, and there were plenty of those.

Occasionally on dark, rainy nights, birds would fly into the light and fall to the ground dead. The lighthouse keeper's children would sometimes have to carry away hundreds of dead birds the day after a storm. If a goose or duck happened to be among the fatalities, it would end up on the dinner table that night. At some lighthouses, the problem of birds hitting and breaking the glass became so common that wire mesh was installed to keep the damage to a minimum.

Today the lighthouse is nicely restored, its electronic equipment to monitor the rocket launches has been removed, and its basic function is once again to shine its light seaward. Two modern-day, one-thousand-watt searchlight beacons have replaced the original first-order Fresnel lens, now handsomely restored and on display at the Ponce de Leon Inlet Lighthouse.

The best way to see the lighthouse is to take a bus tour around the space center (check at the space center for more information). None of the buses stops at the lighthouse, but the "Blue Tour" drives by it and pauses for pictures. The Coast Guard has the authority to give tours of this (or any other) lighthouse, but tours are difficult to arrange because the light is in a very restricted area of the Cape.

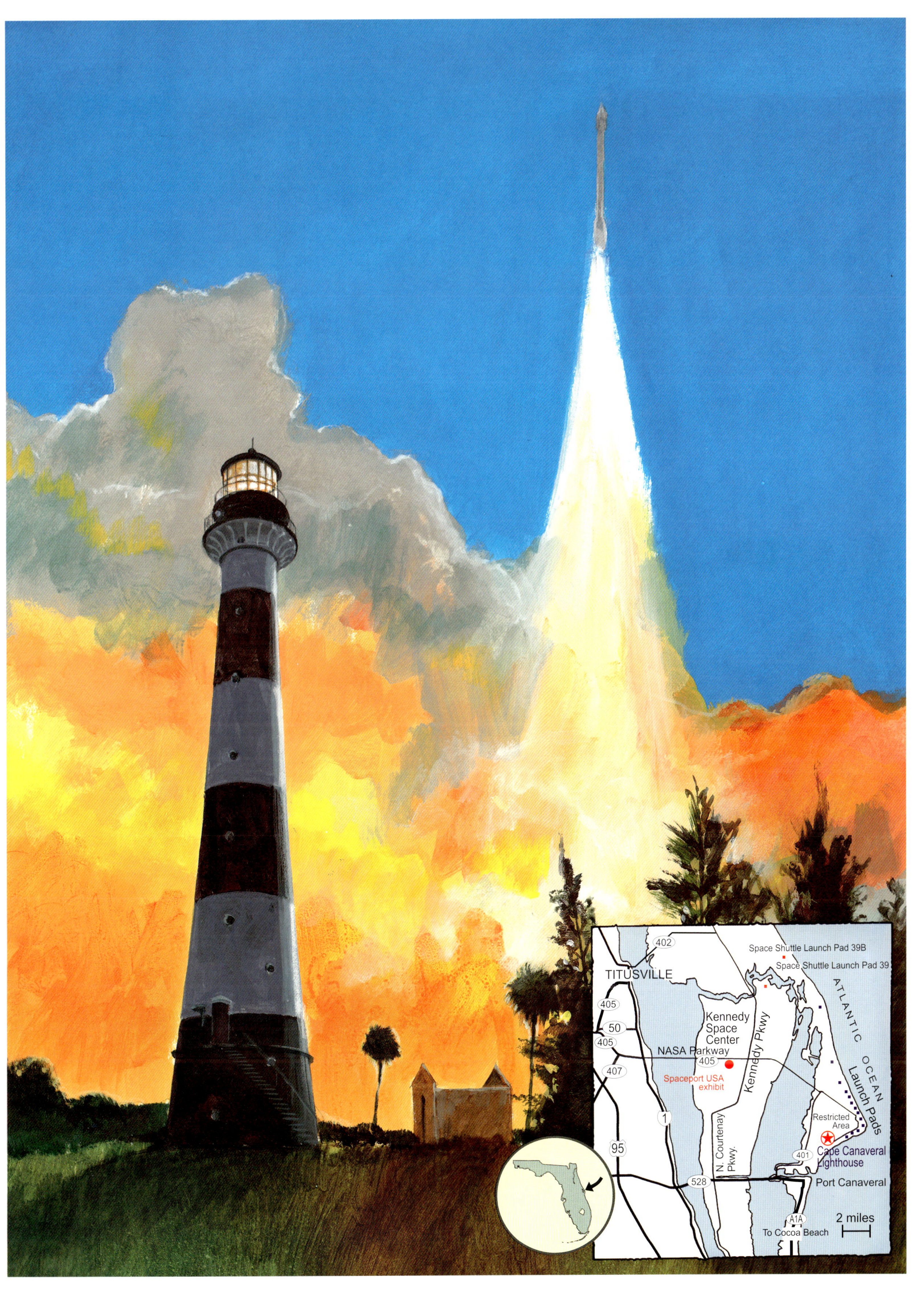

Space Shuttle Launch Pad 39B
Space Shuttle Launch Pad 39
402
TITUSVILLE
ATLANTIC OCEAN
405
50
405
407
Kennedy Space Center
NASA Parkway
405
Kennedy Pkwy
Spaceport USA exhibit
Launch Pads
Restricted Area
1
95
N. Courtenay Pkwy.
401
Cape Canaveral Lighthouse
528
Port Canaveral
A1A
To Cocoa Beach
2 miles

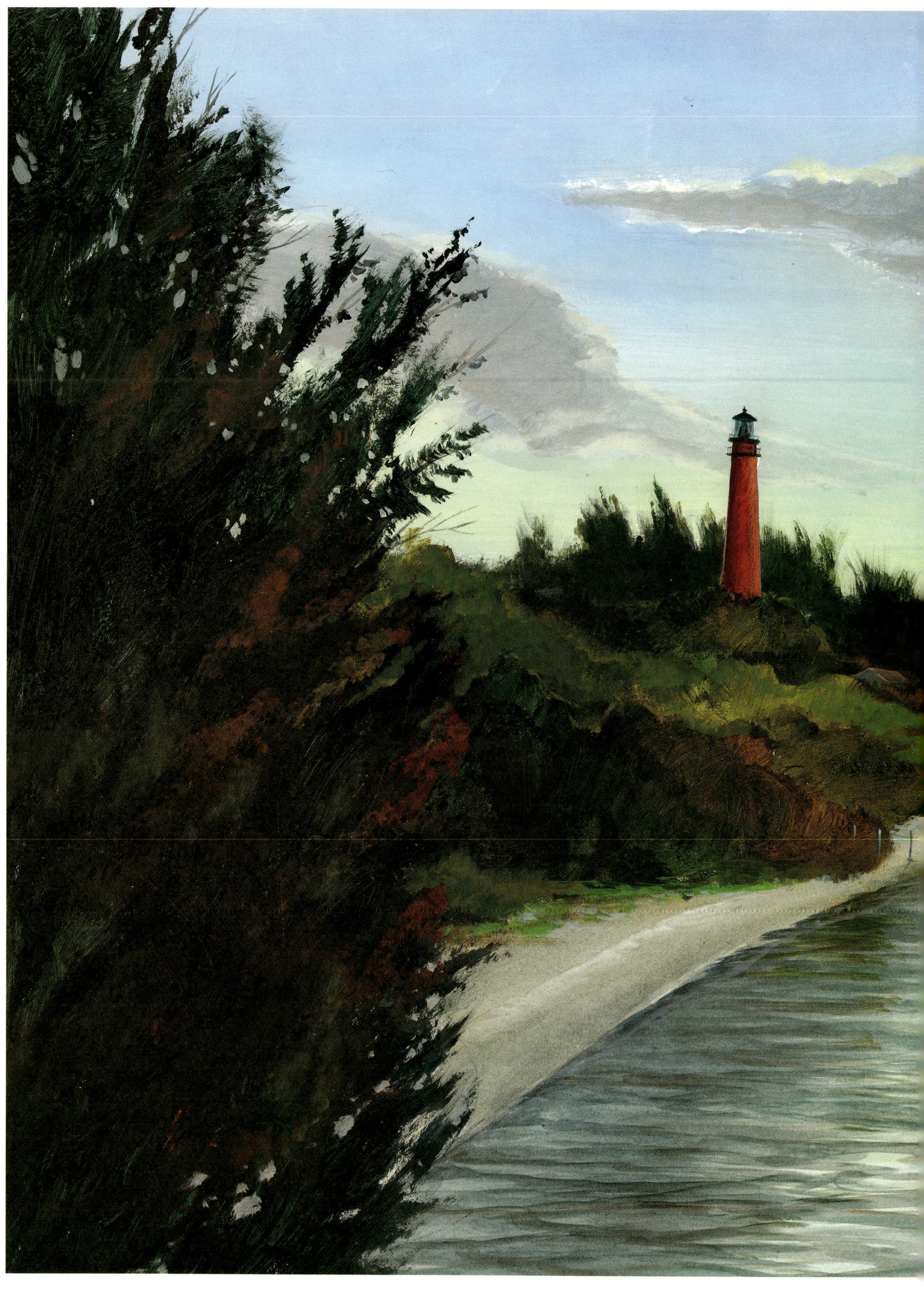

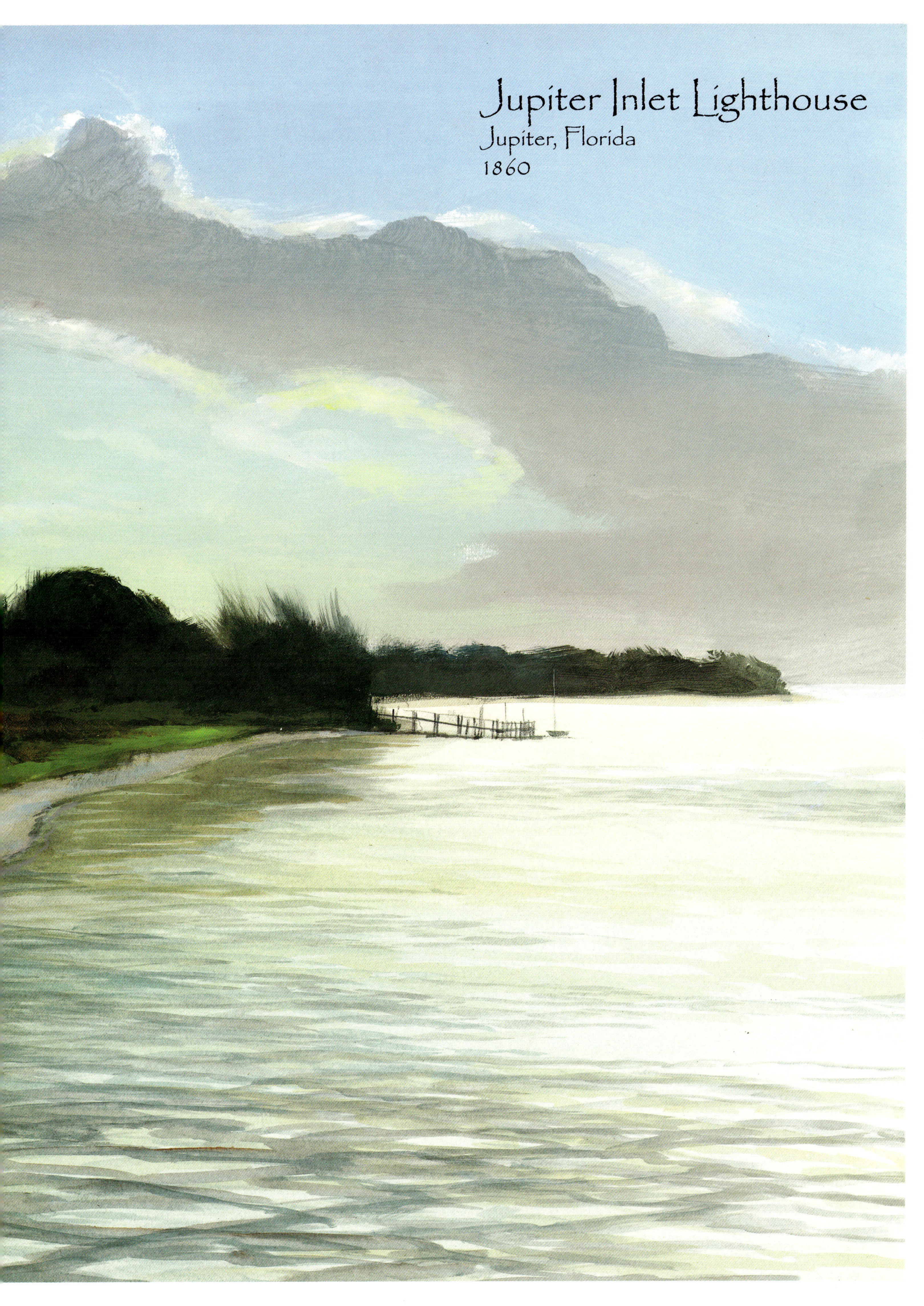
Jupiter Inlet Lighthouse
Jupiter, Florida
1860

Work began on the Jupiter Inlet Lighthouse in 1854, but there were many delays. Even though no battles between settlers and Indians occurred here, because of the horrible Indian attack at the Cape Florida Lighthouse in 1836, any threat of violence was taken seriously. Work progressed slowly and cautiously.

Shortly after the lighthouse was finished in 1860, it was darkened by the Civil War. It seems that the Union found this a convenient inlet to unload supplies and munitions, so the Confederates dismantled part of the illuminating mechanism and hid it in the area of Lake Worth Creek. This made access to the area at night a little more difficult for Union soldiers. After the war, the lens was retrieved and reinstalled. By this time, Seminoles and settlers in the area had made peace with one another and were quite friendly.

Despite the presence of the lighthouse, shipwrecks still occurred offshore. Such was the case one October day in 1872, when one man's loss became another man's find. One hundred fifty thousand dollars worth of cargo went overboard. Most of it sank, but some drifted ashore and ended up in the hands of the Seminole Indians. What remained went to the few settlers who lived in the area. As one crate began to wash ashore and was about to be retrieved by one of the Indians, the lighthouse keeper read the markings on the crate and yelled out in a loud voice, claiming it as his own. That's how the assistant keeper's wife came to own a brand new Wheeler and Wilson sewing machine, a useful luxury that she put to use for years.

Entertainment was not what it is today and there was little in the form of amusement but an event sometimes took place on weekends that would entertain residents of the lighthouse and nearby towns. The young assistant lighthouse keeper, Dwight Allen, would gather a crowd and boldly walk on the pitched roof of the 105 foot high lighthouse. After his onlookers grew to a number he thought sizable enough, he would end his exhibition by doing a handstand at the very peak of the tower, much to the delight of his audience and especially the young women he was trying to impress.

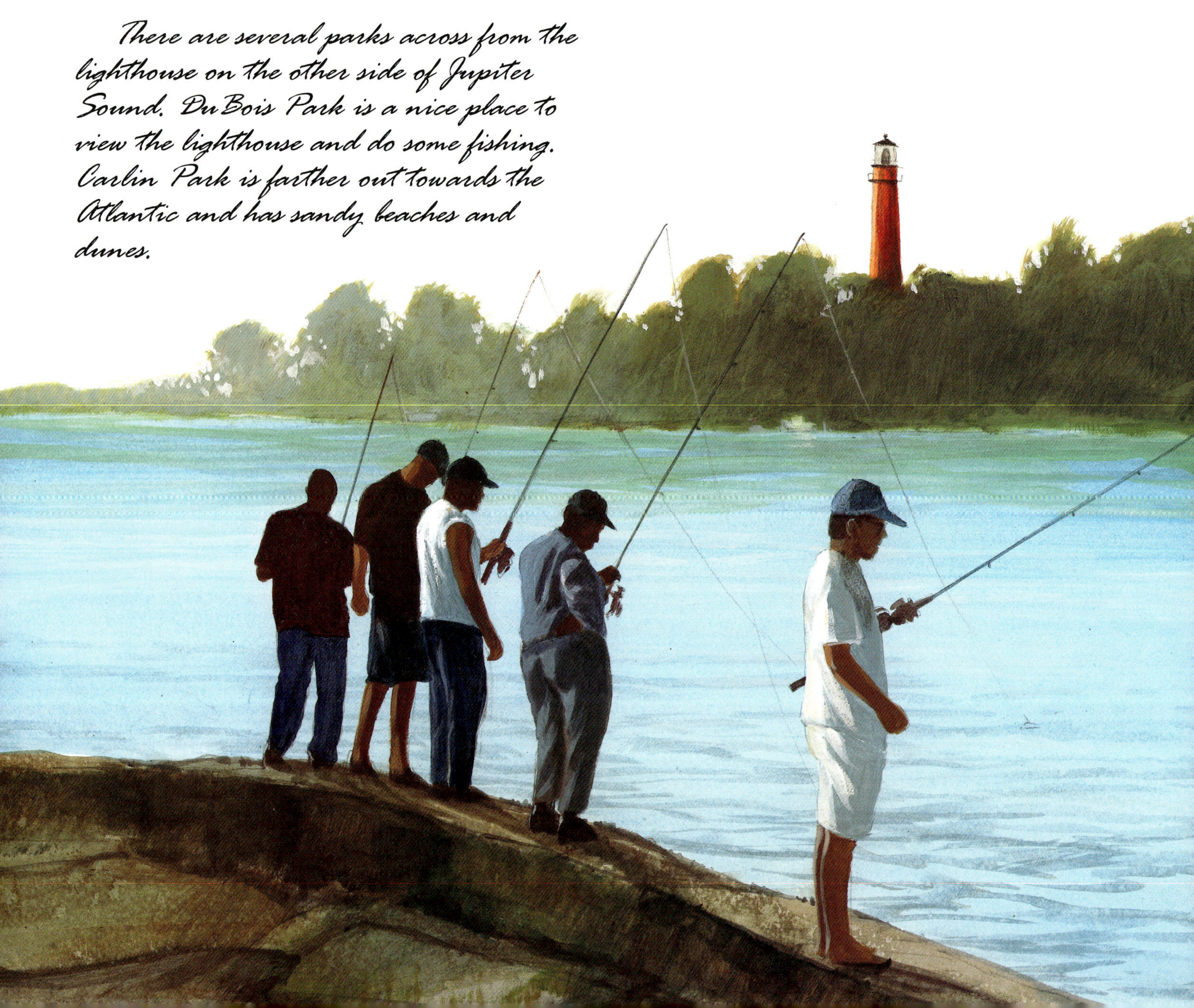

There are several parks across from the lighthouse on the other side of Jupiter Sound. DuBois Park is a nice place to view the lighthouse and do some fishing. Carlin Park is farther out towards the Atlantic and has sandy beaches and dunes.

The migration of birds was a problem for many Florida lighthouses, especially along the Atlantic Coast. Wire screens were installed at this light to keep birds from crashing into the panes of glass. These large migrations seem to be a thing of the past, but the Jupiter and Cape Canaveral Lighthouses were especially hard hit in previous times. During the early 1900s, ducks came here in such abundance they would sometimes cover the entire width of Jupiter Sound. Each morning, bucketfuls of dead birds would be collected at the base of the light. Offshore lights still have bird crashes, but city lights in general have reduced the number of hits. Insects were also fierce at Jupiter. Even at the top of the lighthouse, the bugs were so thick that by morning, they would sometimes have to be scraped off the glass by the bucketful.

Hurricanes were an ever-present danger in the summer months. During the hurricane of 1928, Jupiter's brick tower was reported to have swayed seventeen inches. I don't know who got out there and took that measurement—maybe it just seemed that way. Nevertheless, brick structures can sway quite a bit.

The original two-story keepers' house measured only twenty-six by thirty feet and housed three families. Sadly, it burned to the ground in 1927 and was never rebuilt.

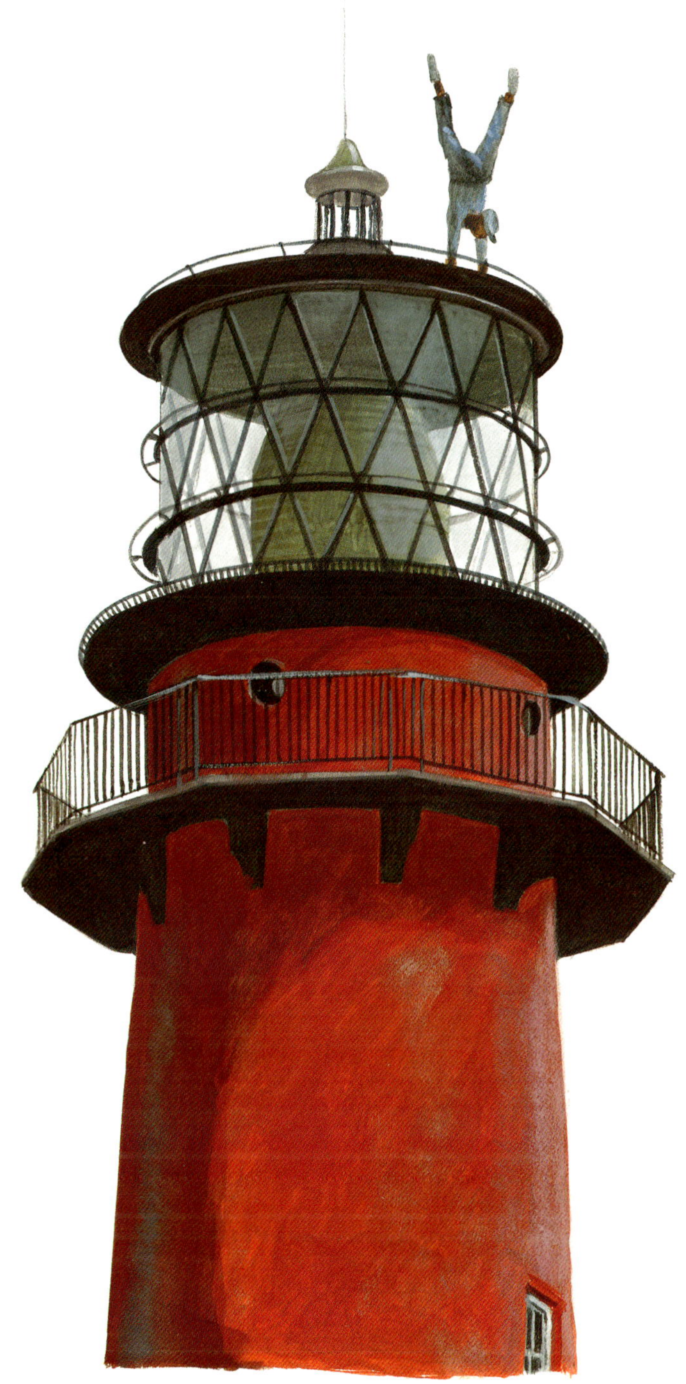

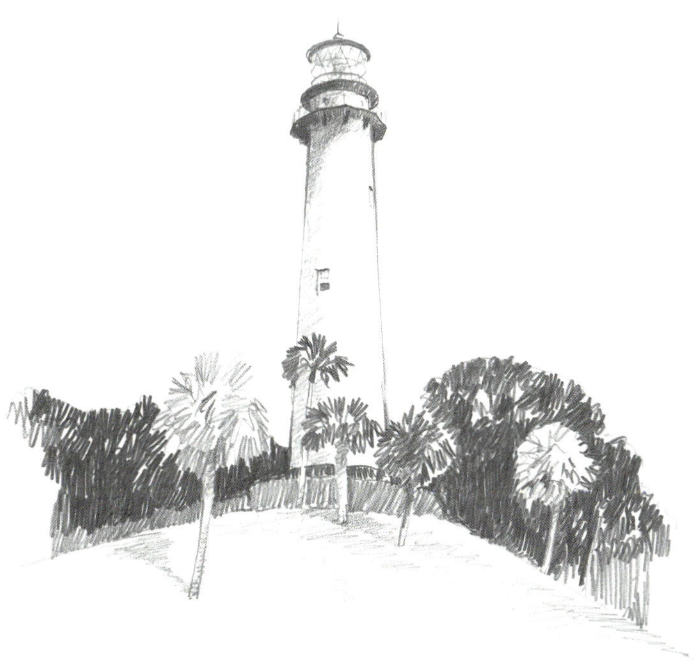

Not far from the lighthouse is a natural feature in the landscape, called Blowing Rocks Preserve, that's fun to visit. If you get there during high tide when there is a good surf, the water sprays up to fifty feet skyward through "blow holes" that have been formed in the Anastasia limestone along the shore.

The lighthouse is open to the public Sunday through Wednesday from 10 a.m. to 4 p.m. The Florida History Center and Museum and the historic DuBois home are also close by.

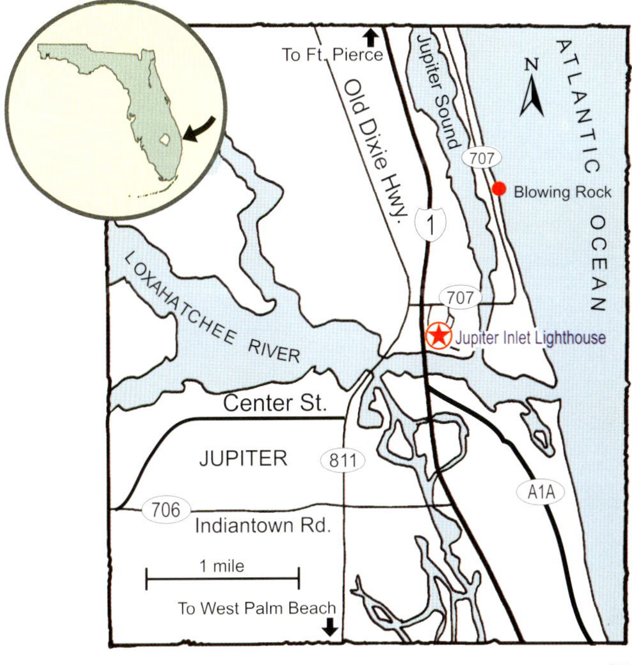

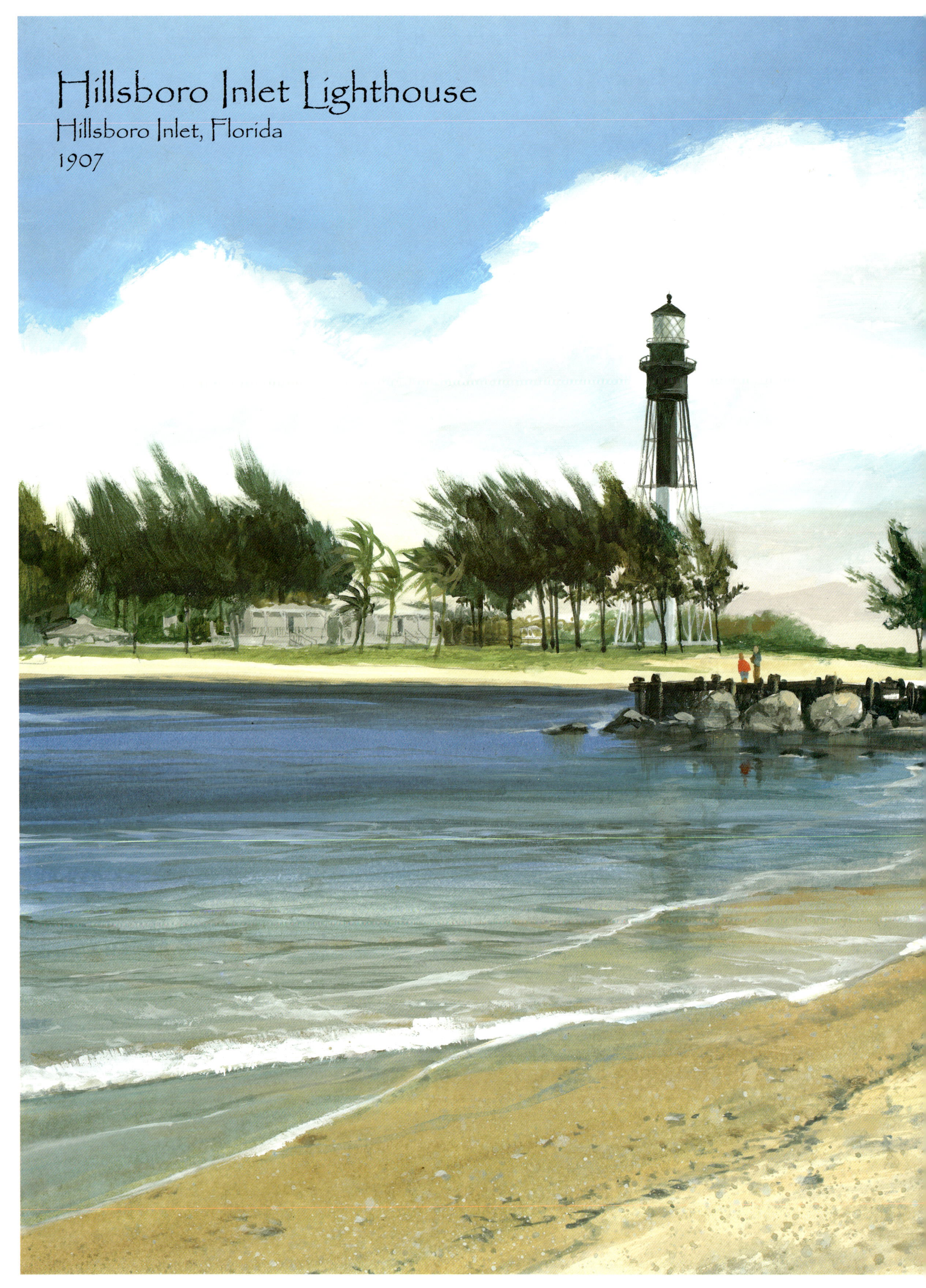
Hillsboro Inlet Lighthouse
Hillsboro Inlet, Florida
1907

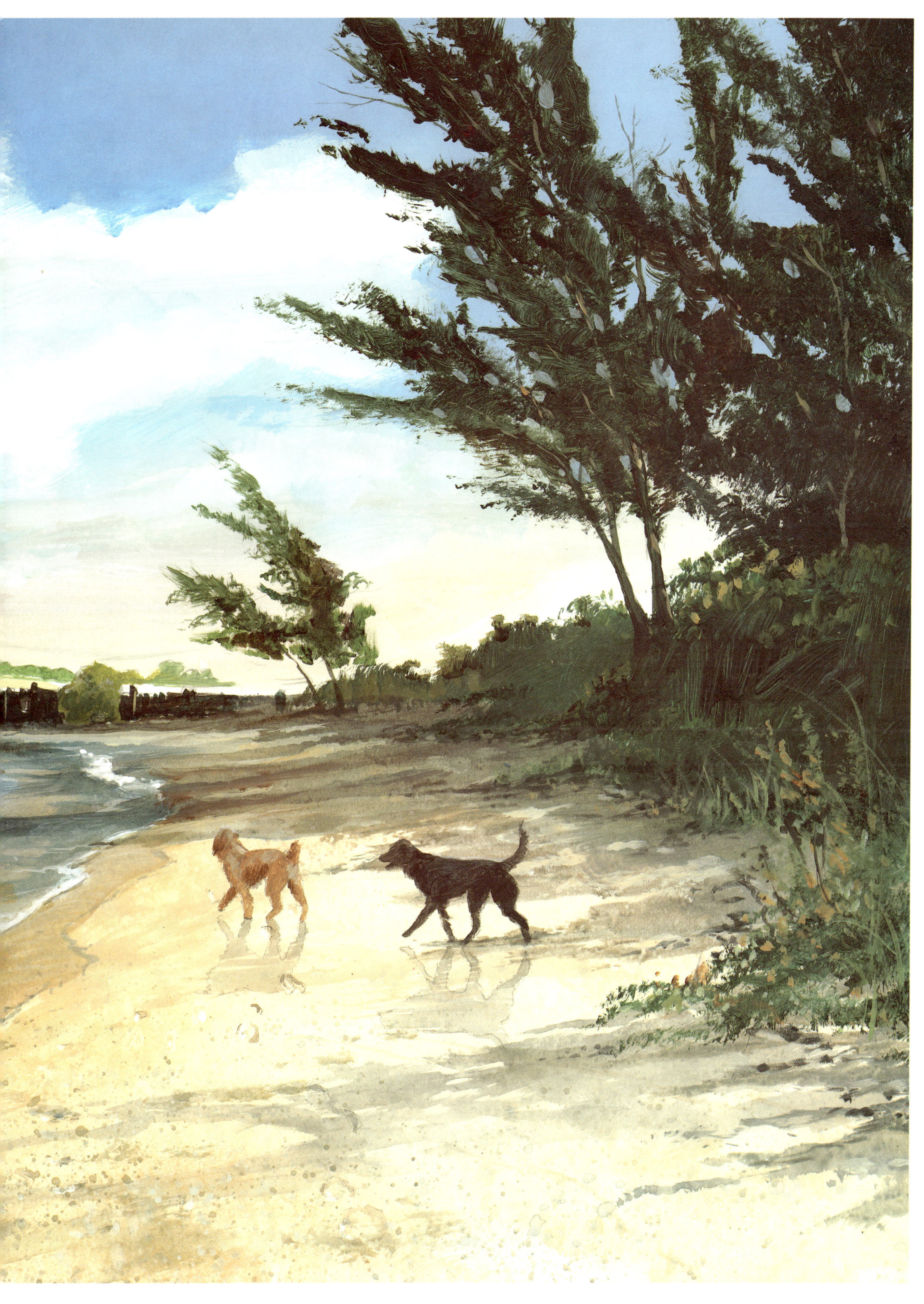

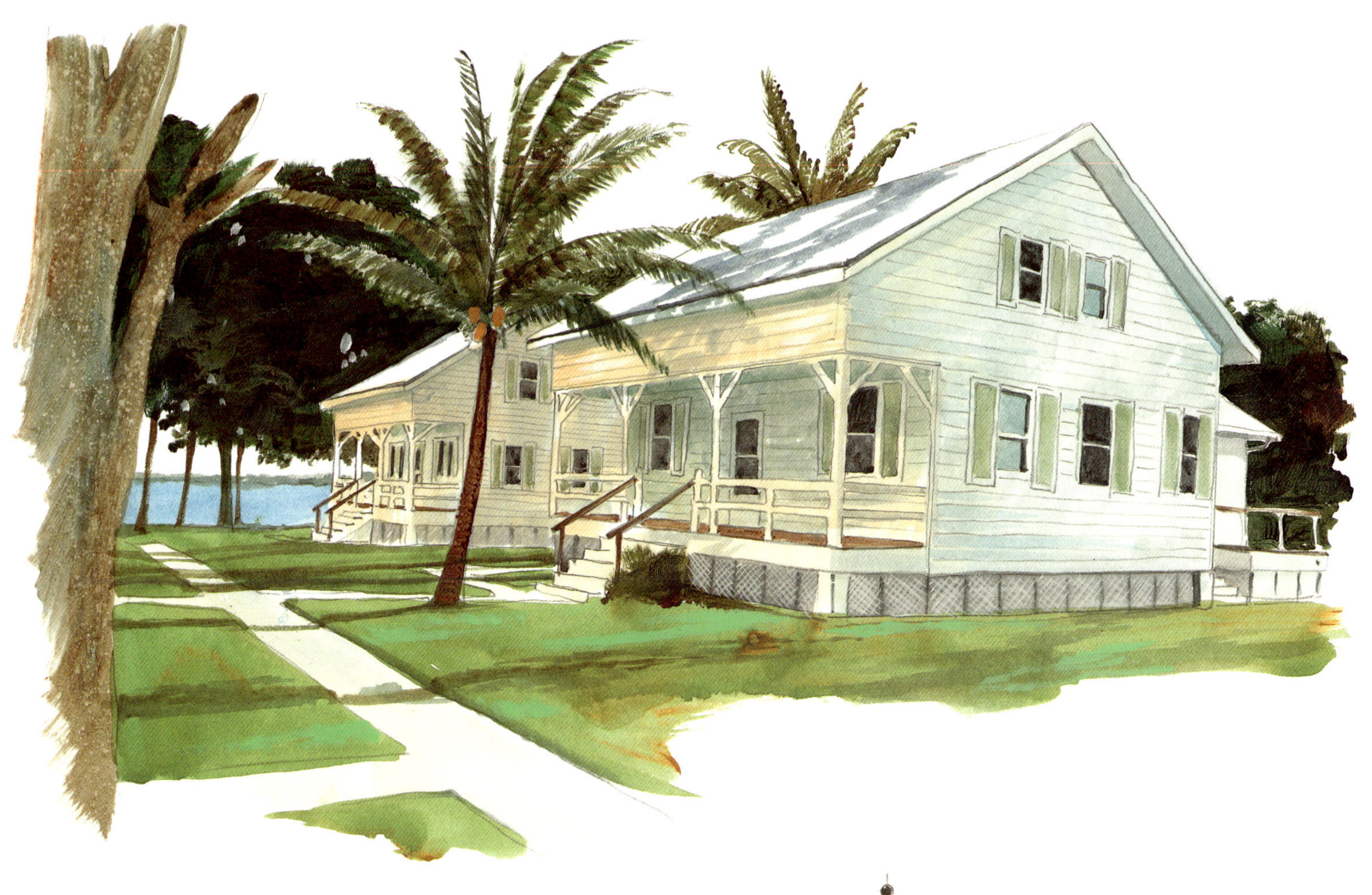

Originally there were three sturdy keepers' houses on the property. Today only two cottages remain. They're used by the Coast Guard as visiting officers' quarters.

The Hillsboro Inlet Lighthouse has weathered many hurricanes, including the one in 1926 that took away about six hundred feet of beach. The erosion was so great that much of the area around the lighthouse was washed away, exposing the concrete pilings that support the structure. Fortunately the lighthouse had a strong foundation. Many attempts were made to stop the beach erosion, including the use of wooden barriers and piled up brush along the shore, but they failed until huge granite boulders were placed from the lighthouse out into the ocean.

The task of building a lighthouse foundation was intensive. Sand was removed down to the bedrock. Holes were then made in the solid rock using chisels, pickaxes, and heavy drills. Bolts were then set into the holes and fixed firmly in place with molten lead. Even in brick and granite lighthouses this method was frequently used. For some lighthouse foundations, massive steel screws were driven into the soft limestone to anchor the lighthouse. Either method proved effective.

Like other skeletal lighthouses, this one was fabricated in Detroit, but others like it were built in New Jersey and New York. They were first assembled to ensure that everything fit properly, then dismantled, packed, and shipped to their final destinations. The cast-iron central tube measures nine feet across and has a double-thick wall with a few inches of space between the walls. This added strength to the tower and insulated it, keeping it a bit cooler in the summer. The lighthouse stands 136 feet tall and became unmanned in 1974.

The diamond-shaped, curved panes of glass in the lantern room of the Hillsboro Inlet Lighthouse are unusual and were very difficult to produce at the time. They were used because they prevented the light from being cut off by any horizontal window framing as the beacon rotated. The clamshell lens, also found in the lighthouse at Cape San Blas, was an improved version of the more traditional beehive Fresnel lens design. Made in 1907 in France, this lens had 356 polished optical glass prisms held in place by a brass framework and was nine feet in diameter. It would cost several million dollars to duplicate this lens today, so smaller beacons with plastic lenses are now used.

The clamshell lens mechanism sat in a circular raceway holding five hundred pounds of liquid mercury that floated the heavy lens so it could easily turn without the use of ball bearings. Unfortunately, the mercury would evaporate in the hot Florida sun, poisoning the air inside the lantern room, although no one realized the dangers back then. The mercury was also handled frequently by the lighthouse keeper when he cleaned it by filtering, adding to the danger.

Hillsboro Inlet was and still is a treacherous stretch of waterway, especially where it meets the Atlantic. It was windy the day I visited the lighthouse, and even the larger boats were having trouble navigating their way through the pass.

During World War II, many ships were sunk along Florida's Atlantic coast. German submarines would sit offshore and use the lights of the town to silhouette passing ships, making them easy targets. The tanker *Lubrofol* was sunk by a German submarine off the coast of Hillsboro Inlet, leaving the beaches fouled with oil. The Hillsboro Inlet Lighthouse was used as an observation platform to help spot submarines as were other Florida lighthouses, but it was a difficult task. Air patrols were the most effective tool to find submarines, and because of those patrols, several submarines were sunk; one still sits in three hundred feet of water just south of Hillsboro.

The lighthouse and grounds are closed to the public. Just to get close, you have to pass through the private Hillsboro Club, and they aren't very fond of sightseers. You can get a good look at the lighthouse from the bridge, but the best view is from the beaches across the inlet. The Hillsboro Inlet Lighthouse Association is working with the Coast Guard and hopes to open the lighthouse to the public in the future.

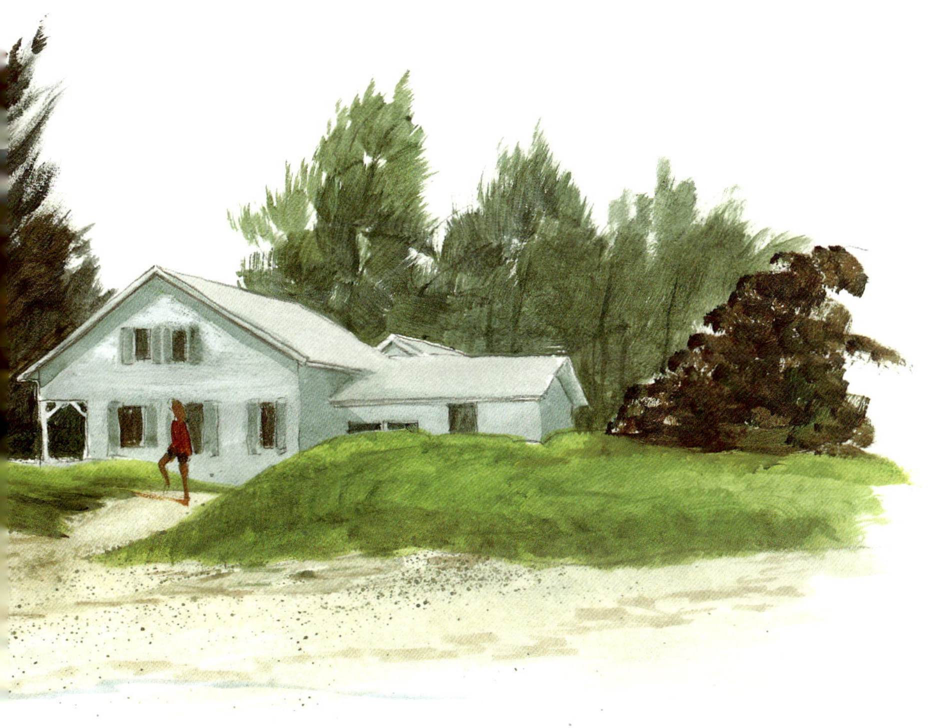

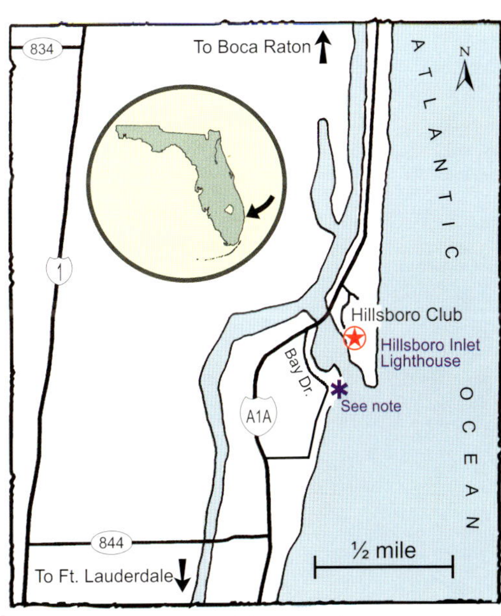

* This is a residential area but there are a few access areas. If you can get to the beach, you'll find it a rewarding place to view the lighthouse.

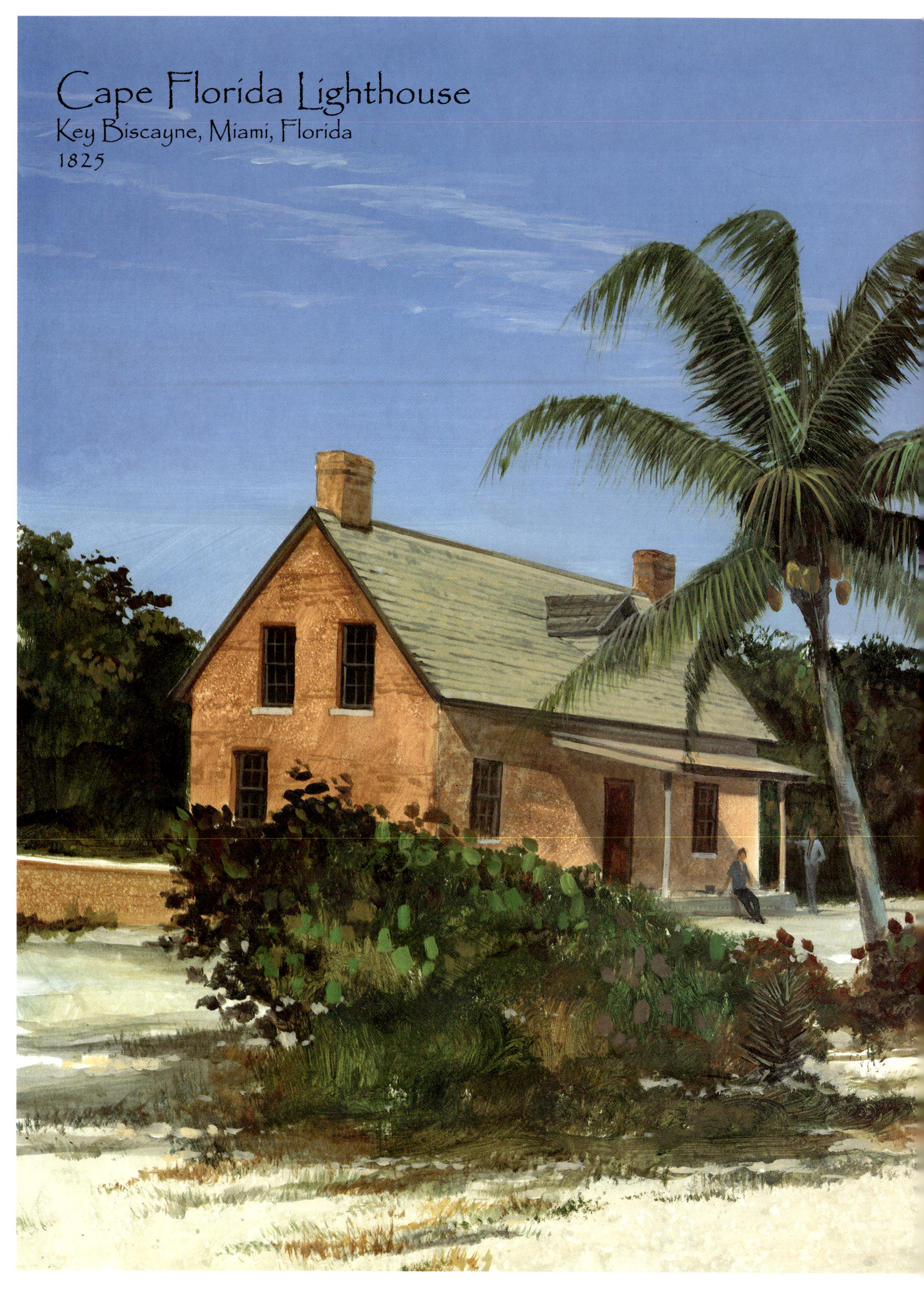
Cape Florida Lighthouse
Key Biscayne, Miami, Florida
1825

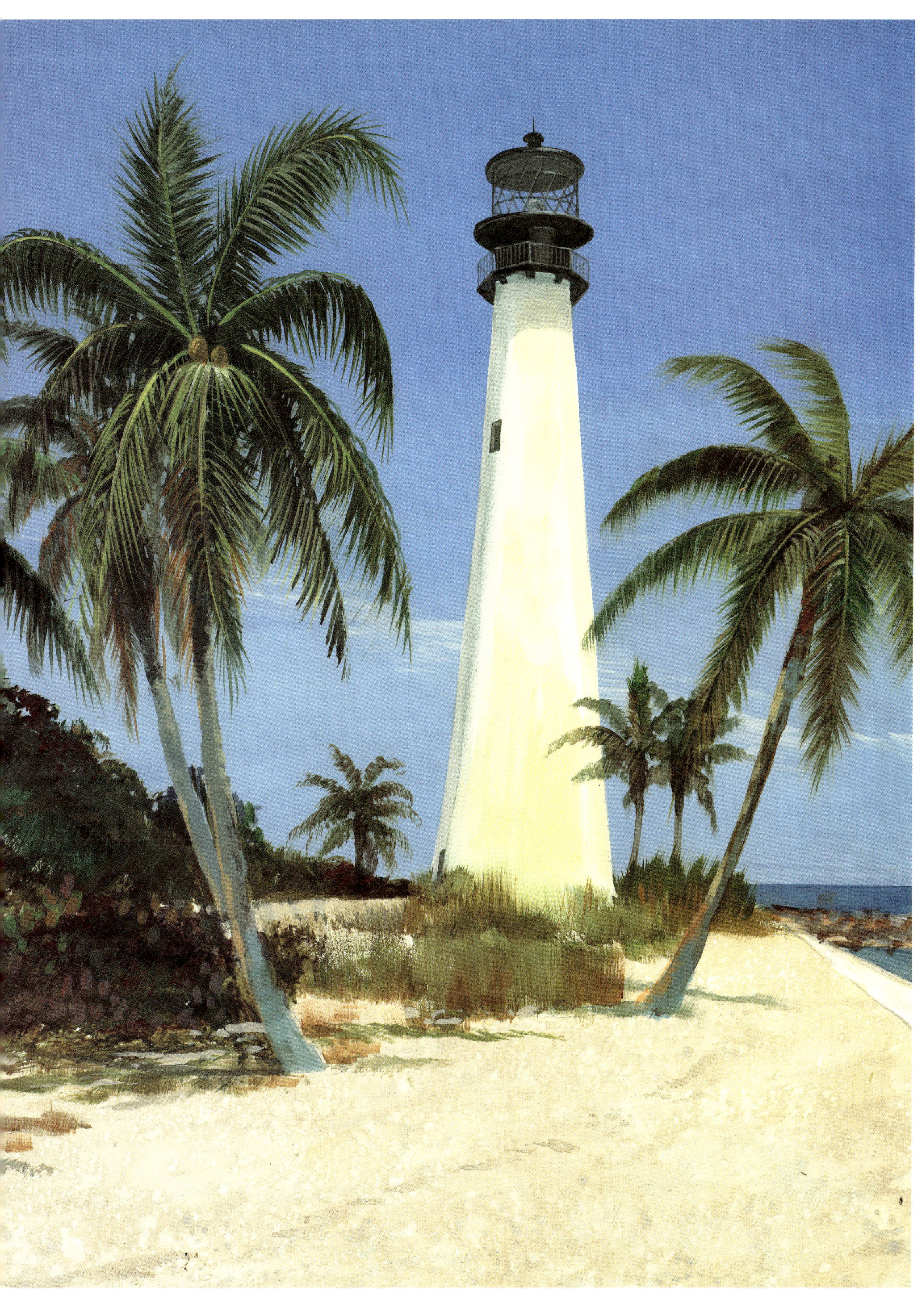

Key Biscayne marks the spot of the first seacoast lighthouse established in Florida. There were two other lighthouses built before this one—in St. Augustine and in Key West—but they were harbor lights. This lighthouse didn't mark the entrance to a harbor but rather warned coastal shipping of the dangerous offshore reefs.

I visited the Cape Florida Lighthouse on a hot sunny day. The biggest problem at the lighthouse today might be the traffic in getting there: I had to drive down four-lane highways, pass high-rise apartments, and maneuver through a myriad of exclusive little shops selling everything from ice cream to high fashion. But tragic events that took place here in 1836 make traffic congestion seem a very small inconvenience.

After entering the park, I walked to the beach where children played in the white sand while others swam or sunbathed in the warmth of the afternoon. As I stood by the freshly whitewashed lighthouse (it was red brick for years but now has been painted its original color), I tried to imagine what it was like on what would become the most horrible and ghastly day in lighthouse history.

On the very spot I was standing, looking skyward, the day was much like it was over a century and a half ago. The winds gently blew in from the Atlantic Ocean, the sky was clear and bright, and the water was a radiant blue. It was peaceful and serene. Brown pelicans soared in groups close to the water with wings almost touching the surface. The lighthouse keeper had gone to Key West, leaving his assistant, John Thompson, in charge. With him was an elderly man named Aaron Carter who also helped out at the lighthouse and was most likely Thompson's slave. Together they went about the business of caring for the lighthouse and grounds, but there was an uneasy feeling in the air. The Second Seminole War had begun a year earlier, and although no threats of violence had been made towards lighthouse keepers, times were troubled.

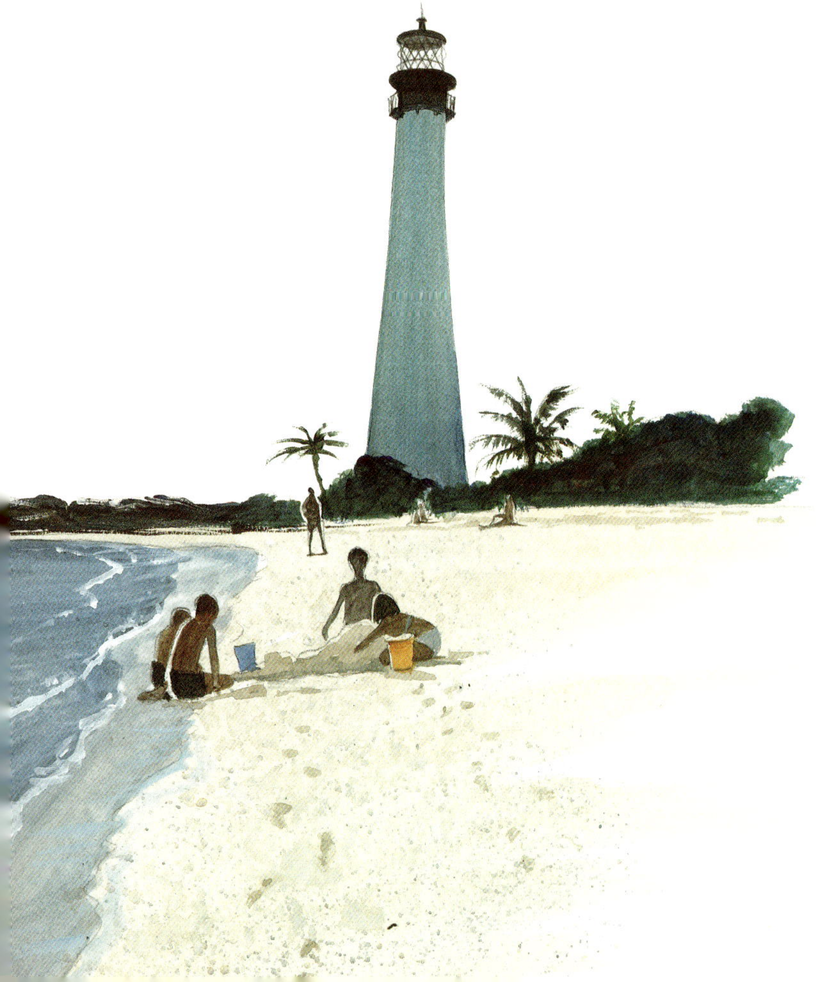

The trouble had begun months earlier when a group of white men killed the Indians' chief, Alibama. William Cooley, a settler in an area just north of what is now Miami, was justice of the peace at the time. He tried the accused men but the case was dismissed for lack of evidence, making the Indians less than happy. Quite a bit less in fact. While Cooley was away from home, Indians attacked his house, killing the children's tutor. Mrs. Cooley ran from the house with her baby in her arms but a bullet ripped through her and the baby, killing them both. Cooley's nine-year-old son was clubbed to death, his eleven-year-old daughter was shot to death, his property was plundered, and his house burned. Cooley returned home and buried his family, then left the area with about sixty other people, escaping only with their lives. They went to Cape Florida—all the time knowing they were still in danger—then sailed south to Indian Key, where there was more protection. Cooley even returned to Cape Florida to help out at the lighthouse for a time; the Seminoles had moved inland and there was no bloodshed for the next five months.

Around four o'clock in the afternoon on July 23, 1836, a nightmare was about to occur. Thompson was walking from the detached kitchen to the keeper's house when a group of Indians appeared about twenty feet away. He ran for the lighthouse, calling to the elderly Carter to follow. At that moment, a volley of rifle balls pierced his clothes and hat. Many rounds also hit the lighthouse door, but Thompson and Carter both managed to make it inside. No sooner had Carter succeeded in locking the door behind him than the Indians had their hands on it. Thompson raced to a window of the lighthouse with three loaded muskets and began shooting at the Indians who were gathered around the nearby keeper's house, throwing them into confusion. Then, as the keeper later noted in his journal, for a second time they "began their horrid yells."

Thompson managed to keep the Indians at bay until dark, but then they set fire to the door of the lighthouse while showering Thompson with a heavy barrage of bullets. Flames from the fire ignited a 225-gallon tank of oil, forcing Thompson and Carter to retreat to the top of the lighthouse. Thompson managed to take his musket and a keg of gunpowder with him. The two men tried to cut away the interior wooden stairs, but the rising flames quickly forced them onto the outside gallery, exposing them to more gunfire.

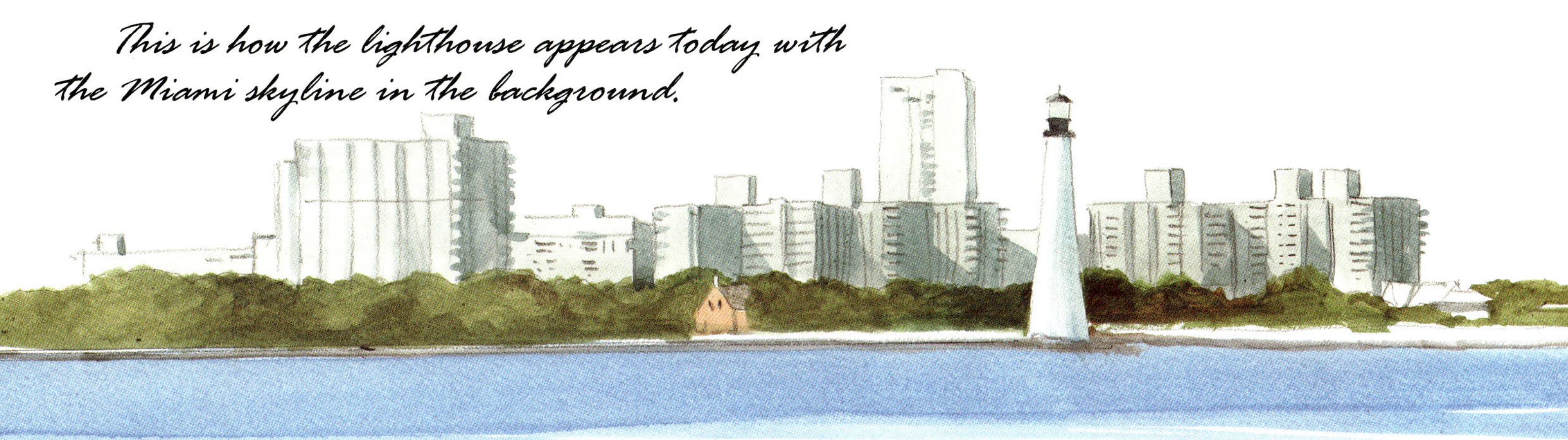
This is how the lighthouse appears today with the Miami skyline in the background.

They had little choice: They could either stay inside the scalding hot lantern room and burn to death or move to the outside catwalk and be shot to death.

The lantern room was full of flames, and glass was bursting and flying in all directions. To end the nightmare, Carter tried to jump to his death from the catwalk but was shot dead before he could get over the railing. Thompson's flesh began to roast, and in an effort to put an end to his horrible suffering, he rolled the keg of gunpowder into the flames. It instantly exploded, shaking the tower from top to bottom. Instead of blowing Thompson into eternity, however, the blast managed to extinguish the flames and collapse what was left of the stairs, leaving Thompson no chance of escaping the tower even if the Indians left.

It was still too hot to retreat into the lantern room, so Thompson had to simply lie on the circular walkway. All his oil-soaked clothes had been burned off his body, and his hair had been singed from his scalp. He was unable to stand or walk because his feet had been shot to pieces with three rifle balls in each foot. Thinking he was dead, the Indians plundered as much as they could fit into their canoes and Thompson's sloop and left as mosquitoes feasted on Thompson's peeling, charred, raw skin all through the night.

When Thompson awoke the next morning, there was little to do but suffer. Carter's body was beginning to smell awful in the summer heat, and Thompson regretfully rolled it off the tower. Everything he owned had been stolen or burned to the ground.

What Thompson didn't know then was that the sound of the explosion had been heard twelve miles away aboard U.S. naval vessels *Motto* and *Concord*. The ships' concerned crews sailed to the still-smoldering lighthouse and were amazed to find the lighthouse keeper still alive. Sailors tried to use a kite to get twine to the top of the tower in order to then hoist up a rope, but that plan failed. Meanwhile, Thompson lay in the sweltering heat with no food or water. It wasn't until a full day later that a ramrod and string were successfully fired from a musket and landed on the gallery railing. Thompson gathered it and then hoisted up a larger rope. Two sailors raised themselves to the platform and Thompson was finally lowered to the ground.

Thompson's recovery was miraculous, and later that same year he was appointed assistant lightkeeper at the Garden Key Lighthouse in the Dry Tortugas. Later, an inspection of the damaged Cape Florida Lighthouse revealed faulty construction. Although some lighthouses at that time were designed with hollow walls, this one was not. The contractor had built it hollow in order to double his profits by using only half the bricks that had been paid for.

It was not until 1847 that the lighthouse was repaired and back in operation—now with solid walls—and in 1855, an extra thirty feet were added to its eighty-foot tower. During the Civil War, the lighthouse was once again damaged and was out of operation until 1867. Ten years later, the new offshore reef lighthouse at Fowey Rocks put the Cape Florida Light out of business. Abandoned, it deteriorated and stood only as a day marker for a full century until 1978, when it was once again restored and relit.

The lighthouse is part of the Bill Baggs Cape Florida State Recreation Area. It's open to the public, and the beaches at the park are nice for swimming.

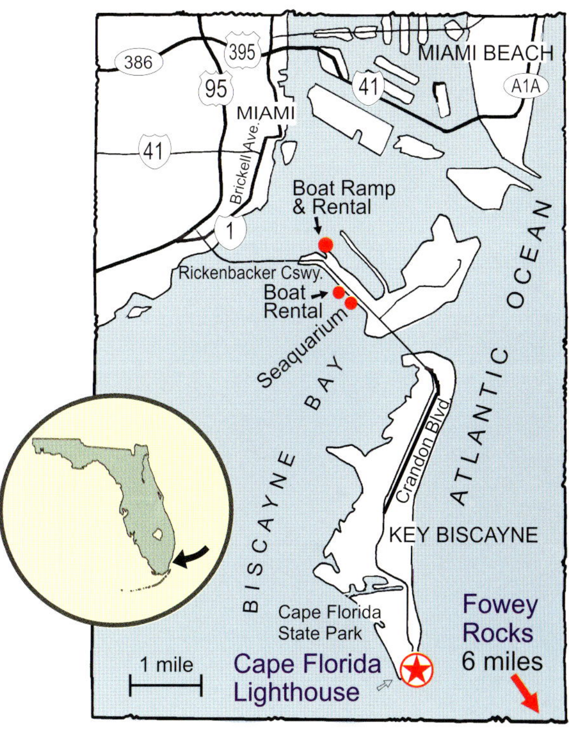

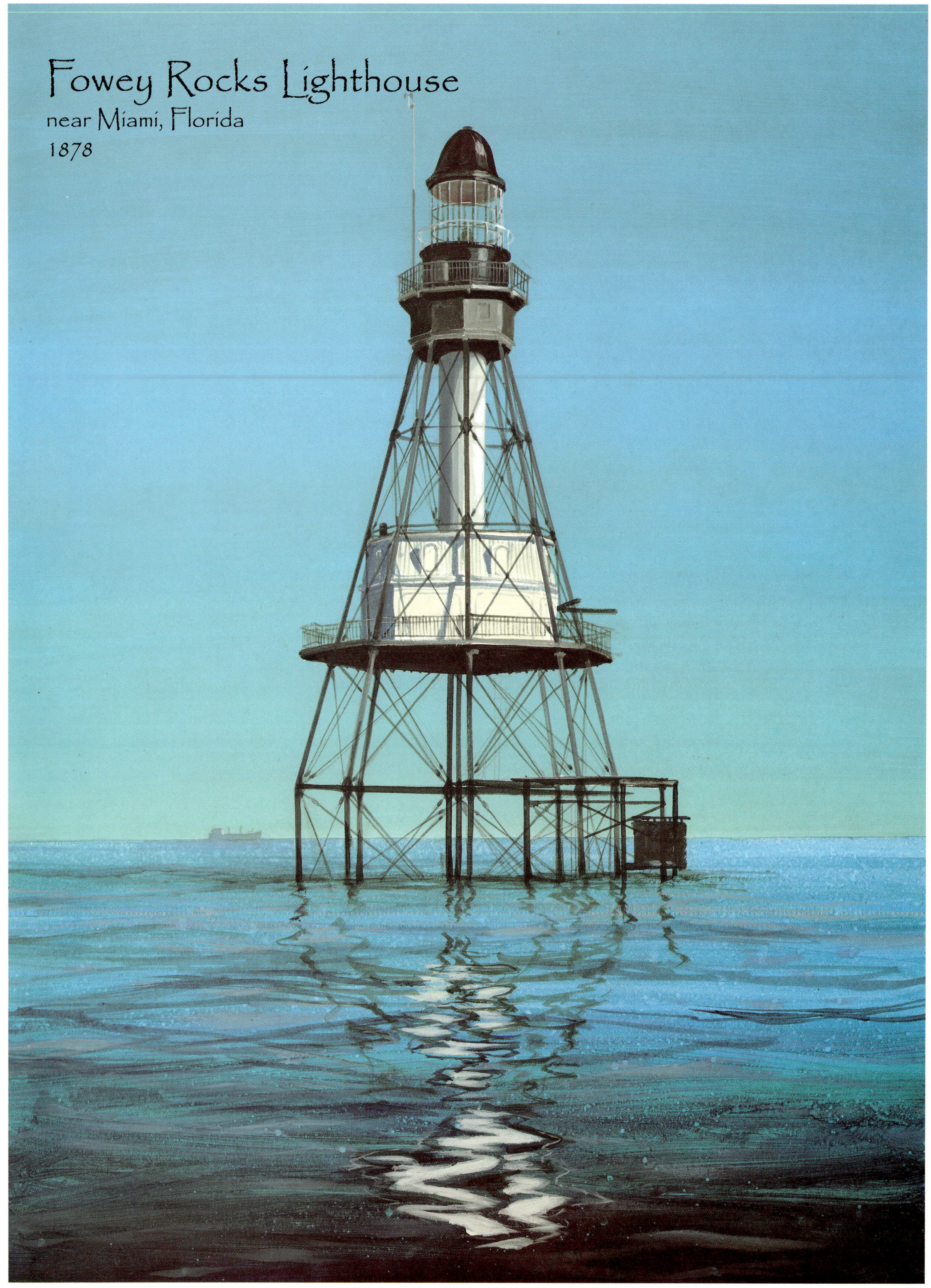
Fowey Rocks Lighthouse
near Miami, Florida
1878

Even with the aid of the nearby Cape Florida Lighthouse, ships continued to run aground. To correct the problem, this iron-pile lighthouse was built about six miles southeast of Cape Florida directly on the reef that was claiming so many ships. It's the sixth and northernmost in this chain of offshore reef lighthouses that extends down to Key West. Like most of the reef lighthouses in southern Florida, it was named after a ship that wrecked in the area, the HMS *Fowey*.

At the start of the construction of Fowey Rocks, a large wooden platform was built on the reef to hold workmen and materials. It was not an easy task to fabricate a scaffold at sea, especially back then. There were no nearby lumber yards or home improvement centers where you could drive in and pick up what you needed. As unbelievable as it may seem, the piles for the working stage were built from local mangrove trees. All the mangroves I've ever seen are thin and twisted and are not likely candidates for any type of building material. However, the red mangrove and the less common buttonwood mangrove (which grows further inland) *can* grow to a height of seventy-five feet. Most likely, these were used for the job.

From this interim stage, the iron pilings for the base of the lighthouse were driven ten feet into the coral reef. The depth of the water here is only about five feet, making it easier to work in some ways, but it also meant that the surf could be rough, making delays inevitable. Workers had to be carried to the site in a steam-powered launch: Steam engines took a long time to fire up and were slow moving. It wasn't the same as zipping out to the site in a twenty-foot fiberglass boat with twin 150-horsepower Mercury engines. Weather, wind, and waves played a major part in delaying construction on all reef lighthouses. The first month at Fowey Rocks went smoothly, but during the second month conditions were so bad that the workmen pitched tents and lived on the platform so they wouldn't have to be ferried over rough seas every day.

The temporary platform must have swayed, creaked, and groaned in the heavy surf. Swimming was not a skill most people had in those days, and here were men several miles out to sea with only a steam barge to rely on to bring them materials and food. Sometimes days went by when seas were too high for the supply boat to reach the construction site. The men basically had nothing to do but sit on their precarious perch and wait. The work was so difficult that the lighthouse took two years to build at a cost of $163,000.

Disaster was always a possibility with such a project, and late one night it was on the way. A large steamer was spotted barreling in the direction of the platform and before the captain of the *Arakanapka* realized what was happening, his ship had slammed into the reef just yards from the platform. The ship broke into pieces and sank. Weeks later, the *Carondelet* gave a repeat performance, clobbering itself on the reef, again just yards from where the workmen watched in horror. The crew of the *Carondelet* had thrown most of her cargo overboard in order to lighten the load, much to the delight of people on the shore, who helped themselves to the bounty as it washed ashore.

Today, the 110-foot lighthouse still warns ships that pass Miami of the dangerous reefs in the area. It was automated in 1967 by the Coast Guard, eliminating the need for a lighthouse keeper. Electricity, supplied by batteries charged with the help of solar panels, powered the lighting and automatic lamp changers that were once lit by mineral oil and kerosene.

The octagonal, two-story, eight-room keepers' house had an iron exterior trimmed inside with wood. Originally, casement windows were used on the upper floor, and the lower floor had green painted shutters, but they have long since been boarded up. With its Victorian flavor, it must have once been even more handsome than it is today. A large tank for holding kerosene and another to hold fresh water were also slung under the lighthouse, but now they too are gone.

You can barely see Fowey Rocks Lighthouse from the Cape Florida Lighthouse, and the only way to get there is by boat. Boat rental places come and go, but there are some on Key Biscayne at the Rickenbacker Marina (next to the Rusty Pelican) at 3301 Rickenbacker Causeway. That's the closest place I found to rent or launch a boat. If you go out there, you might enjoy seeing the stilt houses in the bay. Just be cautious as the waves can grow larger than you might expect.

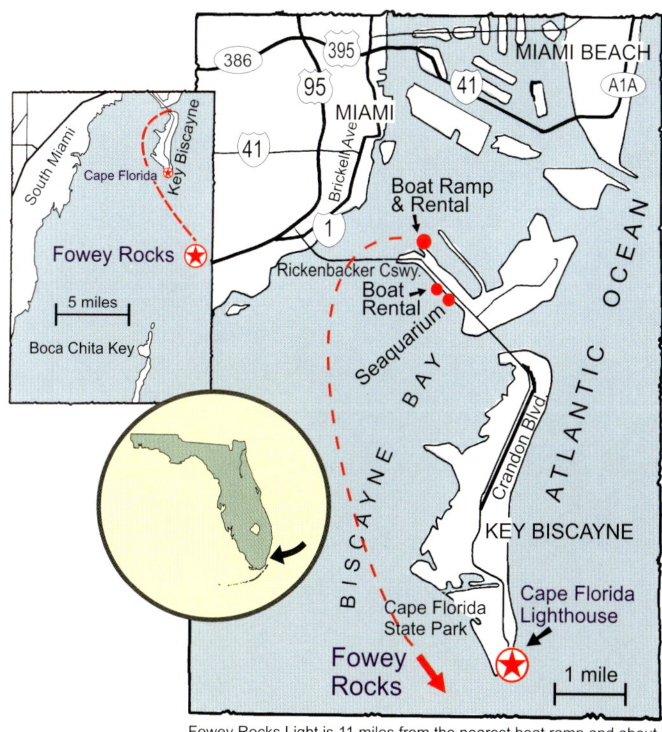

Fowey Rocks Light is 11 miles from the nearest boat ramp and about 6 miles from the Cape Florida Lighthouse.

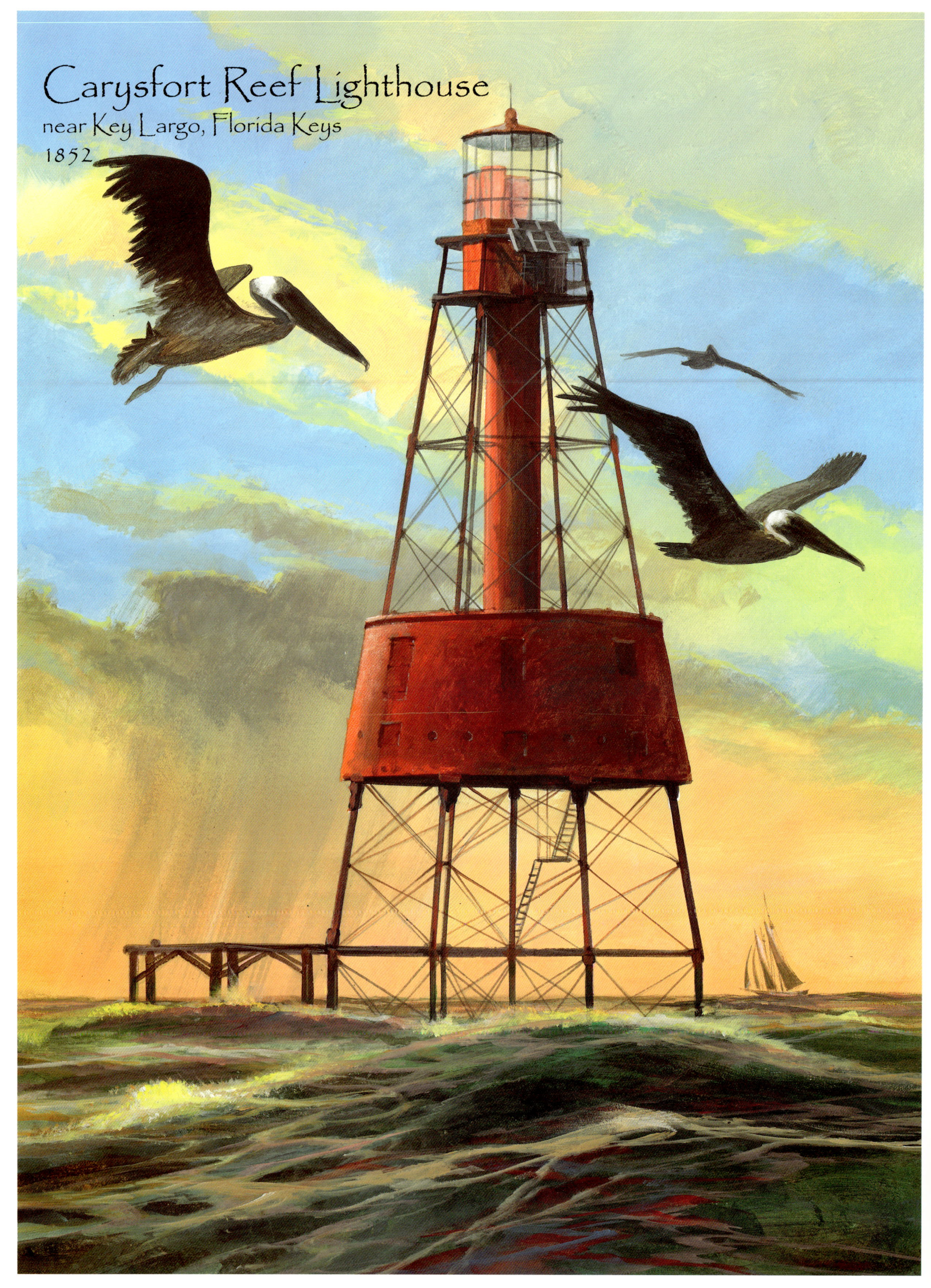
Carysfort Reef Lighthouse
near Key Largo, Florida Keys
1852

Carysfort Reef Lighthouse, like Fowey Rocks just to the north, got its name from a ship that wrecked in the area. Many of the stories of these lighthouses are similar, but just for a moment, imagine you are a lighthouse keeper at a reef lighthouse in the 1850s. Pristine, azure blue waters and crystal clear blue skies surround you. You watch beautiful white cumulous clouds build up in the afternoon and distant rain showers move along the horizon. The fishing is unlike at any other place in the world, with sea creatures plentiful and ready for the taking at the drop of a hook and sinker.

No one bothers you with annoying phone calls at suppertime, trying to sell you something you don't want. It's just you out there with your two assistants. There's plenty of time to reflect on life, catch up on your reading, and enjoy every sunset with an unobstructed view. You have a little world of your own, and you are its ruler. It's a solitary life, but one of tranquility with few needs and wants. What more could you ask for?

Of course, the Keys, are still a remote string of islands with no bridges connecting them. Not until 1912 was the first railroad built to link the Keys, so the reef lighthouses were more remote than most. You are living on a tiny cast-iron island. What happens if you're chipping rust from the ironwork with a chisel and hammer and you slip, fall, and break your arm? The only medicine you have at the lighthouse has come in a wooden crate from the Lighthouse Board. There is no phone to call for help. The boat that hangs on the davit or the occasional passing ship is your only lifeline to the mainland. You might not even be able to leave at all if the surf is too rough. Even if you can get to a hospital, care is minimal compared to today's standards.

What happens when those clear blue skies turn dark? The wind can blow so fiercely that the lighthouse begins to sway. The azure blue water has begun to churn, and white caps cover the ocean as far as you can see. The surf is beginning to break under those thin, cast-iron poles holding up the lighthouse. As day turns to night, the swells rush against the floor you are living on, rising and falling twenty feet. As you climb the winding staircase to tend the light, carrying a bucket of oil, you can hear the wind thrash against the iron walls of the narrow tube that reaches skyward. When you get to the lantern room, a torrent of rain cascades in sheets down the sides of the glass cage, making you feel as if you are inside some sort of cylindrical waterfall where nothing beyond is visible. The noise of the wind is deafening, and you fear the glass might at any moment implode, showering you with razor-edged shards.

A category five hurricane has come knocking at your door, but you had very little warning except for a dropping barometer and a lack of sea birds that sometimes circle around. You have at other times noticed their absence before a large storm but you thought little about it until now. There was no radio to warn you, no AM or FM broadcasts. (Radio broadcasts won't appear until 1921.) There was no short-wave transmission from ships at sea warning of the impending hazard nor telegraph to tap out a Morse code signal of danger. (Shortwave radios and telegraphs haven't been invented yet.) You have no communication with the outside world. The lighthouse could come apart at the seams and no one would know.

If you survive this hurricane and life returns to normal, then you might want to catch up on your reading, but on your last monthly journey to shore, you didn't find any new books waiting for you. The Lighthouse Board usually sends you a rotating library several times a year, but it was delayed. With your meager salary, you can't really afford to buy such luxuries. The few books you do have, you have read over and over and know by heart.

Every remote lighthouse was issued a medicine chest, which contained the following items. Your guess is as good as mine what most of these things were used for.

8 oz. Sweet spirits of nitre
8 oz. Arnica
8 oz. Essence of Jamaica quinine
8 oz. Cough mixture
12 oz. Rochelle salts
8 oz. Senna leaves
8 oz. Castor oil
4 oz. Carbolated oil and laudanum
2 oz. Glycerine
4 oz. Chloroform liniment
1 oz. Lactopepin
3 oz. Saltpeter
2 oz. Sulphur zinc
100 Quinine pills
2 oz. Laudanum
2 oz. Calverts carbolic acid
1 oz. Iodoform
100 Opium and camphor pills
1 oz. Dover's powders
4 oz. Spirits of camphor

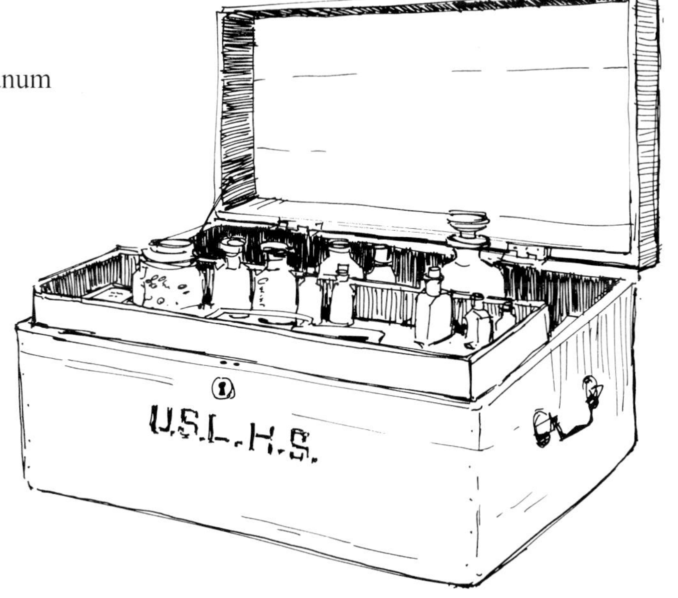

By now the sunsets that were so enjoyable in the past are simply a sign that a long night spent tending the lamp is ahead. All those meals you could leisurely enjoy without interruption are not that enjoyable since there is no real refrigeration of any kind. You try to keep some of your food cool in metal containers suspended in the ocean, but this doesn't keep things fresh for long. So food such as apples, carrots, and potatoes spoil quickly, leaving you with a limited selection of dried or canned foods. You eat basically the same thing over and over again. Fresh fish is the exception with grouper, yellowtail, and snapper readily available and plentiful. Lobster along with conchs are also abundant (but knowing how to swim was not as prevalent as it is today), so unless you know how to swim you might be out of luck there. Of course you have no diving gear, snorkel, or facemask anyway, as they haven't been invented yet. You will have to rely on traps or spears for those lobsters.

Even on a good day, you might be wishing you could hear from a friend, but the only friendly thing in sight is a sailing ship passing about five miles off the horizon. There is no e-mail to check when you get bored. You can't find out what's happening on the six o'clock news. A loved one could be seriously ill and you might not even know about it for a month. You did hear about the Indian attack at the Cape Florida Lighthouse and about how the assistant keeper there was practically roasted alive while the structure burned. You wonder if something similar could happen to you some dark night. Perhaps pirates will use your beacon to guide themselves to your door, overpower you for some small booty, and leave you for dead. Who would help you? Such thoughts sometimes go through your mind as you work through the night hours.

You and your two assistants are quite on each other's nerves. One of them has eaten more than his share of the dried bacon and the last egg, which was quite unfair and has led to hard feelings. You have not spoken to one another for almost two weeks.

Today when I drive down the highway, my automobile air conditioner cools me from the day's heat. I can stop at any one of hundreds of restaurants or convenience stores for something good to eat or drink. All along the Keys, I can rent a reliable boat with an outboard motor that takes me to the reef lights at speeds of forty miles per hour, compared to a trip that once took hours. While enjoying these modern conveniences, I have thought about the durable and rugged people called lighthouse keepers. For all the hardships they endured, they earned an annual salary of perhaps $480, but with few exceptions, they were a proud and steadfast breed who took their jobs seriously and who considered it an honor to be keepers of the lights.

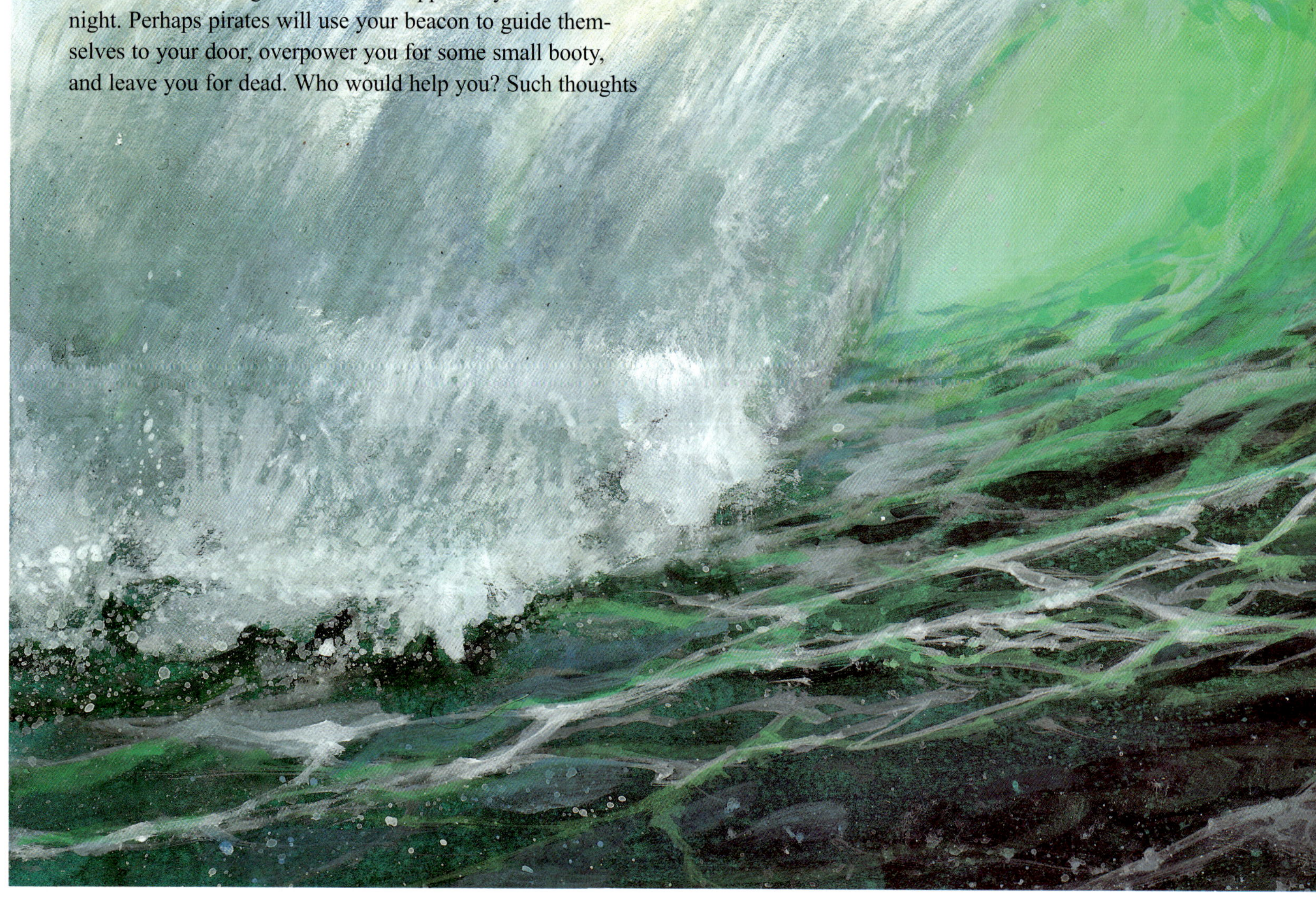

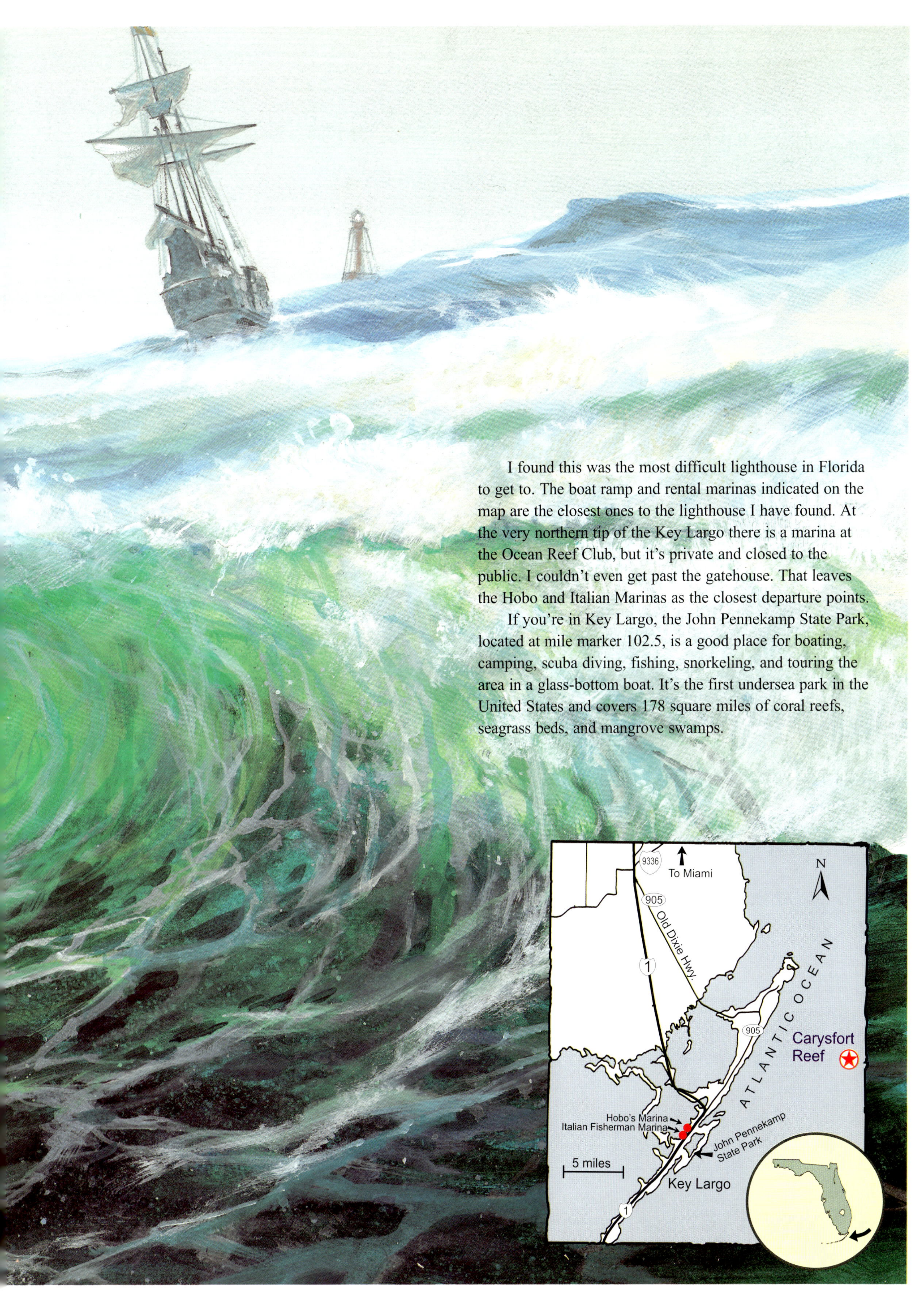

I found this was the most difficult lighthouse in Florida to get to. The boat ramp and rental marinas indicated on the map are the closest ones to the lighthouse I have found. At the very northern tip of the Key Largo there is a marina at the Ocean Reef Club, but it's private and closed to the public. I couldn't even get past the gatehouse. That leaves the Hobo and Italian Marinas as the closest departure points.

If you're in Key Largo, the John Pennekamp State Park, located at mile marker 102.5, is a good place for boating, camping, scuba diving, fishing, snorkeling, and touring the area in a glass-bottom boat. It's the first undersea park in the United States and covers 178 square miles of coral reefs, seagrass beds, and mangrove swamps.

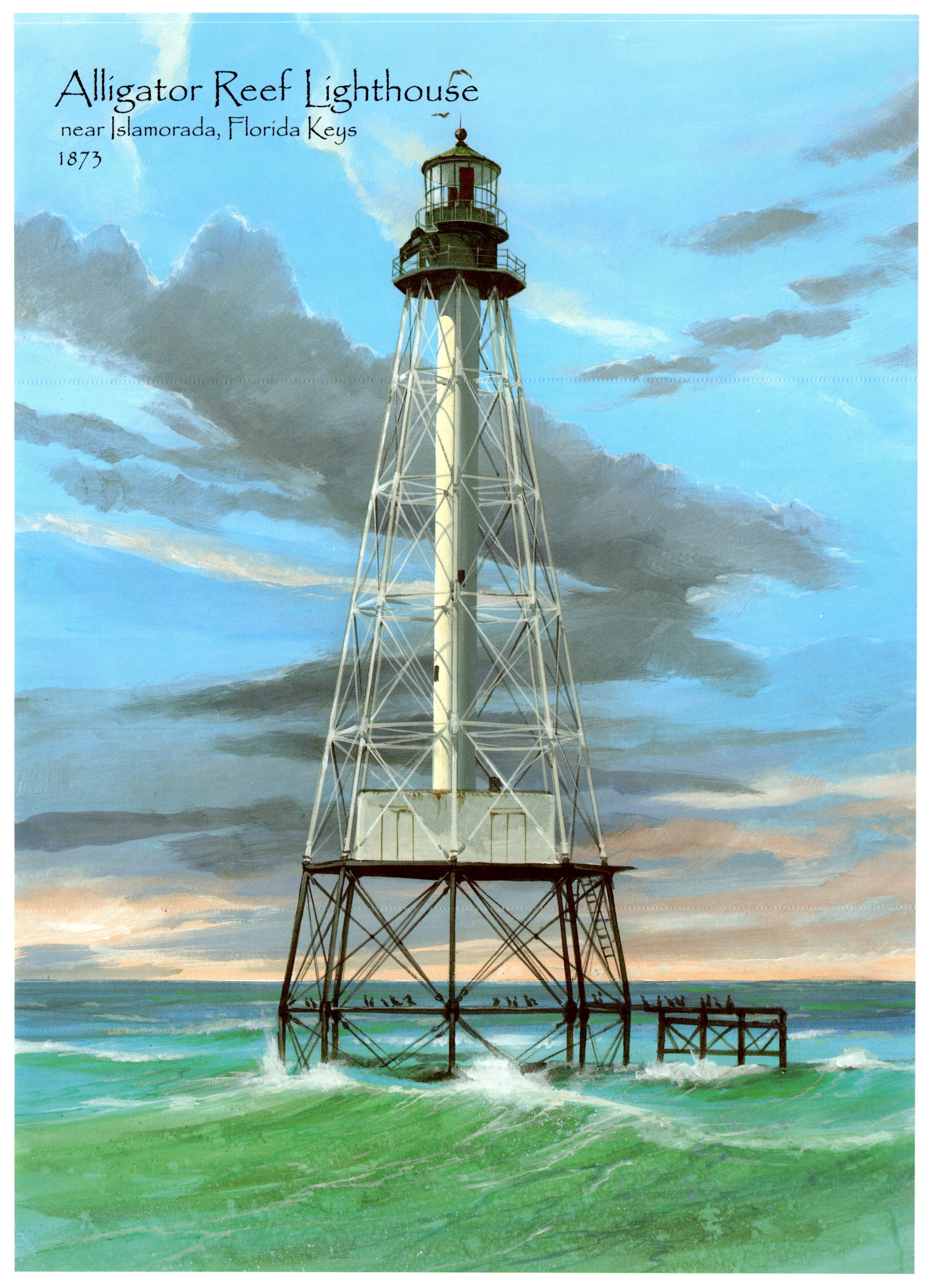
Alligator Reef Lighthouse
near Islamorada, Florida Keys
1873

Piracy was rampant in the early 1800s. No ship was safe with so many pirates sailing the waters around the Keys and southward to the West Indies. The slave trade was also big business during this time, and the U.S. government wanted to put an end to both slave trading and piracy. One of the ships commissioned to help with this cleanup effort was the U.S.S. *Alligator*, for which the lighthouse and reef are named. The *Alligator* was assigned to patrol the areas around Florida and the West Indies but made trips as far away as Africa to capture several slave ships. One dark night in November 1822, the *Alligator*, while cruising the coast on what was then known as Carysford Reef, went hard aground, burying her hull in the sharp coral. For three days the crew labored to free the schooner, but with all efforts exhausted, the crew abandoned the ship and made an encampment at a nearby key. Fortunately another American ship, the *Ann Maria*, was sailing the area. Her crew saw the *Alligator* on the reef and tried but failed to remove the ship from its position. The captain of the *Alligator* ordered all government property onboard his ship, including twelve cannons, transferred to the *Ann Maria*. The *Alligator* was then blown up to keep pirates from using anything that remained. To this day, two sections of the ship's hull still lie on the ocean floor, including some rigging, cannonballs, and gun carriages, all encrusted in the coral that was responsible for destroying her.

In 1852, in an effort to make navigation safer, day markers were placed along the Keys. Each one was simply an iron pole thirty-six feet high with nothing more than a large barrel fastened to the top. They were all painted a different color and could be seen for a couple of miles with the naked eye and maybe ten miles with a telescope. They were later upgraded with painted metal cylinders and included a letter on each one. Despite these markers, more than six hundred vessels shipwrecked and were lost to the reefs along the Keys between 1848 and 1858. These ships had a combined value of twenty-two million dollars.

A lighthouse was clearly needed. In 1857, the Light House Board recommended that one be built on Alligator Reef, but nothing was done because major events, such as Florida's secession from the Union in 1861 and the Civil War, kept getting in the way. Finally in 1870, Congress decided to allocate enough funds to build a lighthouse, but it wasn't completed and lit until 1873.

The 136-foot-tall lighthouse cost $185,000 to build. It was completely assembled in Cold Spring, New York, then taken apart and shipped to the Keys. Two and a half miles offshore, piles were driven ten feet into the coral with a steam-powered pile driver. The massive hammer, though it weighed two thousand pounds and was dropped from a height of eighteen feet, managed to wedge the piles into the coral only about one inch with each strike.

Living quarters at the lighthouse were divided into four rooms. There were two doors on each wall of the house instead of windows. Privacy wasn't a major concern and neither were insects. In general, there were few insects that far out in the ocean, but mosquitoes did reach the light and would sometimes be a nuisance if the winds were blowing from the Keys. Below the living quarters, large drinking-water tanks were suspended. Every few years, the keeper would have to clean them, then melt paraffin and apply it to the inside walls to protect the metal from rust and to keep the water cleaner. The tanks were then filled by a tender; afterwards rainwater would keep them full. These tanks were removed after the lighthouse became automated in 1963.

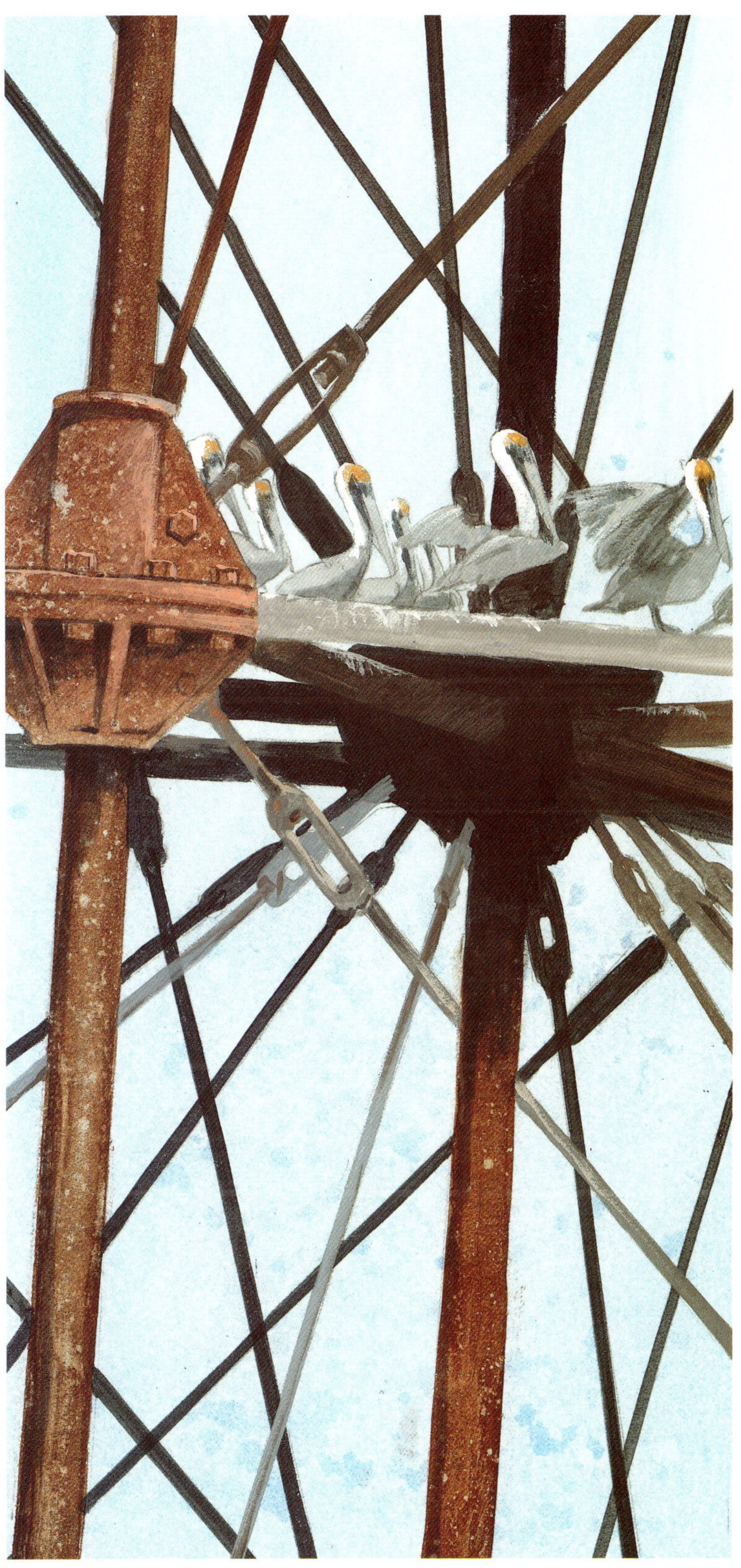

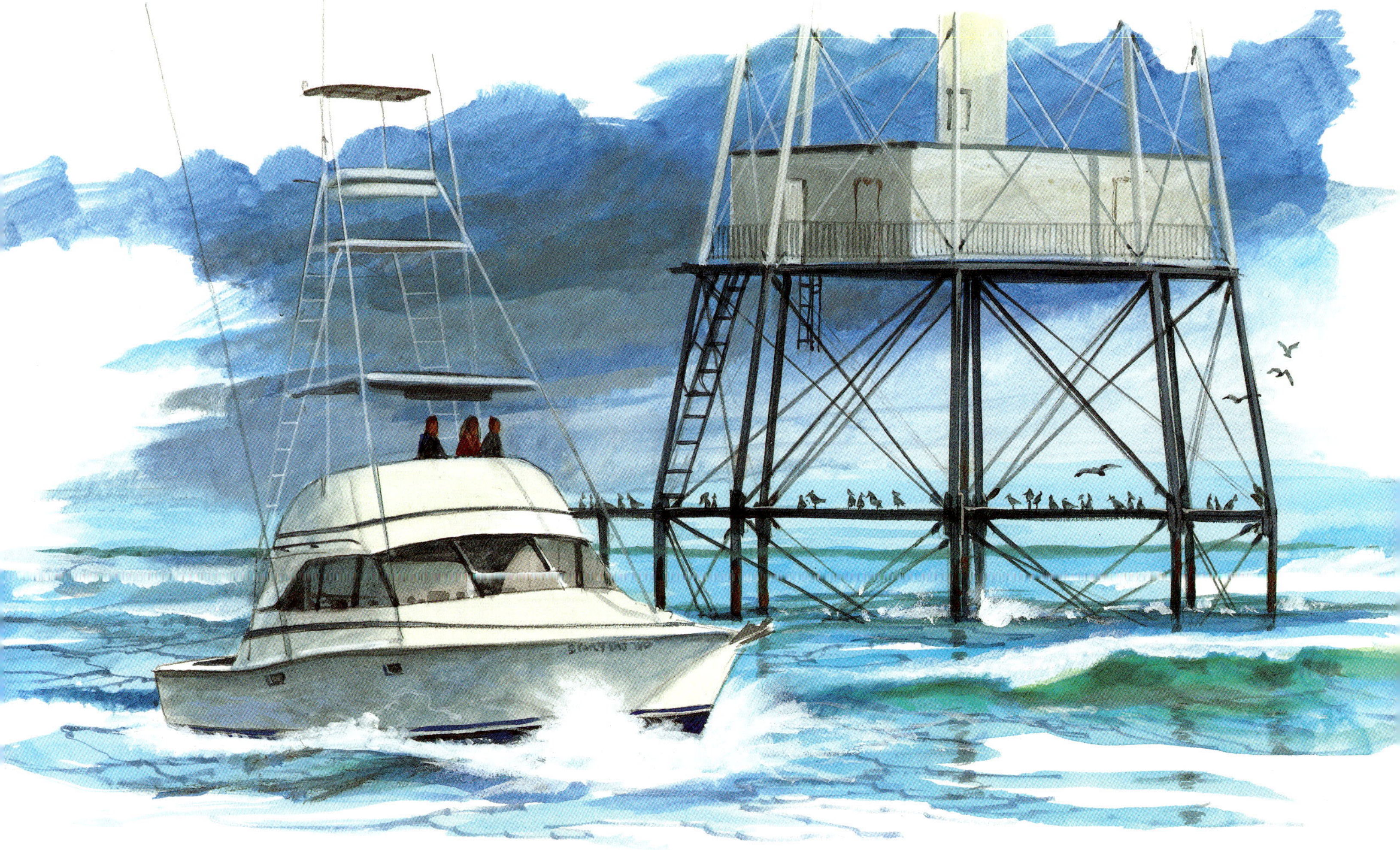

It's quite shallow by the lighthouse, making it a good place to snorkel if the water is not rough.

If conditions are calm, you can rent a small boat to get to the lighthouse. If it's rough, then a larger boat like this is the alternative. Just talk to people around the marinas. You can usually find a friendly boat owner willing to take you to the lighthouse for a fee. Their love of the water and willingness to share their experiences often are much better than going out alone.

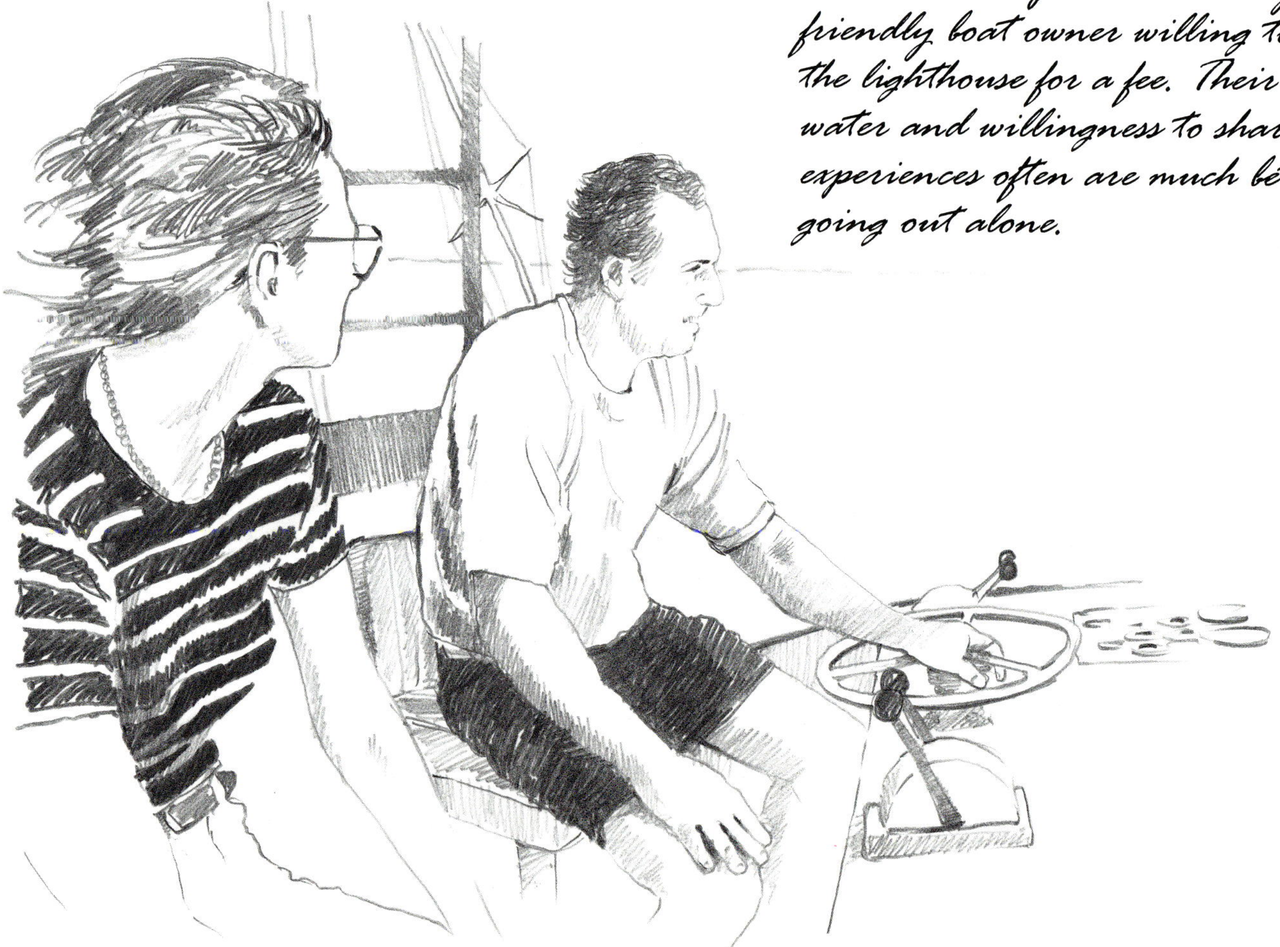

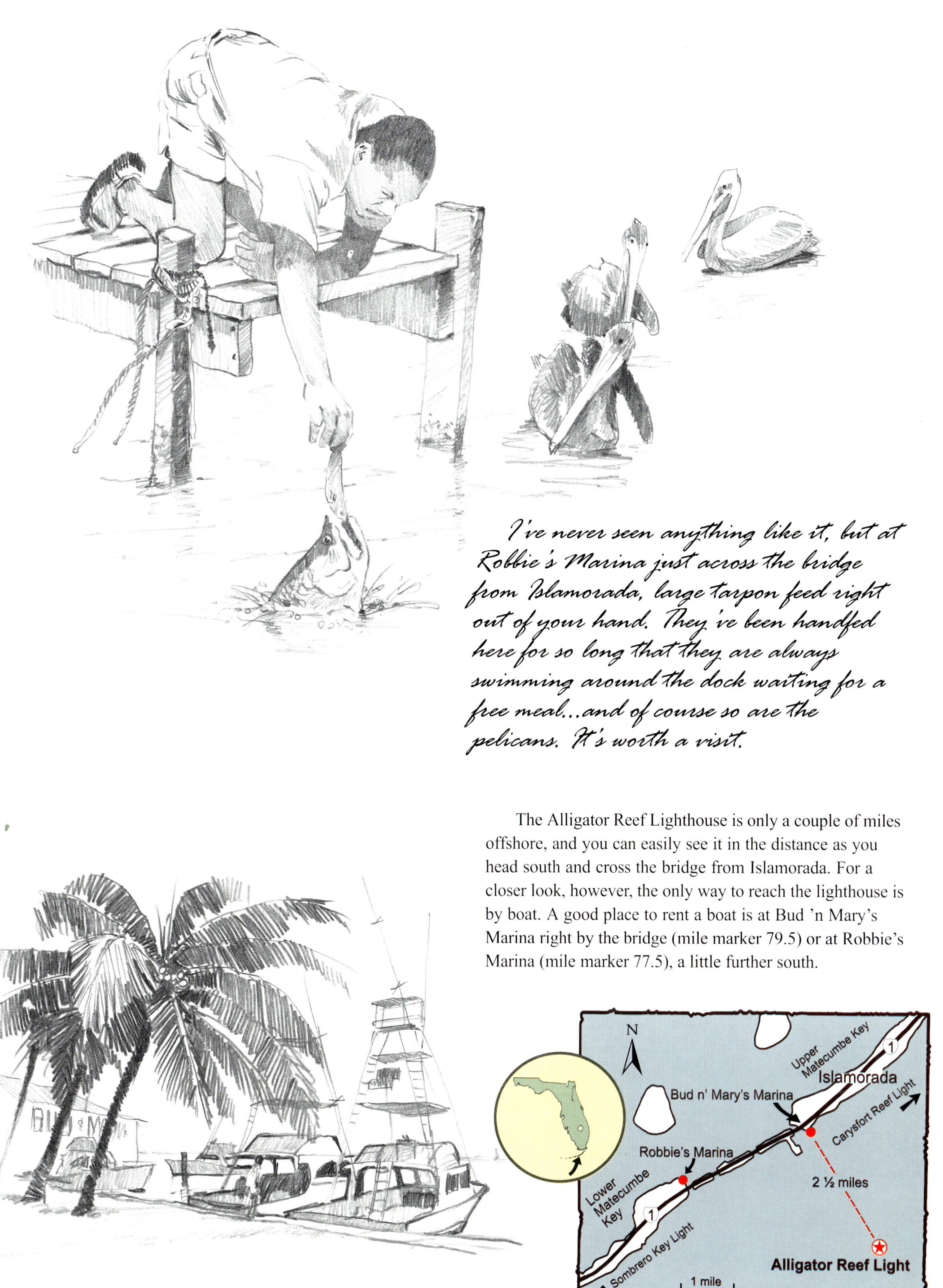

I've never seen anything like it, but at Robbie's Marina just across the bridge from Islamorada, large tarpon feed right out of your hand. They've been handfed here for so long that they are always swimming around the dock waiting for a free meal...and of course so are the pelicans. It's worth a visit.

The Alligator Reef Lighthouse is only a couple of miles offshore, and you can easily see it in the distance as you head south and cross the bridge from Islamorada. For a closer look, however, the only way to reach the lighthouse is by boat. A good place to rent a boat is at Bud 'n Mary's Marina right by the bridge (mile marker 79.5) or at Robbie's Marina (mile marker 77.5), a little further south.

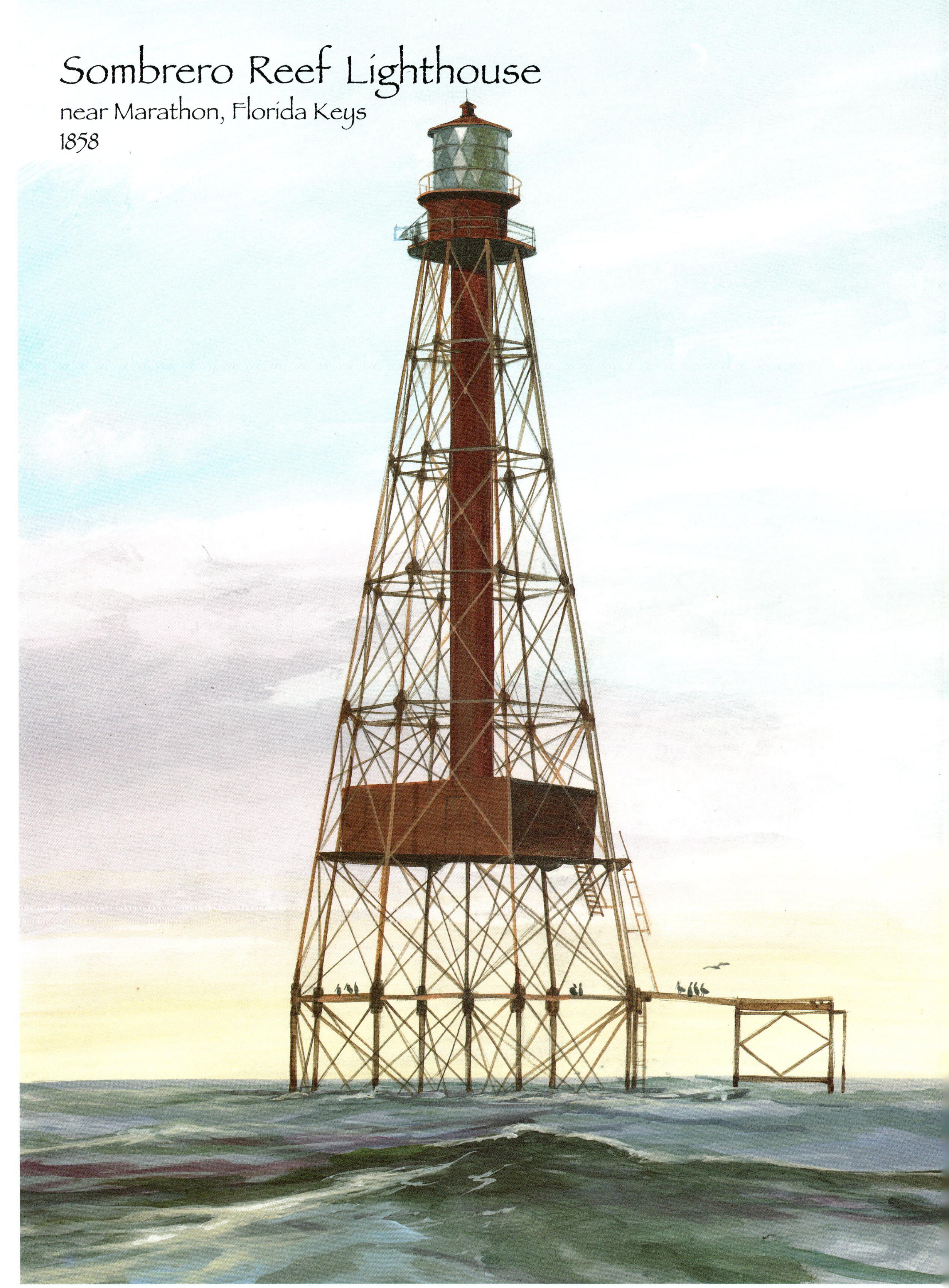

Sombrero Reef Lighthouse
near Marathon, Florida Keys
1858

One hundred fifty years ago, ships became grounded and damaged and sank up and down the coasts of the Florida Keys about every week and a half on the average. Seventy-one ships sank here in 1856 alone. Who knows how many ships went down in earlier times, when records were lost to the sea along with crew and cargo? Today we take it for granted that ships can safely navigate waters with few problems, but it wasn't always that way. Before the electronic age, sailors had to rely on the stars, crude maps, lighthouses, and good judgment to guide them. There was no sonar onboard to tell the depth of the water, and there were no detailed and frequently updated maps or global navigation systems collecting information from a half dozen satellites overhead to pinpoint your location to within a few yards.

Of course, not all the ships that were lost on the reefs were destroyed by accident or because of a lack of vigilance on the part of captains. As new steamships were introduced, older sailing ships began to operate at a loss. Unfortunately, there was plenty of opportunity for ship captains and owners to be less than honest. Many ships were run aground and wrecked intentionally to take advantage of marine insurance. Cargo would be thrown overboard, and salvagers, known as "wreckers," were often in on the scheme. They operated all up and down the Keys, and their goal was to get to a distressed ship in time to gather up whatever they could before a ship went down. For their efforts they either got to keep a percentage of the salvage or were paid in cash for what they had saved. Many were honest men, but many were not and were often in on the scheme of intentional shipwrecking and shared with the owners the illegitimate rewards.

One judge at the time, after hearing case after case concerning salvage, thought that nearly half of the shipwrecks could be attributed to causes other than the perils of the sea. Even after the reef lighthouses in the Keys were built, the number of shipwrecks remained about the same, but because ship traffic had increased, the actual percentage of ships being wrecked on the reefs actually dropped.

Keepers living in lighthouses along the coast always lived with their families, but reef lighthouses had no room for families, only the keeper and his assistants. Close quarters and a lack of contact with the outside world often led to hostilities among the men.

Only one boat was kept at each reef lighthouse, so when one man sailed to Key West for supplies, the others would be left alone without a boat. If there was trouble, the keepers' only salvation was to raise a distress flag and hope that a passing ship would stop. Sometimes a keeper would be caught in bad weather and drown, as was the case at Sombrero Key. Even more ghastly, an assistant keeper once died at this lighthouse, and the keeper, not wanting to be accused of foul play, kept the dead body at the lighthouse in the heat for three days until a ship finally stopped.

The Coast Guard replaced the U.S. Lighthouse Service's nonmilitary lighthouse keepers in 1939. In 1960, the light was automated, leaving Sombrero Key unattended except for occasional maintenance visits. The first-order Fresnel lens was removed in the early 1980s and is now on display at the Key West Lighthouse Museum.

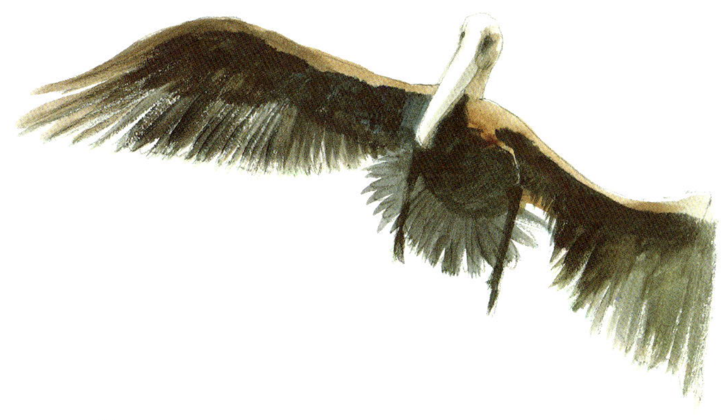

The pelicans are perhaps the most frequent visitors to the reef lighthouses.

Sombrero Key Lighthouse is the tallest of the reef lighthouses—standing at 142 feet tall—and was built at a cost of $153,000. You can just make out the lighthouse on your left in clear weather as you head south on Route 1, crossing the bridge just after Marathon. The only way to get to this lighthouse is by boat. Not all marinas have boat rentals, but they can tell you where to find one. Motel owners can also point you in the right direction. I rented my boat from Bud Boats, which is located at the Buccaneer Resort, 2600 Overseas Highway (mile marker 48.5) in Marathon. Keep in mind that reef lighthouses are a long way from shore, so don't venture out if the weather is rough: It gets a lot rougher out in the open ocean.

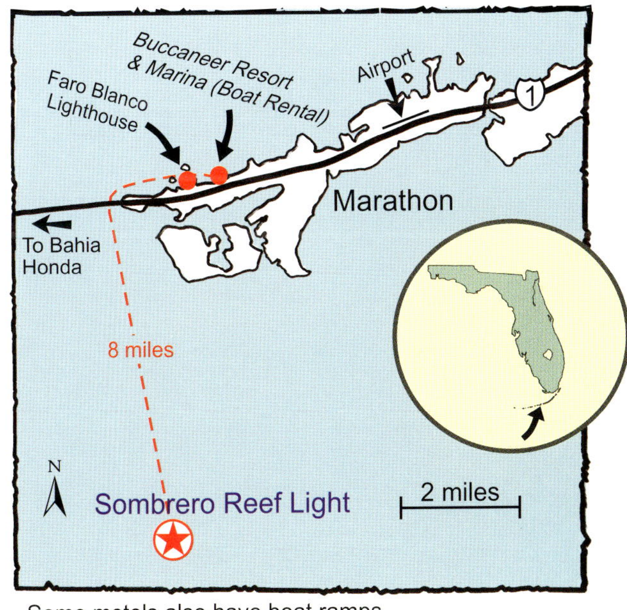

Some motels also have boat ramps.

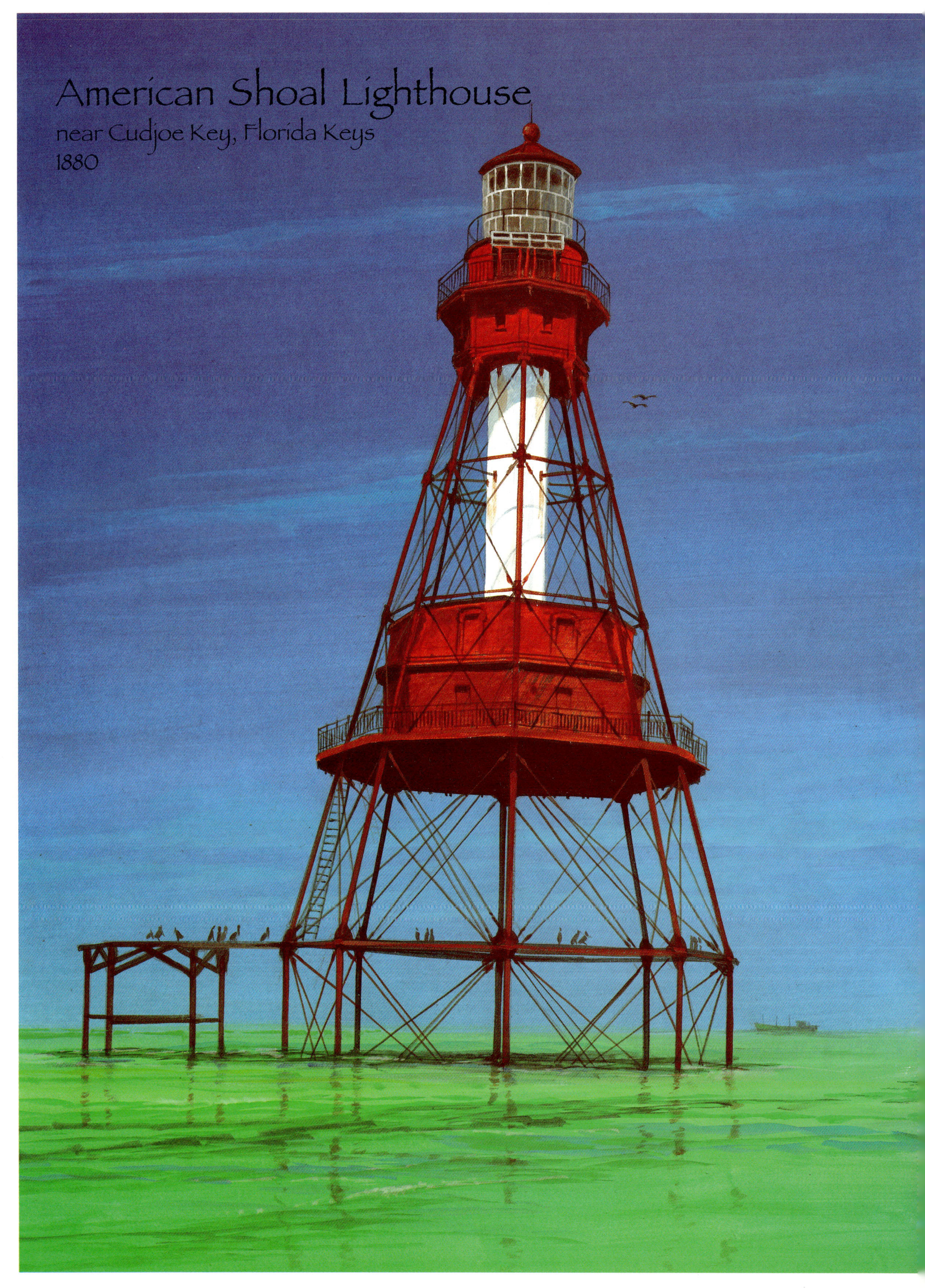
American Shoal Lighthouse
near Cudjoe Key, Florida Keys
1880

This was the last iron-pile lighthouse built in the Florida Keys. It was finished in 1880 and resembles the Fowey Rocks Lighthouse. The entire ironwork structure was built in Trenton, New Jersey, at a cost of $47,000, not including the site construction and lens. The tower was completely assembled at the factory to ensure that everything fit properly before it was shipped to the Keys.

The men who built this lighthouse used Key West as their base of operations even though it was nineteen miles away. Other islands were nearer, but Key West had the accommodations that other islands lacked. There were no roads or railways connecting the Keys at that time, and nothing was accomplished easily. As was the case for some of the other reef lights, a temporary platform was first built using local lumber from locally harvested mangrove trees. Materials were hauled to the site in a steam-powered vessel along with the men, and iron pilings were pounded into the coral an inch at a time with a steam-powered pile driver. Delays could last for days and even weeks because of rough seas. And there were no telephones to check on that order of bolts that hadn't yet arrived from Philadelphia, either.

The lighthouse was automated in 1963, marking the end of an era: lighthouse keeping as it had been practiced for over one hundred years. The Coast Guard regularly services the light in the 109-foot-tall lighthouse, but private contractors are now hired to scrape, paint, and maintain the ironwork. If parts need to be replaced, the Coast Guard's civil engineers fabricate them using original blueprints. It is a constant maintenance vigil to battle vandalism and nature. Strange as it may seem, even though the American Shoal Lighthouse stands seven miles from the nearest land, termites have taken their toll on the interior of the keepers' quarters.

In 1980, exactly one hundred years after the lighthouse was built, it was used by the Coast Guard—along with other reef lighthouses in the Keys—as a lookout post to spot refugees coming from Cuba and to monitor boats that might be carrying drugs. The lighthouse still operates at night, and during the day it serves as a day marker for all the shipping that passes by. Even with the advent of global positioning systems, the familiar lighthouse is welcome reassurance for ships' captains. Divers also like the lighthouse and often use the area to view the over two hundred types of fish that populate the reef.

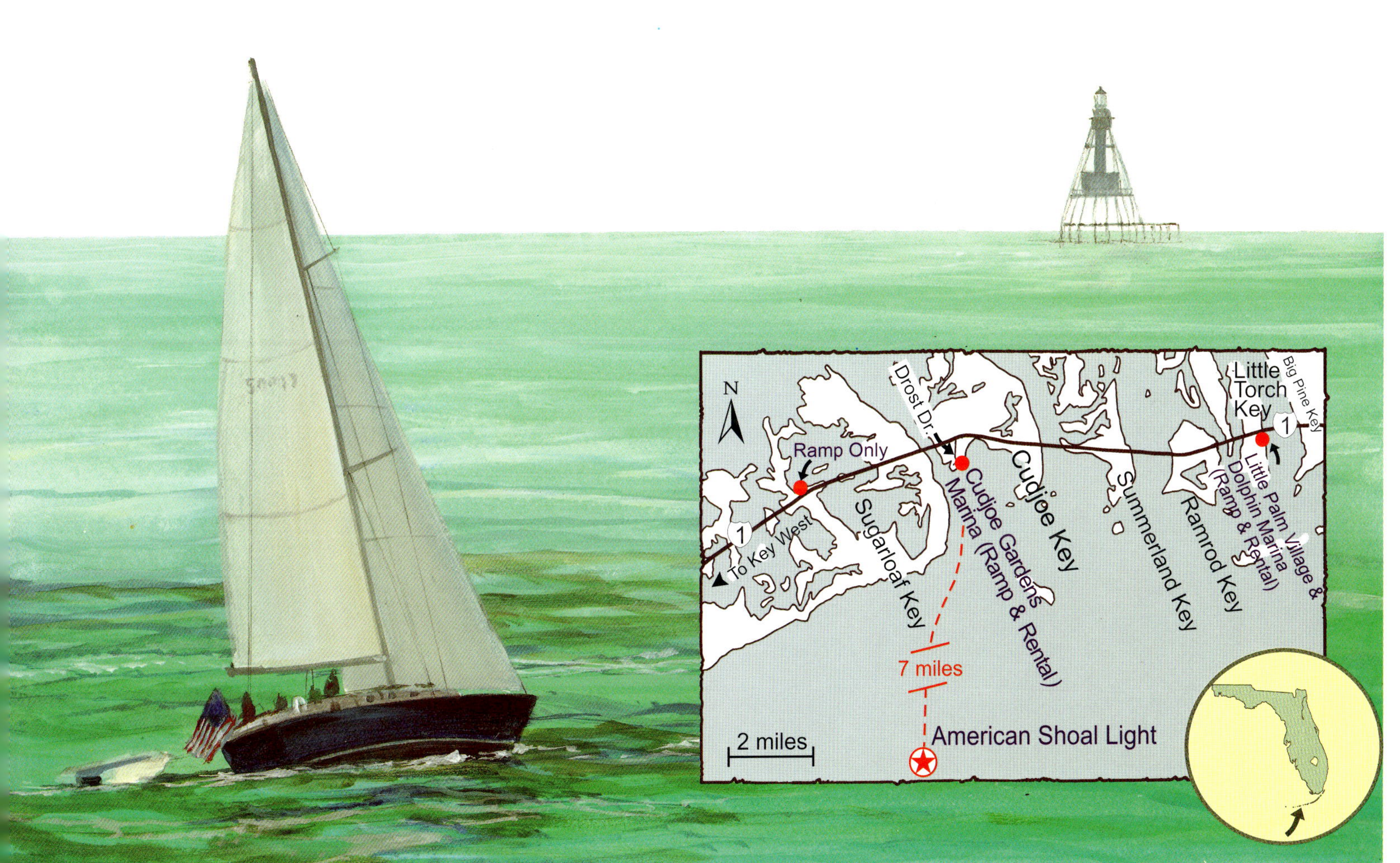

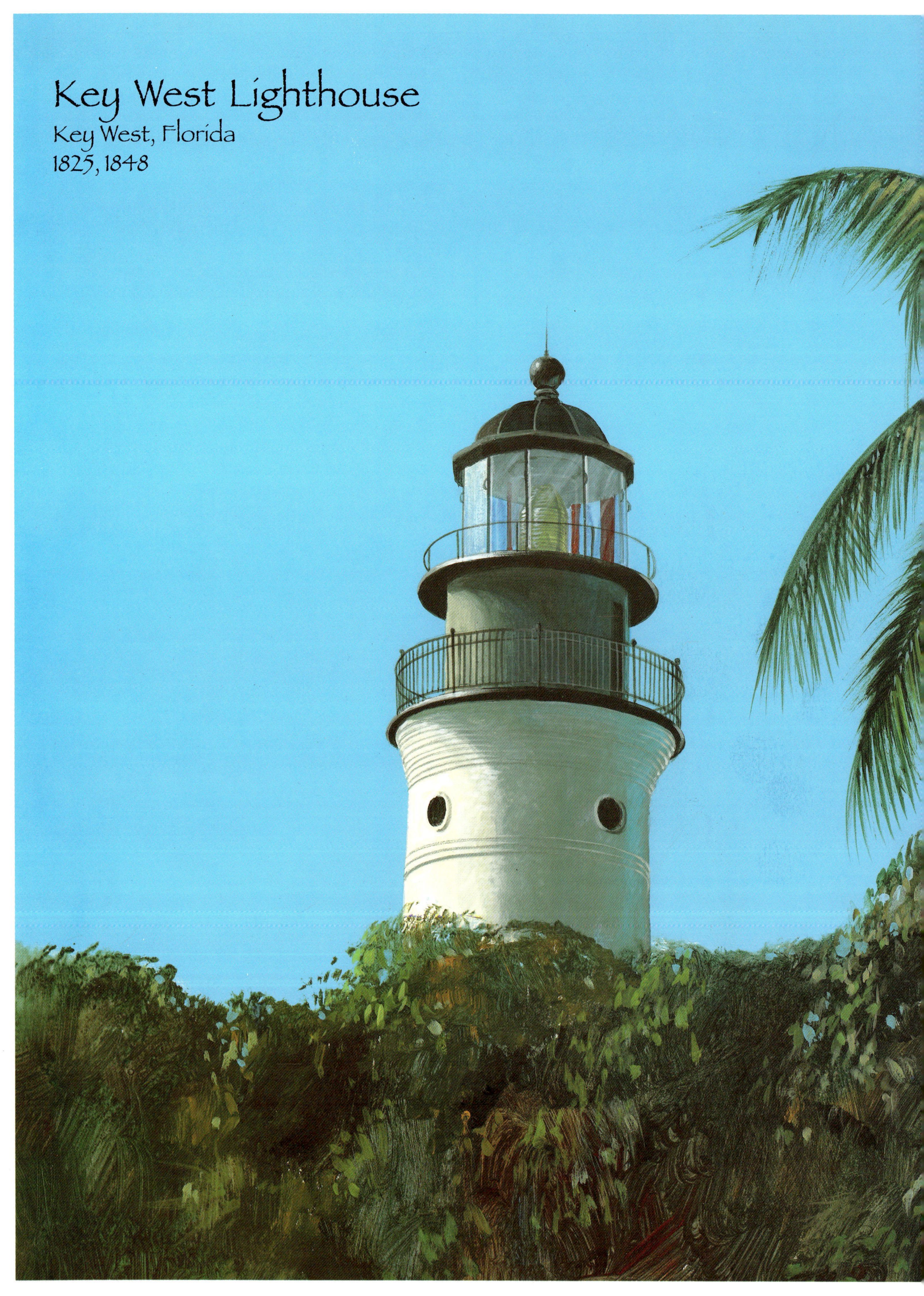
Key West Lighthouse
Key West, Florida
1825, 1848

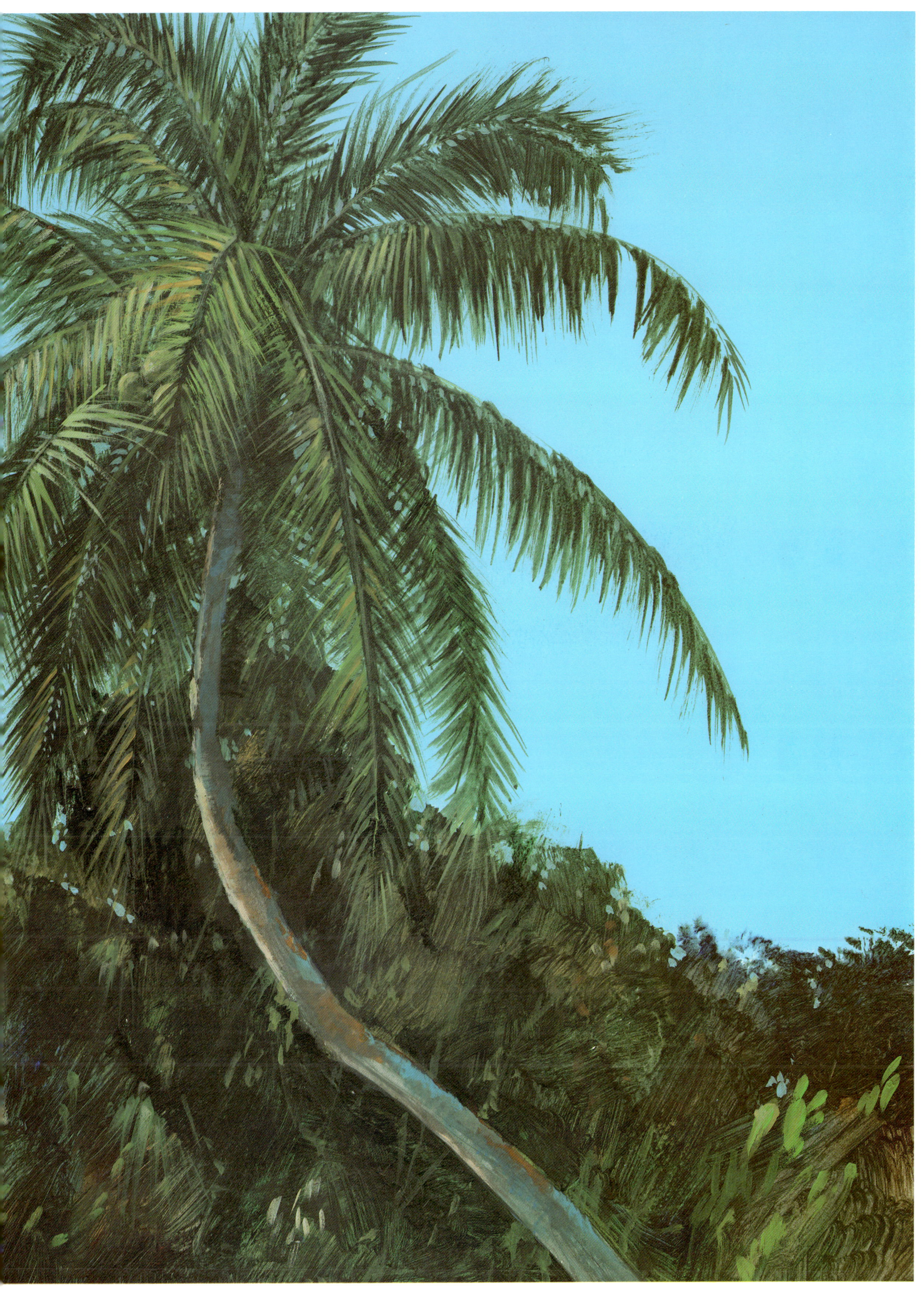

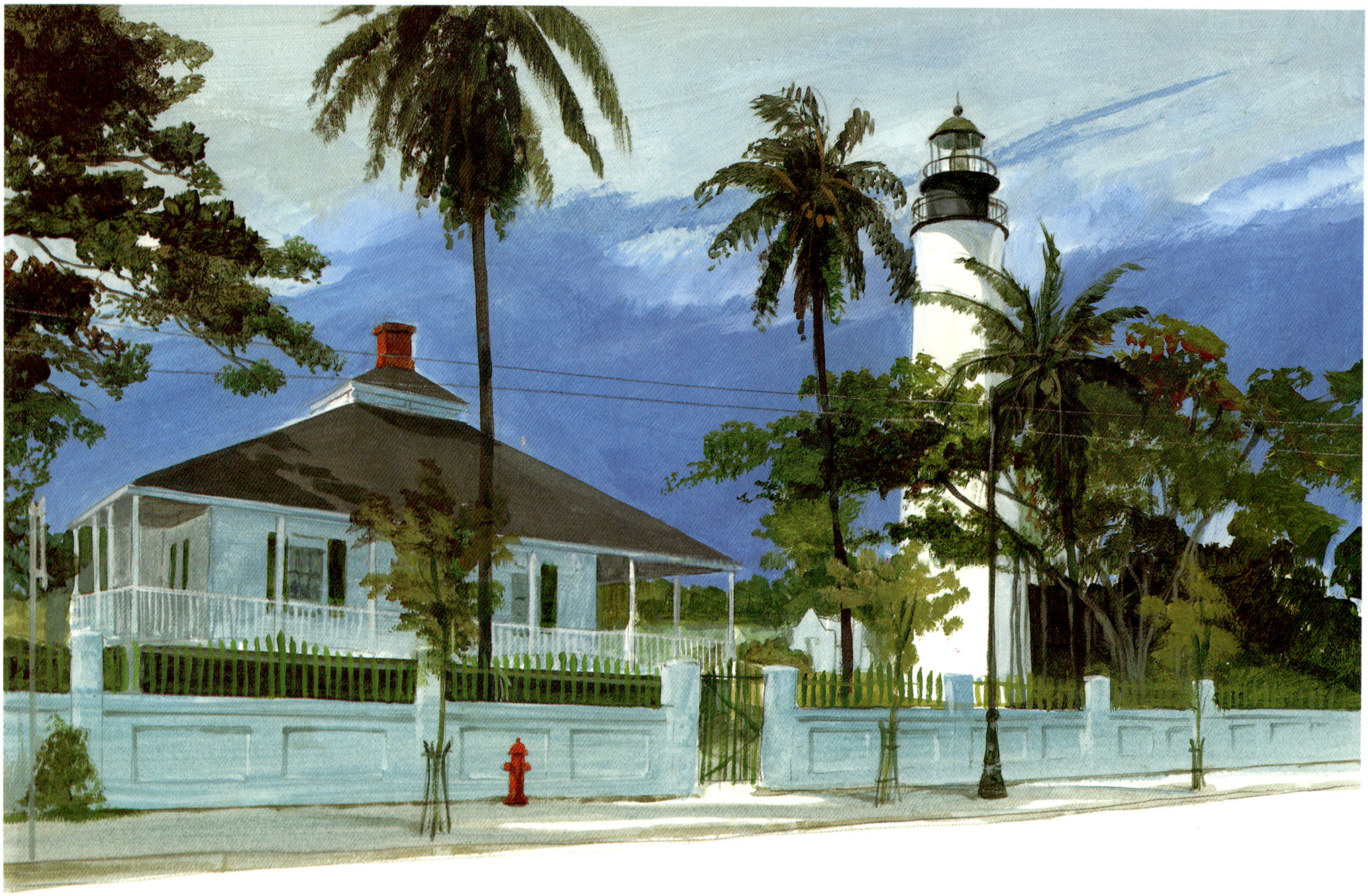

As you drive into Key West, you might get the impression that you've made a mistake in wanting to visit. A little persistence will pay off once you get past the fast food restaurants and strip centers that have sprung up in recent times. Continue to make your way into the heart of Key West, and you'll find that this southernmost town in the United States has a charm like no other place.

Key West has always been a mecca of sorts, and at one time in its history it was the second largest city in Florida, just behind Pensacola. Key West's residents had the highest income per capita in the entire country, due mostly to shipwreck salvaging operations. Sponging and cigar making were big businesses as well. Key West was a booming community with five daily newspapers and one Spanish weekly. In 1890, the state of Florida received ninety-five percent of its internal revenue from Key West, and the lighthouse played an important part in the town's economy by guiding more than six hundred ships into its port every year. In contrast, by 1920 the economy had collapsed, and the city was five million dollars in debt, with eighty percent of its twelve thousand residents on the dole. Today Key West thrives once again because of one thing—tourism.

The unusual banyan tree has aerial roots that grow down from its branches and make secondary trunks.

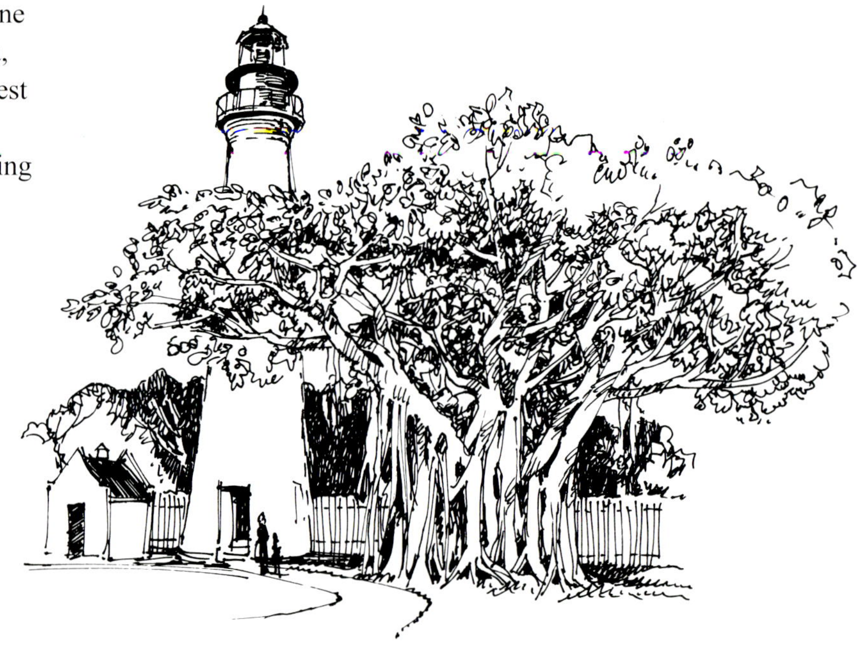

The lighthouse was originally much closer to the shore but instead of the waterfront eroding away, as is the case most of the time, landfill was brought in, leaving the lighthouse further inland. Another lighthouse existed before this one. It was built in 1825 about twelve hundred feet from the present one, but a hurricane destroyed it in 1846 and claimed the lives of fourteen people who had taken shelter inside.

Hurricanes are particularly brutal in the Keys, since there is nothing to buffer the onslaught of either wind or water, and in 1935 one of the worst hurricanes in history hit the area. It destroyed much of the Keys, including Henry Flagler's Overseas Railroad, which was built just a couple of decades earlier. Three years later, the government bought up what was left of the railroad bridges and turned them into the Overseas Highway, putting the economy back on its feet.

The builders of the present lighthouse used foresight in their plans. Using chisels, they gouged their way through the tough coral bedrock, making a round hole several feet deep and using this as a base on which to begin laying brick. This entire brick structure took only 48 days to complete at a cost of $7,247.

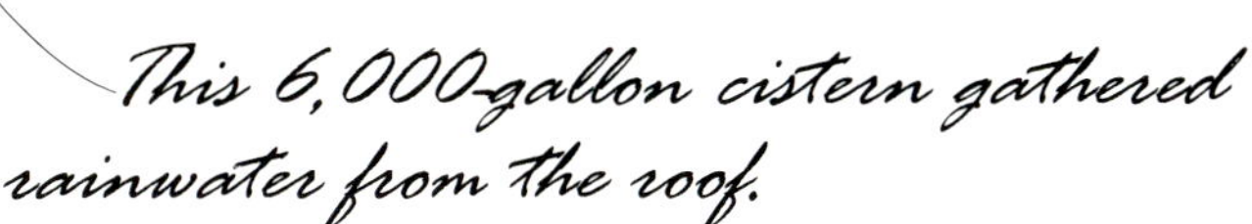

This 6,000-gallon cistern gathered rainwater from the roof.

It's generally not thought that women were assigned as lighthouse keepers, but there were several at Key West. Barbara Mabrity served as keeper until she was "urged to retire" after a remark she made was interpreted as disloyal to the Union during the Civil War. She was eighty-two years old at the time.

The lighthouse was officially taken out of commission in 1969 after 121 years of continuous service. Eighty-three-year-old Mary Bethel was given the honor of extinguishing the light. She had served as assistant keeper alongside her husband for seventeen years and as head keeper for an additional ten years after he died. The light didn't stay dark for long, however. The Key West Art and Historical Society came to its rescue and completed its loving restoration of this beautiful landmark in 1989. You can climb the eighty-eight steps to the top of the eighty-six-foot-tall lighthouse and get a good view not only of Ernest Hemingway's house directly across the street but also of the entire town of Key West. You can also see the working third-order Fresnel lens. The keeper's house is full of original furniture and displays. There is also a first-order Fresnel lens that you can actually walk inside of to see its faceted prisms. Key West is rich in history, so take advantage of all there is to see and do here when you visit.

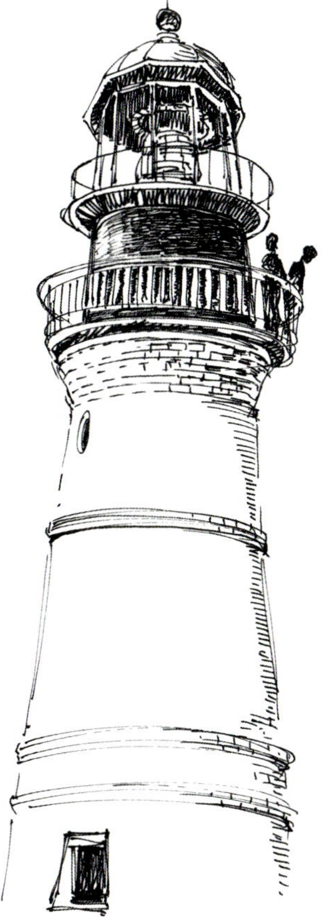

You can see the double rings where the lighthouse was extended an additional twenty feet from its original height.

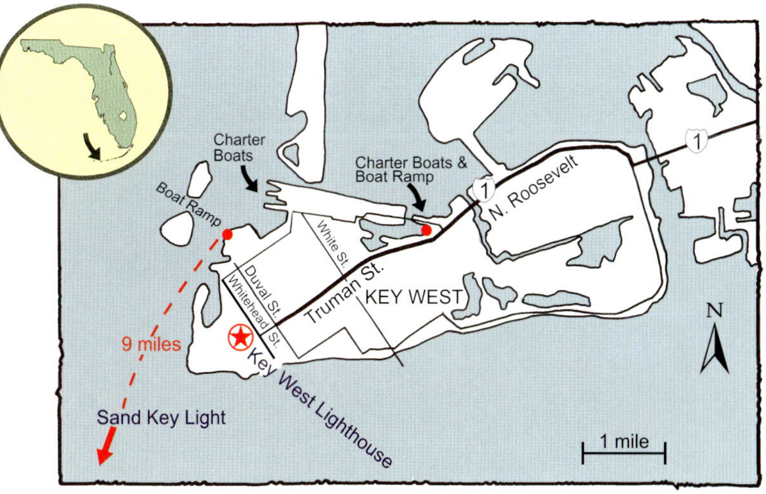

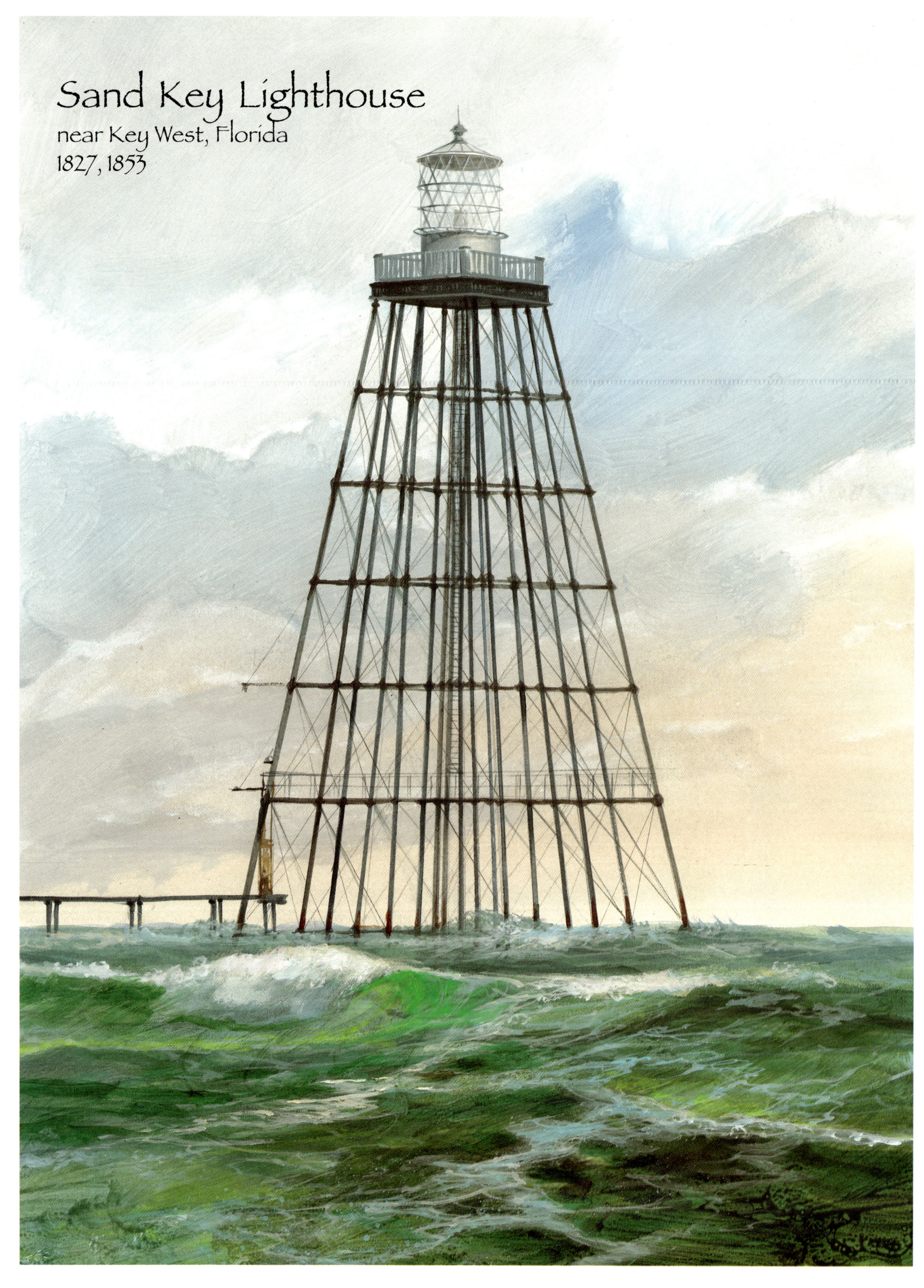
Sand Key Lighthouse
near Key West, Florida
1827, 1853

Sand Key Lighthouse is probably the most convenient of all the reef lighthouses in the Keys to get to. It's also a great place to do some snorkeling, and there are many small boats that regularly take groups of snorkelers to the lighthouse, around which are more than sixty mooring buoys boats are welcome to tie up to.

Like other reef lighthouses, Sand Key was built on a coral reef. A variety of fish—including grunts, yellowtail, snapper, parrotfish, and angelfish—are the main residents on the reef, but you might also see grouper, blue tang, and even the occasional nurse shark.

The reef at Sand Key varies in depth, dropping to ninety feet in some places. In the shallows, you can see brain coral, fire coral, and even artifacts from the original brick lighthouse that was destroyed during a hurricane in 1846. The storm was so severe that the keepers' house was completely washed away and the lighthouse collapsed with the keepers inside.

A lightship was used for seven years until a new wrought-iron, screwpile lighthouse was constructed to replace the brick one. This type of lighthouse was much less susceptible to the forces of hurricane winds because the thin structure offered little wind resistance, and since it was firmly anchored into the coral reef, it was in less danger of being washed away. There is sometimes a white sandy beach around the lighthouse, but with every storm it changes. When I was there, the island had disappeared under the clear, blue Gulf Stream waters, leaving only the lighthouse visible.

The present lighthouse stands 109 feet tall and was built with 450 tons of iron. It was finally lit in 1853 after several funding delays. Inside were nine rooms, each measuring twelve feet square. One of the rooms held two tanks: one held oil; the other held rainwater for cooking and drinking. Two boats were supplied for this lighthouse, which was unusual; most lighthouses had only one.

The light was automated in 1941, and the Coast Guard inspects it every three to five months, making a thorough inspection of the entire structure every six years. Late one afternoon in 1989, as the lighthouse was being renovated, flammable paints and chemicals caught fire, and the lighthouse began to burn. It's hard to believe that a steel structure could be affected by fire, but the keepers' quarters were lined with wood and also contained wood furniture. The fire generated enough heat to buckle and destroy much of the keepers' quarters and to collapse the base of the stairs and stair tower. The keepers' quarters, as well as the spiral staircase and tubular support, have been completely removed. An exposed ladder, where the staircase once was, is now the only way to reach the top of the lighthouse. Today a beacon stands a few hundred yards away and serves as a temporary replacement for a lighthouse that guided ships through the area for over 150 years.

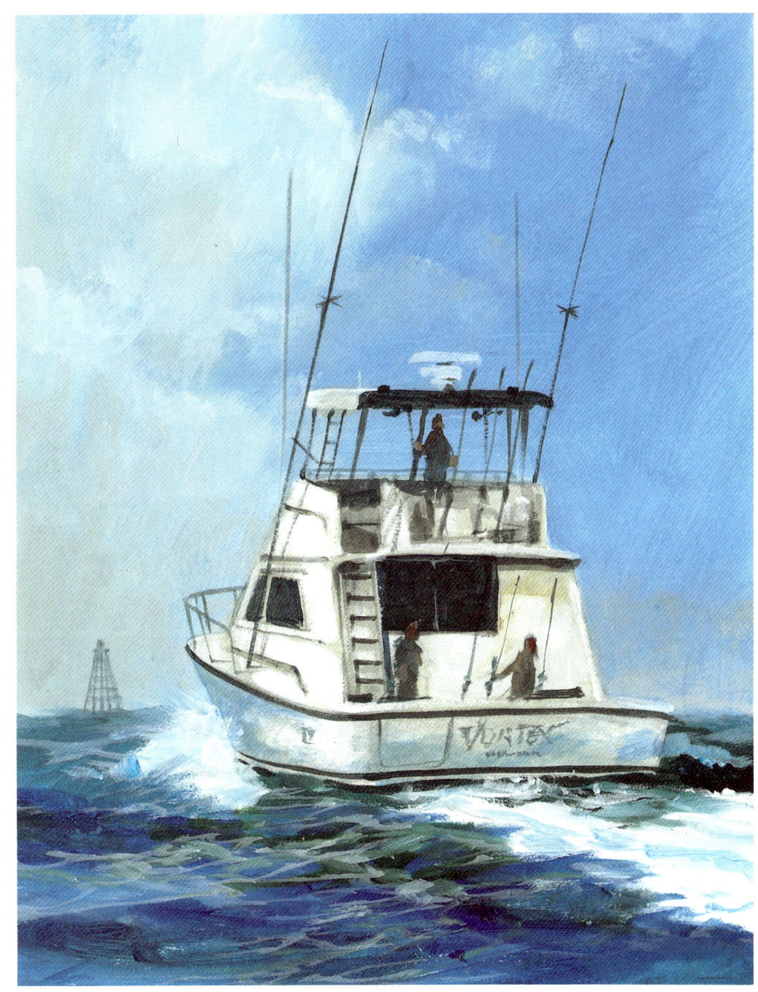

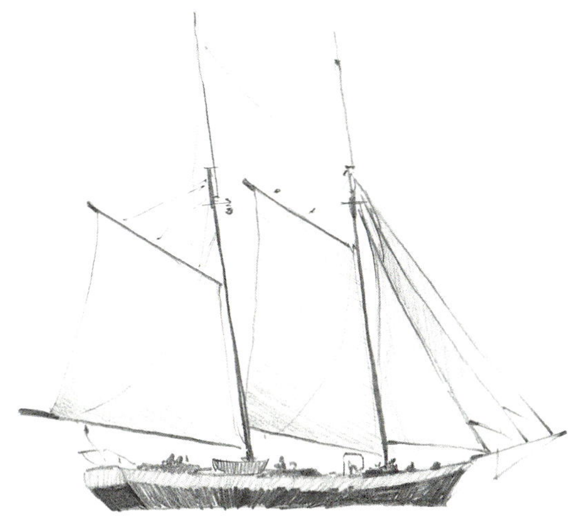

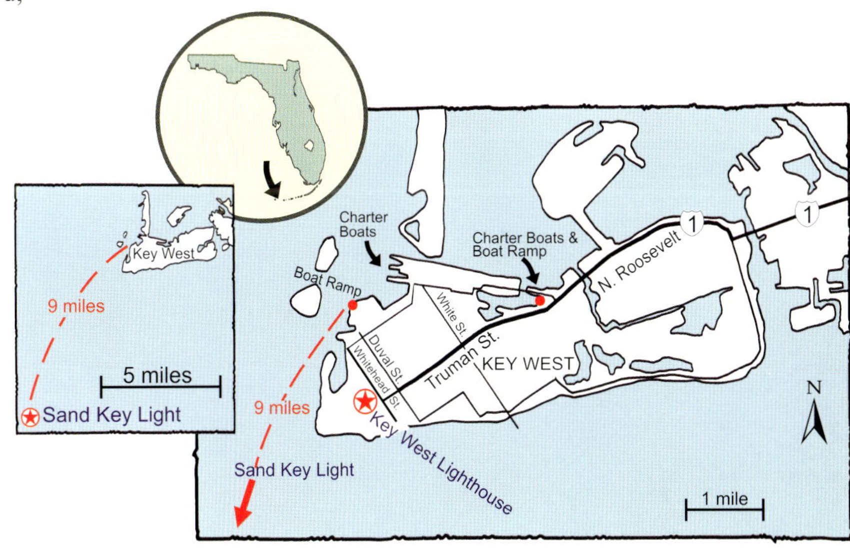

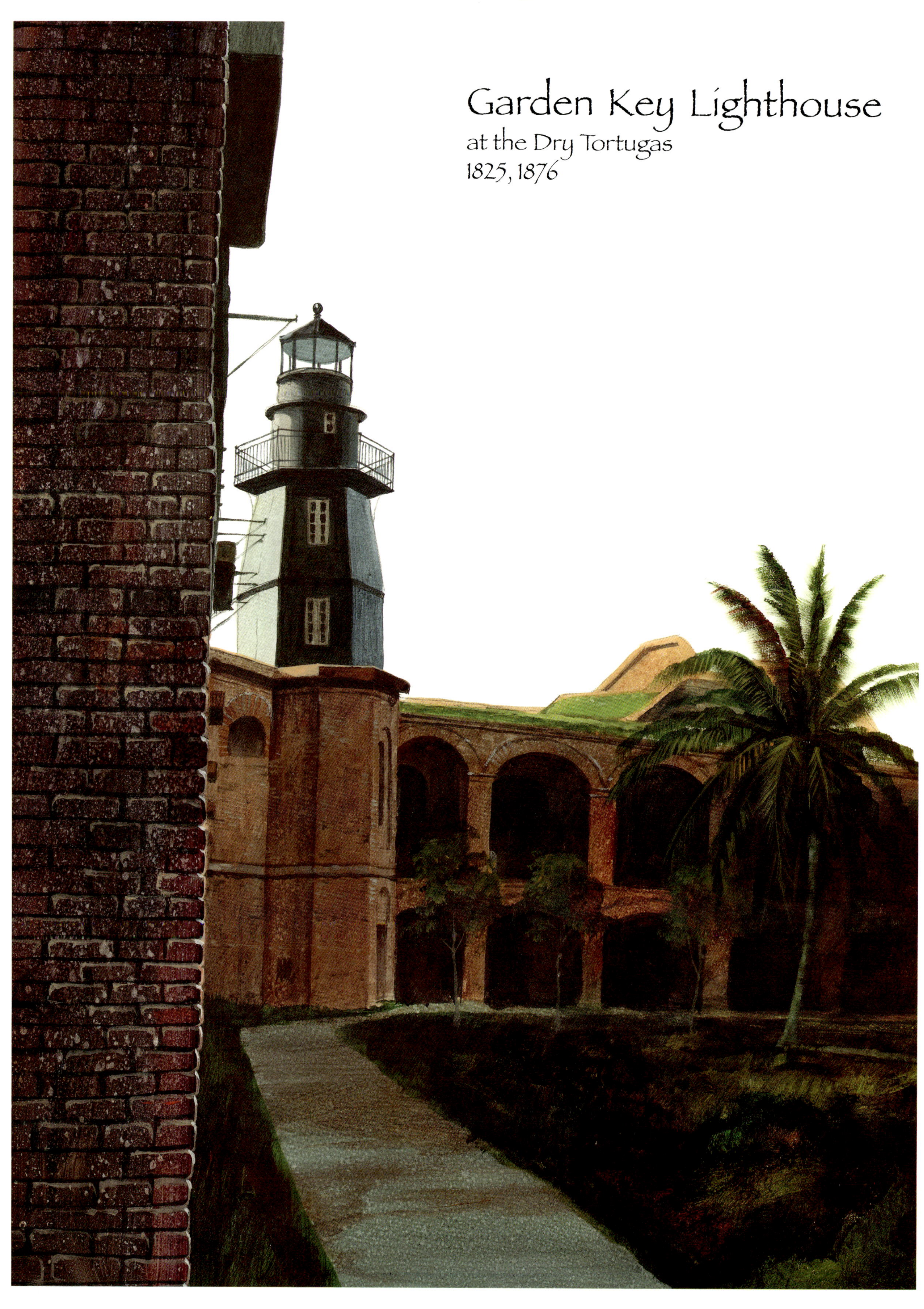
Garden Key Lighthouse
at the Dry Tortugas
1825, 1876

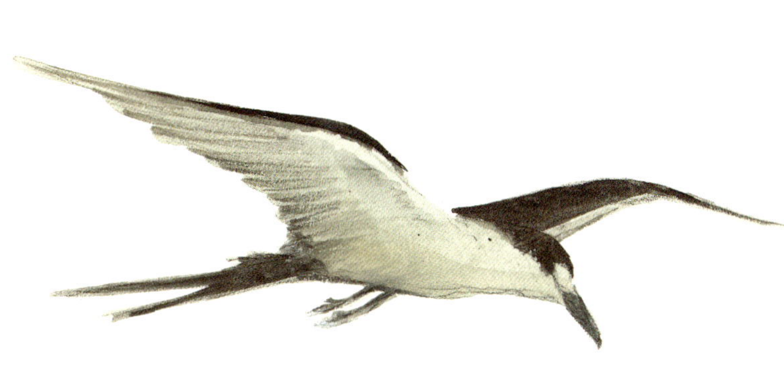

There are a couple of stories here: one about the fort, the other about the lighthouse. Fort Jefferson is located on Garden Key—seventy miles west of Key West—one of the seven islands that make up the Dry Tortugas, which were discovered by Ponce de León in 1513 and named for the many turtles that nested in the area. Construction of the fort began in 1846 and continued for thirty years, but the fort had outlived its usefulness before construction was ever completed.

The largest all-masonry fortification in the Western world, Fort Jefferson was part of a coastal defense buildup after the War of 1812: It played an important part in protecting trade to gulf ports and in denying access and anchorage to any enemy fleet that might attempt a military blockade. Its walls are fifty feet high and eight feet thick around its half-mile perimeter, and over forty million bricks were used in its construction. It also served as a sort of "Devil's Island" for prisoners. Its most notorious inmate was Dr. Mudd, who was imprisoned after treating Abraham Lincoln's assassin, John Wilkes Booth, for a broken leg.

Shipwrecks started to dot the Dry Tortugas around 1622—perhaps even earlier. More than two hundred wrecks have been documented. In addition, many ships involved in privateering, smuggling, and slavery must have gone down as well, but records of such illegal activities were naturally not logged. Salvagers earned a handsome living gathering what they could from all these wrecks. With so many ships sinking, there was little disagreement that a lighthouse was needed.

The original lighthouse at Fort Jefferson was built of brick in 1825 and was painted white, long before the citadel existed. It stood only sixty-five feet tall and immediately spawned complaints from mariners. The keeper at the time wasn't as diligent as most keepers; to add to the problems of an already dim light, he often neglected to clean the windows in the lantern room, leaving them covered with soot. Conditions improved when he was removed from service, but the lighthouse was still quite inadequate. In 1858, a new, taller lighthouse was built on nearby Loggerhead Key and was fitted with a first-order Fresnel lens. In the meantime, the light at Fort Jefferson was reduced to a harbor light, but it took up valuable parade ground space inside the fort. It was eventually replaced with the current lighthouse built in 1876. Made of black, boilerplate iron, it was placed on the wall of the fort. The fifty-six-foot-tall lighthouse is still lit but has not been considered an official aid to navigation since the early 1920s.

Today the fort and lighthouse remain part of one of Florida's most interesting parks. The National Park Service manages the Fort Jefferson National Monument, which entices twenty-seven thousand visitors each year by private boat, ferry, or daily seaplane service from Key West. (The ferry takes about three hours each way.) Spring is when most tourists—many of them bird enthusiasts—visit the island. Nearly three hundred species of birds have been spotted on the Dry Tortugas. Only a stone's throw from Fort Jefferson is where 45,000 brown noddies and over 100,000 sooty terns nest. The islands of the Dry Tortugas are the only place in the United States where you can see these two birds and are the site of the only known nesting colony of frigatebirds in the country.

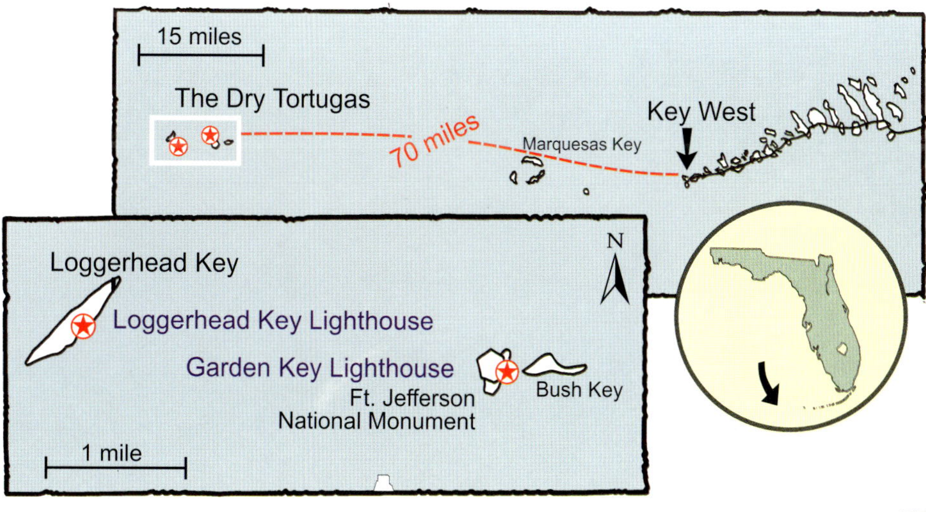

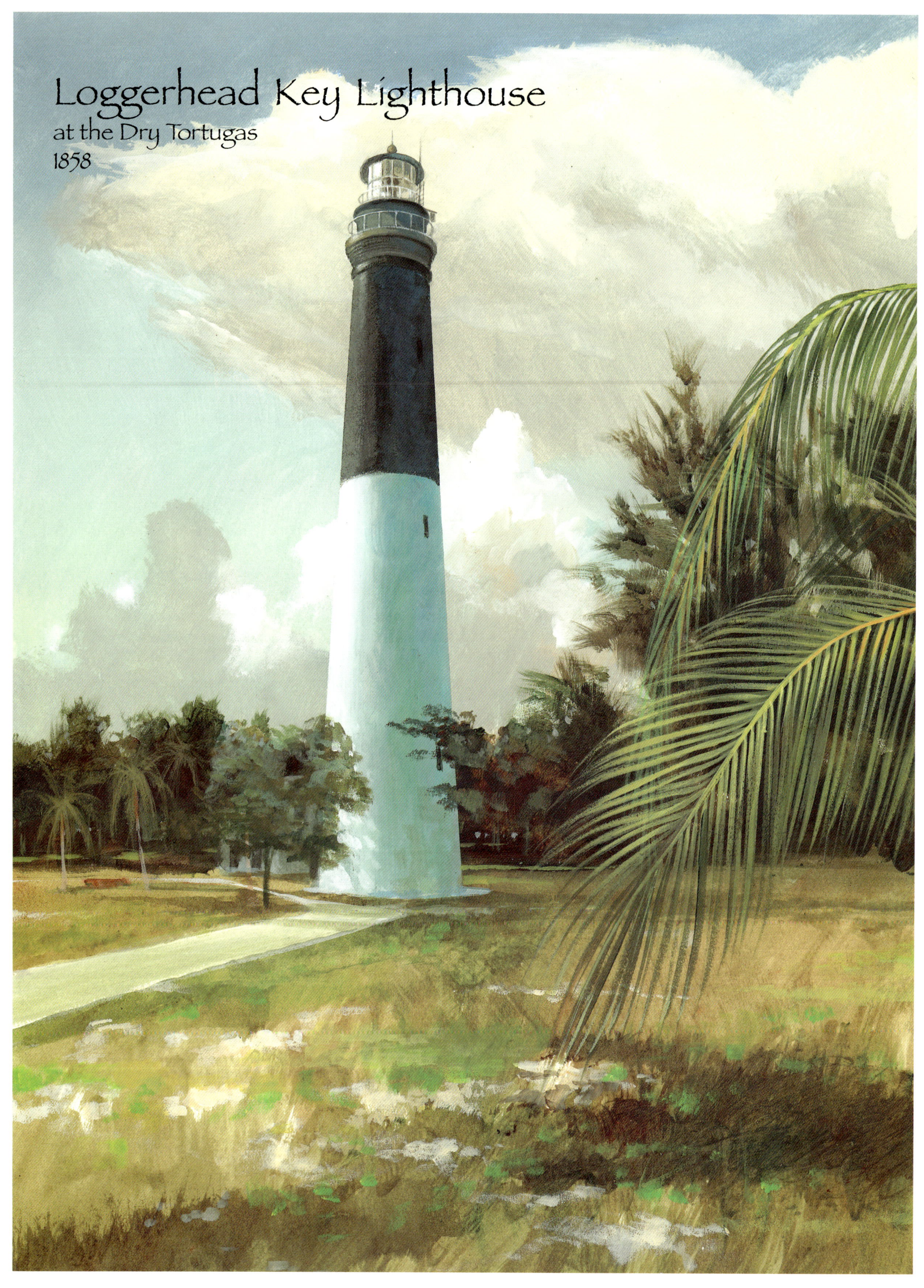

Loggerhead Key Lighthouse
at the Dry Tortugas
1858

Loggerhead Key is a small island that sits seventy miles west off Key West. Florida was sparsely populated at the time the lighthouse was built, and a location such as Loggerhead Key was extremely remote for a keeper and his wife. It was usually hot and humid, with only gulf breezes and occasional thunderstorms to cool things off a bit, and mosquitoes were vicious and abundant, constantly plaguing the lighthouse keeper.

The only source of water was what could be gathered in a cistern from passing rain clouds. In this location, and many others like it, keeping water from becoming putrid was almost impossible. Water collected from the roof of the keeper's house would be polluted before it even reached the cistern. Salt buildup and lead-based paint particles, along with dirt and ever-present bird droppings, would be washed into the water supply. Then the dark interior of the cistern would offer a perfect environment for bacteria to flourish. Efforts were made to quickly scrub the roof clean before an approaching rain shower, but often there was no time. Valves, or "cocks," were installed and could be closed to prevent water from being drained into the cistern. This allowed the roof to be washed clean for the first few minutes of a rain shower. Then they would be opened to let so-called clean water fill the reserve.

The sandy island would not support crops, and it was difficult—if not impossible—to keep food fresh. The sea was often the best place to keep food cool. Perishables such as meat and milk were stored in tight cans that were lowered into the water. It was not an easy life, and the romantic notion of a lighthouse keeper is often a mistaken one.

The lighthouse on Loggerhead Key was built in 1858 because the one at nearby Fort Jefferson was inadequate and of little use to anyone. The lighthouse at the fort was reduced to a harbor light when the new light at Loggerhead Key was lit. It was electrified in 1931, and its three-million-candlepower light made it the most powerful light in the United States at that time. In 1986, a modern optic lens replaced the original first-order Fresnel lens, which is now on display at the Coast Guard Aid to Navigation School in Yorktown, Virginia.

A decade and a half after the 151-foot-tall lighthouse was built, mortar between the bricks started to erode and cracks began to appear because of exposure to wind-driven rain. A new lighthouse was requested. That never happened, but Congress did appropriate enough money for repairs. To remedy the continuous cracking, nine feet of brick work was removed from the top of the lighthouse, and iron rods were inserted for reinforcement. Then, one section at a time, masonry was chiseled out in the lower sections, rods were implanted, and bricks were replaced, but the lighthouse continued to vibrate in strong winds. Despite its problems, the lighthouse continues to stand and function today, marking the entrance to the Gulf of Mexico.

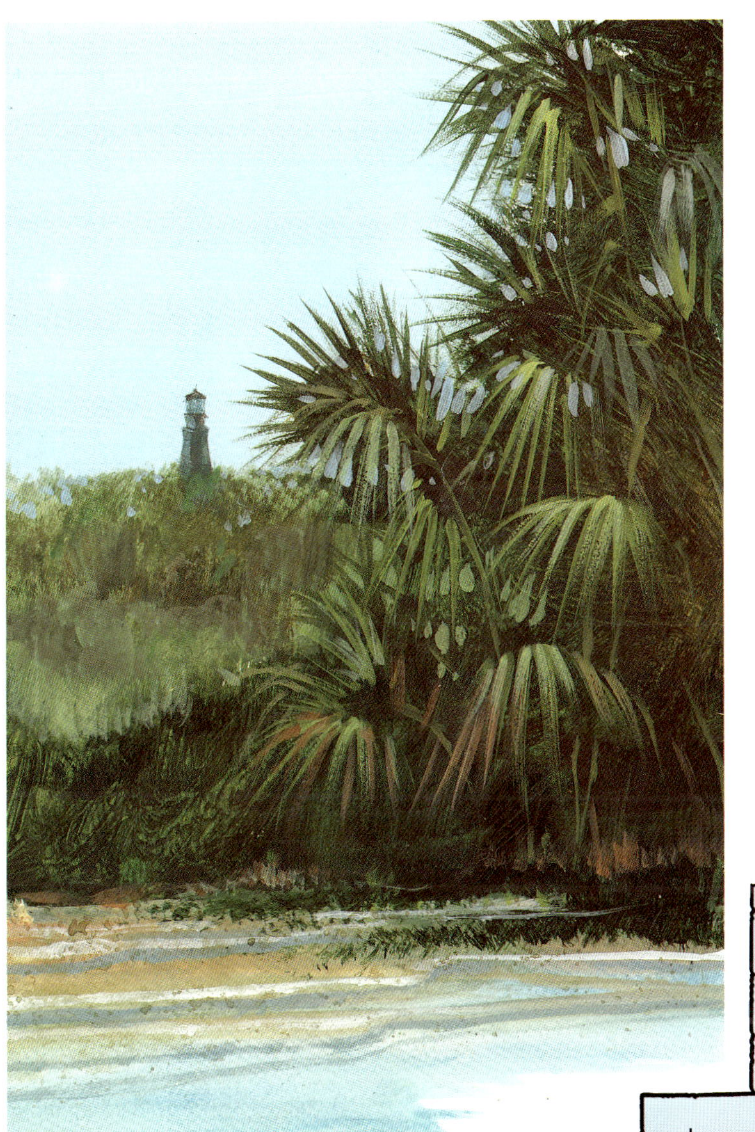

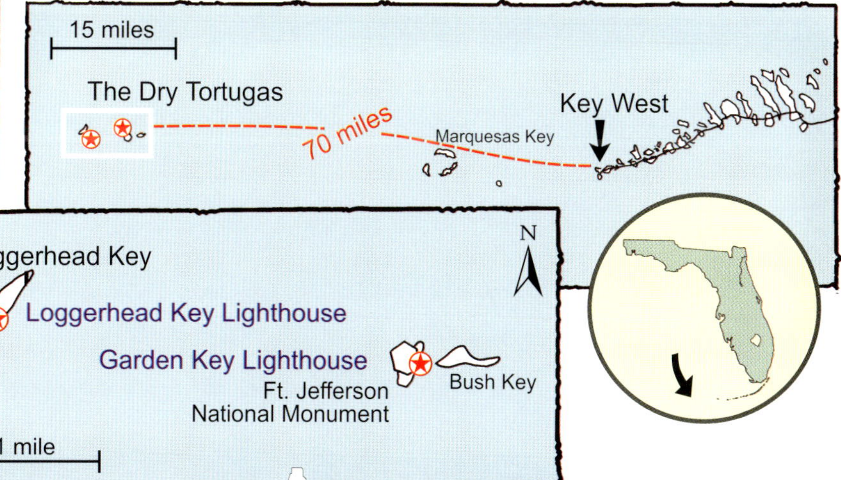

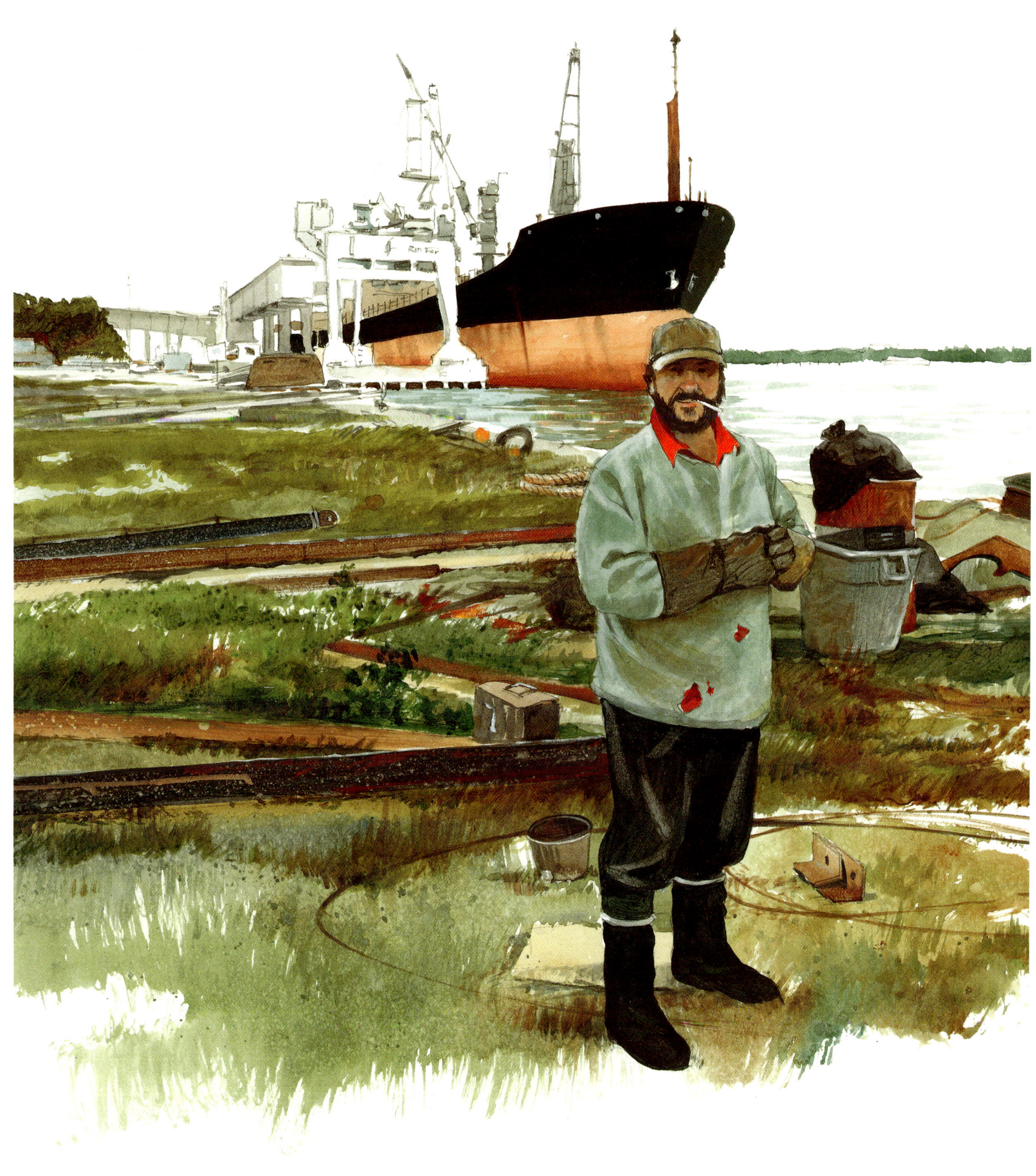

The men who make their living on the sea have had hard lives, and their faces tend to reflect their experiences. Like the routes on a nautical chart, the lines on their faces describe their journeys. Their beards and ragged hair appropriately express the ruggedness of their character.

Sketchbook

Here are a few sketches I've made of interesting people and places while visiting lighthouses.

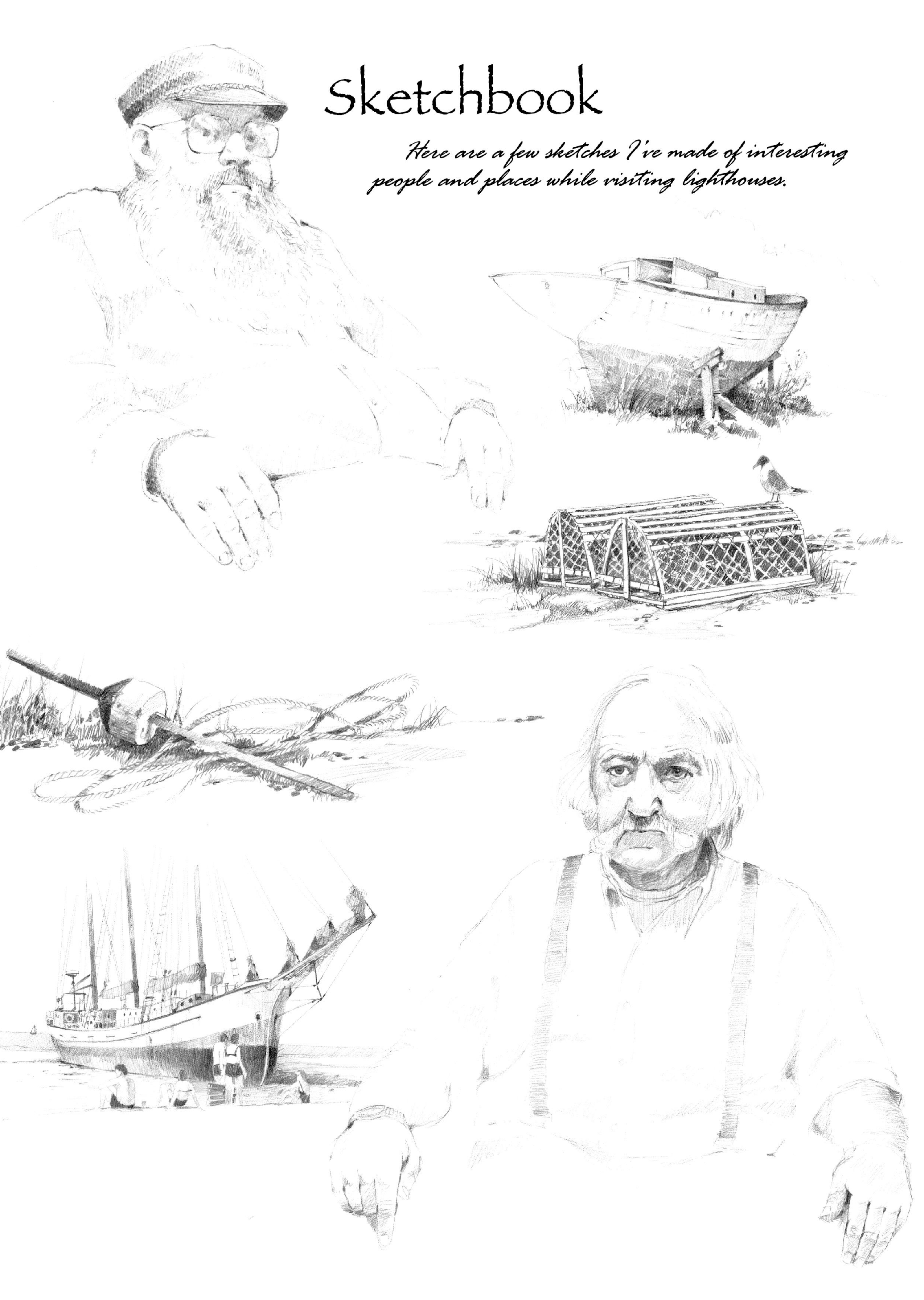

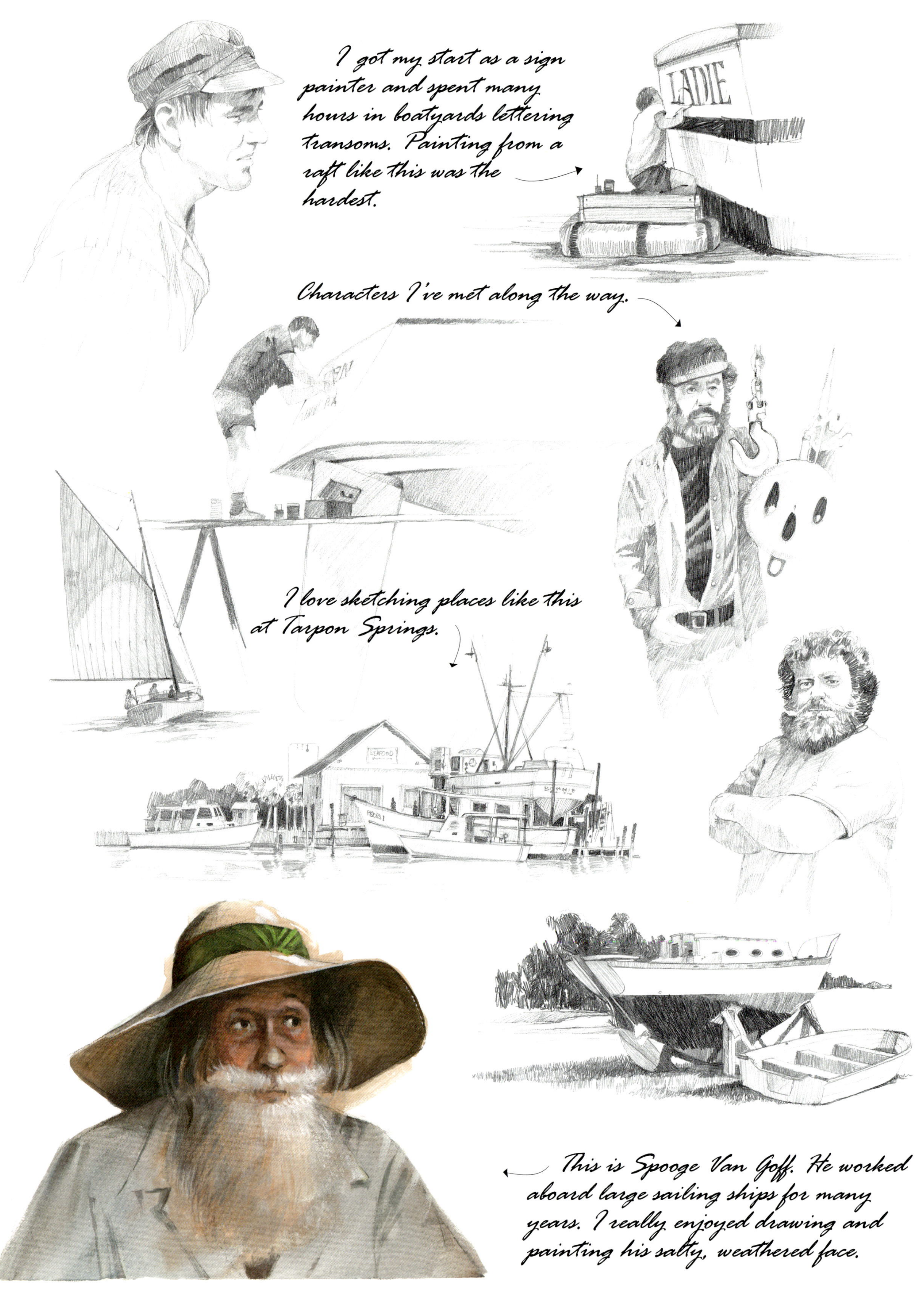

I got my start as a sign painter and spent many hours in boatyards lettering transoms. Painting from a raft like this was the hardest.

Characters I've met along the way.

I love sketching places like this at Tarpon Springs.

This is Spooge Van Goff. He worked aboard large sailing ships for many years. I really enjoyed drawing and painting his salty, weathered face.

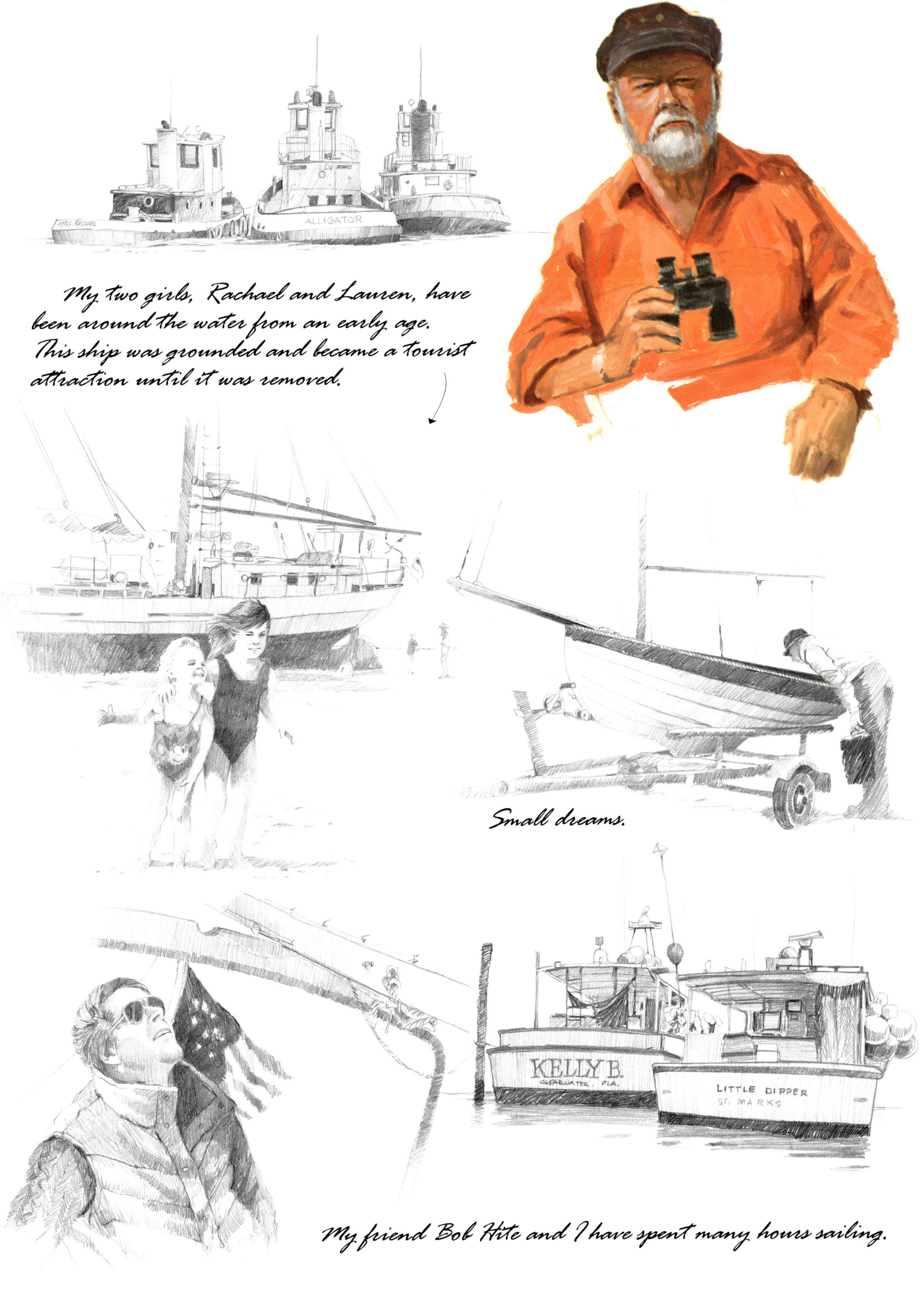

My two girls, Rachael and Lauren, have been around the water from an early age. This ship was grounded and became a tourist attraction until it was removed.

Small dreams.

My friend Bob Hite and I have spent many hours sailing.

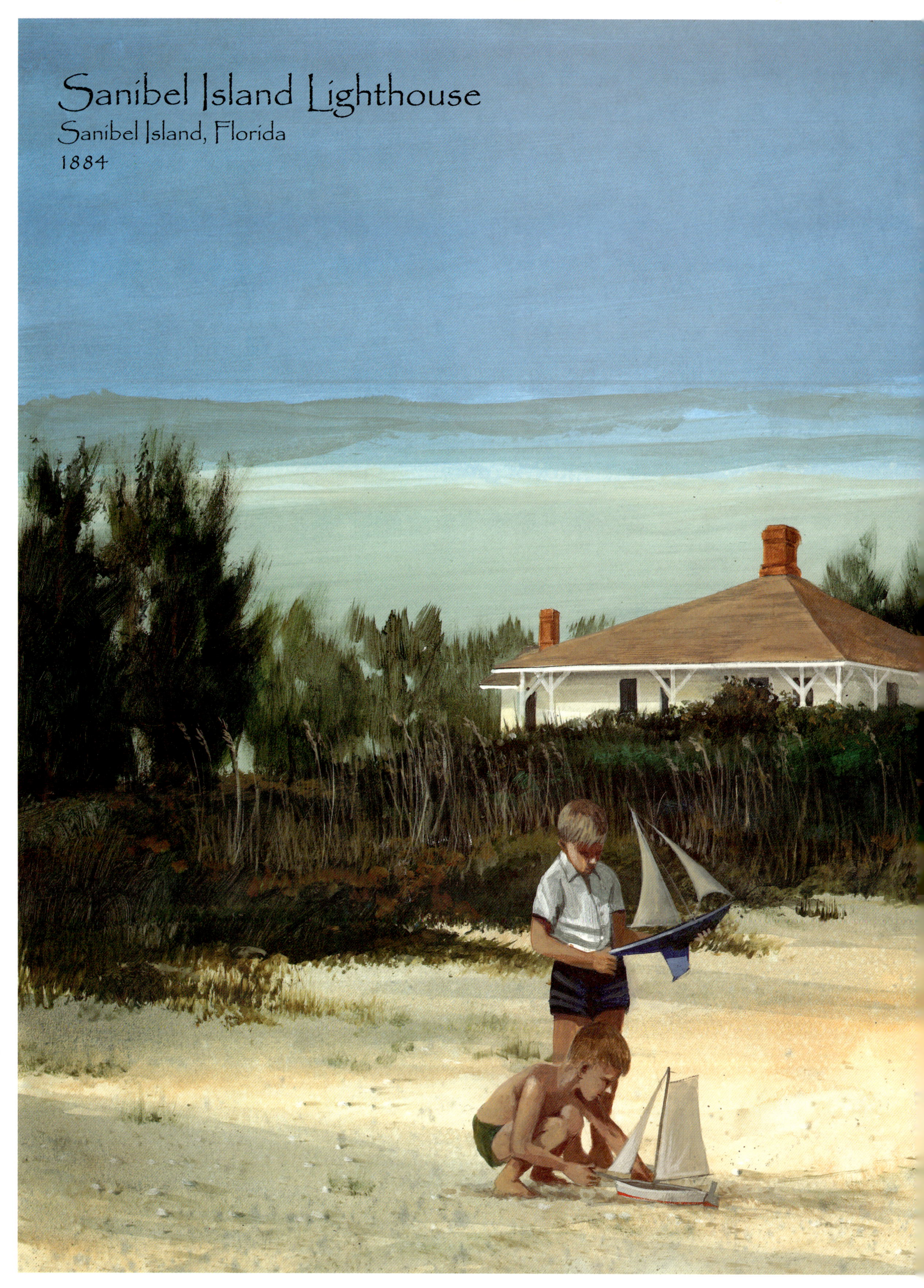
Sanibel Island Lighthouse
Sanibel Island, Florida
1884

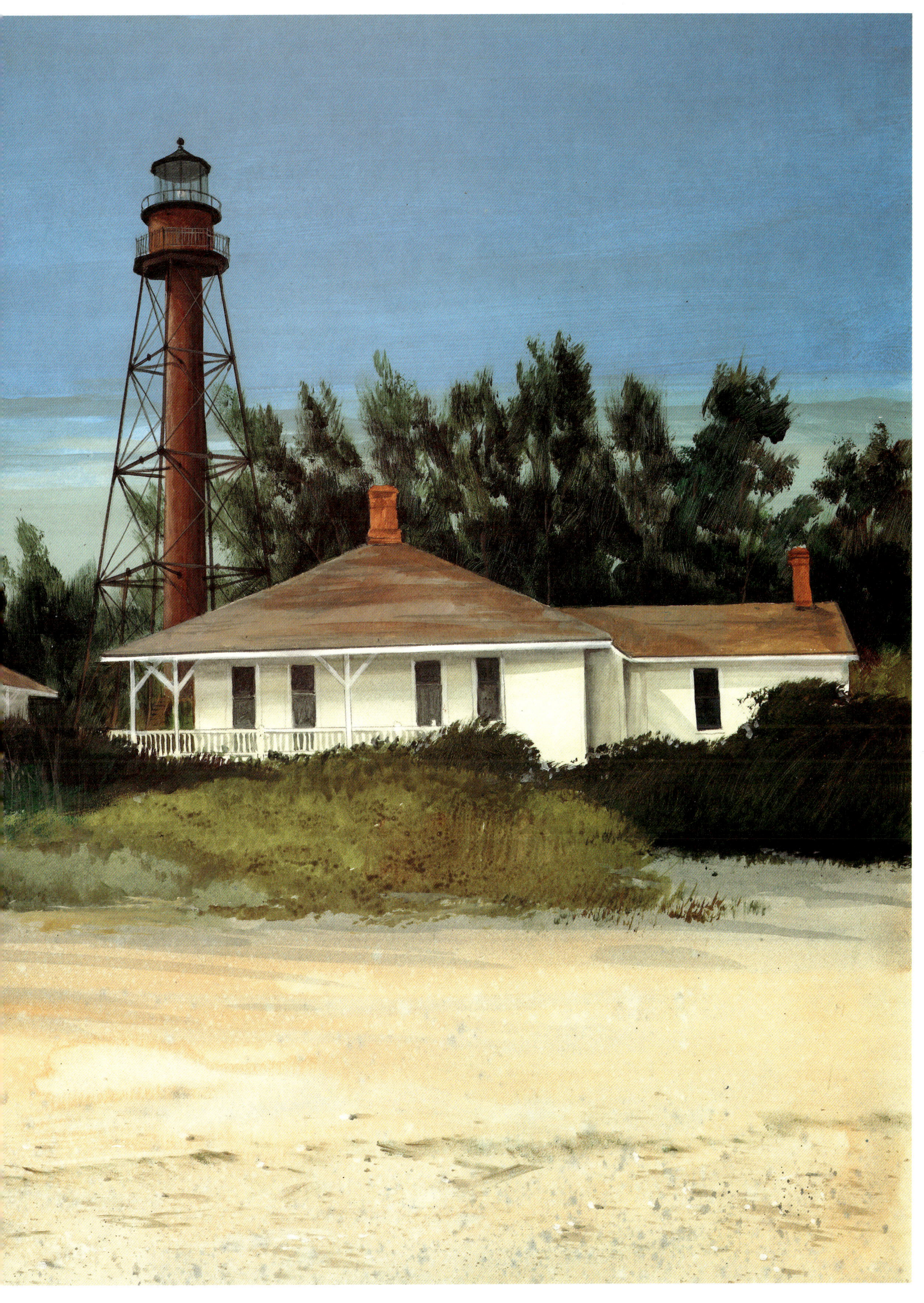

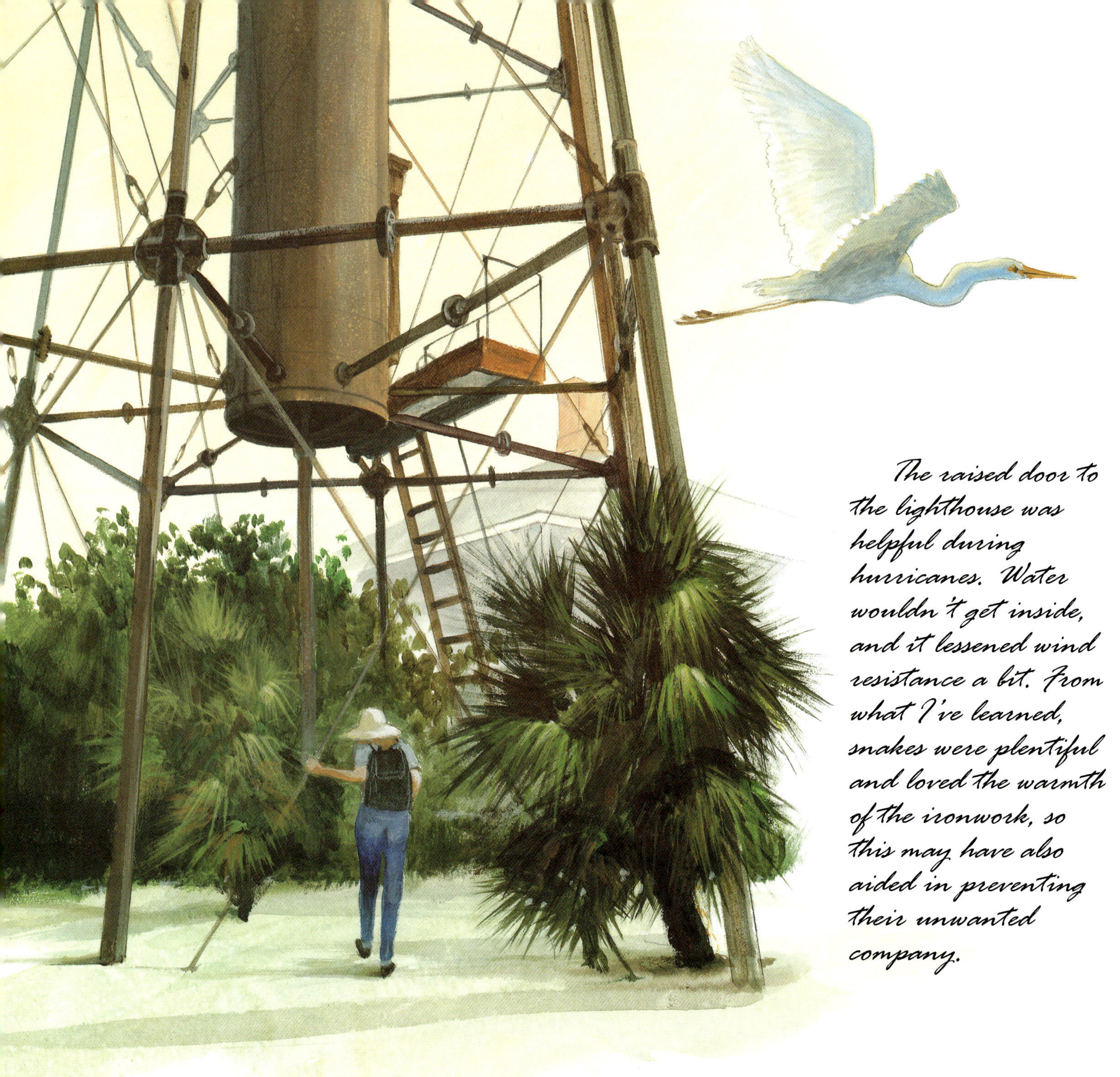

The raised door to the lighthouse was helpful during hurricanes. Water wouldn't get inside, and it lessened wind resistance a bit. From what I've learned, snakes were plentiful and loved the warmth of the ironwork, so this may have also aided in preventing their unwanted company.

A carbon copy of the Cape San Blas Lighthouse in the Panhandle, the Sanibel Island Light was first lit in 1884. It was intended that the lighthouse be erected earlier, but the schooner carrying the iron tower from Jersey City sank just two miles from the island. Divers using newly developed hard hats that supplied them with air salvaged all but a couple pieces of the lighthouse.

As far back as 1833, residents of Punta Rassa, a small town on the mainland, tried to get Congress to build a lighthouse on Sanibel, hoping it would serve to attract shipping and settlement to the area. Ships heading to Key West from New Orleans would have been served by a lighthouse as well as by businesses in the small town. But Florida wasn't even a state at that time, and Congress wasn't interested.

After the Civil War, the port of Punta Rassa began to prosper and became a large export center for cattle which, at that time, were driven in herds overland as there were no railroads in the area. From this port, they were put on ships and sent to other locations. Tampa was also becoming a booming port, and ships heading south from Tampa needed a navigation beacon. Congress finally realized the need and approved the building of a lighthouse, though some years later the town of Punta Rassa literally died out from hardship and disease.

The Sanibel Lighthouse is the last one heading south until you reach the Dry Tortugas, 130 miles away. The lighthouses on the gulf coast are far apart, unlike the lighthouses in the Keys, where there are many more dangerous shoals and reefs.

When the lighthouse was built, Sanibel Island was nearly uninhabited, and the keeper and his family had 670 acres of land set aside for farming. Unfortunately, the sandy soil wasn't good for growing much of anything ... except children. One lighthouse keeper who served there for twenty-two years had thirteen of them, seven from his first wife who died and five more from a widow who already had five children. They added one of their own, making a total of thirteen. Some took over as keepers until 1941, making for fifty years of family service.

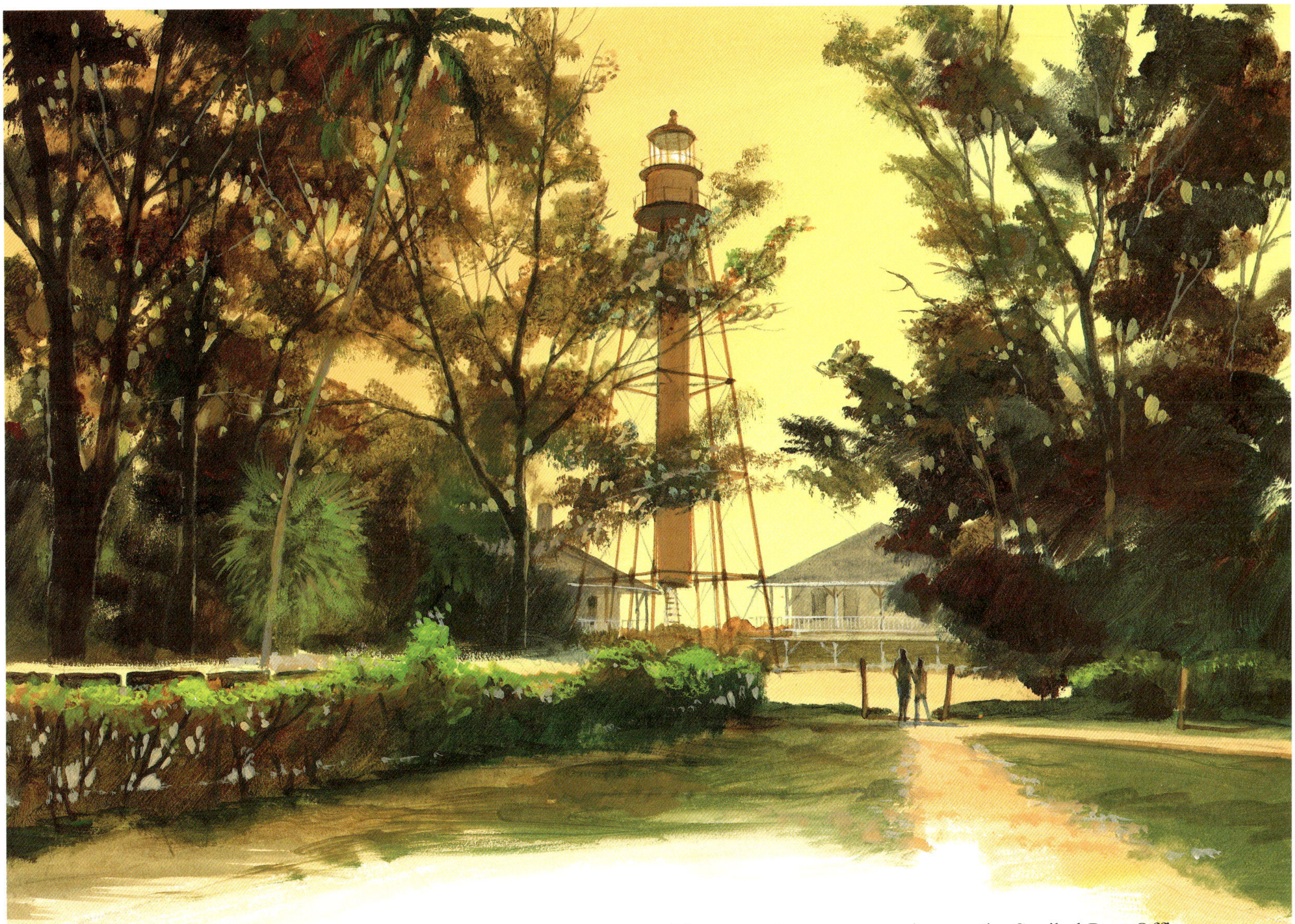

In 1963, a causeway was built from the mainland to Sanibel Island, and now nightmare of congested traffic. Before that time, a ferryboat brought visitors and automobiles over from the mainland. Thomas Edison had a home and laboratory in nearby Fort Myers, where he developed and refined many of his inventions, including the electric light. He and his friend Henry Ford were frequent visitors to Sanibel Island to relax and enjoy the beaches.

The beaches around the lighthouse are very lovely with white sand, sea grapes, and sea oats. The beaches are accessible *if* you can find the elusive parking spot. The lighthouse isn't open to the public and the keepers' houses are fenced in and are used by National Wildlife Refuge employees. You can walk all around the site, however, and it's a popular place for shelling and swimming.

Back in 1949, the lighthouse was automated, long before many other lighthouses were mechanized. The ninety-eight-foot-tall lighthouse has a modern light beacon. One of the original lenses is now displayed at the Sanibel Historical Museum, where you can also see the Sanibel Post Office, an old store, house, and tea room, all built in the mid 1920s.

If you like bird watching, the J. N. "Ding" Darling National Wildlife Refuge is towards the northern end of Sanibel extending into Captiva Island. Its 6,500 acres are one of the best places in the South to view shorebirds such as ibis, herons, egrets, roseate spoonbills, white pelicans, and dozens of songbirds. Many other native wildlife species, including alligators, also call this refuge home. Photographers and naturalists come from all over the world to visit this haven for wildlife. It's worth visiting if you can tear yourself away from the shops on the island. A trip to the Edison home in Fort Myers is also a wonderful place you won't want to miss.

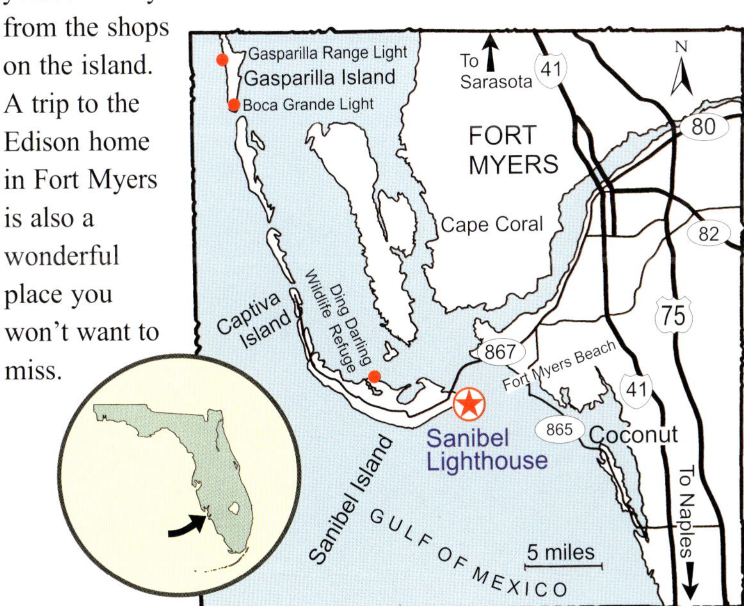

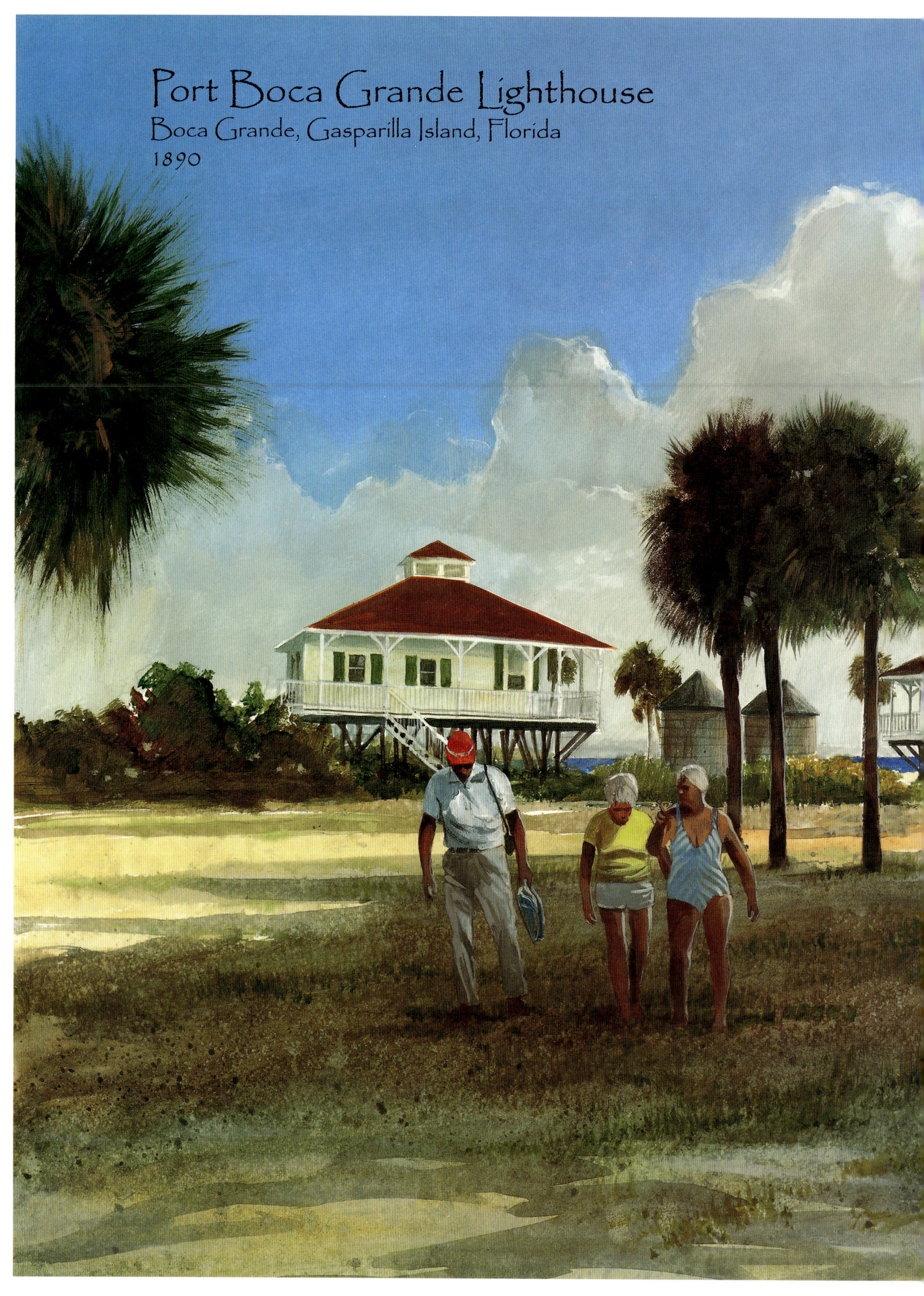
Port Boca Grande Lighthouse
Boca Grande, Gasparilla Island, Florida
1890

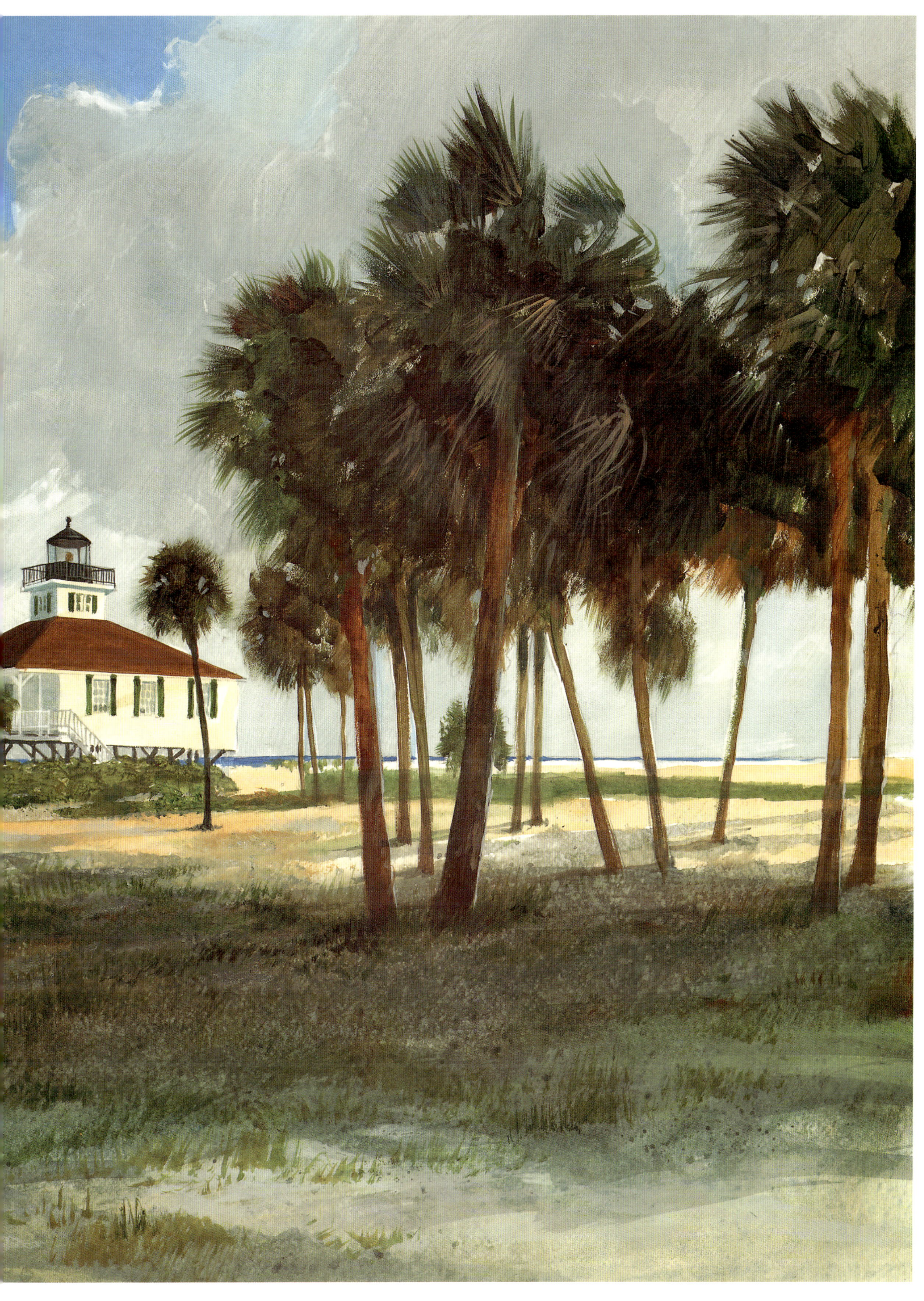

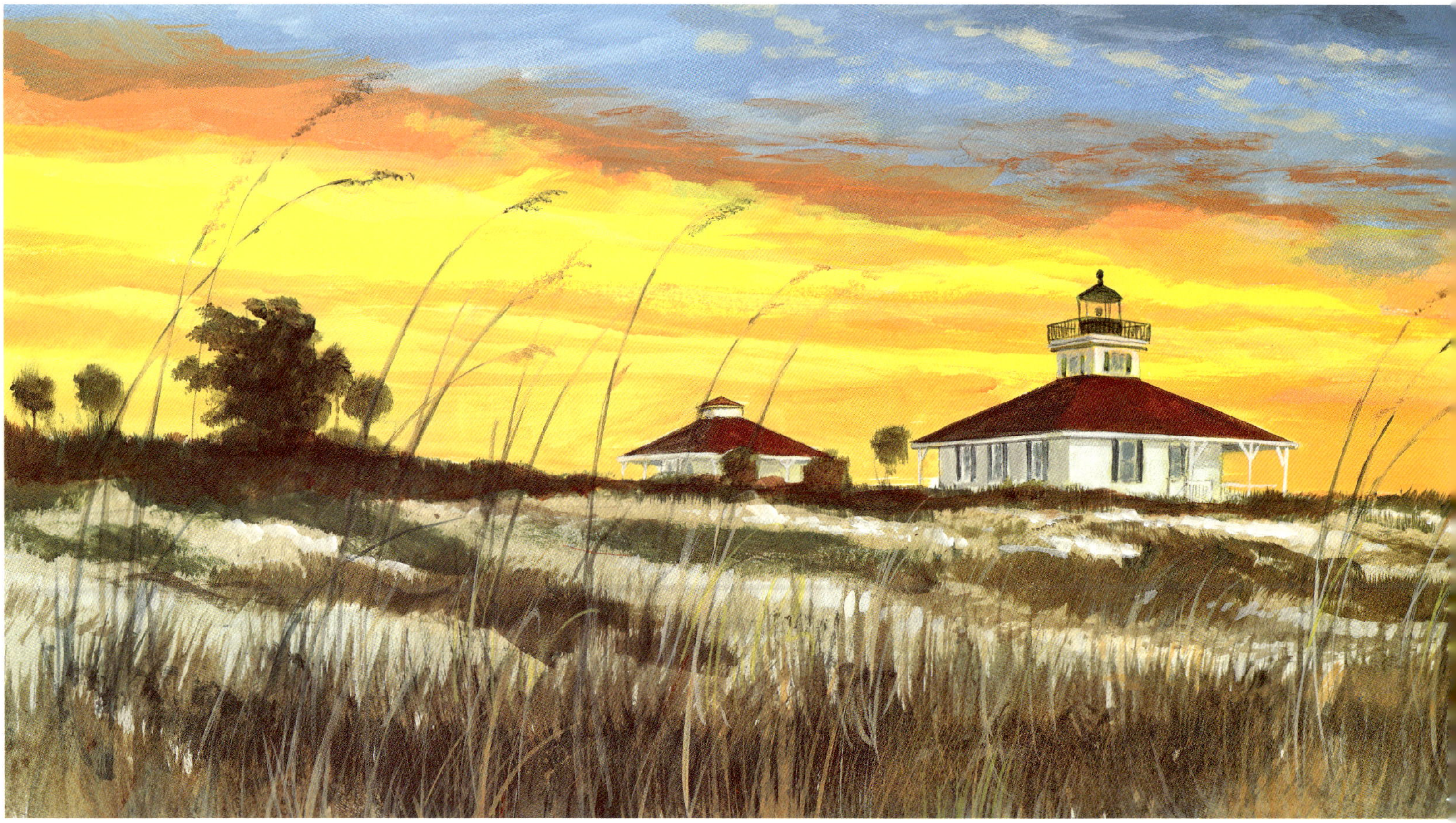

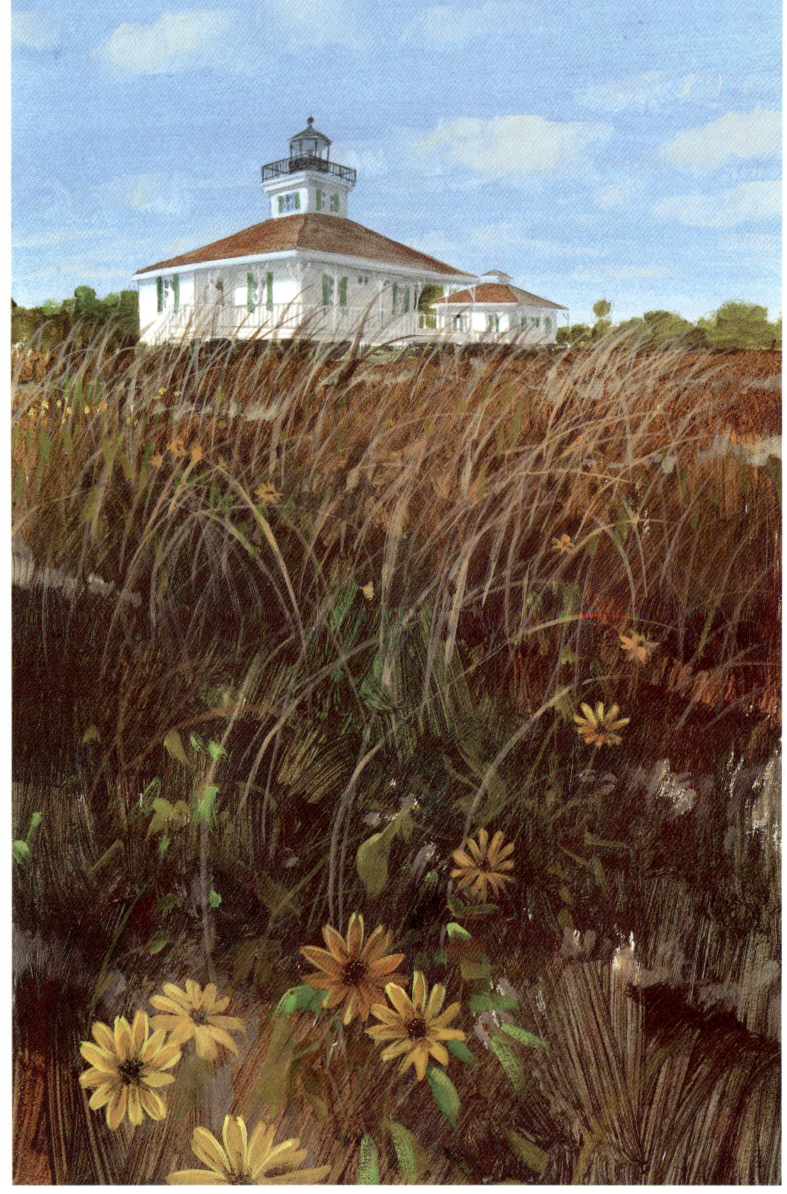

The history of Gasparilla Island goes back to the days of pirates and specifically to José Gaspar. It has been argued for years whether he actually even existed. One artifact that disputes his existence is old charts that predate Gaspar's supposed lifetime. They list Gasparilla Pass as Friar Gaspar Pass. The story of Gaspar, however, seemed to grow in the early 1900s, told by fishermen. Of course, fishermen don't have a great reputation for remembering details, and when newspapers started to write about the Gaspar legend, it became more and more accepted as truth. Pirates certainly did exist in this area and most likely visited these islands in the 1700s. The legend of Gaspar is so firmly embedded in the folklore of the entire region that it's best to let it live, as it adds to the notoriety and interest of the area.

The Boca Grande Lighthouse, built in 1890 and the oldest structure on Gasparilla Island, once helped to guide hundreds of oceangoing ships into its port for the huge phosphate industry that sprang up in the early 1900s. Phosphate is an important element in the making of fertilizers, which enable farmers to raise crops on the same land year after year. Many other products, such as detergents and explosives, incorporate phosphate as well. It's even an ingredient in soft drinks. Since Florida has approximately seventy-five percent of the phosphate deposits in the United States, the port naturally thrived. The railroad brought in not only phosphate, sometimes a hundred carloads at a time, but also visitors from the North.

The lighthouse served as a home for the lighthouse keeper and his family, and the twin building next to it served as home to the assistant lighthouse keeper. The keeper would take care of the light until midnight, and then his assistant would tend to the light for the rest of the night.

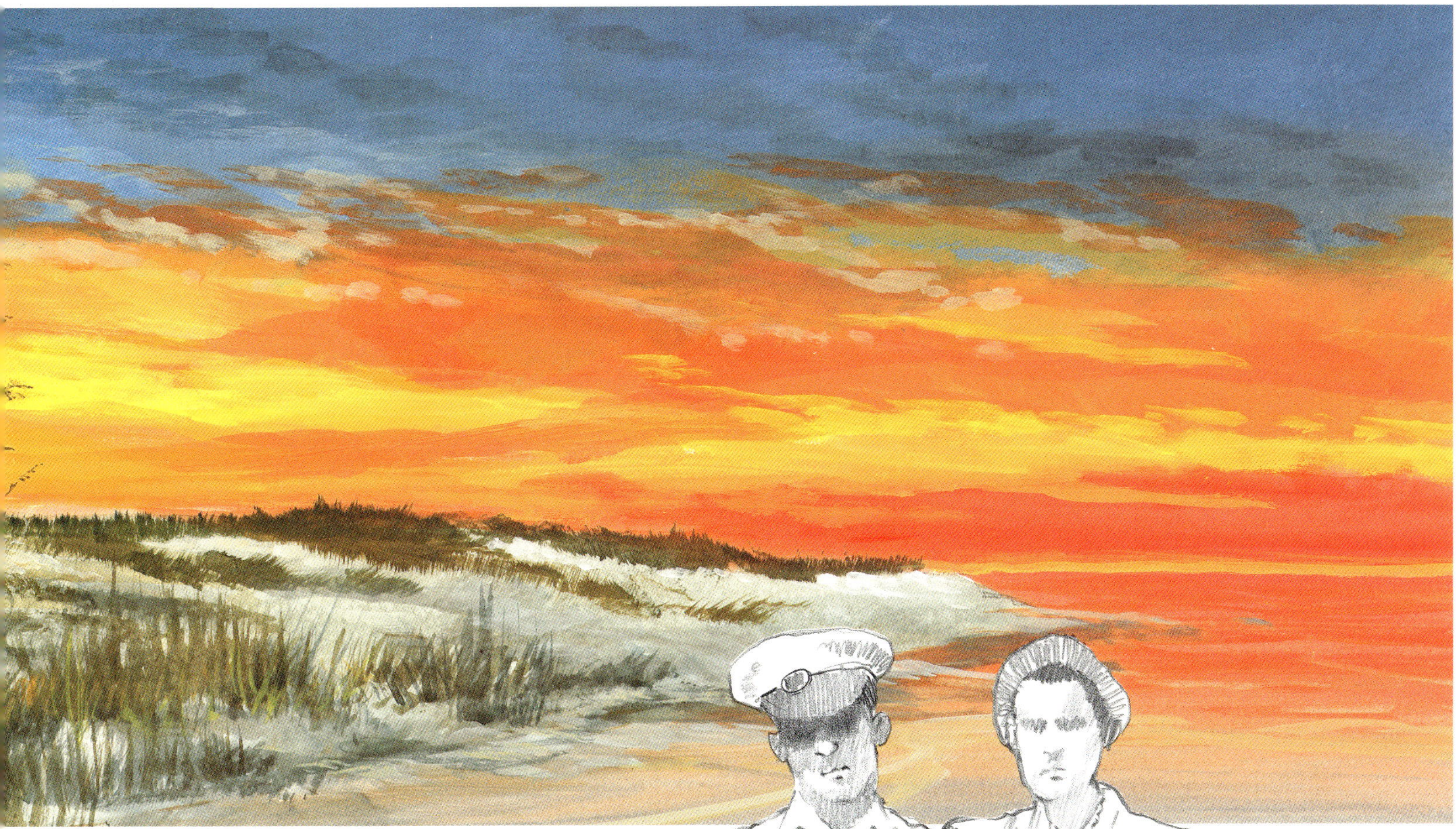

Near the lighthouse stood what was known as the quarantine house. Built in 1895, it was the second oldest building in Boca Grande. It once stood next to the lighthouse and was painted bright yellow with green shutters. It still exists but has been moved to a different location. Since contagious diseases, especially yellow fever, were prevalent at the time, all ships that came into the area were required to raise a yellow flag. They would moor in a certain area, then wait for the doctor to row out, board the ship, and inspect for sickness before being allowed to come into port.

With the opening of the elegant Gasparilla Inn in 1911, Boca Grande became known for its good hotels that catered to a rich clientele. There was even a streetcar on the island that provided service from downtown to the tip of the island where the port was. The hotel to this day is still the resort of choice on the island. A bridge for cars wasn't built until

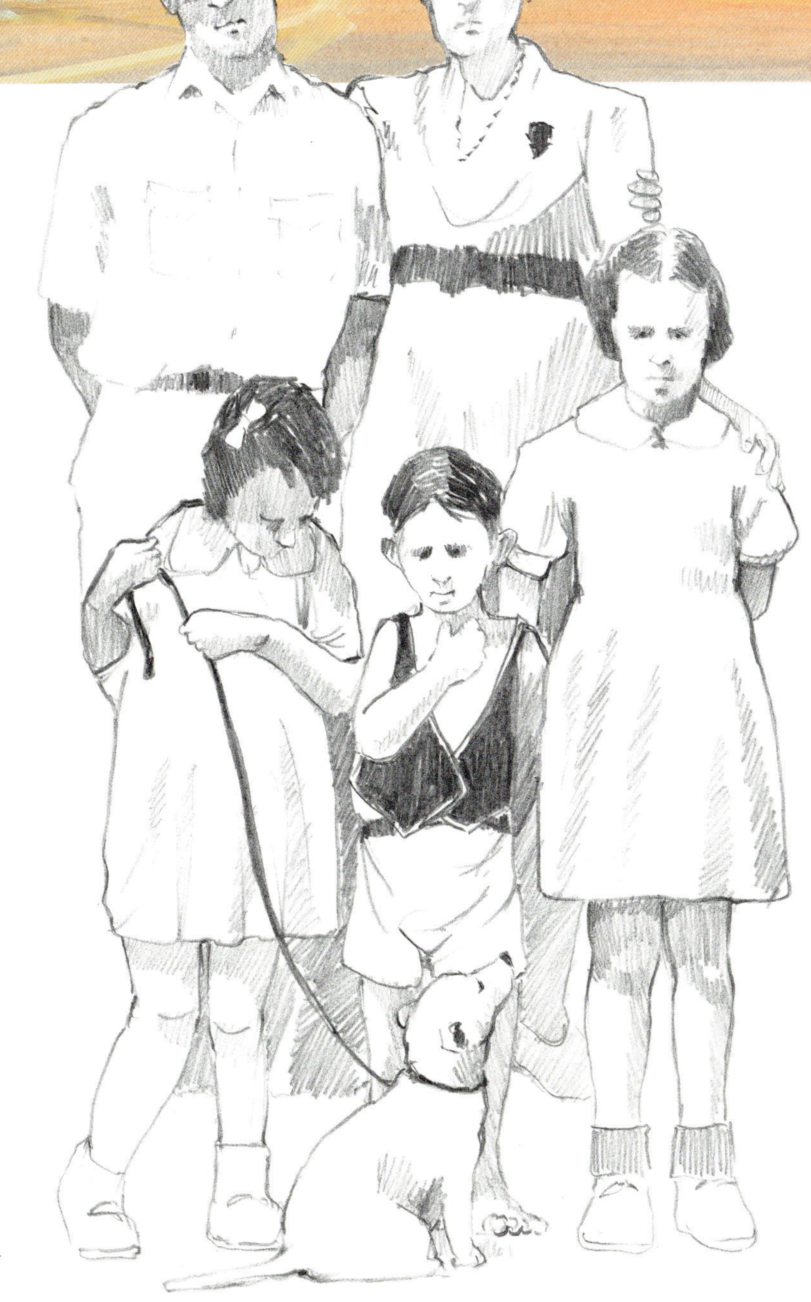

This was the family, with their watchdog Brownie, who lived at the lighthouse from 1932 to 1941.

1958, so the only way to get to the island before then was either by railroad, built in 1909, or by ferryboat.

In the early 1970s, new terminals in Tampa with larger and more modern facilities, along with a port to handle deeper draft vessels, left Boca Grande behind the times. It meant the end of the railroad in Boca Grande; operations ceased in 1981. The one remaining train terminal left here is just a hundred yards from the lighthouse and is used to offload fuel oil for a power company. Stored in large tanks, the oil is transferred to river barges, then towed to the power plant near Alva.

Most lighthouses around the country became automated in 1960, marking not only the end of an era but also the abandonment and deterioration of many lighthouses. Such was the case at Boca Grande. In 1966, the Coast Guard removed the Fresnel lens from this light and used it at the nearby Gasparilla Light, leaving the Boca Grande Lighthouse dark and discarded. For twenty years it served little purpose except as a picnic spot for tourists and as a hangout for teenagers. By 1970, it fell into ruin and almost into the sea from beach erosion. A year later, just before it was too late, 35,000 cubic yards of sand were placed around the lighthouse in an attempt to save it. The federal government

This is a four-place lampchanger inside the Fresnel lens. When one of its 250-watt lamps burns out, another one automatically rotates into place.

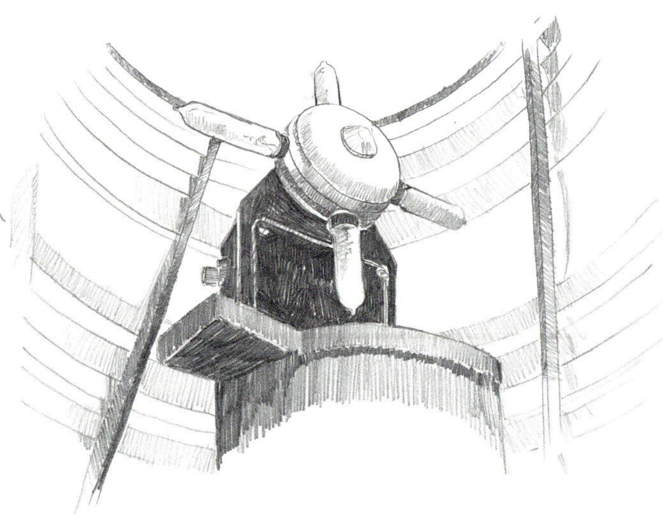

The Coast Guard reinstalled the original third-order Fresnel lens in 1986 when the lighthouse was recommissioned.

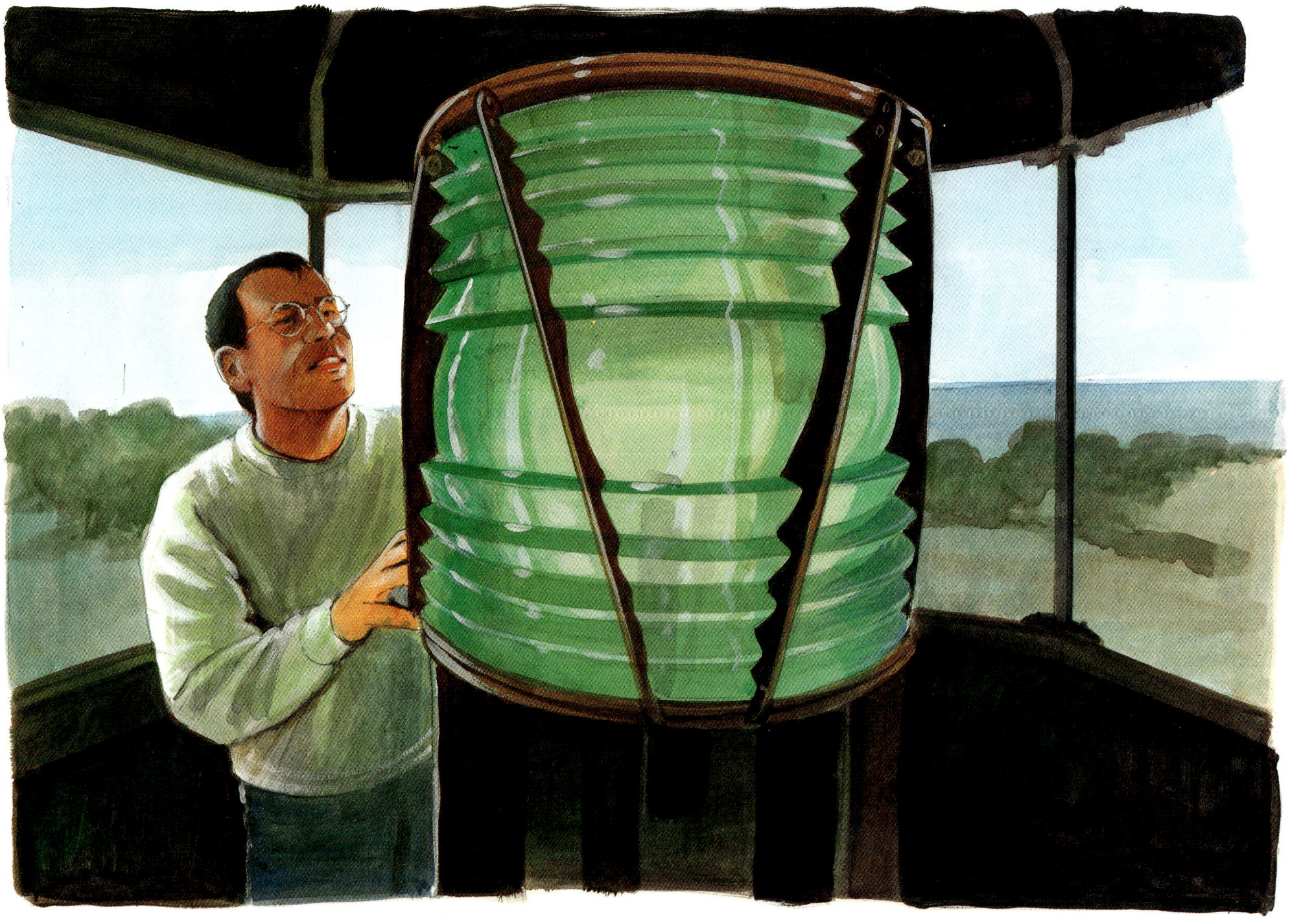

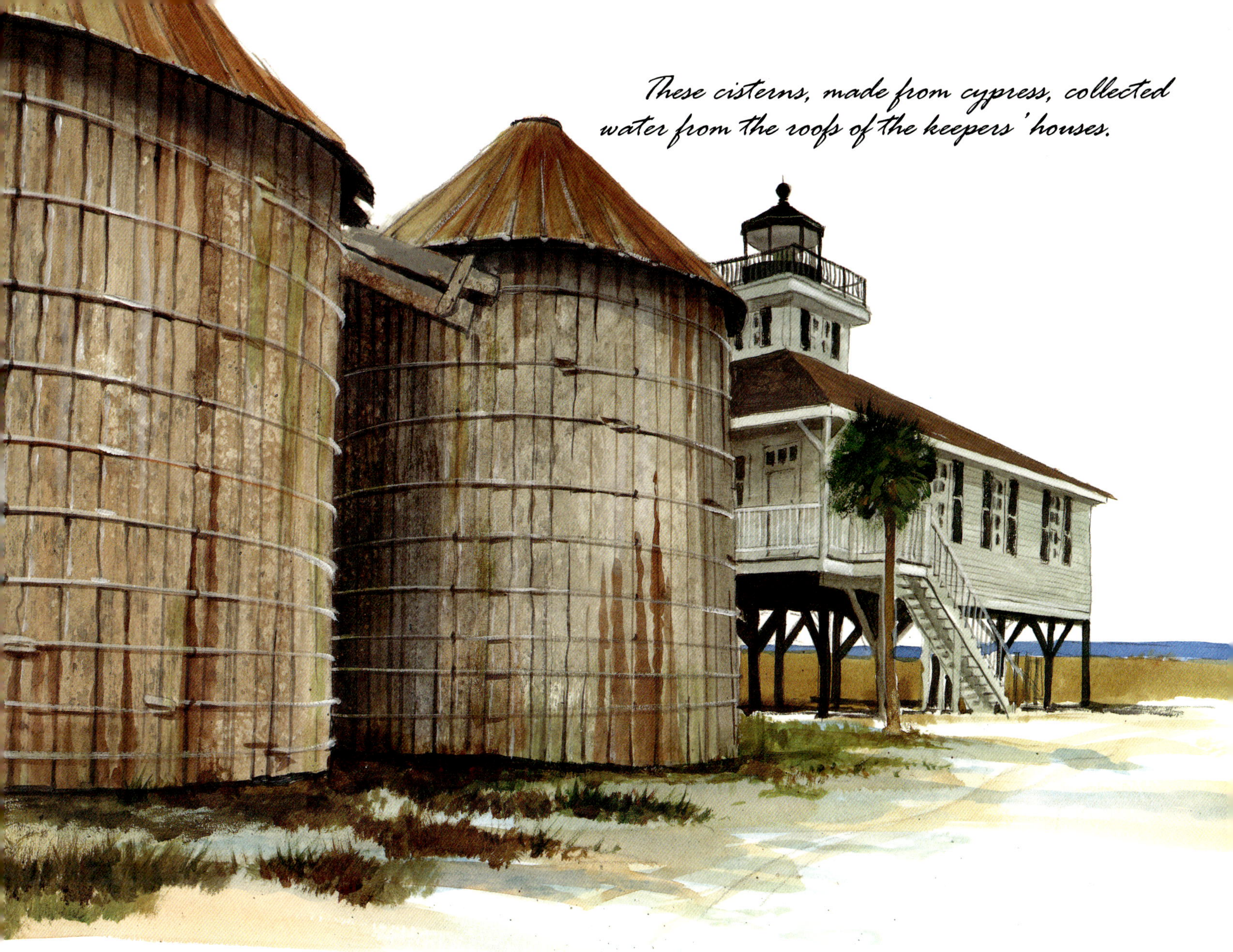

These cisterns, made from cypress, collected water from the roofs of the keepers' houses.

turned it over to the county, and in 1980 it was placed on the National Register of Historical Places. Five years later, the area's residents took up the cause to restore the lighthouse with the help of the state.

The lighthouse is open to the public and has displays of earlier times. The area is fenced, but you can see the outside of the lighthouse from the nearby park and beach. The assistant keeper's house serves as a house for the park ranger.

Tarpon fishing in this area is world renowned, and every year during the second weekend of July, sport fishermen come from all over the world to compete for $100,000 in prizes. Tarpon, known as "silver king," can weigh two hundred pounds. Fishermen in the competition no longer keep these stately fish after a catch but release them after measuring, weighing, and photographing them. Today taxidermists can create an accurate fiberglass trophy model from that information. If you're thinking of joining in on the competition, the entry fee is about $3,700.

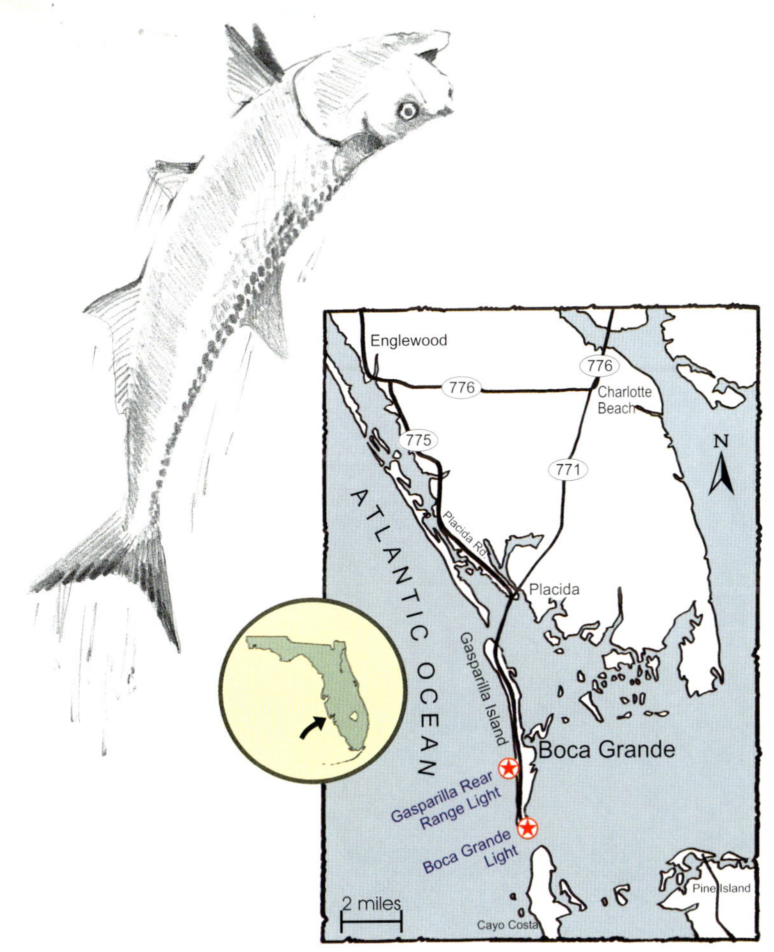

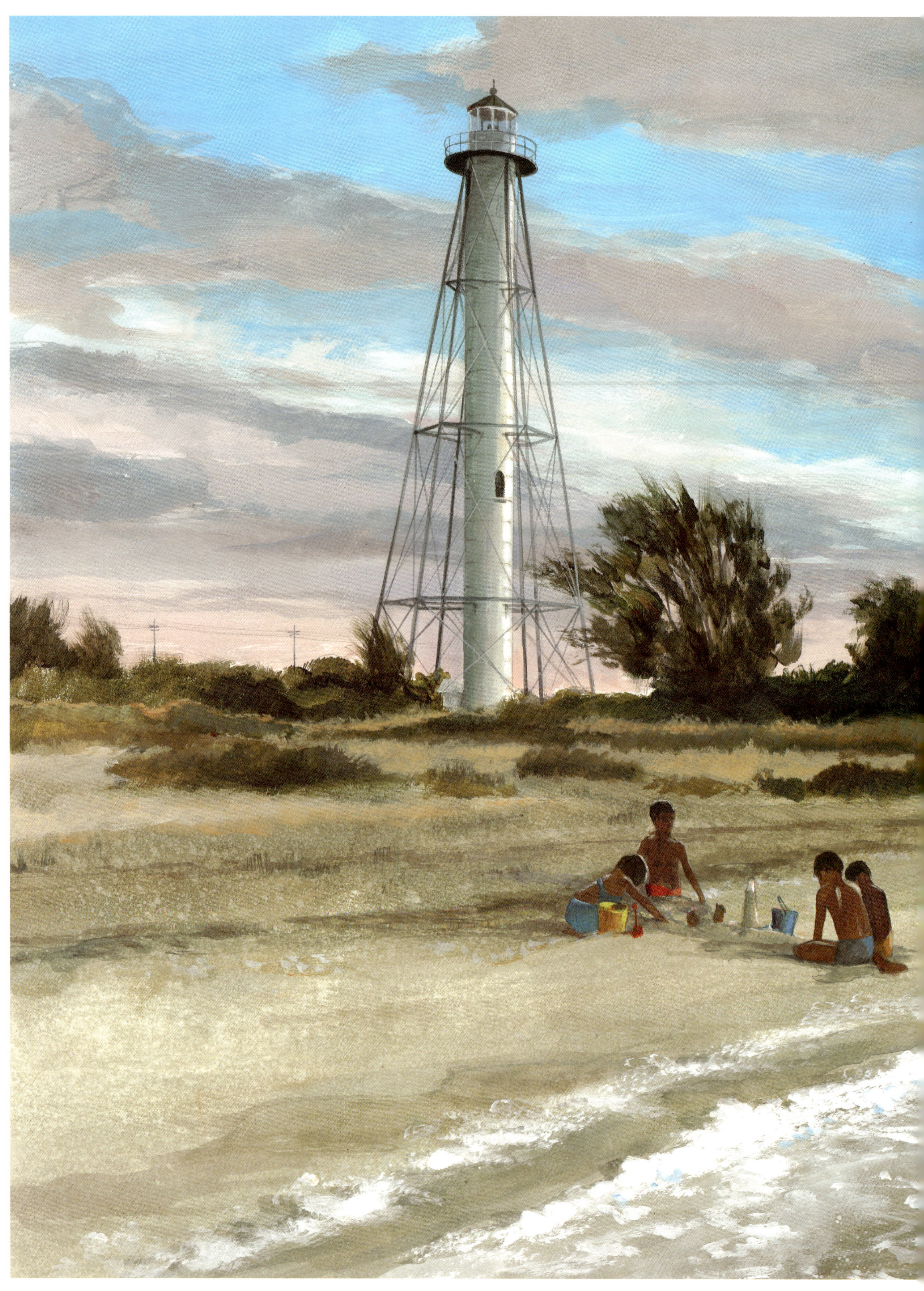

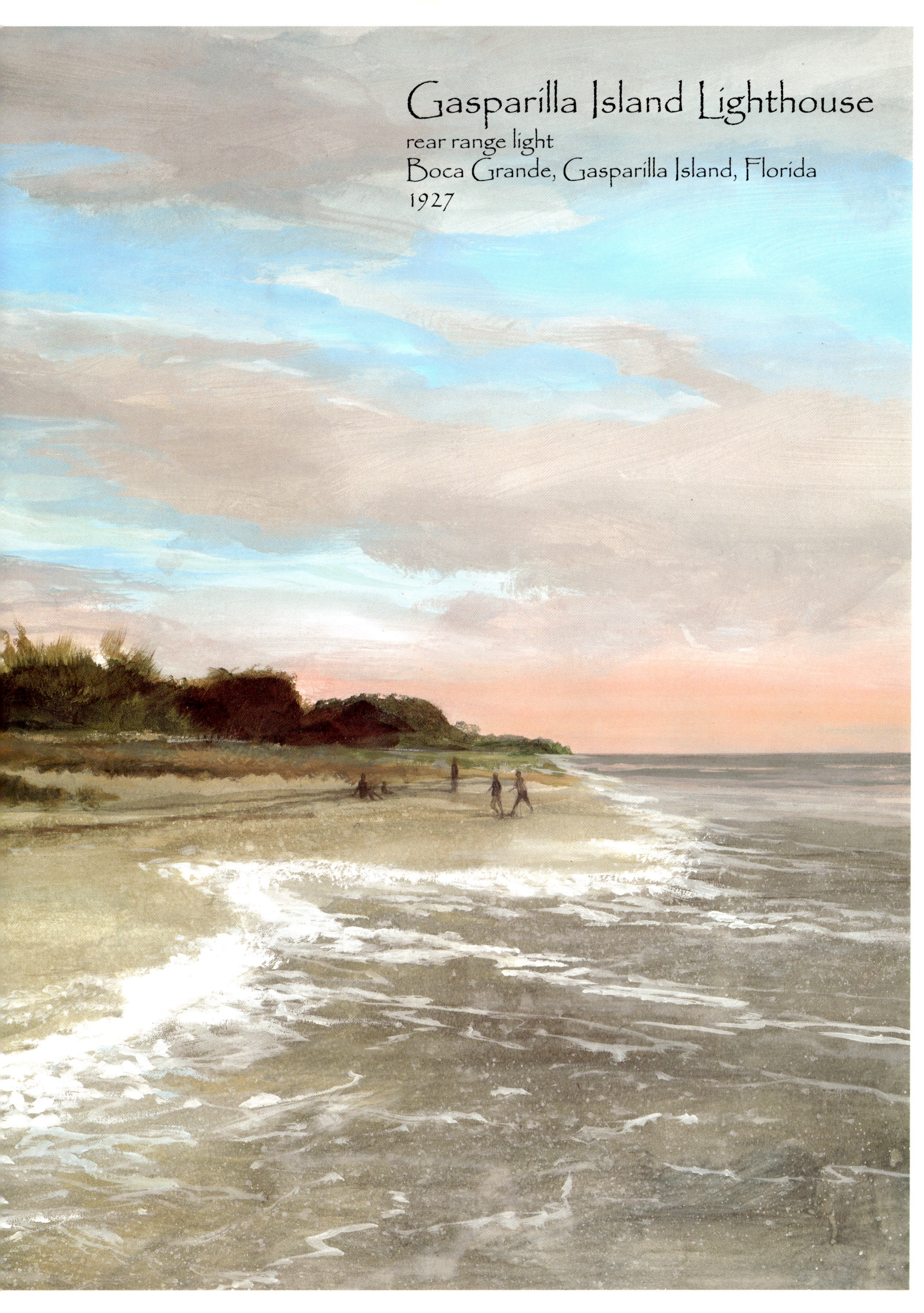

Gasparilla Island Lighthouse

rear range light
Boca Grande, Gasparilla Island, Florida
1927

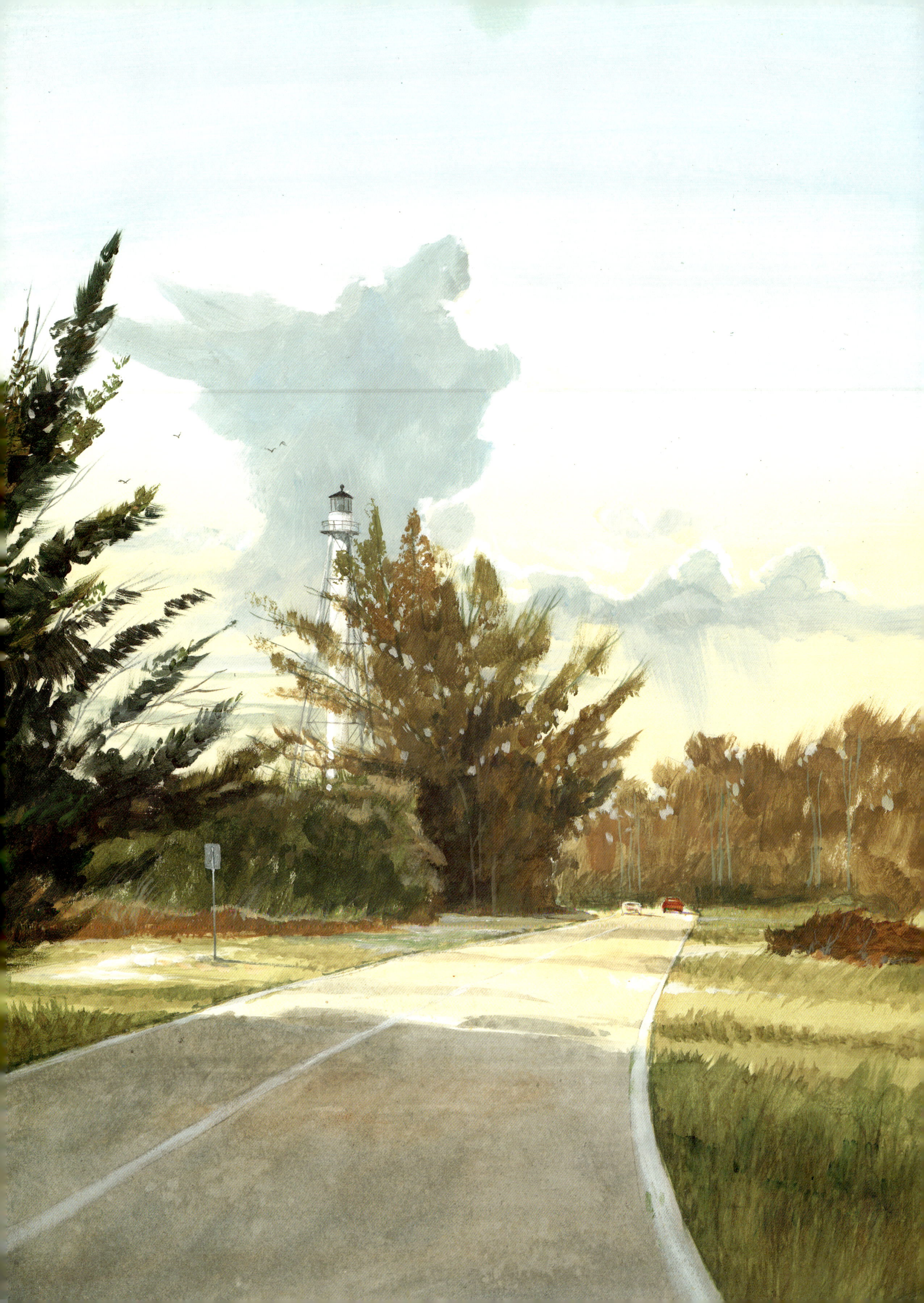

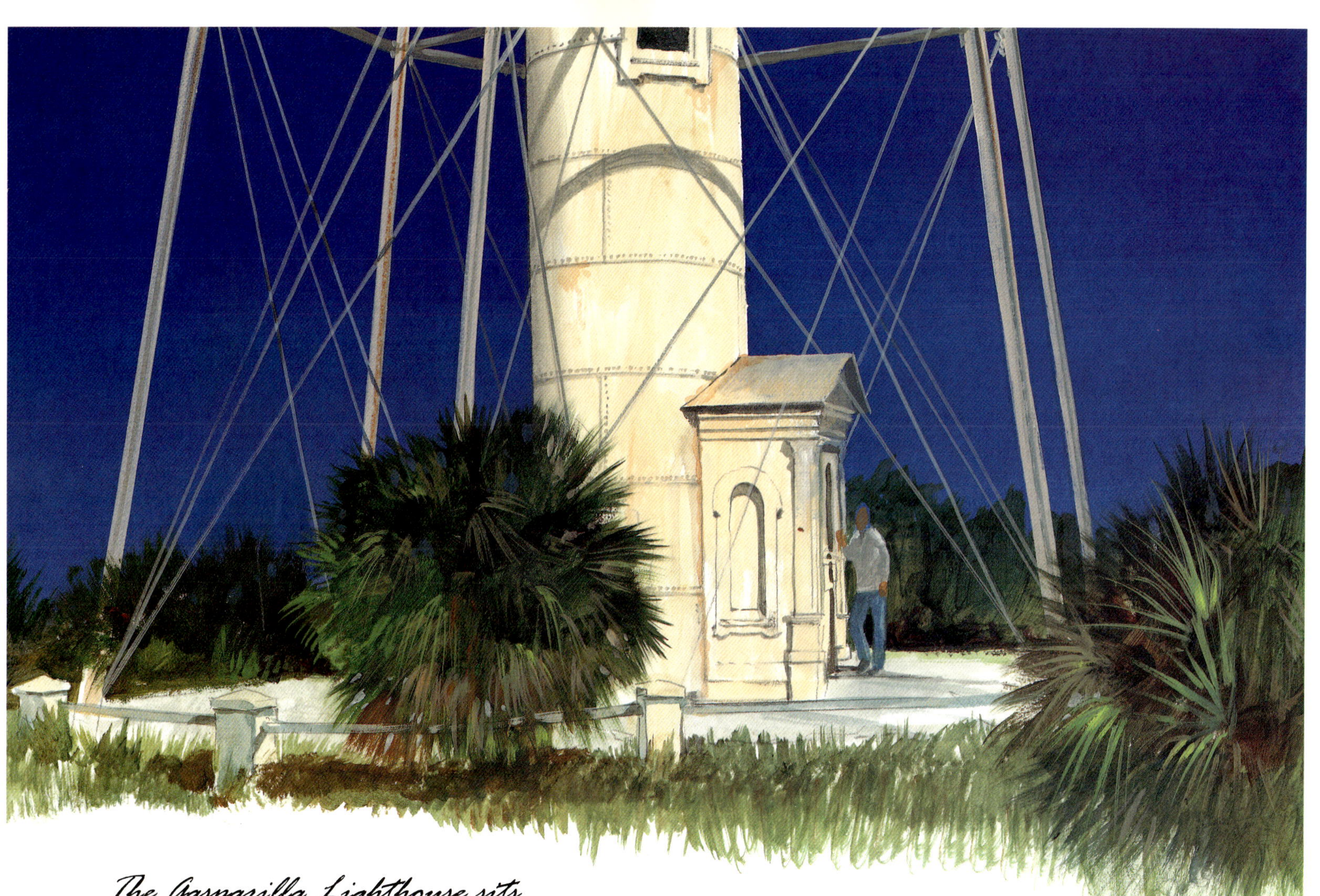

The Gasparilla Lighthouse sits right on the beach. It's a great place to have a picnic, go swimming, and build a castle in the sand.

A rear range lighthouse is used in the same way that you line up the sights on a gun. When one lighthouse is directly behind the other, then a captain knows he is in the middle of the channel. The Gasparilla light serves this purpose. Built in 1927, it stands 105 feet tall and had to be moved once because the beach had eroded dangerously close to it. Fortunately, these cast-iron skeletal lighthouses were bolted together, making disassembly possible. The lighthouse has a narrow lantern room just under the light, making it look somewhat out of proportion, so it doesn't rank up there with the most attractive lighthouses in Florida. The Boca Grande Lighthouse a mile down the road, however, makes up for its companion's lack of style.

Boca Grande is the town, Gasparilla is the island, but most people know this place simply as Boca Grande. It was a thriving port when phosphate was discovered and mined in Bartow, directly east of Tampa. The Peace River ran from the area of the mining down to Port Charlotte, near Boca Grande. River barges were used to deliver goods to the port for shipping until 1909. At that time, a railroad was completed from Bartow to Boca Grande, making it possible for phosphate to be shipped directly to Boca Grande by rail.

The island not only grew economically because of the phosphate industry; it also became a popular social spot during the winter for residents from the North. The railroad offered special excursions from New York to accommodate the many wealthy tourists. To this day, tarpon fishing continues to bring in many sport fishermen, and the area is known worldwide for its Annual Tarpon Tournament. The tarpon has become the symbol of the area—maybe even more so than the lighthouses—and images of tarpon can be found just about everywhere in town.

The lighthouse is not open to the public, but the grounds are, and you can walk right up to it. There is a wonderful beach and parking only a few hundred feet away. Nearby downtown Boca Grande has many quaint shops and restaurants to enjoy.

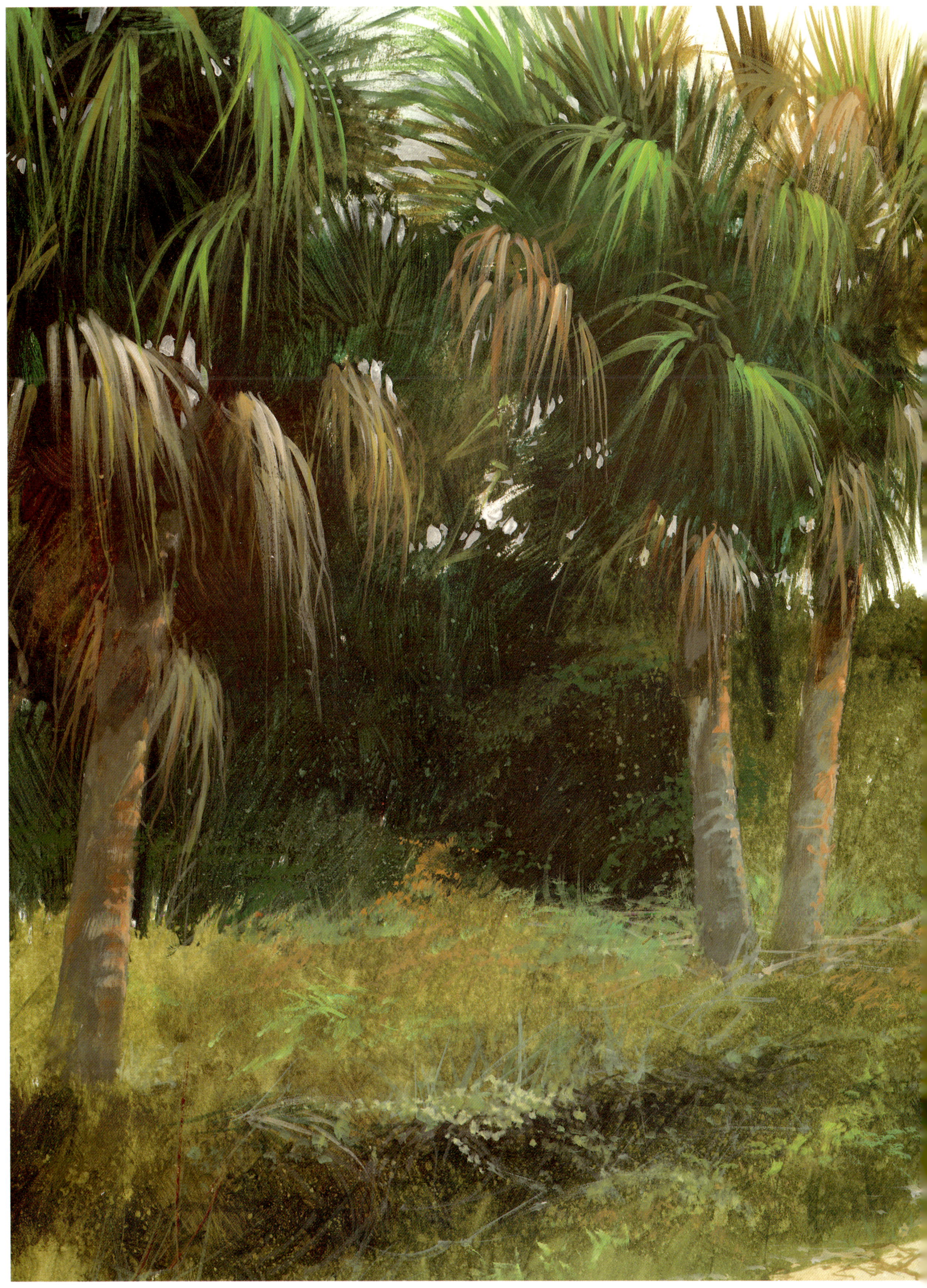

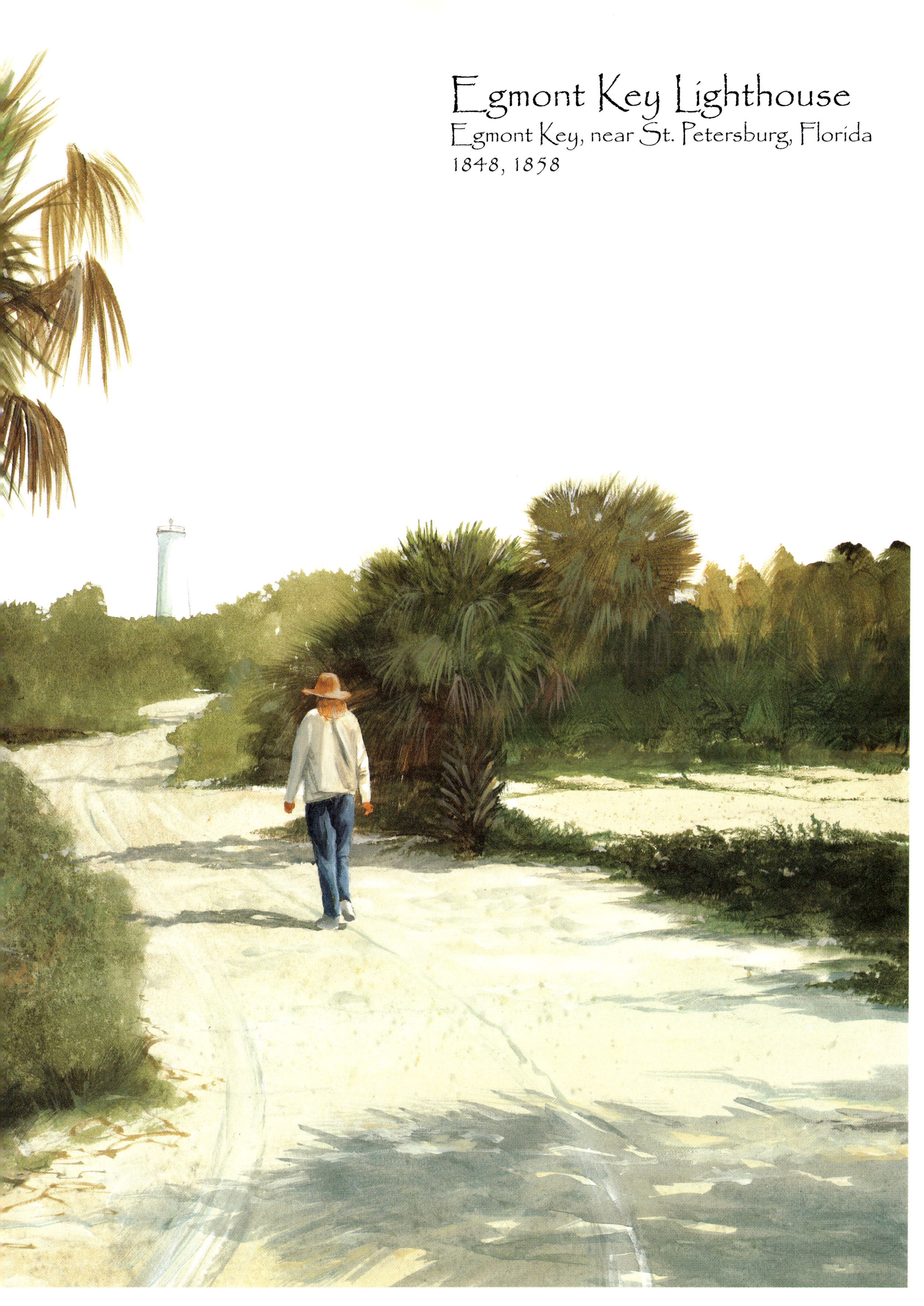

Egmont Key Lighthouse

Egmont Key, near St. Petersburg, Florida

1848, 1858

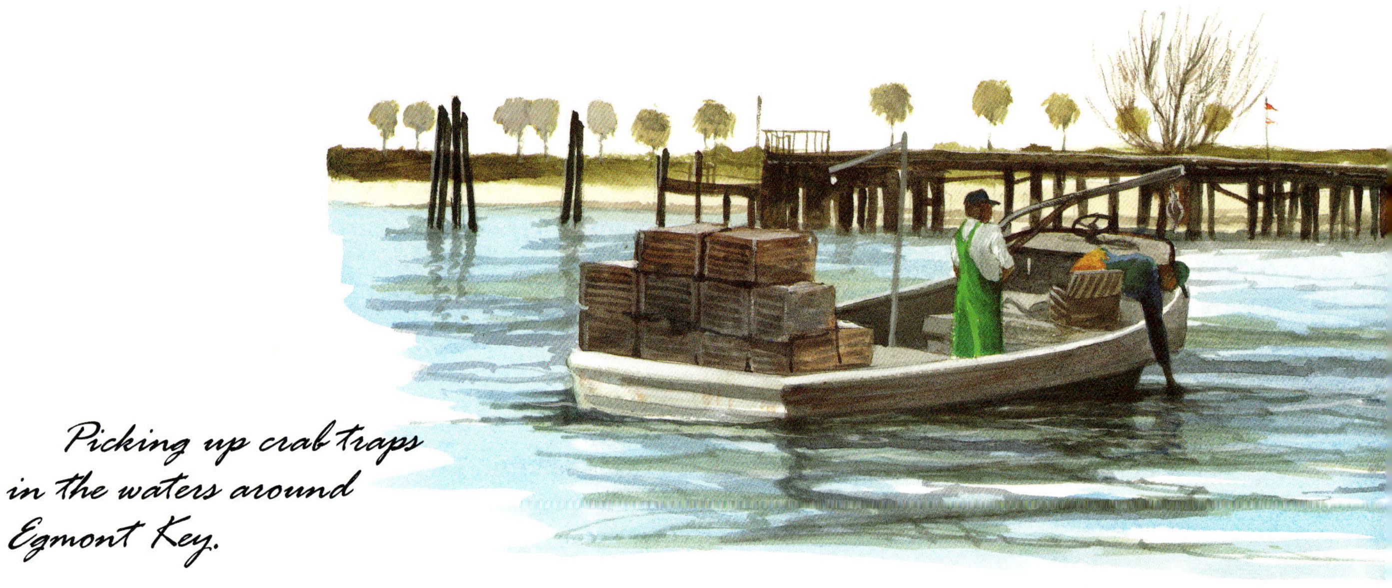

Picking up crab traps in the waters around Egmont Key.

The lantern room was removed in the 1940s. That shortened the lighthouse to 70 feet and made the tower much less attractive, but it's just as functional and requires less maintenance.

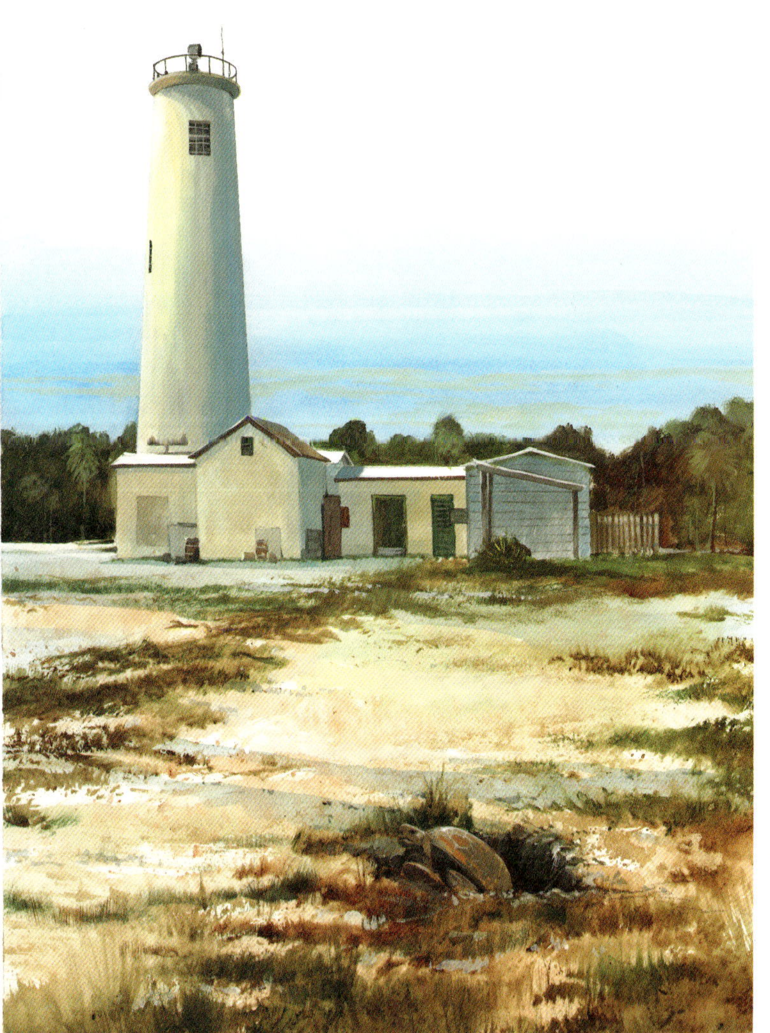

The island of Egmont Key was quite significant in earlier times. Hernando De Soto and other Spanish conquistadors passed by here in the early 1500s, and it was a prison camp for Indians during the Third Seminole War in 1856-1858. Over three hundred Indians, including the famous Billy Bowlegs, were kept here while waiting to be transferred to the West. During the Civil War, the island served as a base for Confederate blockade-runners who traded with Caribbean merchants, selling cotton and tobacco and buying coffee, tea, and much-needed war supplies. That was short-lived, however, because the Union Navy captured the island and used the lighthouse as a lookout for enemy ships. Confederate prisoners were kept on the island, along with nearly two hundred escaped slaves. Yellow fever visited Egmont Key in 1887, and a hospital was established. Ten years after the epidemic, it was time for the Spanish-American War, and a large fort was built on the island. Over one thousand tents housed soldiers and wounded troops returning from Cuba, but the invasion never came to the area as anticipated, and the fort's soldiers never saw any action.

When the year 1916 rolled around, the island's military population grew to about six hundred people, and there were about seventy buildings, including a school and movie theater as well as tennis courts, brick roads, electricity, telephones, and even a small railroad that ran the length of the narrow, mile-and-a-half-long island. Today the massive concrete fort has been undermined by the gulf and makes an eerie spectacle against the clear ocean waves. Little remains that is recognizable on the island except the fort, some brick roads half buried in the sand, and of course the lighthouse.

Gopher turtles love to build tunnels in the hot sand around the lighthouse.

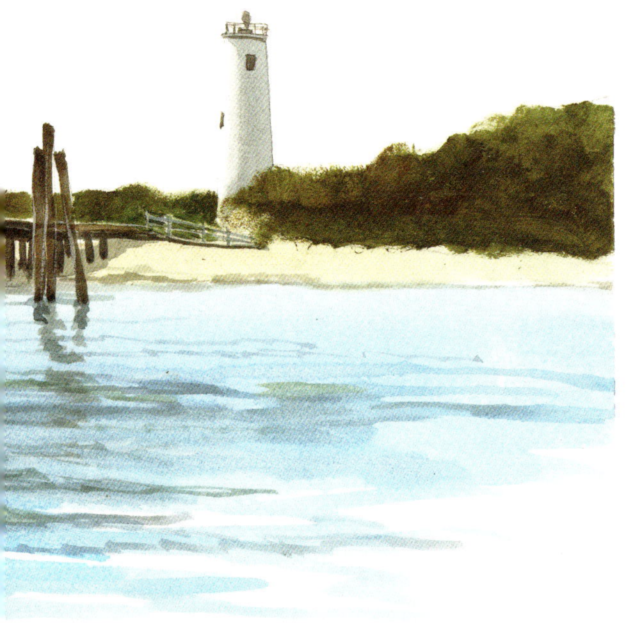

A few small wooden cottages exist on the island that are used to house members of the Tampa Bay Pilots Association. These men board large freighters and guide them under Tampa Bay's Sunshine Skyway Bridge into the port of Tampa.

Two lighthouses have been built at Egmont Key. The first, built in 1848, was destroyed by a hurricane. Ten years later, another was built and still stands today. The lighthouse is not open to the public, but you can walk throughout most of the island and enjoy the beaches except for certain nesting areas. The Coast Guard, whose job it is to maintain lighthouses, began automating all of them in the 1960s: Egmont Key's light was automated in 1989.

The island is a national wildlife refuge and state park. It's a wonderful place to a have a picnic or to explore, with its brilliant white sandy beaches, unspoiled by tourists. In fact, if you go there, you may find you have the entire island to yourself except for a few pilots and the park ranger, who also serves as lighthouse keeper. The currents from Tampa Bay in this area can be ferocious if you're in a small boat, so be watchful. Unless you have a boat, nearby Fort DeSoto is the closest place from which you can see the lighthouse. There you can also visit the fort and enjoy the beaches or fish at the pier.

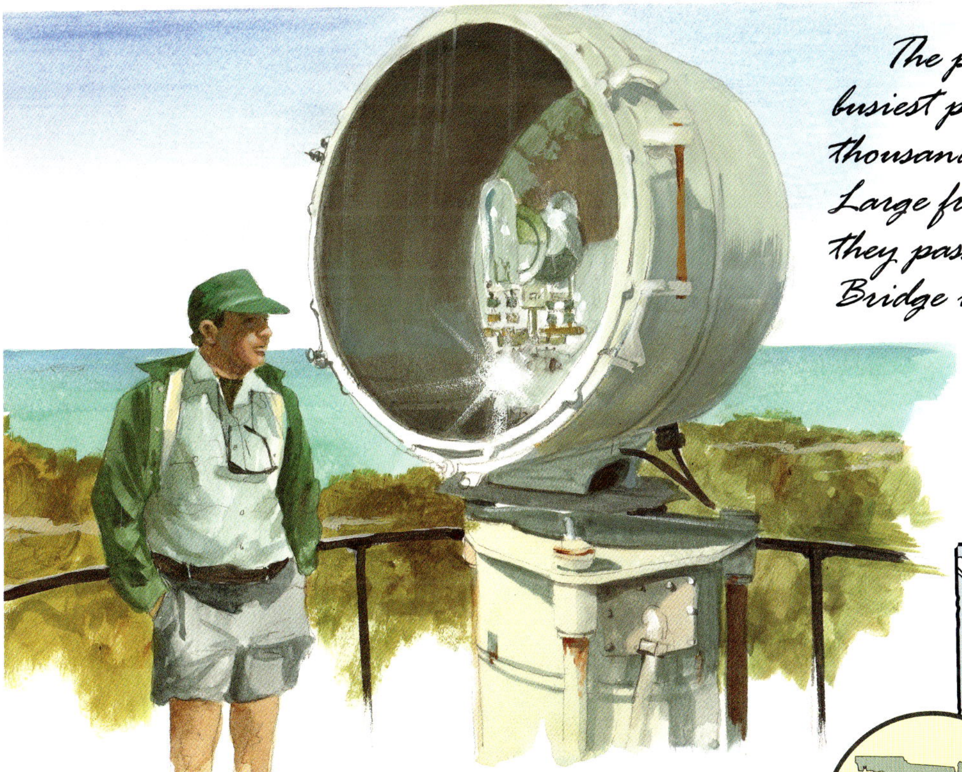

The port of Tampa is the largest and busiest port in the state, with four thousand ships entering it every year. Large freighters see the lighthouse before they pass under the Sunshine Skyway Bridge into Tampa Bay.

A park ranger stands beside the 200,000-candlepower rotating marine beacon that replaced the original kerosene lamp and Fresnel lens.

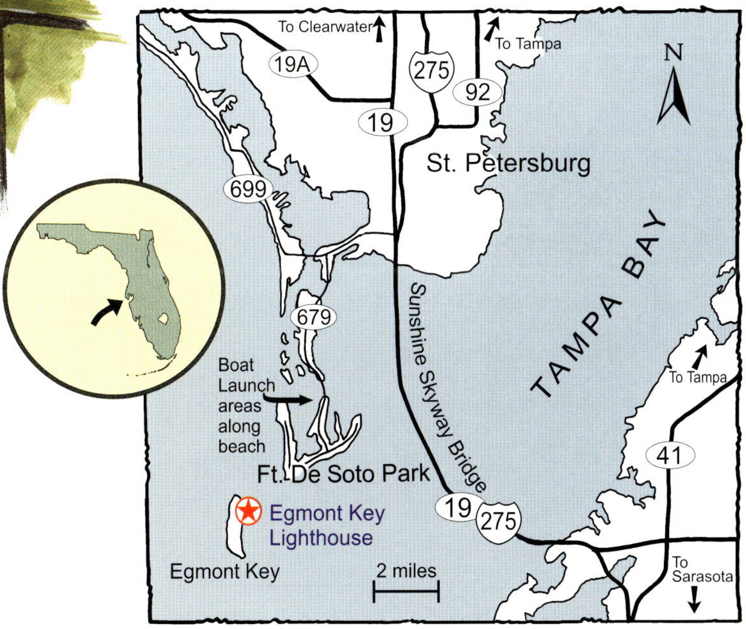

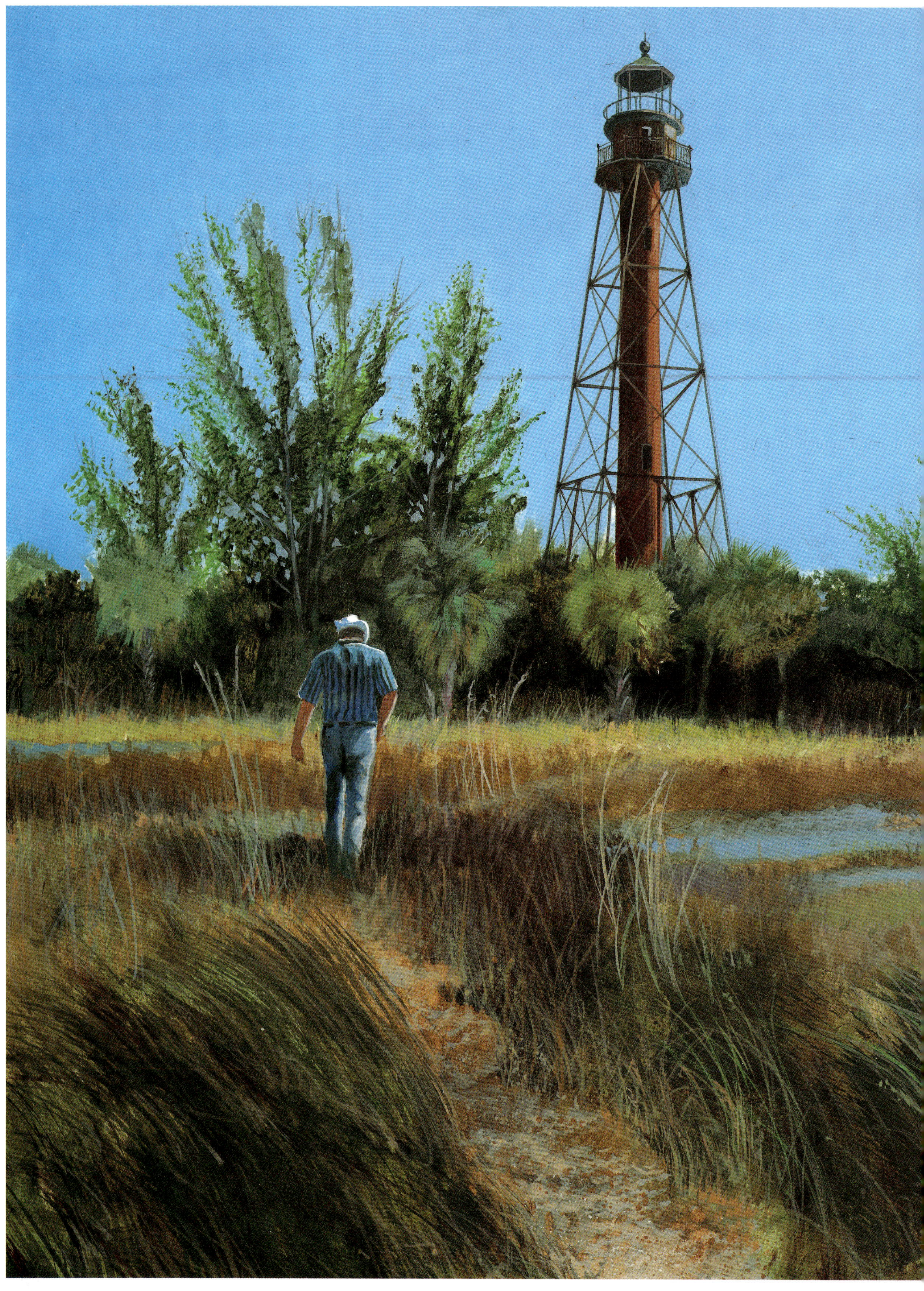

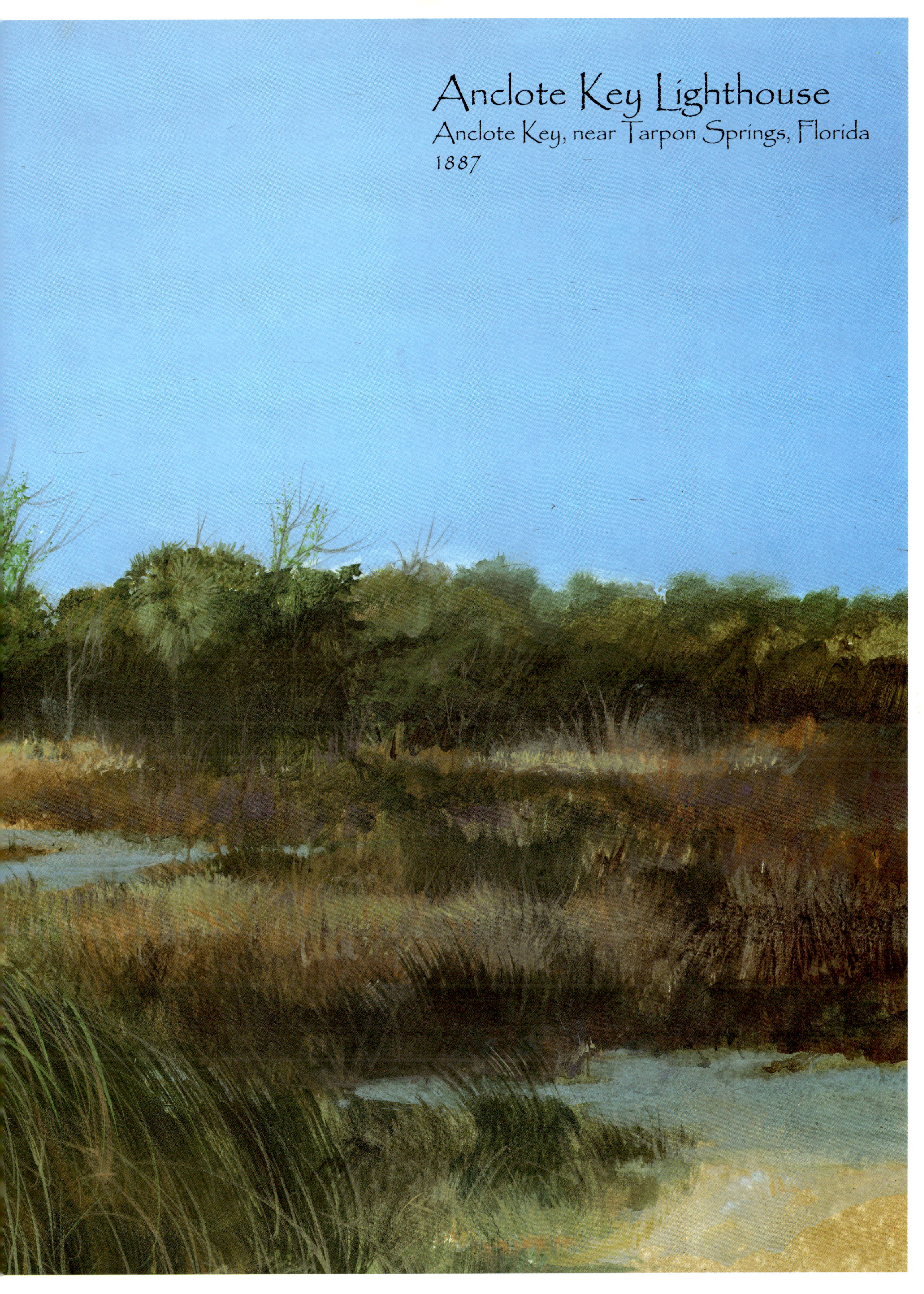

Anclote Key Lighthouse

Anclote Key, near Tarpon Springs, Florida
1887

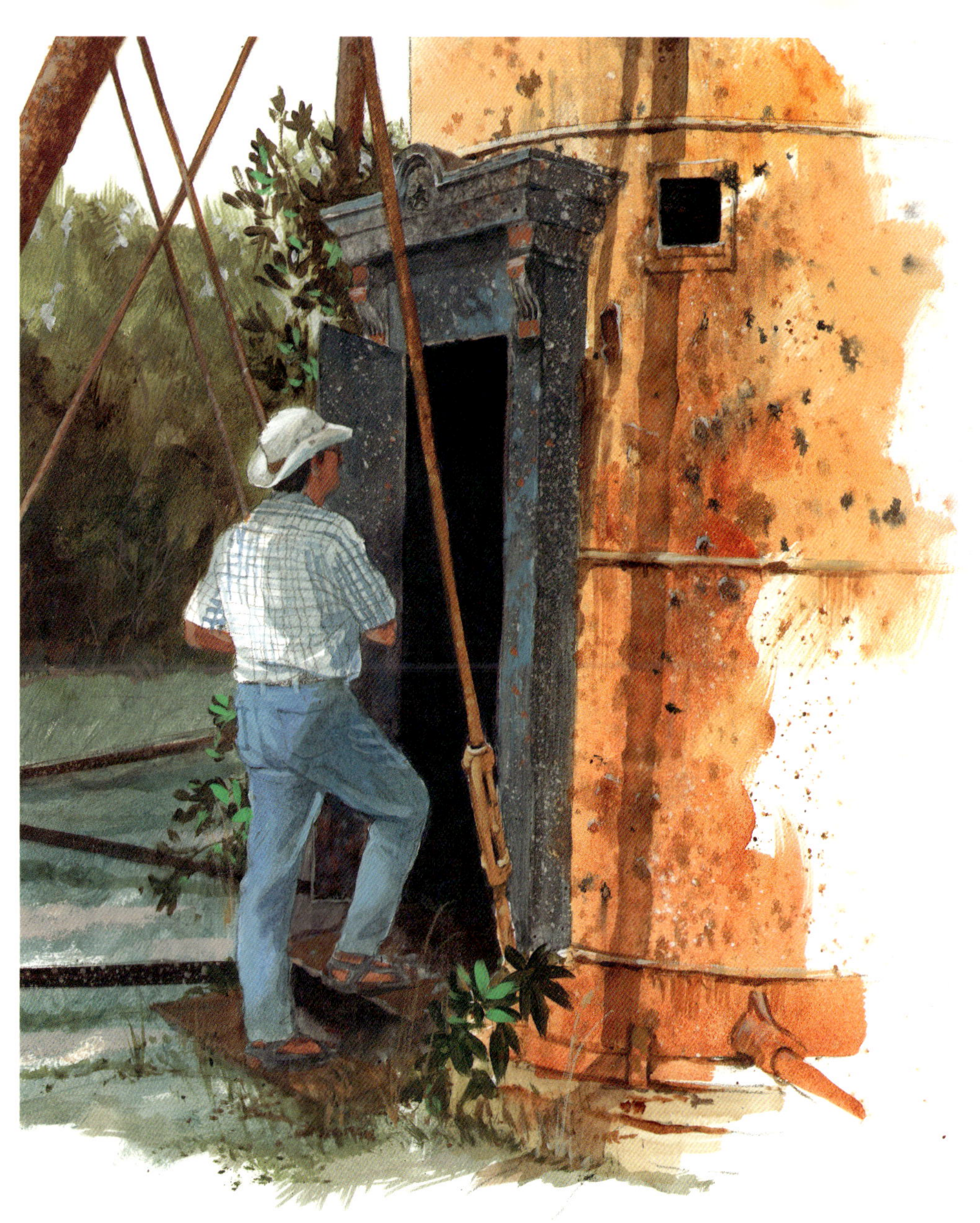

My friend Harvey explores what remains of the 110-foot-tall Anclote Key Lighthouse. The door had been welded shut, but vandals made the effort to haul a cutting torch to the island by boat and cut it open. For decades, the lighthouse has been open because of vandalism. Now, sadly, only the shell remains.

I find it hard to understand the purpose of trying to destroy such a special place. I remember climbing the lighthouse as a boy and touching with awe and respect what was then left of the Fresnel lens.

Built in sections, the heavy, cast-iron rods with turnbuckles tied everything together. Since they didn't have much surface area like brick lighthouses, skeletal lighthouses easily withstood hurricane winds.

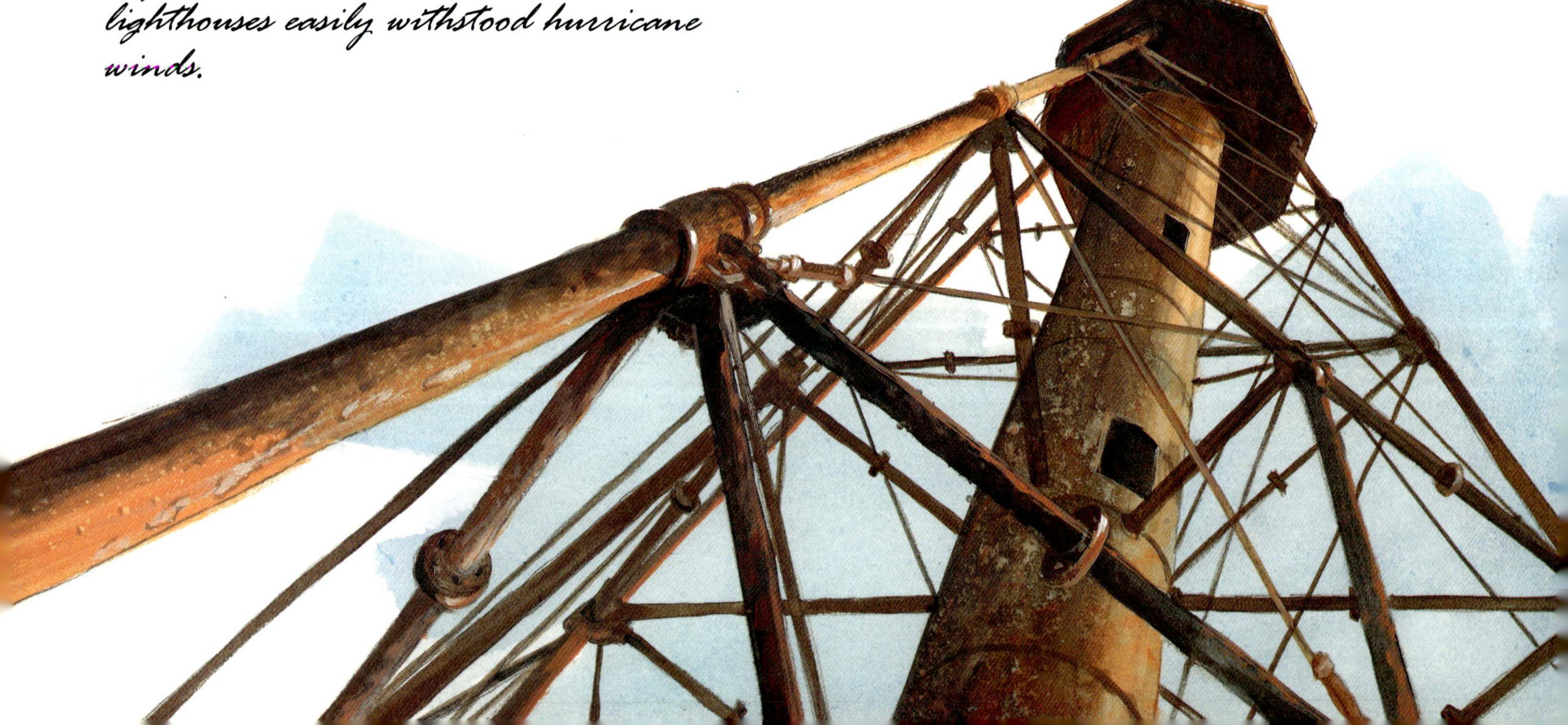

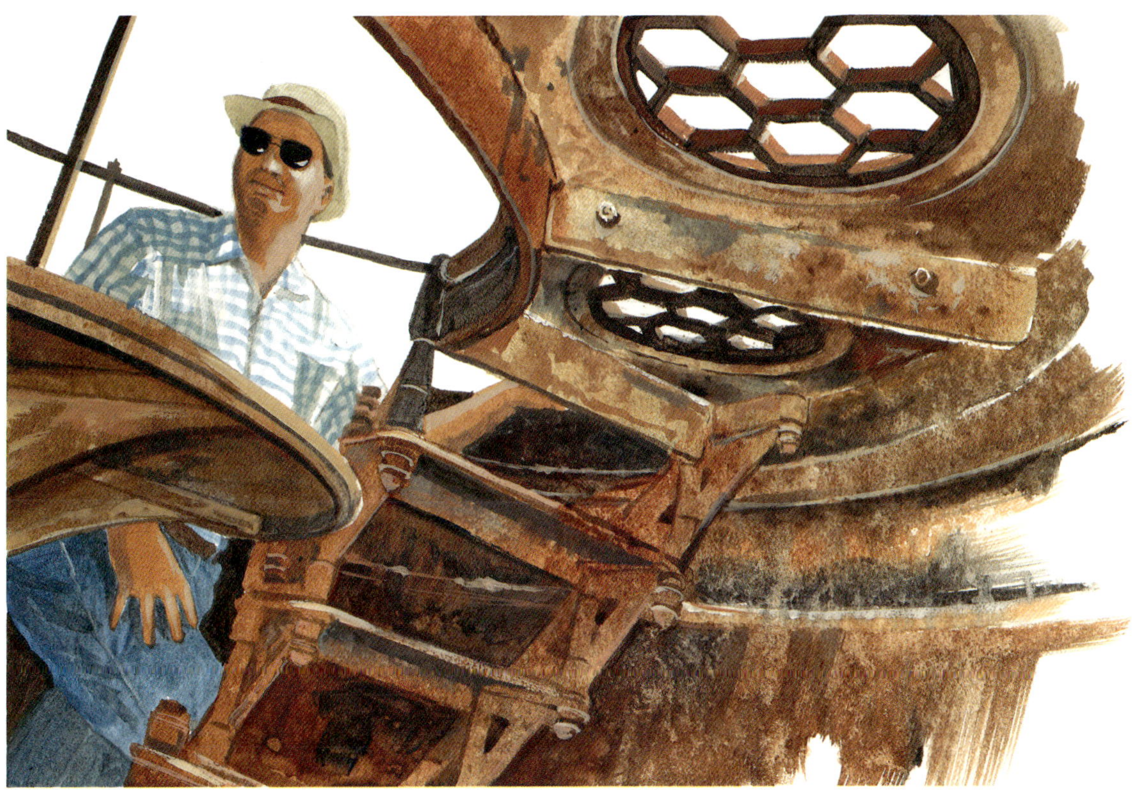

These bee-hive-shaped frames once held thick pieces of glass that allowed light down into the watch room below, but not one piece remains. Vandals have destroyed the glass along with everything else in sight.

Cast iron was used as a building material for lighthouses instead of steel for several reasons. Steel, an alloy made from iron and carbon, wasn't produced in large quantities until the 1850s and was more expensive than cast iron. Steel is much stronger than cast iron and is not brittle, but it lacks one major advantage of cast iron: iron weathers better than steel. Cast iron, or iron, is a single element and doesn't allow for water molecules to replace any other molecules, as happens with an alloy. For that reason, water can't permeate it molecule by molecule, like it does with steel; basically, rust stops at the surface. Had lighthouses been made of steel, they would have long since rusted away.

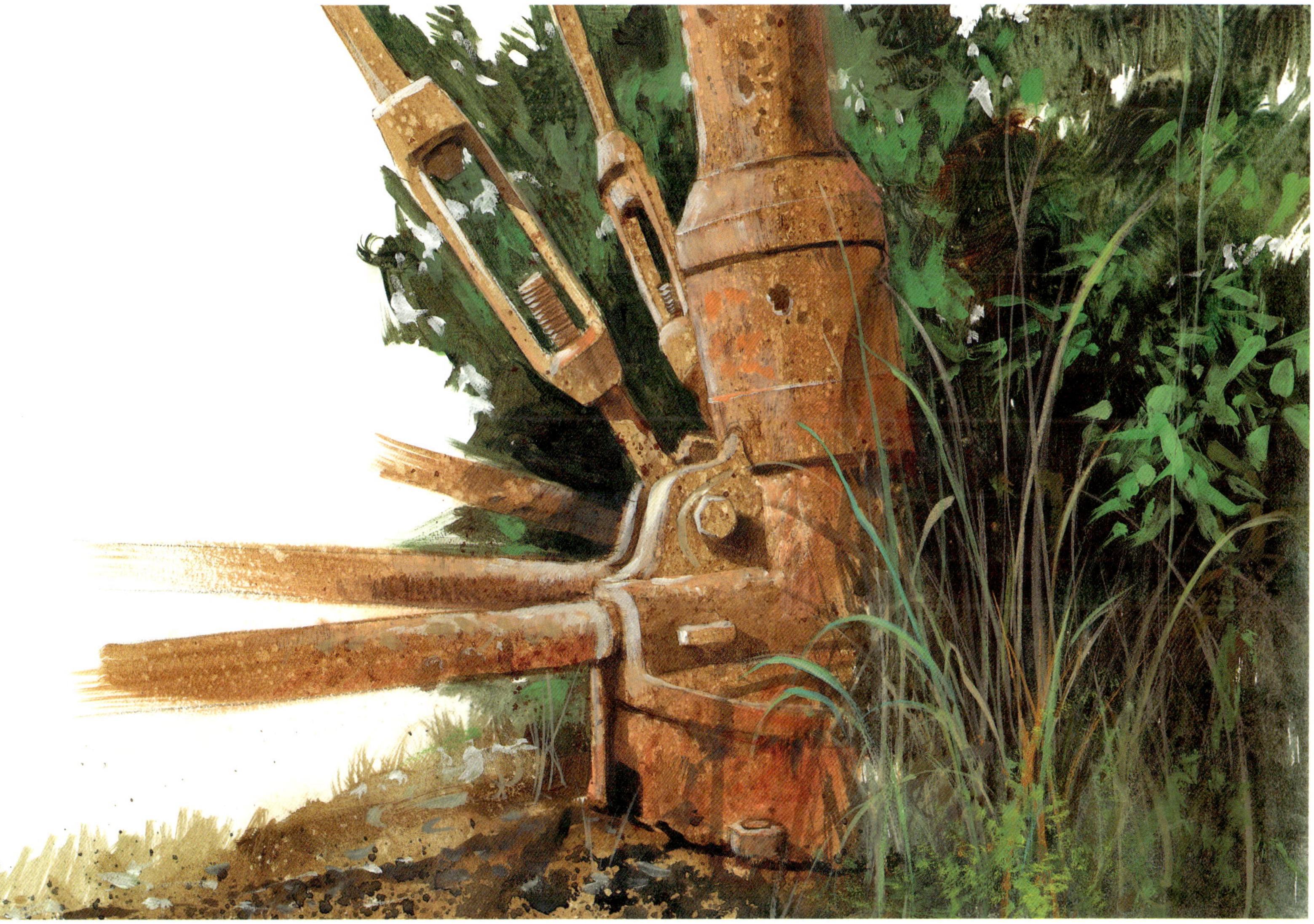

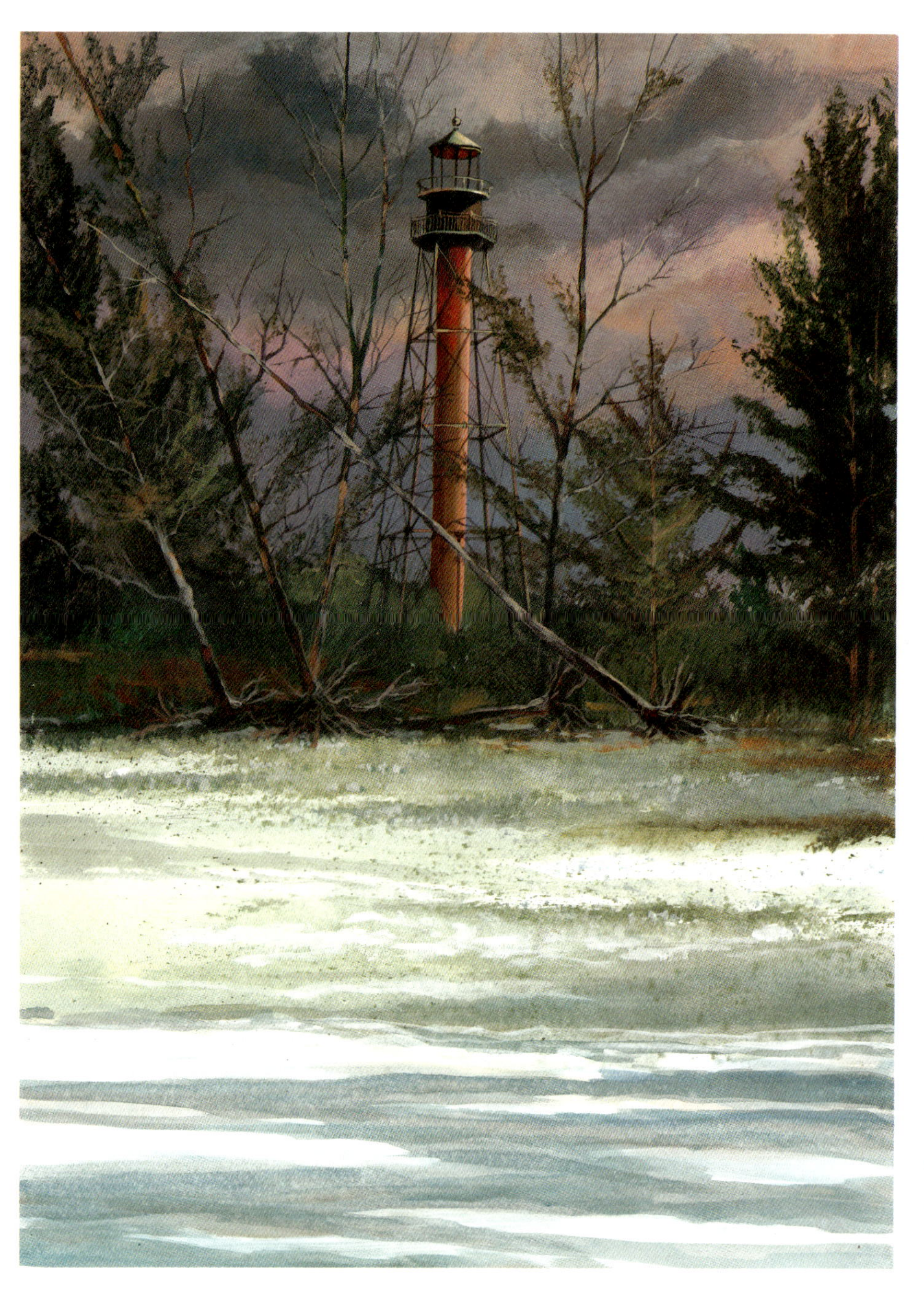

The worst enemy of the lighthouse, besides modern electronics, has been beach erosion. Shifting sands at the Anclote Key Lighthouse have undermined Australian pines. A powerful hurricane on this sandy beach could easily eliminate another hundred feet of beach. Most lighthouses that no longer exist were lost this way.

Despite the vandalism to this lighthouse and some erosion, the beach is still as beautiful and peaceful as ever. Shrimp boats pass here on their way to and from Tarpon Springs, and residents enjoy fishing just off the island. Today the lighthouse marks the island like an exclamation mark, guiding more families to Anclote Key for a picnic than ships to port.

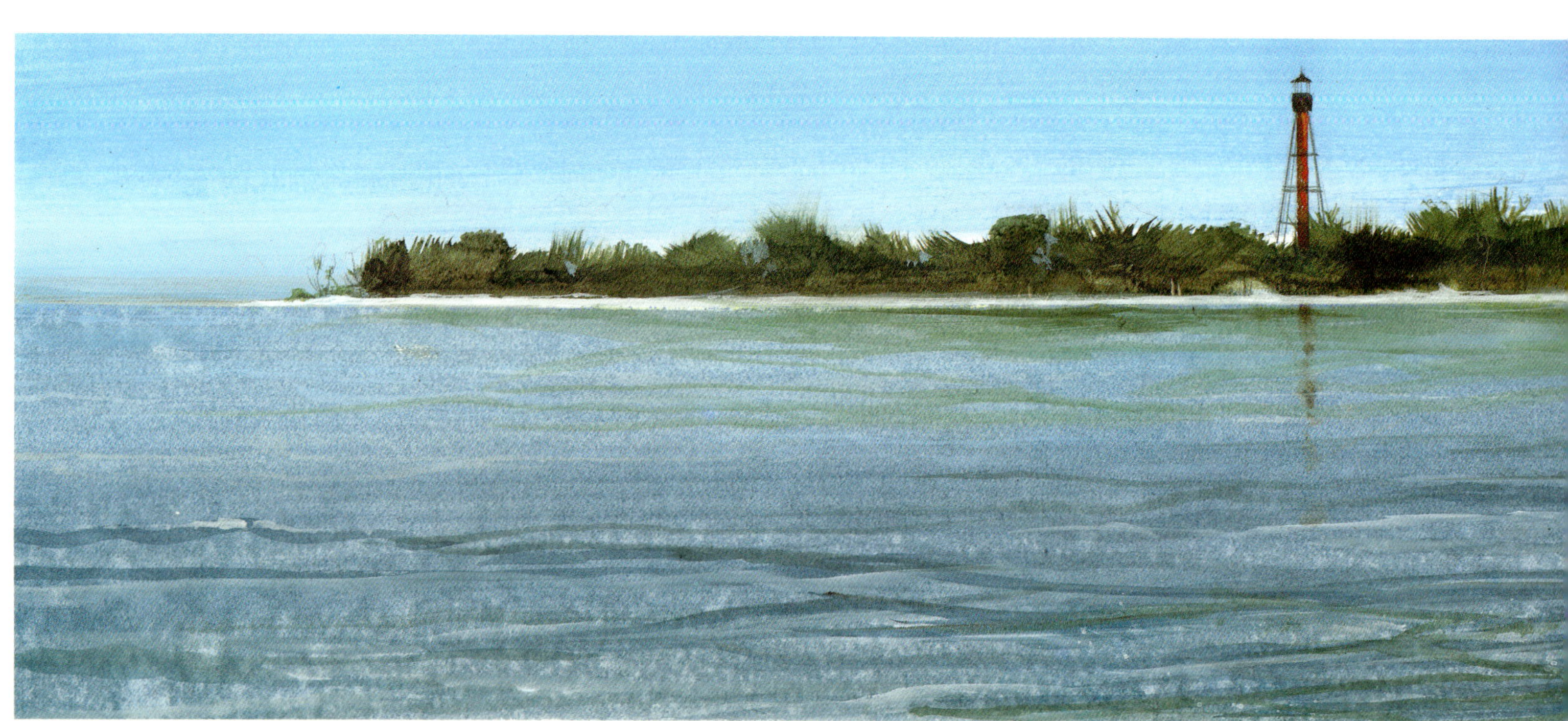

This type of skeletal lighthouse was developed in the early 1860s for several reasons. Sandy soil along Florida's coasts made difficult to build adequate foundations to support the heavy weight of brick lighthouses. A cast-iron skeletal structure was much lighter, so its foundation didn't need to be as massive. If erosion threatened, skeletal lighthouses could be disassembled and moved since they were bolted together in small sections. Skeletal structures also cost less to build than brick ones.

Originally, there were two keepers' houses and several other outbuildings by the lighthouse. Four hundred feet of cedar picket fencing painted white surrounded them.

Lighthouse keepers were generally men and women of few words, especially when it came to filling out their daily logs. On October 6, 1889, the keeper at the Anclote Key Lighthouse, referring to his child, wrote, "Baby was taken very sick at 5 P.M." The next day he wrote, "Baby boy died this morning at 2:30 o'clock. Keeper and wife went over to bury him today." On August 30, 1890, his log entry read, "Baby born. Keeper's wife. Bad weather." If nothing else, it shows how rugged these people must have been out of sheer necessity.

I grew up and still live in Clearwater, Florida, just a few miles south of Tarpon Springs and the Anclote Key Lighthouse. Thirty years ago, my parents would sometimes pack a lunch and take our small boat out to the 180-acre island. There we would spend the day on the white sand beaches, swimming and collecting shells. The lighthouse was automated in 1952 and was therefore unmanned and officially closed to the public, but I remember it always being open because of vandalism. People found a way to tear down the fence and break open the heavy steel door. I can remember going up to the top of the light and looking at the small, third-order, pineapple-shaped Fresnel lens, which even then was badly damaged. The lighthouse was decommissioned in 1985, and today there is nothing left of the lens. All the windows have been knocked out. People have even stolen bricks from the old oil house and the many brick walkways for their own use. Efforts are being made to restore the old lighthouse, but when I did these paintings, nothing had been done.

The nearby town of Tarpon Springs is a small, active community, mainly of Greek heritage, and is best known for its sponge industry. Tourism seems to be the predominant industry with 750,000 tourists visiting the old sponge docks each year. The quaint shops are still full of those souvenirs—shell lamps and bins with dried seahorses and sand dollars—I used to love as a boy. The restaurants and bakeries all serve up delicious traditional Greek pastries, and although tourism overshadows industry, Tarpon Springs remains the largest natural sponge market in the world, with annual revenues over five million dollars. Today all but a few of the colorful sponge boats are gone, along with their traditional hard hat divers. They have been replaced by more ordinary-looking boats with scuba divers. Many shrimp boats now make Tarpon Springs their home port as well. Instead of using the Anclote Key Lighthouse to guide them, boats now use a tall smokestack with a flashing strobe light from the power plant at the mouth of the river as a day marker and lighthouse.

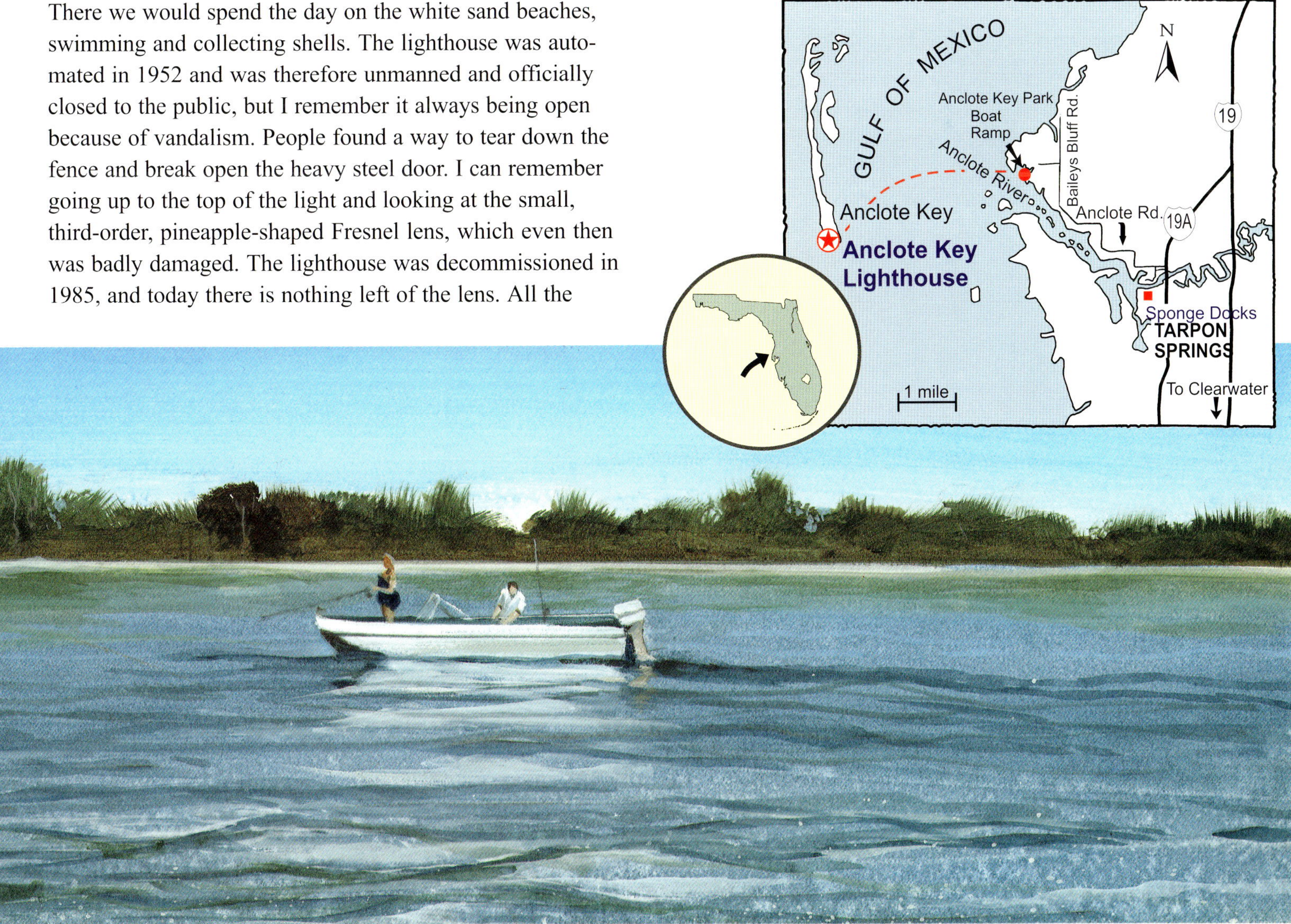

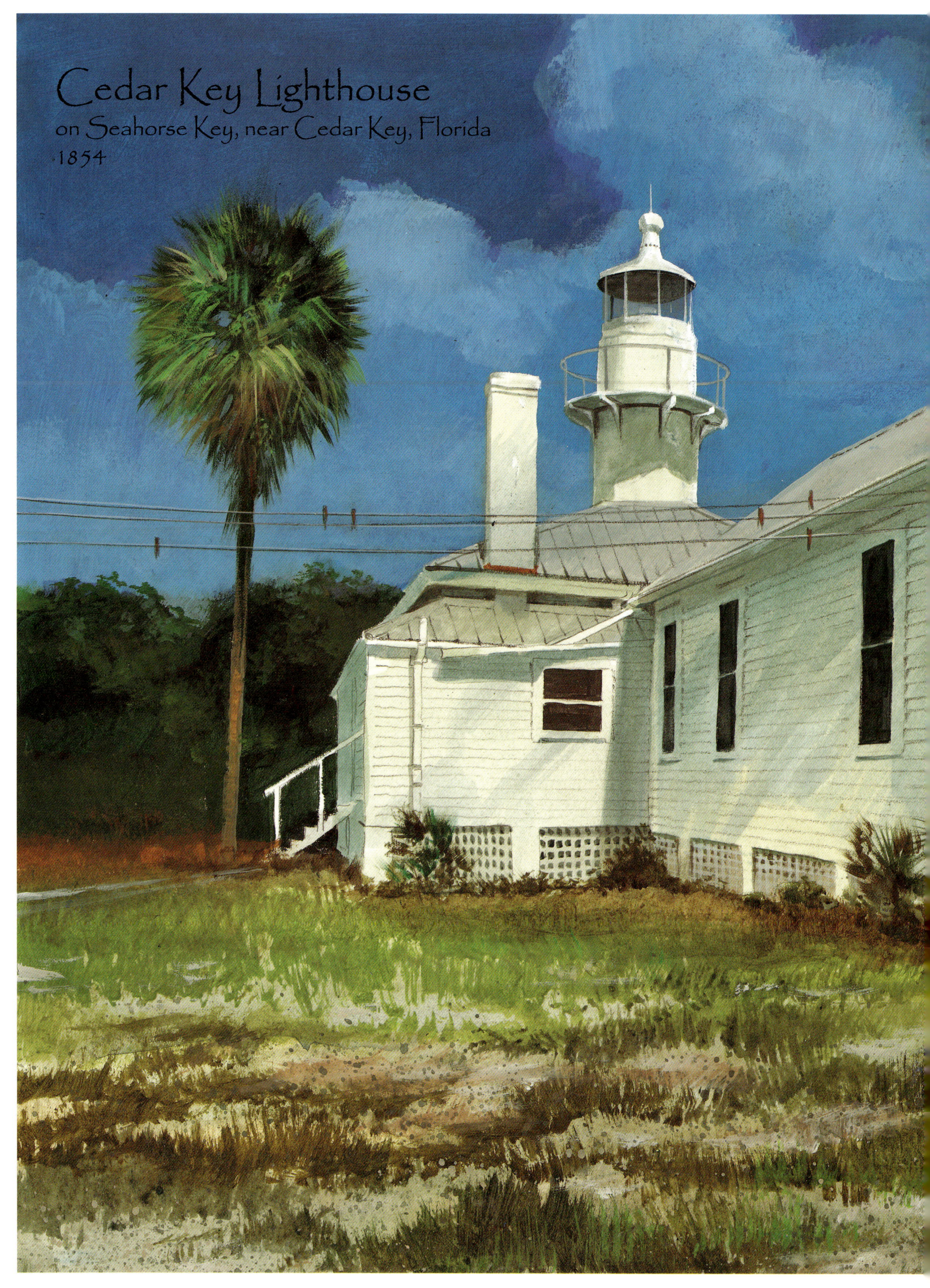
Cedar Key Lighthouse
on Seahorse Key, near Cedar Key, Florida
1854

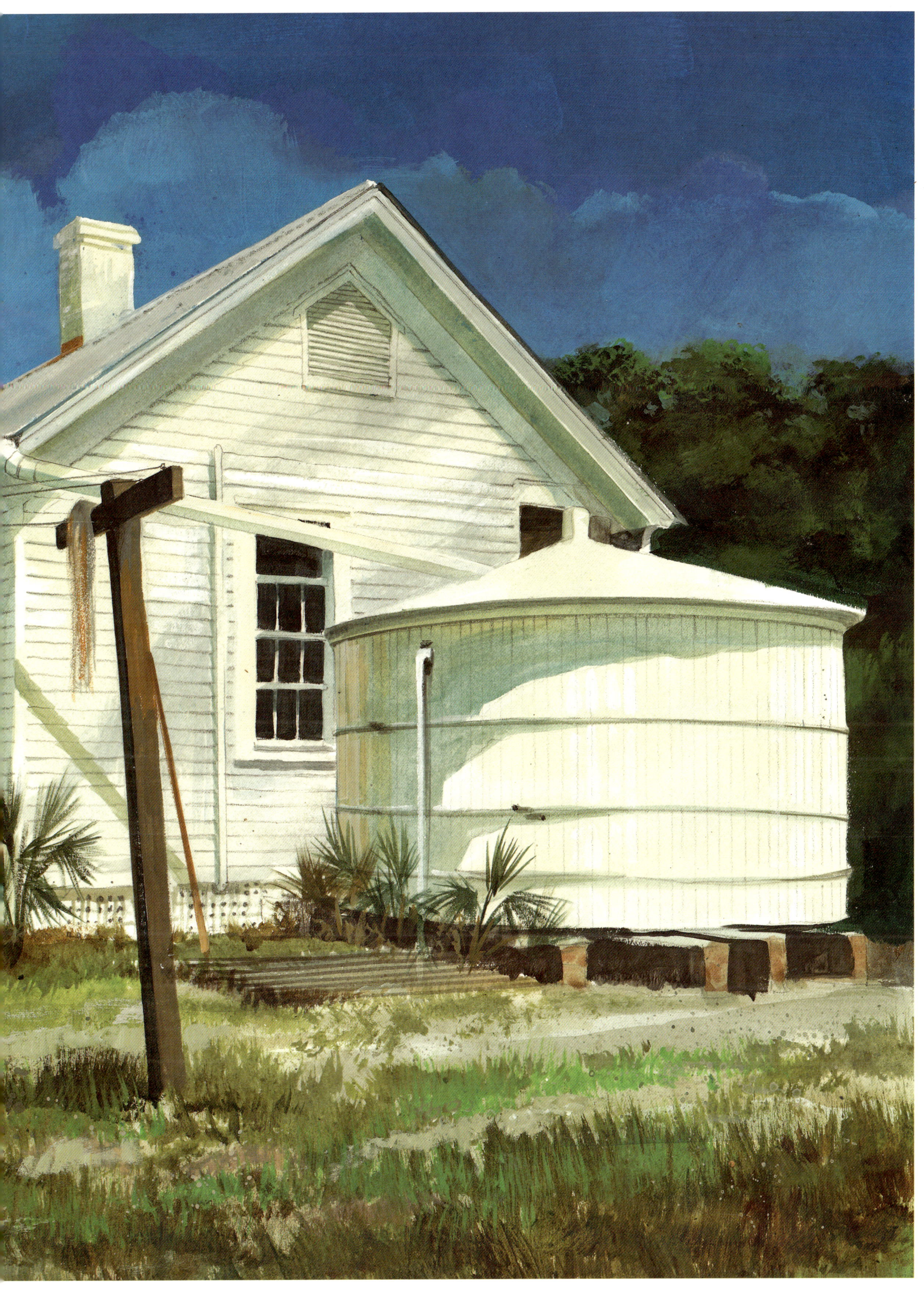

The Cedar Key Lighthouse is actually located at Seahorse Key, about four miles offshore from Cedar Key. The island is a mile long and no more than half a mile wide at its widest point. Pelicans take advantage of this national wildlife refuge and use every available space around the lighthouse as a major nesting area. A steep path leads up to the lighthouse, where signs strongly discourage people from trespassing. If the signs don't dissuade you from exploring, the overwhelming smell of thousands of birds and their fish dinners will!

Cedar Key itself is one of the least populated areas in Florida. It was once a busy port, and the first cross-state railroad ran from here to Amelia Island on the Atlantic coast. Cedar Key now seems to be frozen in time. The nearest major town, Gainesville, is sixty miles away. You won't find a K-Mart, convenient stores, or fast-food restaurants anywhere nearby. A small, family owned grocery store, a few nice galleries, and some good, locally owned seafood restaurants are what you'll discover here.

In 1839, Congress authorized the construction of a lighthouse in the hope that development would bring settlers to the area, which would in turn help drive the Indians from the coast. But it wasn't until 1854 that the lighthouse actually became a reality and was lit for the first time. Built on a dune forty-five feet high, the lighthouse itself extends seventy-five feet above sea level. Sometime later, wood-frame housing extensions were added to each side of the brick lighthouse for the keepers and their families.

At the time of the Second Seminole War from 1835 to 1842, before the lighthouse was built, federal troops used Seahorse Key as a detention center for Indians being moved to the West for resettlement. Many Indians were housed at relocation camps in Tampa until they could be sent on their long journey west to Oklahoma. Indians who tried to leave the camps were placed in chains and put on ships that brought them to Seahorse Key. On the island there was little chance of escape, and it remained a stockade until the end of the Seminole War. It is hard to realize this was happening at the time my great-grandparents were growing up.

The 1880s marked the high point in the expansion of Cedar Key. Cotton production, sugar harvesting, and lumbering up the nearby Suwannee River just to the north were responsible for the growth of the area as an emerging port, but the event that put Cedar Key on the map was the building of the Eberhard Faber Mill. The mill produced cedar blanks, which are pencils without lead. Other mills turned out lumber and railroad ties.

As the Civil War started in 1861, the light at Seahorse Key was extinguished, and the island was once again turned into a prison. Because of the war, the railroad to Fernandina was destroyed, and a blockade along the gulf severely limited the use of the port at Cedar Key.

Brown pelicans nest in trees in large colonies, building their nests ten to twenty feet above the ground. Both parents share the duty of raising one to three chicks. During the three and a half months it remains in the nest, each baby pelican will eat 150 pounds of fish. When I was there in June, the trees were filled with these hungry young birds.

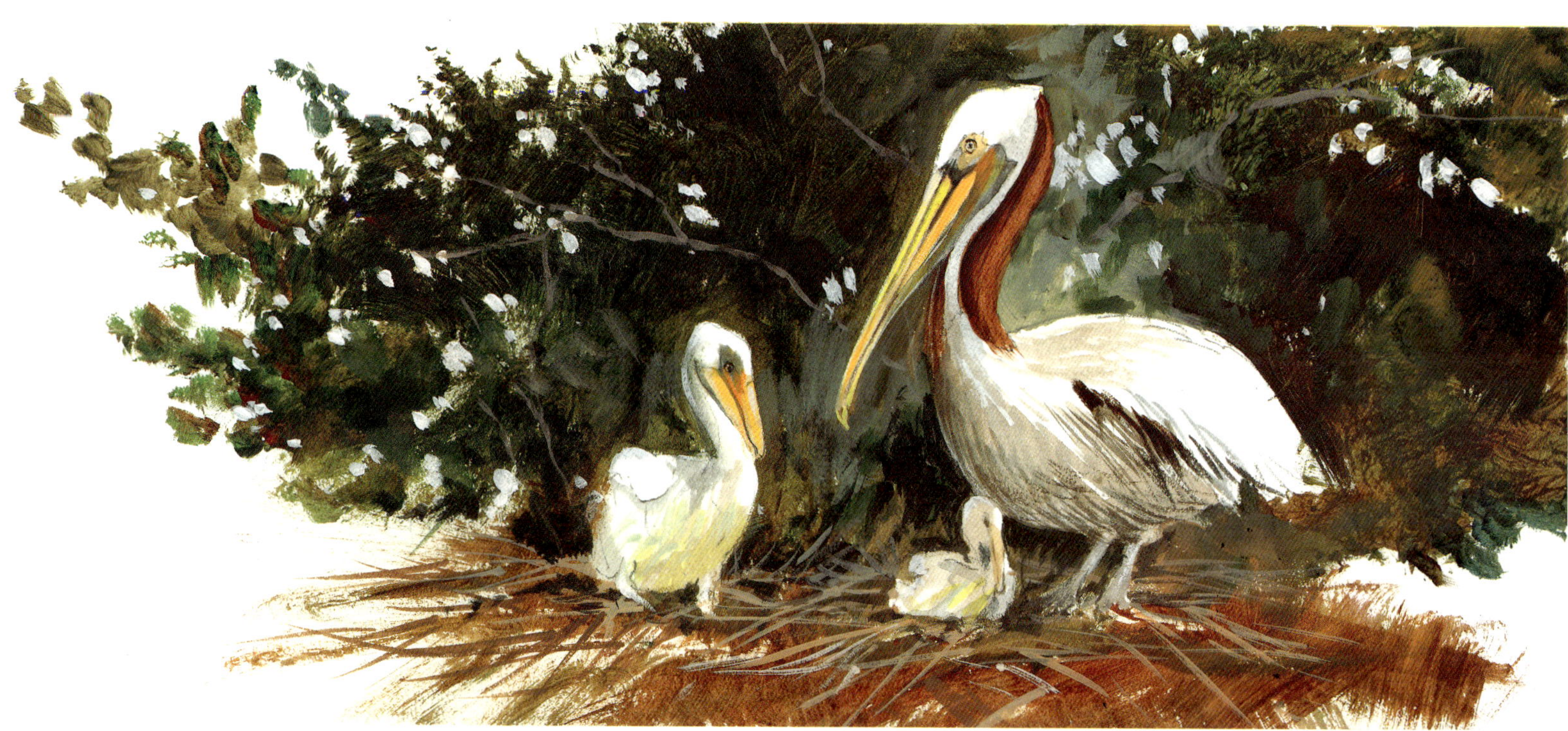

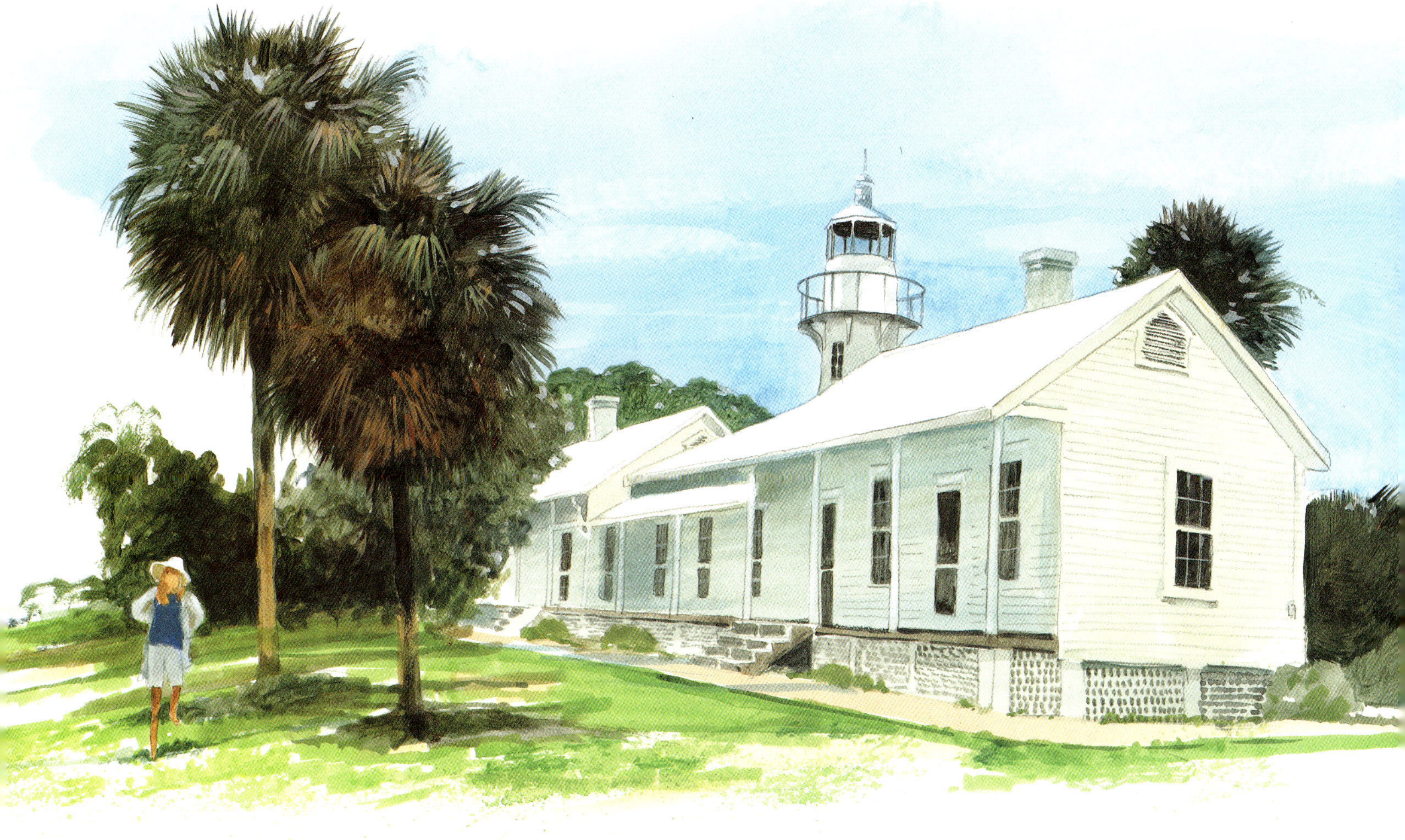

After the war, Henry Plant considered building his railroad to Cedar Key, but he couldn't reach a satisfactory agreement with the town and decided to lay tracks to Tampa instead. This sealed the fate of Cedar Key. With a larger, deep-water port and a new railroad at Tampa, Cedar Key quickly began its decline. The once-thriving lumber industry had already begun to falter because most of the trees had been harvested. A vicious hurricane in 1896 wiped out what cedar trees were left in the area and destroyed all the cedar mills. The factories were never rebuilt, and twenty-five hundred jobs were lost. By 1913, ships ceased to use the port at Cedar Key, and the town never recovered, either as a port or as an industrial area.

Today Cedar Key remains one of Florida's hidden treasures with its old Florida charm. You can't see the lighthouse from Cedar Key; it's a little too far away for that. The only way to get there is by boat. I'm not a fisherman but from what I can see, the fishing is pretty good here. Fishing—along with tourism—is certainly the major source of income for Cedar Key's residents. Some things have changed, however. In 1878, fish brought two cents a pound, mullet two cents apiece, and turtle six to eight cents a pound. If you visit today, don't expect to find prices quite like those of the old Florida.

Today the University of Florida in Gainesville operates the lighthouse as a center for marine biology research. It is the oldest lighthouse still standing on Florida's west coast.

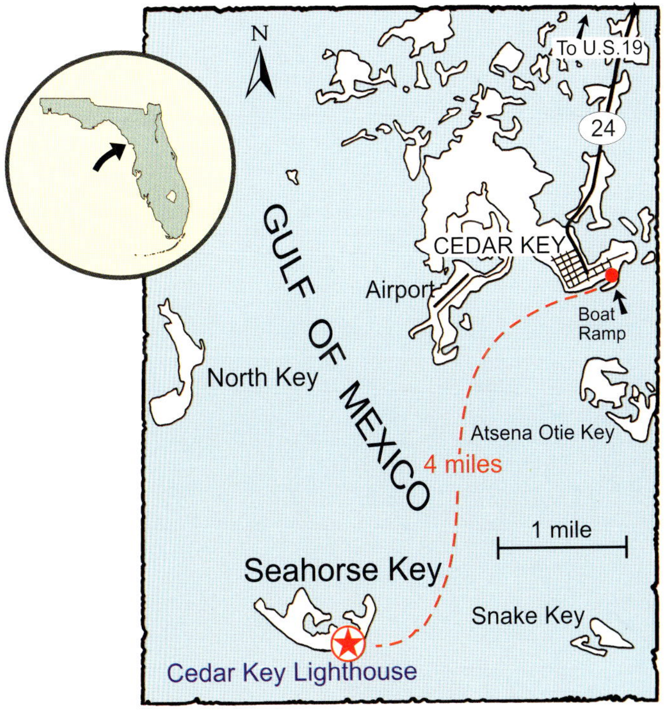

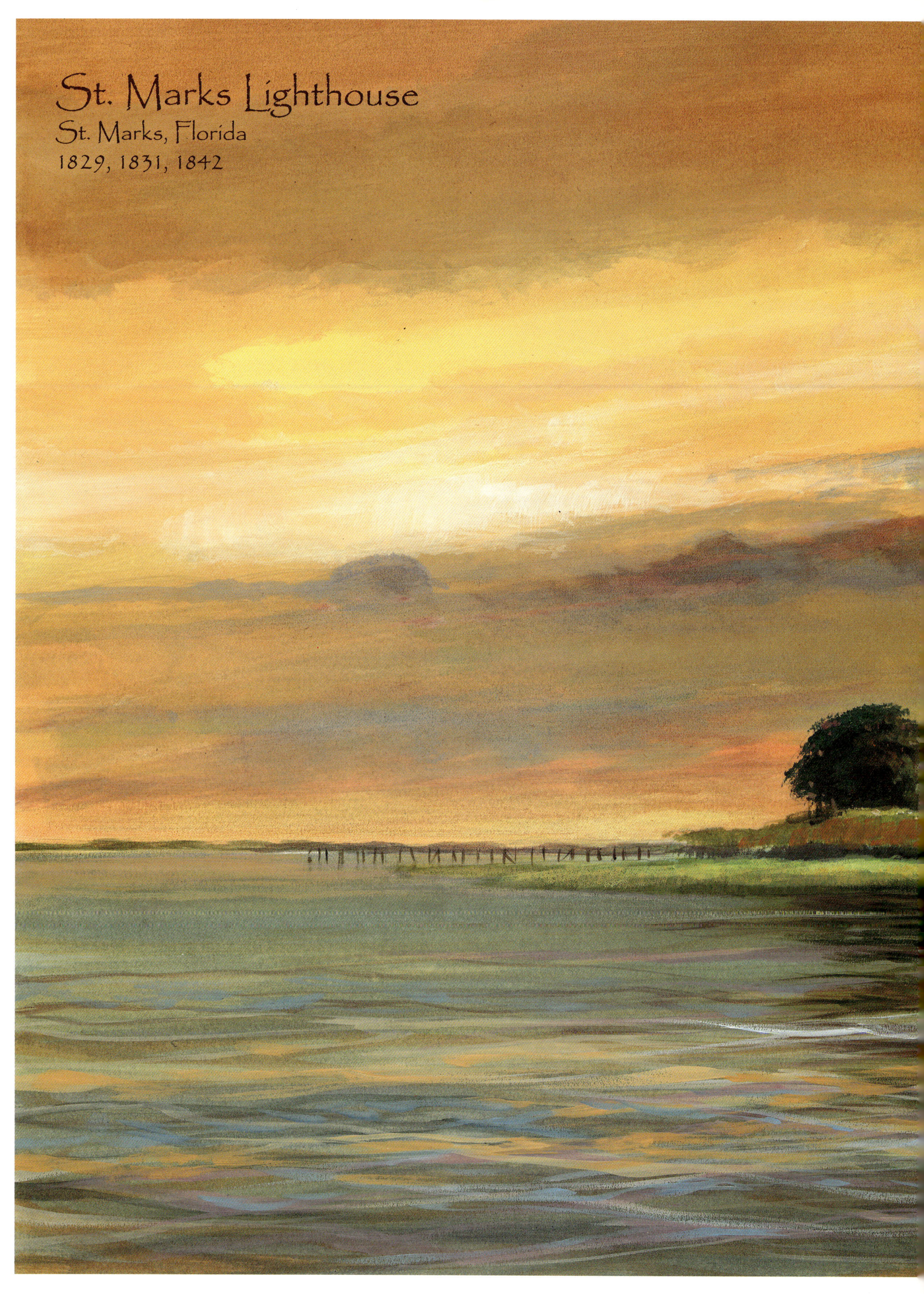
St. Marks Lighthouse
St. Marks, Florida
1829, 1831, 1842

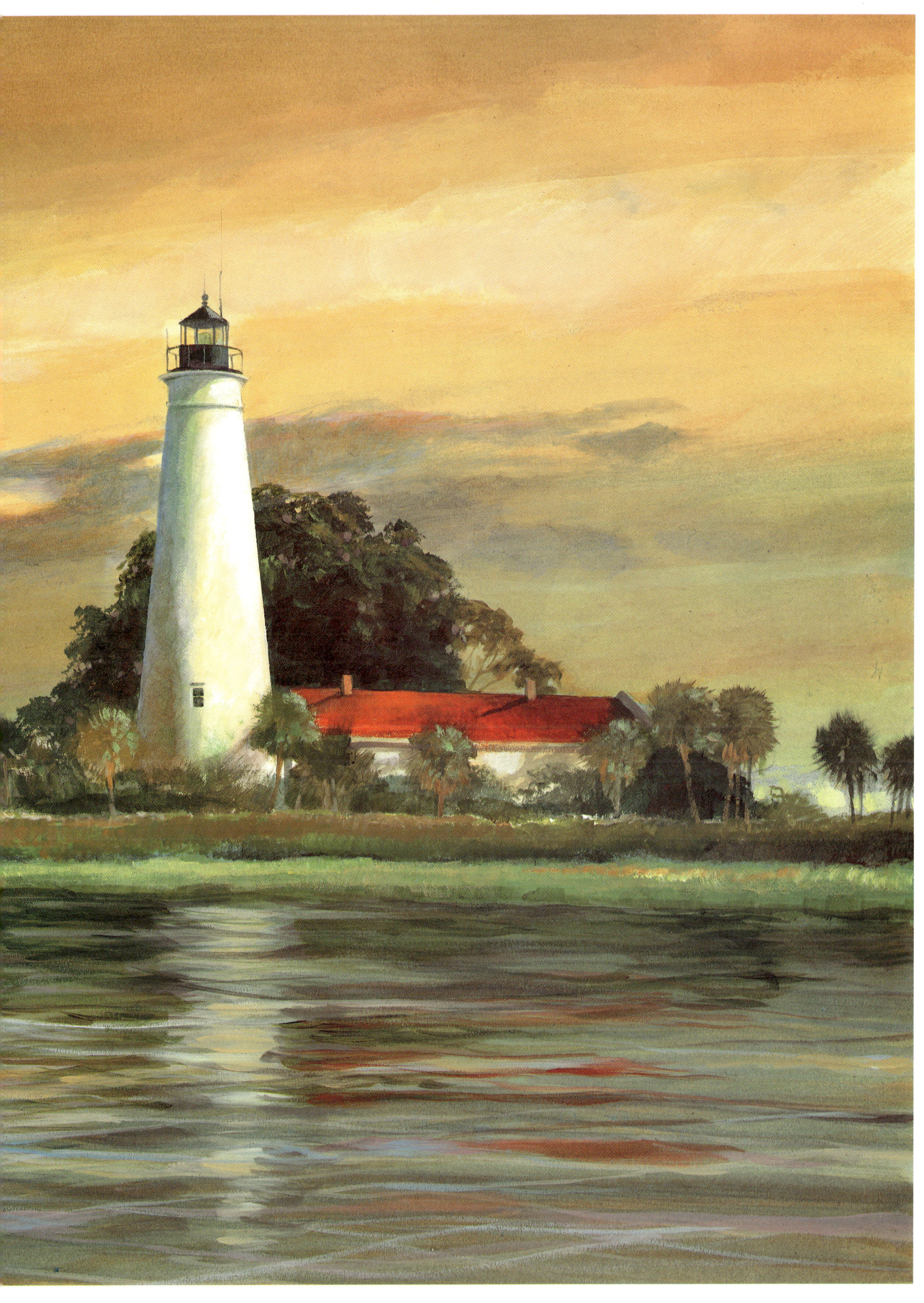

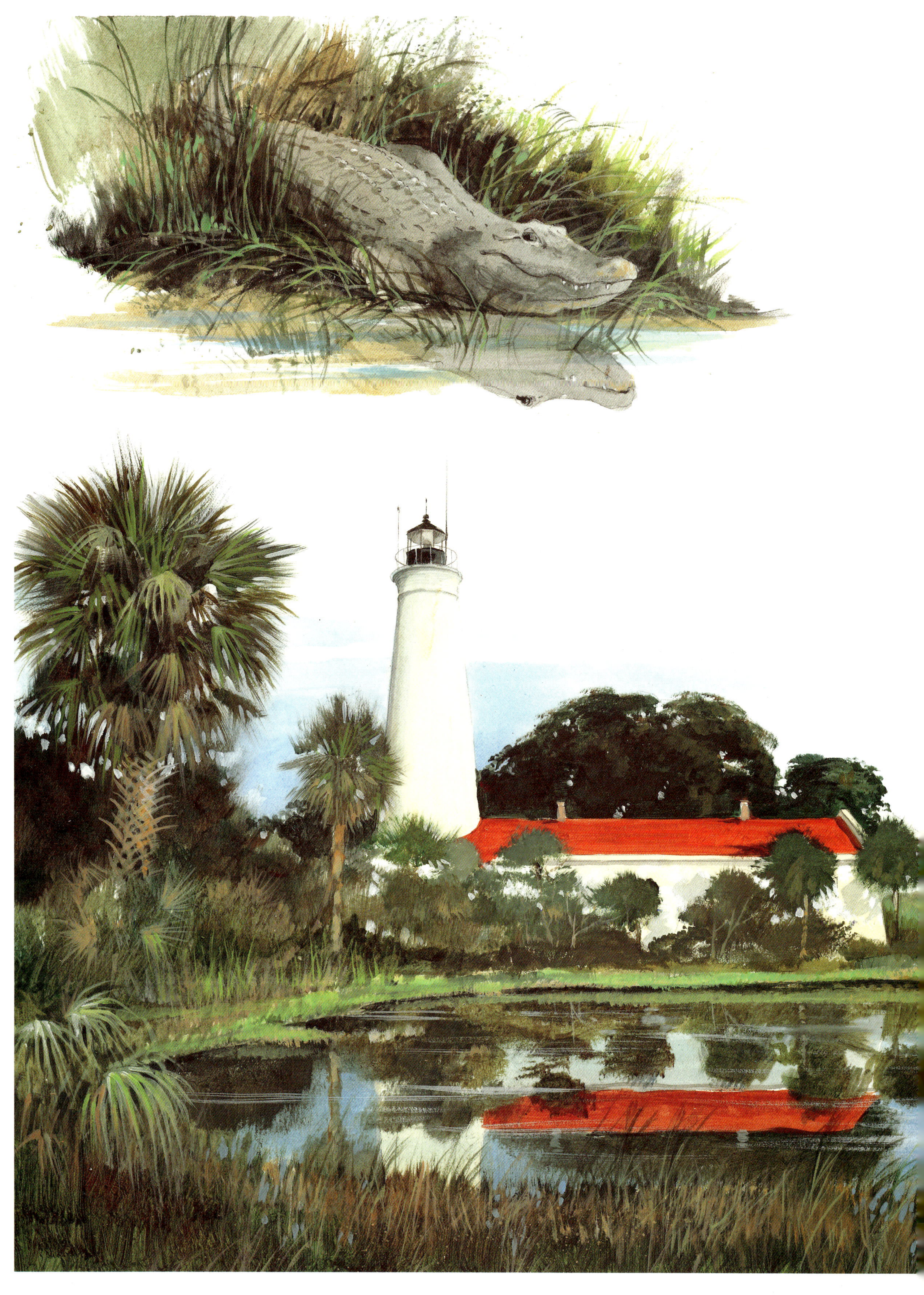

I've always thought that alligators have this Mona-Lisa-of-the-wild kind of smile. You can't tell if they're happy, angry, full, or hungry. Their eighty teeth can exert three thousand pounds of pressure per square inch when they close their jaws, so I never assume they're full. Over a million alligators are roaming around Florida now, and you can find them just about anywhere. Even with this healthy population, only about three people in the state are attacked each year.

In the wild, alligators can live up to thirty-five years of age and can grow up to fourteen feet long. The female lays twenty to fifty eggs and is very protective of her offspring. Alligators don't like salt water, but the ponds and wetlands by the lighthouse are fresh. There's a good chance you will see them sunning themselves on the edge of the ponds or just off the road. One thing is very important—don't feed them. As they become familiar with humans as a source of food, they become less apprehensive and more aggressive. Your arm, instead of that marshmallow or piece of bread, could end up being lunch.

The lighthouses at St. Marks—like all other Florida lighthouses—have had their share of problems. The first one, built in 1829, was so poorly constructed that it was not accepted by the lighthouse board. Lighthouse plans called for solid walls, but the contractor built it with hollow walls, so another lighthouse was built in 1831. Beach erosion toppled this second structure, and another one was built in 1842. That's the one still standing today on a twelve-foot-deep base of limestone rocks taken from nearby Fort San Marcos de Apalache.

A brutal hurricane swept over the St. Marks area in 1843 and flattened everything in sight except the lighthouse tower. The keeper and his family survived by clinging to the upper levels of the tall structure, but fifteen others who had sought shelter in the dwelling drowned.

During the Civil War, the Confederates tried to blow up the lighthouse and seriously damaged the base of the tower. Despite all its problems, St. Marks has survived and stands like a jewel in the midst of a sixty-five-thousand-acre wildlife refuge. Each time I have been there, it has been warm and sunny. Egrets and herons were everywhere, quietly fishing for their breakfast. I have never experienced such a peaceful place, the stillness and silence broken only by the occasional hum of a mullet boat motoring by. Thank goodness there are still places like this for us to enjoy. St. Marks National Wildlife Refuge was established in 1931 to set aside an area for thousands of wintering waterfowl. Levees, bridges, and culverts were constructed to create a huge network of freshwater pools for these winter visitors.

The lighthouse was automated in 1960 and is maintained by the U.S. Coast Guard, as are all lighthouses. I was lucky enough to be there when two Guardsmen were checking the light. They allowed me to follow them to the top of the eighty-foot-tall lighthouse where the fifth-order Fresnel lens glimmered in the sunlight, looking much like a sculptured glass pineapple. St. Marks is one of those special places where you can sit for a very long time and just absorb the beauty of the surroundings punctuated by the lovely white tower. Of the thirty Florida lighthouses, this is the one that best fits the description "picture-perfect." The way the dark oak trees cradle the white lighthouse makes for a magnificent contrast.

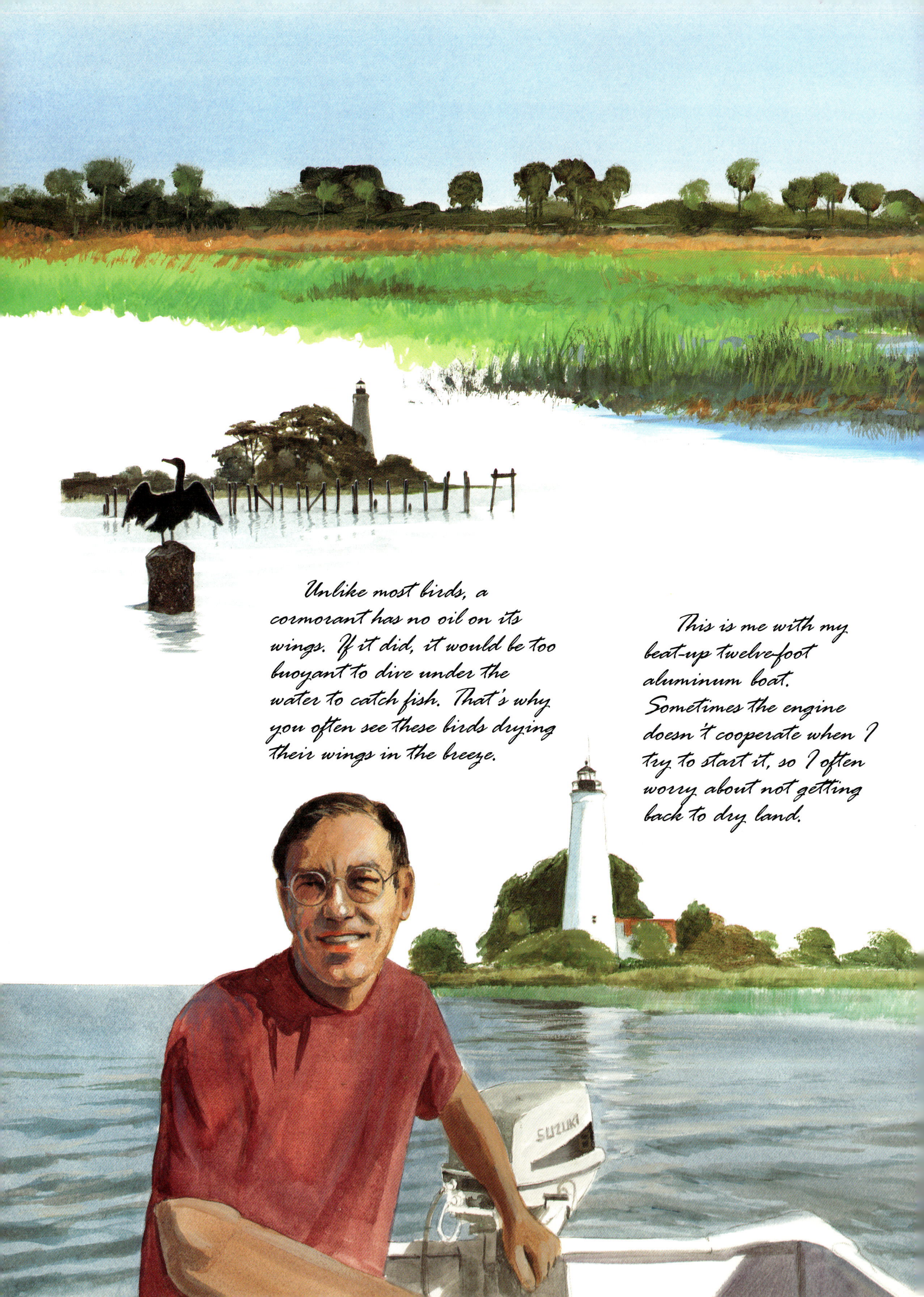

Unlike most birds, a cormorant has no oil on its wings. If it did, it would be too buoyant to dive under the water to catch fish. That's why you often see these birds drying their wings in the breeze.

This is me with my beat-up twelve-foot aluminum boat. Sometimes the engine doesn't cooperate when I try to start it, so I often worry about not getting back to dry land.

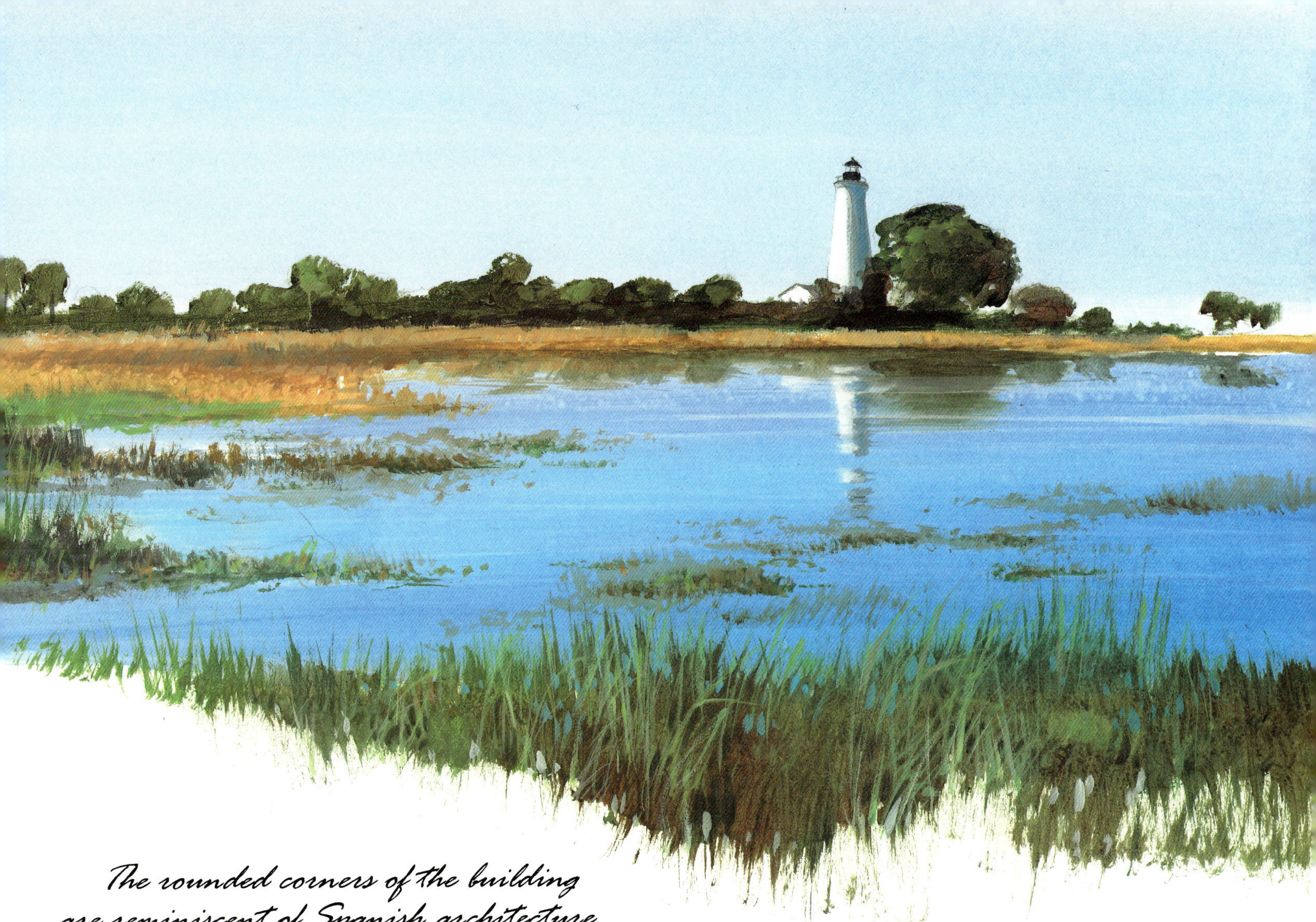

The rounded corners of the building are reminiscent of Spanish architecture.

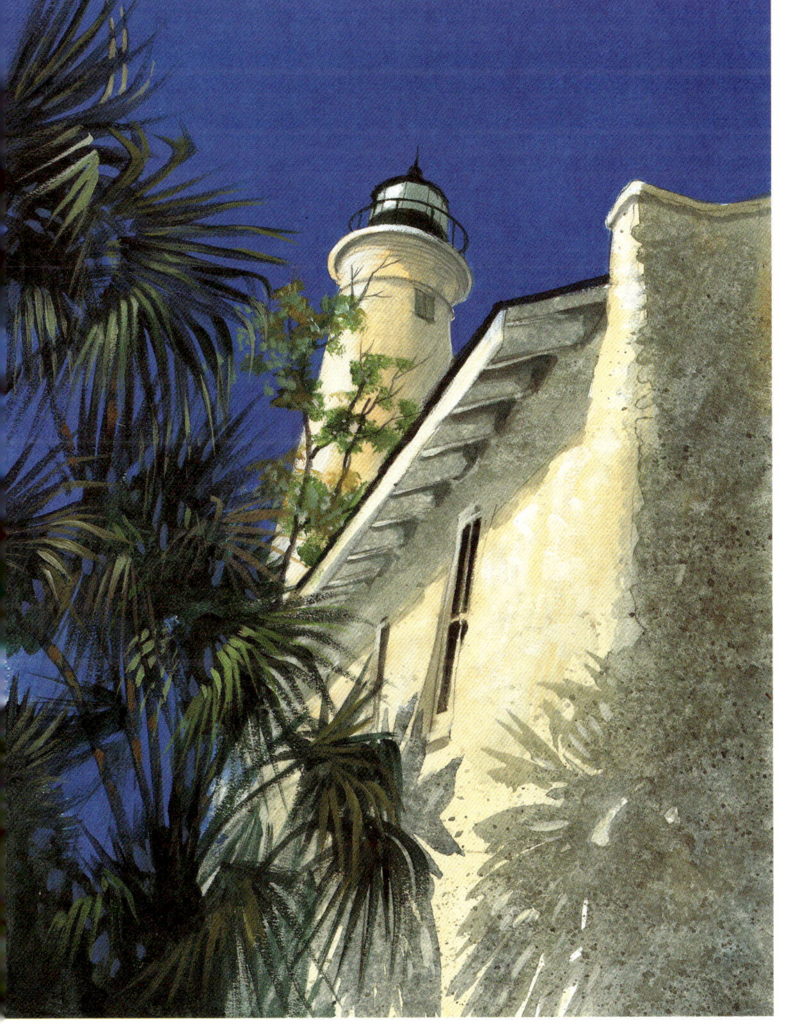

After gaining admission to the refuge at the visitors center, it is a seven-mile drive through the wetlands until you come to the lighthouse. If you have a boat, there is a ramp so you can go fishing or simply motor out and view the lighthouse. The interior isn't open to the public except on special occasions, but a trip to the site is certainly worth the effort. Bring your lunch and enjoy the day.

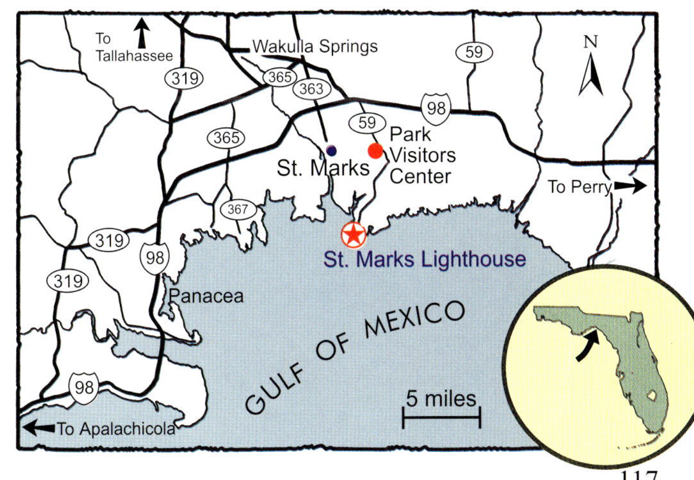

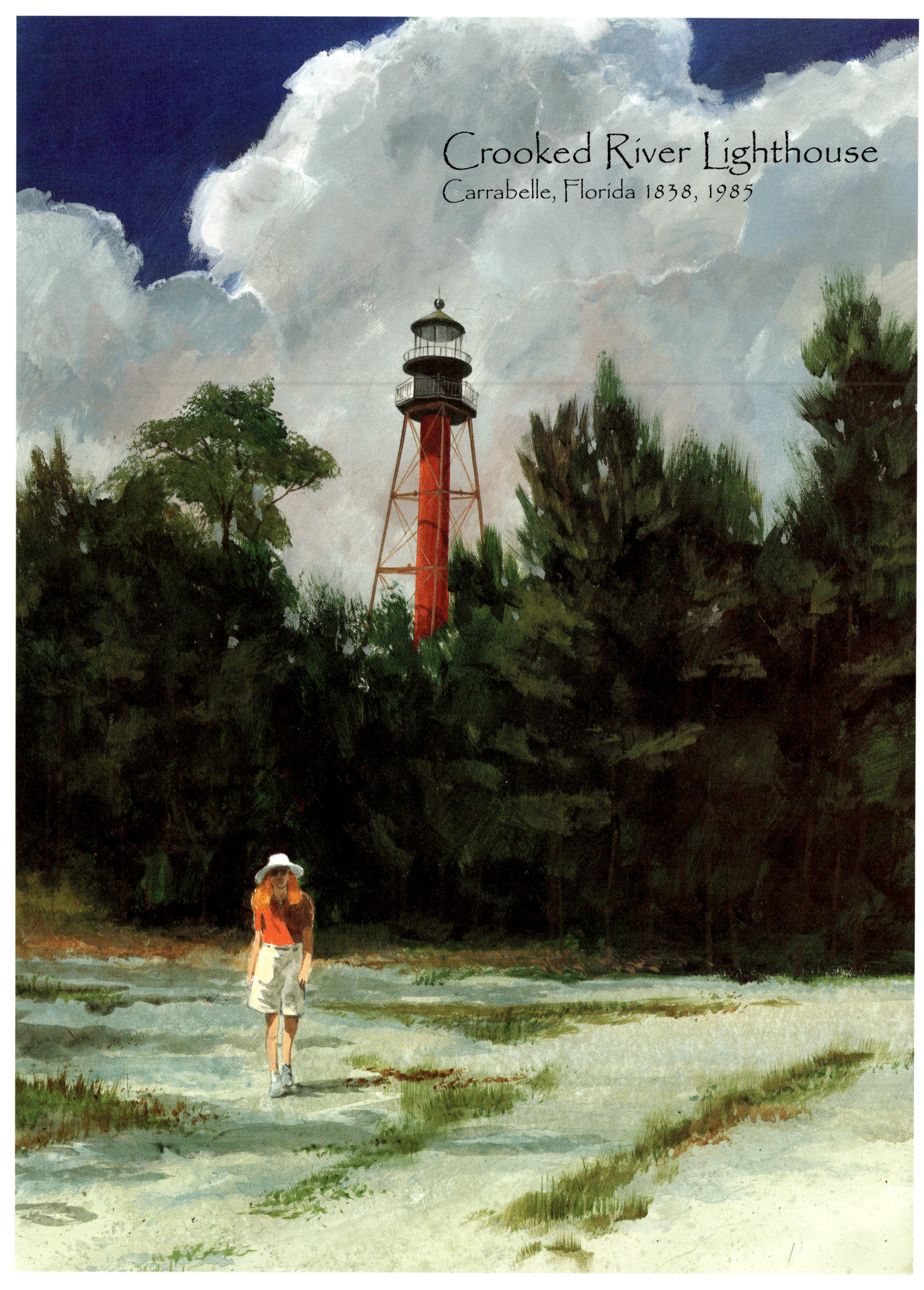
Crooked River Lighthouse
Carrabelle, Florida 1838, 1985

Carrabelle, with its population of several thousand people, hasn't grown much since its early days. It had a good start in the late 1800s with cotton from Georgia and hardwoods from Central America. Florida's extensive pine forests and several area saw mills also meant more business. Processing lumber made Carrabelle a busy port, but like Cedar Key and Apalachicola, the town didn't evolve as was hoped, due in part to the development of railroads in other parts of the state. Today it's a pleasant community where fishing, both sport and commercial, is the main activity. This area of Florida has been called the "Forgotten Coast." I hope it will stay that way for a long time. It's unspoiled and handsome and one of the few places left with no high-rises along the shores (at least not yet). It gives you a sense of what Florida was like years ago. The police station in Carrabelle is famous for being the smallest in the world—a phone booth in the middle of town.

Lighthouses were an important part in the development of any seaport, and the first lighthouse to guide ships into the port of Carrabelle was built on Dog Island, a barrier island just offshore from Carrabelle. Constructed in 1838, it became the victim of a storm that toppled both the tower and the keeper's house thirty-five years after they were built. During the time it was operational, the lighthouse also suffered damage during the Civil War, a fate typical of many lighthouses.

After the loss of the first lighthouse, twenty-two years went by with no light to guide ships into the area. Then in 1895, a new lighthouse was completed on the more stable and protected mainland just north of Carrabelle. It's exactly like the lighthouse on Anclote Key near Tarpon Springs. Called a skeletal lighthouse, it was quite an advancement over brick lighthouses. These iron structures used less material and were less expensive to build. Since they were prefabricated in the North, they could be disassembled and moved at a later time if beach erosion threatened. Their surface area was less than that of a solid brick lighthouse, so they weathered hurricane winds far better. Most importantly, a skeletal lighthouse weighed less than a brick one, so its foundation didn't need to be as substantial. A single brick weighs 4.5 pounds, and there are over 130,000 bricks in a lighthouse like the one at Ponce de Leon Inlet. That adds up to about three hundred tons for the bricks alone, not to mention thousands of barrels of cement, iron stairs, and a Fresnel lens which, with its heavy glass and iron base, could weigh as much as three tons.

Even though the lighthouse is 103 feet tall, it's hard to see from the road. You have to keep a sharp eye out for it, since it's hidden behind the Florida pines that surround it. It looked much different when it was first built, as there were no trees at all around the light then. Two keepers' houses with large porches stood on each side of the lighthouse, but they have long since disappeared. At the time they were built, the lighthouse, oil house, and keepers' houses cost forty thousand dollars.

Carrabelle and Dog Island played an important part in the war effort during World War II, serving as a huge military training facility. Over thirty thousand troops were stationed at what was then called Camp Gordon Johnston. The camp contained over eleven hundred buildings, as well as a bombing range, bazooka range, live grenade practice area, and bayonet and knife course. An area covered with barbed wire, obstacles, shell holes, and trenches served as a training ground where six machine guns fired live ammunition just thirty inches above the ground while troops crawled underneath. On the 159,347 acres of land that this military center occupied, there was even a street fighting course called Harbeson City that was constructed from an old logging village to simulate a Nazi-occupied village. Small landing craft also used the beaches to practice assaults as an important part of the training here. Nothing is left of the military training center now.

The area around the lighthouse is starting to be developed with small houses near the now-dark lighthouse, and other lots are for sale. It looks to me as if the area at the lighthouse itself has become a nighttime hangout for teenagers. Although there is a fence around the lighthouse to keep vandals out, the structure seems quite susceptible to abuse. It would make a wonderful tourist attraction if only the area were tidied up and developed, perhaps with a gift shop. I believe this lighthouse might deteriorate into a memory if it's not cared for in the future.

Dog Island, like all barrier islands, continues to shift and move. It's a natural thing, and there's not much to be done about it. These sandy beaches come and go, sometimes growing very large but just as often washing away because of hurricanes. Still, people continue to build homes on barrier islands at their own risk.

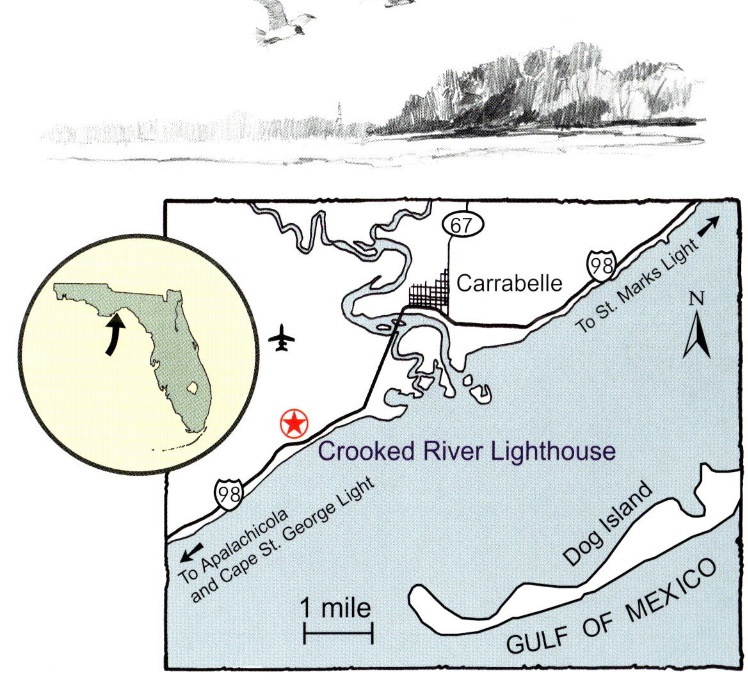

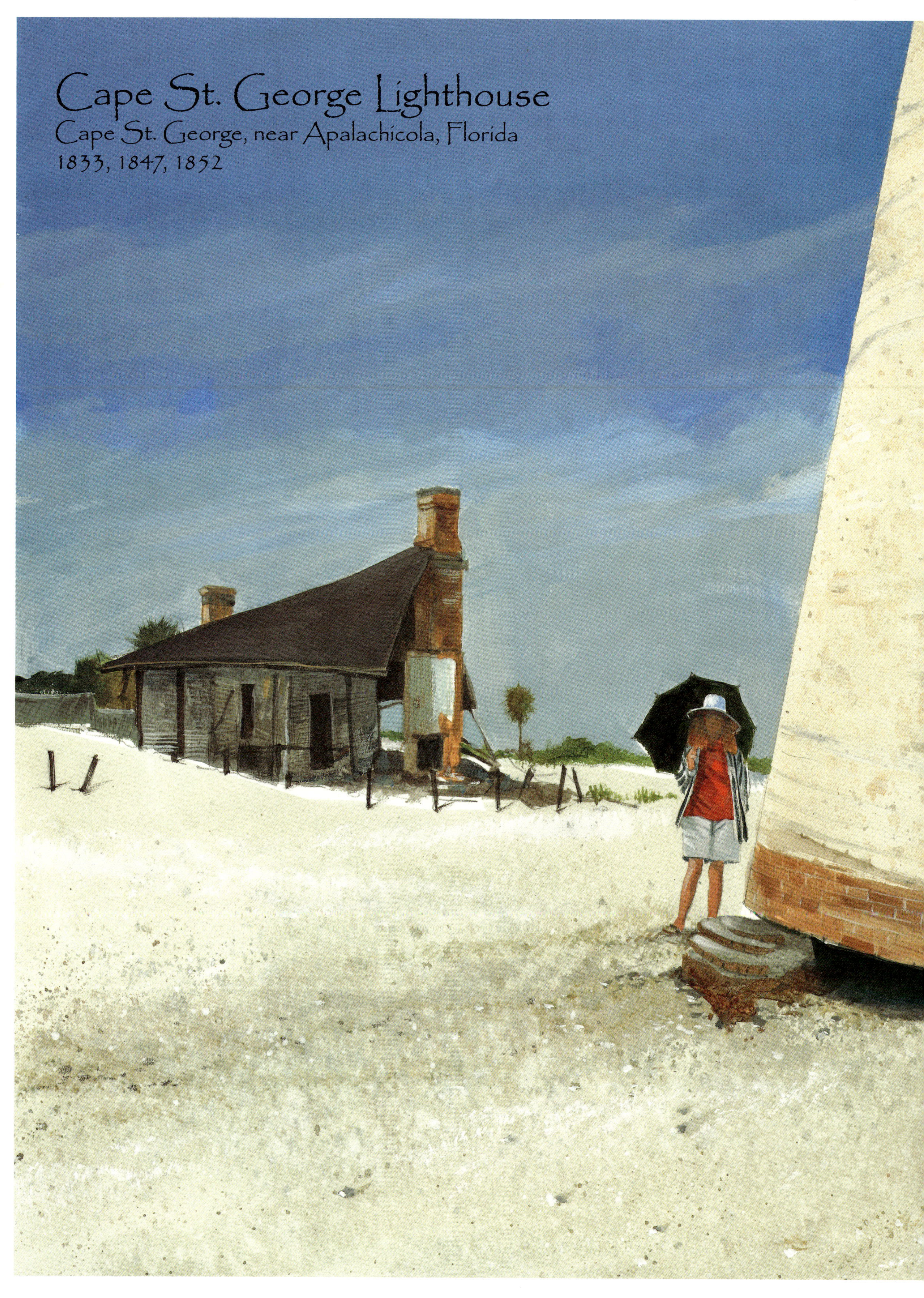
Cape St. George Lighthouse
Cape St. George, near Apalachicola, Florida
1833, 1847, 1852

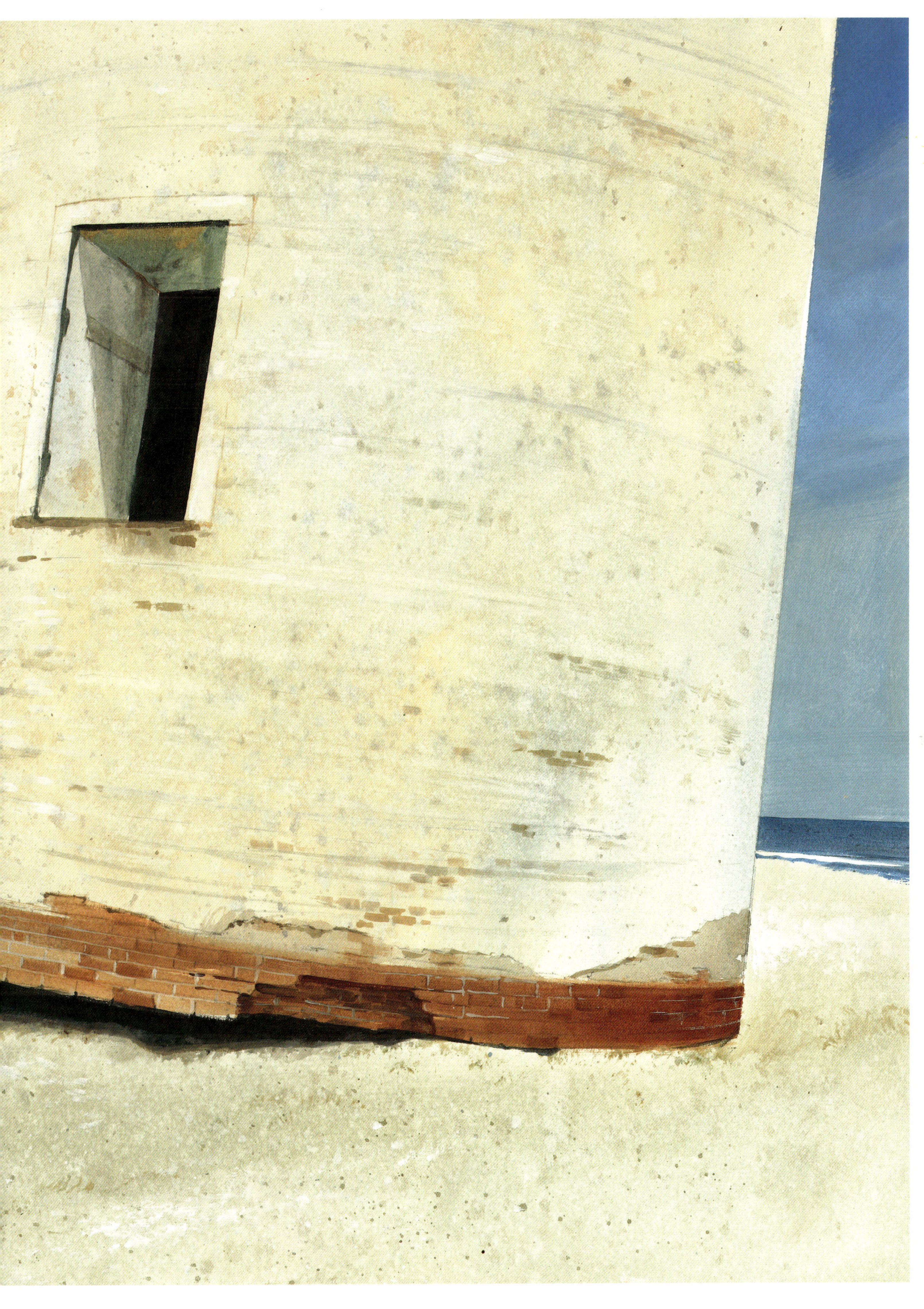

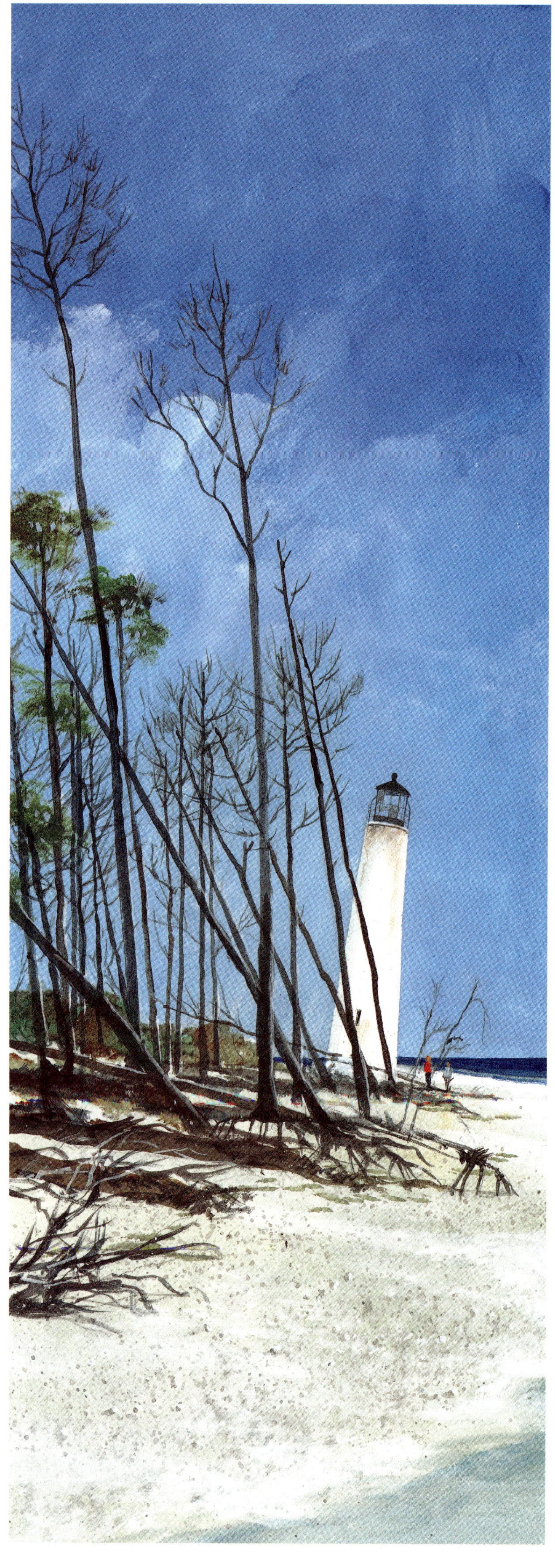

The Cape St. George Lighthouse was one of the more interesting adventures I had while visiting Florida lighthouses. Not having done my homework as I should have before my wife Sarah and I arrived, I quickly found out that my car would be of no use in getting to the lighthouse. Fortunately, we were towing our boat. Unfortunately, our boat is only twelve feet long, and the lighthouse is nine miles offshore. At Apalachicola, I asked a man by the boat ramp to point the way, since the lighthouse was not visible and the island was barely visible. Accompanying his directions was a stern warning about the quickly changing temperament of the bay, especially with summer storms. After considering our options, we put in the water and headed for the island, having to negotiate every wave with caution, which made for a long and exhausting excursion. A slightly larger boat would have done just fine; we were a little undersized and underpowered.

After what seemed like forever, we finally landed on the protected back side of St. George Island, where the water was calm and smooth. The lighthouse was still not visible even after we landed. That required a two-mile walk across the island, then south down the beach. The fine powdery sand path made walking difficult. Add to that the intense heat of the sun, and the trek was less than comfortable. Fortunately, there were no mosquitoes despite the lack of a breeze, although I'm sure at times they're ferocious. If we hadn't traveled so far in that little aluminum boat of ours, I might have had the notion to turn back before we fell victims to heatstroke, but our persistence finally paid off. We came to a small dune and just beyond saw the blue gulf waters breaking up on the unspoiled beach. There wasn't another person in sight. Stepping out into the surf to cool our feet, we looked in all directions but still saw no lighthouse. Remembering the conversation back at the dock, I thought the man who gave us directions had said to go left. We did and soon came to a forest of pine trees with four to five feet of their roots exposed from beach erosion. Then we finally came upon the spectacular sight of this leaning tower.

There have been three lighthouses on or near this site. The first one was built in 1833. The second was built in 1847 and stood only four years. The hurricane that destroyed it also destroyed the lighthouses at Cape San Blas and St. Joseph Bay to the north and at Dog Island just to the south near Carrabelle. The lighthouse built in 1852 at St. George is the one I've painted. At the beginning of the Civil War, the light was extinguished and the lens removed and hidden. The Union captured Apalachicola by ship in 1862 and used the keepers' houses as housing and recreation areas for soldiers. After the war, the lens was found, and the light was relit in 1899.

A hurricane in 1985 took out the dune line, and in 1992, Hurricane Andrew added to the erosion problem. The lighthouse that once stood fifteen hundred feet from the gulf

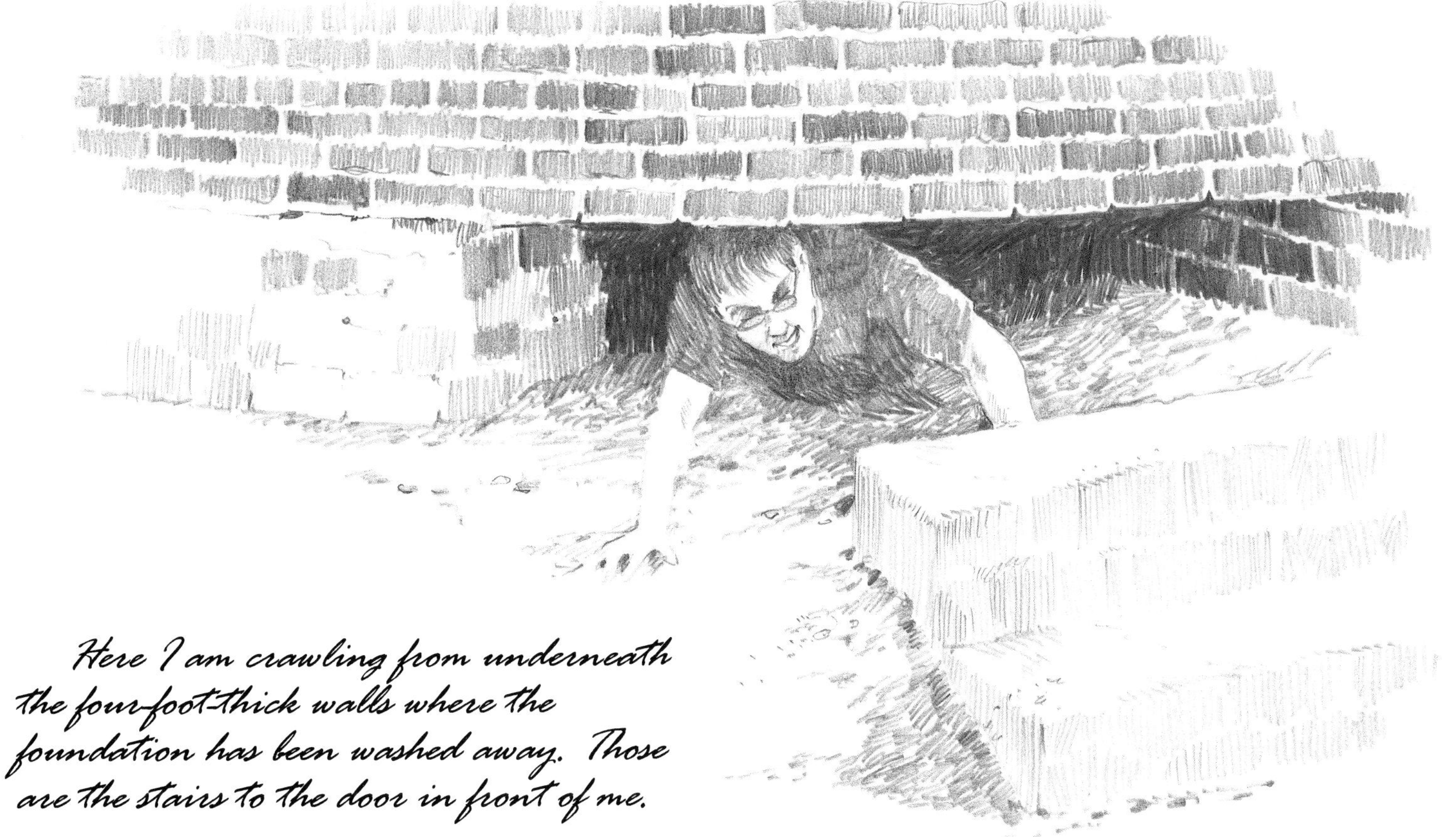

Here I am crawling from underneath the four-foot-thick walls where the foundation has been washed away. Those are the stairs to the door in front of me.

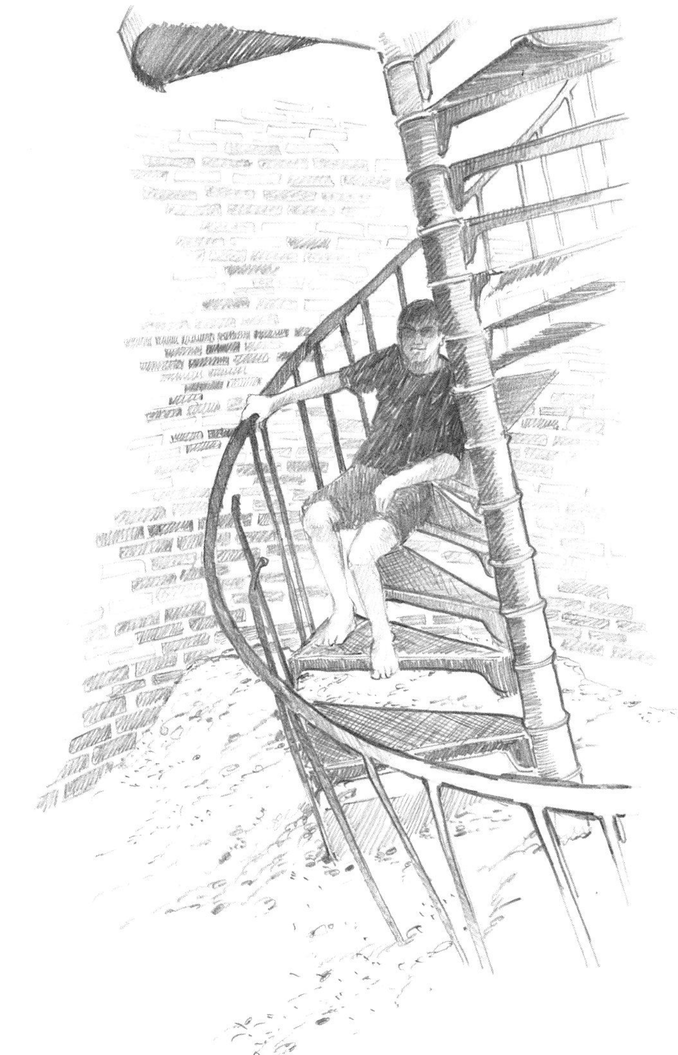

The staircase has been ripped from its pinning and rests on the floor where sand has washed in and piled up in a small dune. Some of the steps have cracked and separated from the center pole. The twisted ironwork leans against the inside wall of the lighthouse, which keeps it from collapsing altogether.

I walked up about eight steps, then my common sense took over, telling me to retreat slowly from this unstable situation. This would be a bad place to be in trouble, with no one around and miles from the mainland. I didn't want to end up like one lighthouse keeper who fell to his death from the tower while painting in 1875.

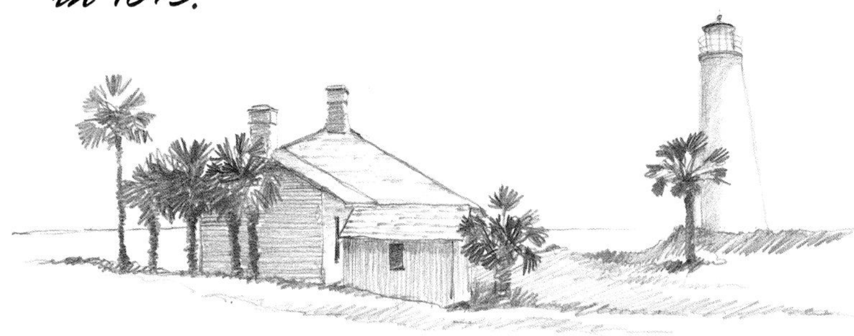

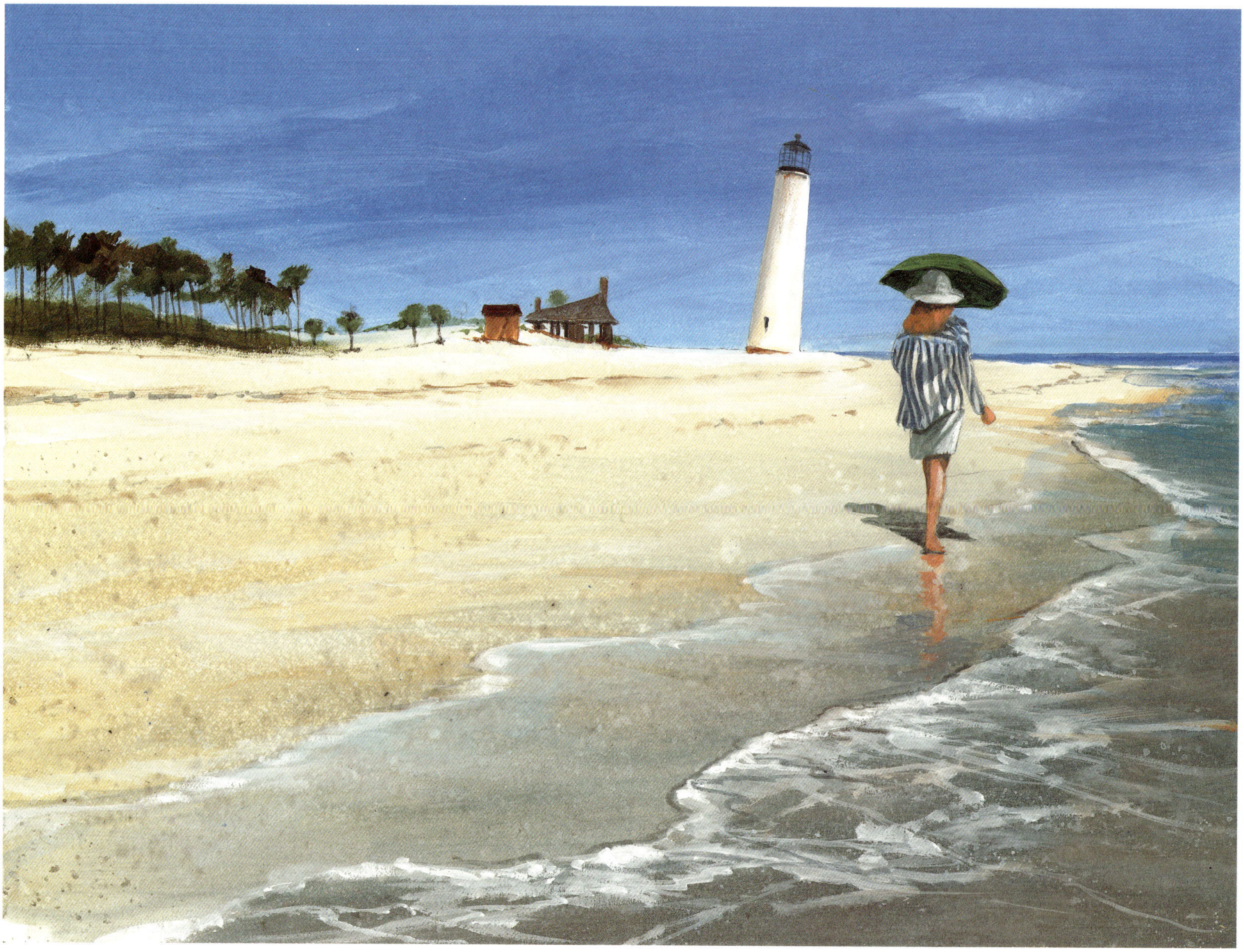

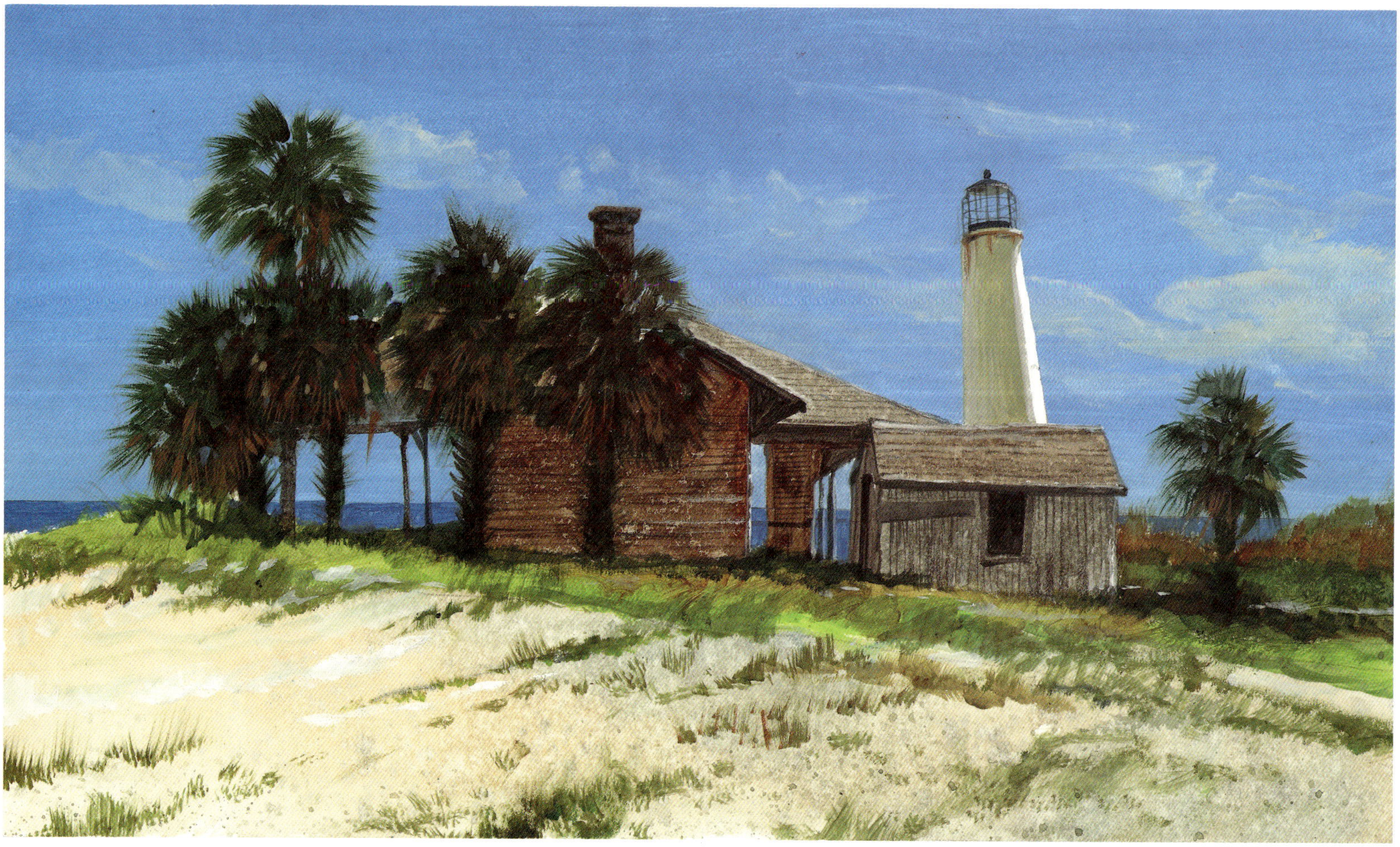

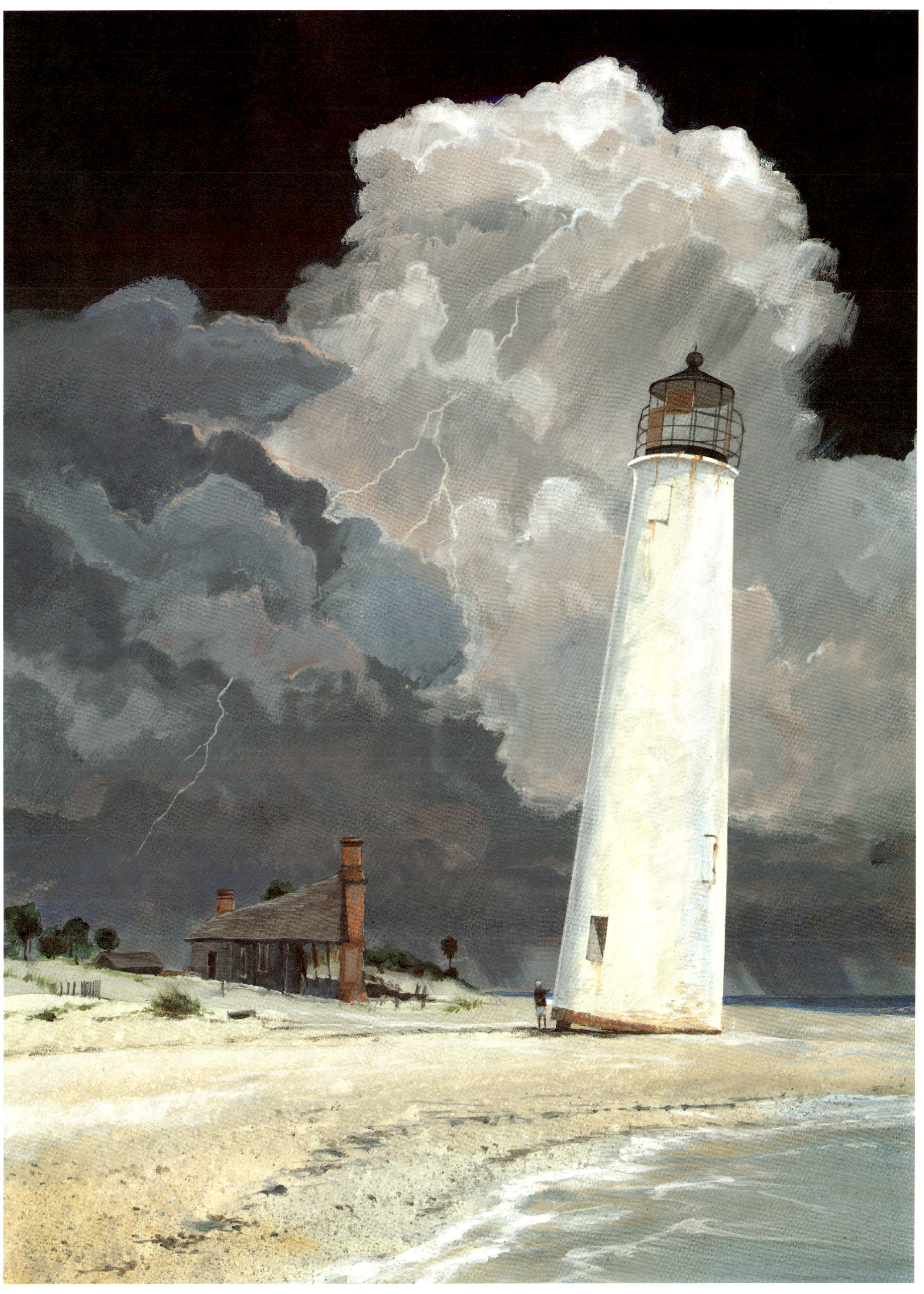

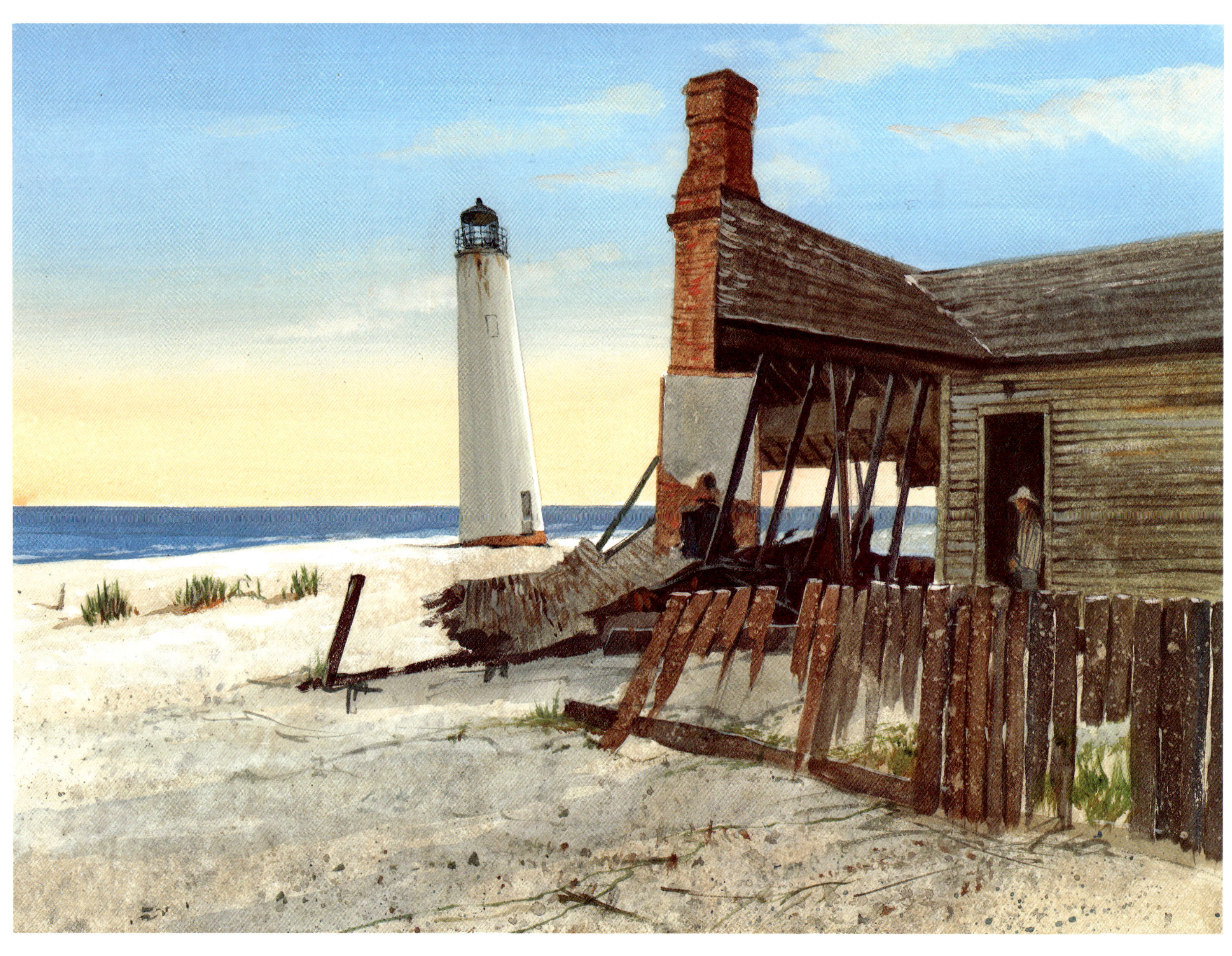

The keeper's house is in a state of collapse. Since I did this painting, the roof has fallen in. The assistant keeper's house burned sometime in the 1940s. These are the last remnants of a long-lived tradition, and it won't be long before they're completely gone. It was a strange feeling standing there, knowing that lighthouse keepers dedicated their entire lives to this place. Children grew up here and even went to school on the island. Now Nature is reclaiming this land.

now has water lapping at its base during high tide and leans at an angle of fourteen degrees—another few degrees and the second oldest lighthouse on the gulf coast will topple. At the time I did these paintings, efforts were under way to save the light. After seeing it, though, I get the feeling that unless something is done quickly, these might be the last paintings done of it before it collapses.

This area of Florida has a long history. Even before Europeans reached the shores of the Panhandle, Indians lived here. Pottery fragments dating as far back as A.D. 750 have been found on St. George Island, and it is believed that there were Indians here as long ago as ten thousand years.

Cotton was shipped through this port in the early 1800s as it was at Carrabelle. Apalachicola, with forty-three cotton warehouses at the time, became the third-largest cotton port on the gulf coast, just behind New Orleans and Mobile. The Apalachicola River extends three hundred miles to Columbus, Georgia, which made Apalachicola the perfect place to transfer cotton to mills in New England and overseas to mills and lace manufacturing centers in England, France, and Belgium.

The comforts of air conditioning we enjoy today can be traced back to Apalachicola and the yellow fever epidemic of 1841. John Gorrie, a local physician, thought that cooling his patients would give them a greater chance of recovering, and he began to design a device that would lower the temperature of the air. By 1851, he had built a machine that cooled the air and created ice as a by-product. It was

Gorrie's invention that formed the basis for today's air conditioners.

During World War II, this area was used as a training camp similar to the one at Carrabelle, and rows of metal huts lined the beaches. At that time, St. George Island was twenty-eight miles long. In 1954, however, a channel was cut through the island, creating two separate barrier islands, making it easier and quicker for shrimpers to get out into the gulf. Now the islands are known as St. George Island, a resort community accessible by bridge, and Little St. George Island, a state park and the site of the lighthouse. The smaller island is ten miles long and can only be reached by boat. Shelling is good here, loggerhead sea turtles nest on the beach during the summer, and many birds visit, especially during spring and fall migration periods. Pine trees on the island were once used to gather turpentine. The stills operated in the early 1900s and again from the 1940s into the early 1950s.

Keeper Edward G. Porter lived on the island and took care of the lighthouse for twenty years until his death in 1913. He loved the island so much, he bought the entire 1,640 acres for $500 and raised his six children there.

The oil house has totally collapsed since I was there. All that remains is a collection of bricks covered by the shifting sands.

Today Apalachicola is known for its oysters, and about ninety percent of commercially harvested oysters come from here. People began harvesting oysters here way back in the 1850s, and it's still one of the main industries along with shrimping. Additionally, Tarpon Springs, known as the sponge capital of the world, once shared its fame with Apalachicola. From the mid-1870s until the early twentieth century, Apalachicola's sponging industry ranked third in the state. The sponging industry was brought to this country by the Greeks, who first started harvesting sponges here in Apalachicola. Their migration headed south to Carrabelle, Cedar Key, and finally Tarpon Springs.

The atmosphere of downtown Apalachicola will take you back to the turn of the century. The lack of shopping malls is delightful, and I think the residents would like to keep it that way.

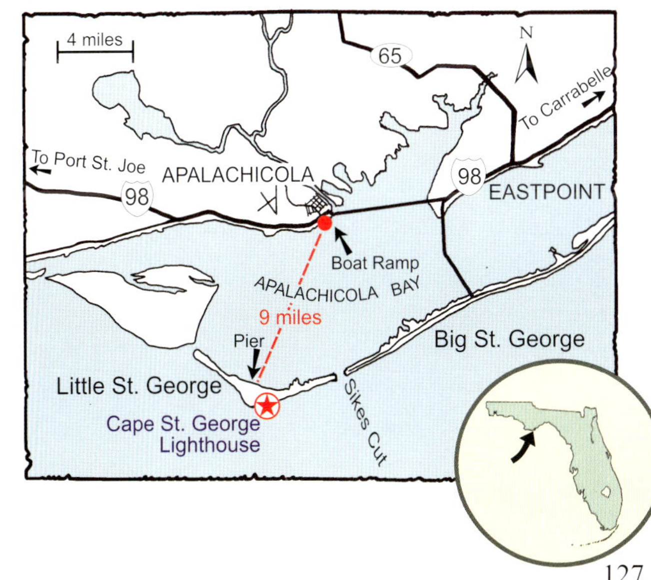

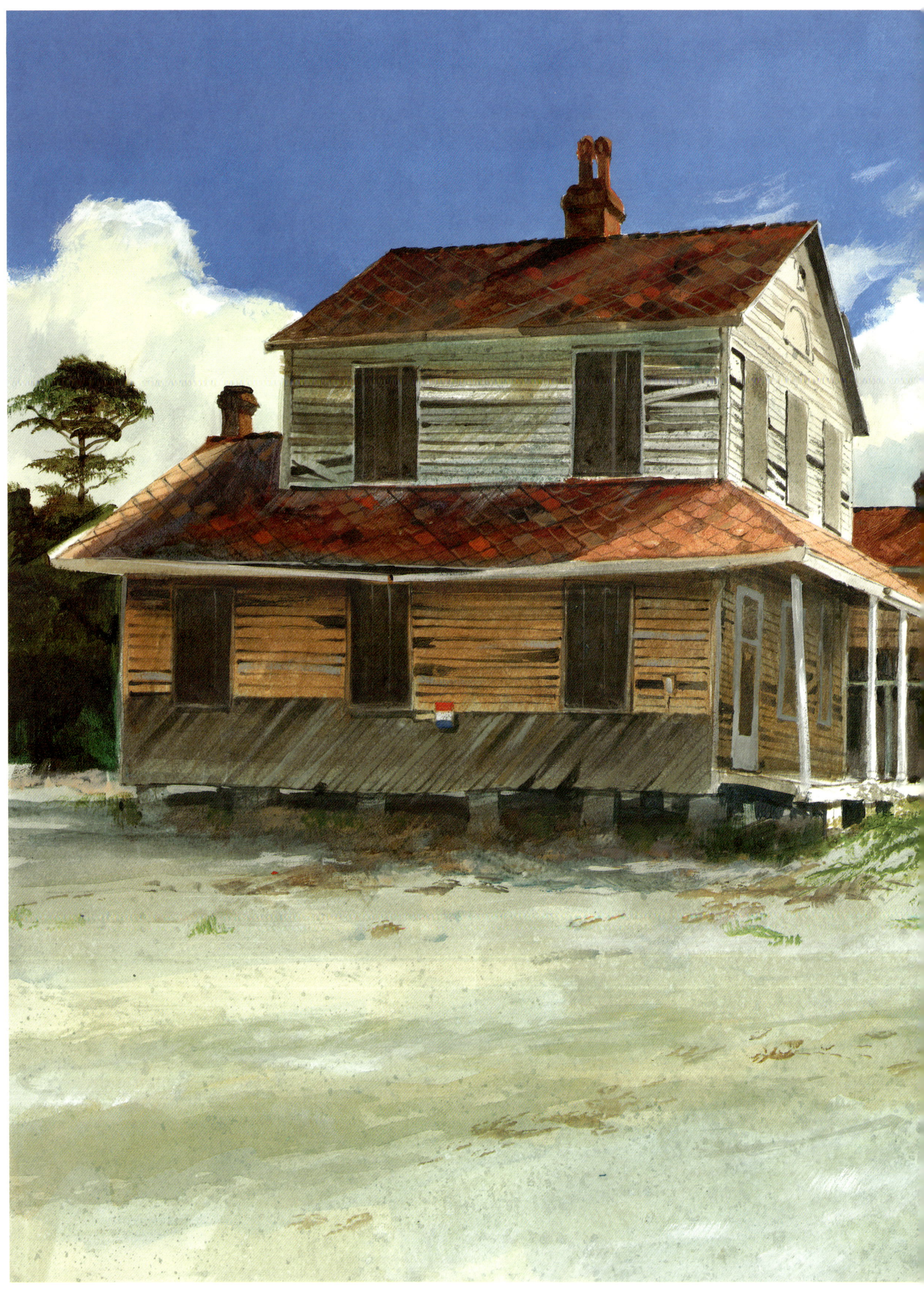

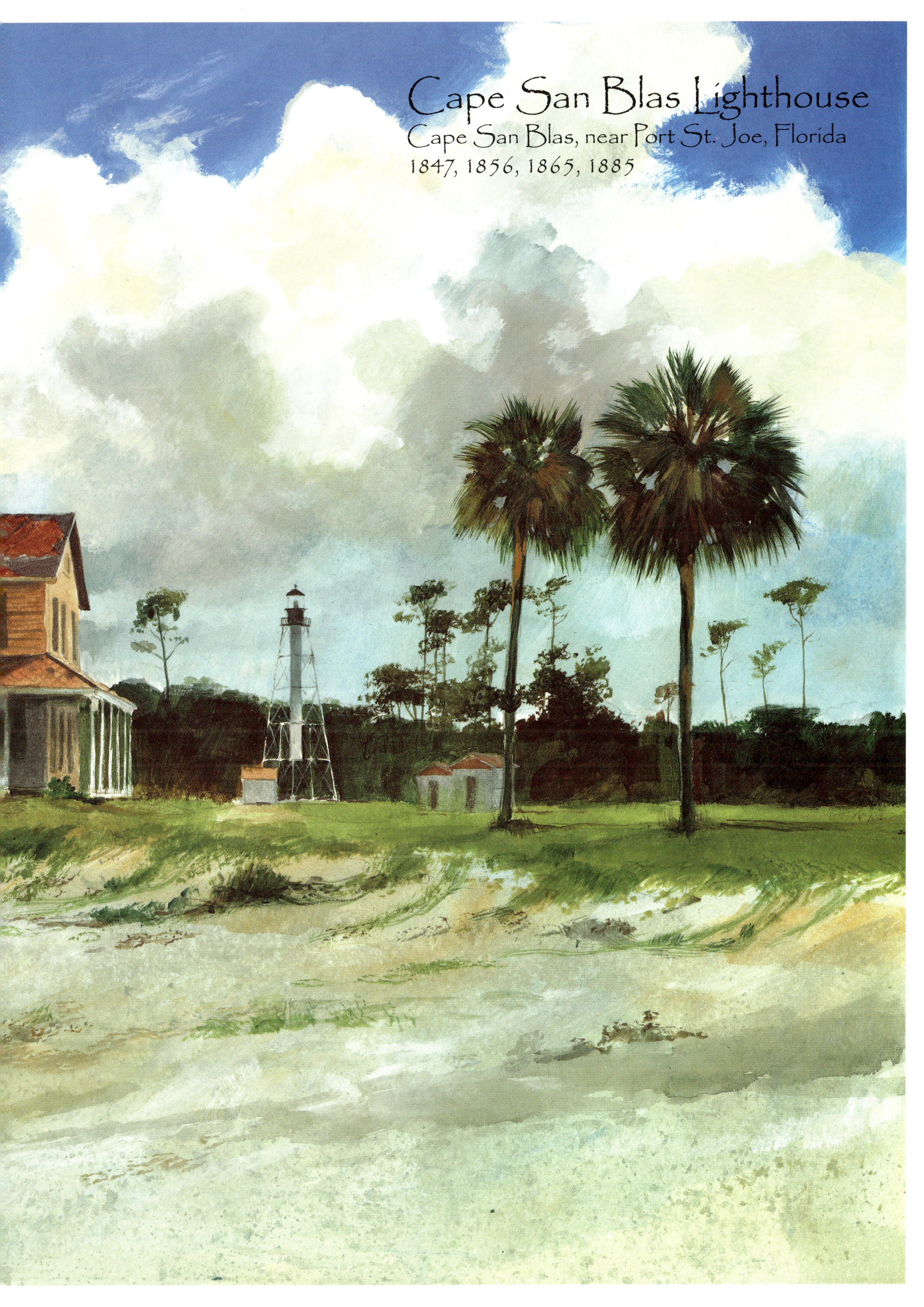

Cape San Blas Lighthouse

Cape San Blas, near Port St. Joe, Florida

1847, 1856, 1865, 1885

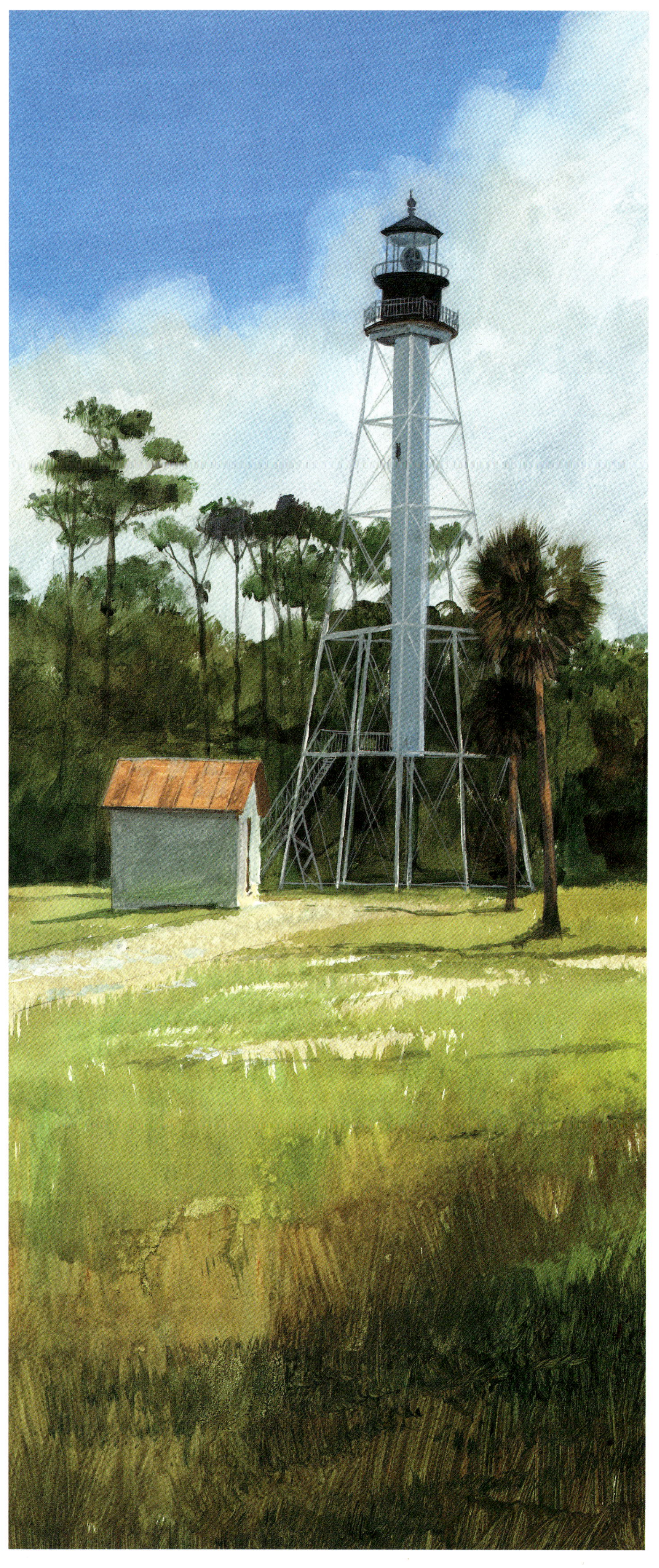

The lighthouses at Cape San Blas and at Sanibel Island are identical.

The lighthouses at Cape San Blas were more plagued by bad luck and bad decision making than any of the lighthouses in Florida. The first light was built in 1847, and a hurricane toppled it only four years later. An epidemic of yellow fever, a horrible disease spread by mosquitoes, caused the rebuilding of the lighthouse to take five years. It was finally finished in 1856. Several months later, another storm with a fourteen foot tide destroyed that lighthouse. A third one was soon built just in time for the Confederates to severely damage it and the keepers' houses when the Civil War began. It was not lit until after the war in 1865. Now erosion was its enemy once again. By 1882, the lighthouse stood in eight feet of water. With its foundation undermined, the brick structure fell into the sea. For three years, a light was shown at the top of a hundred-foot-high mast as a lighthouse substitute. Then the decision was made to install a skeletal iron structure rather than another brick one. It was prefabricated in the North, and the ship carrying it sunk in shallow water off the coast of Sanibel Island near Fort Myers. The ironwork was salvaged and finally delivered to Cape San Blas. There, in 1885, it was put in place nine hundred feet inland. Problem solved—not exactly! Eleven years later, erosion ate up so much of the beach, the ninety-eight-foot-tall lighthouse had to be disassembled and moved. That still wasn't enough, and in 1918, the lighthouse had to be moved again, this time a quarter of a mile north of where it first stood and 1,850 feet inland.

Like most lighthouses, Cape San Blas was remote, and it took the keeper a full day to travel to Apalachicola, just twenty-four miles away. This mule-and-wagon journey was made only twice a year to pick up supplies, and it meant being away from the lighthouse for three days: one day's travel each way and one day to rest the mules. Today the same trip takes forty-five minutes each way by car.

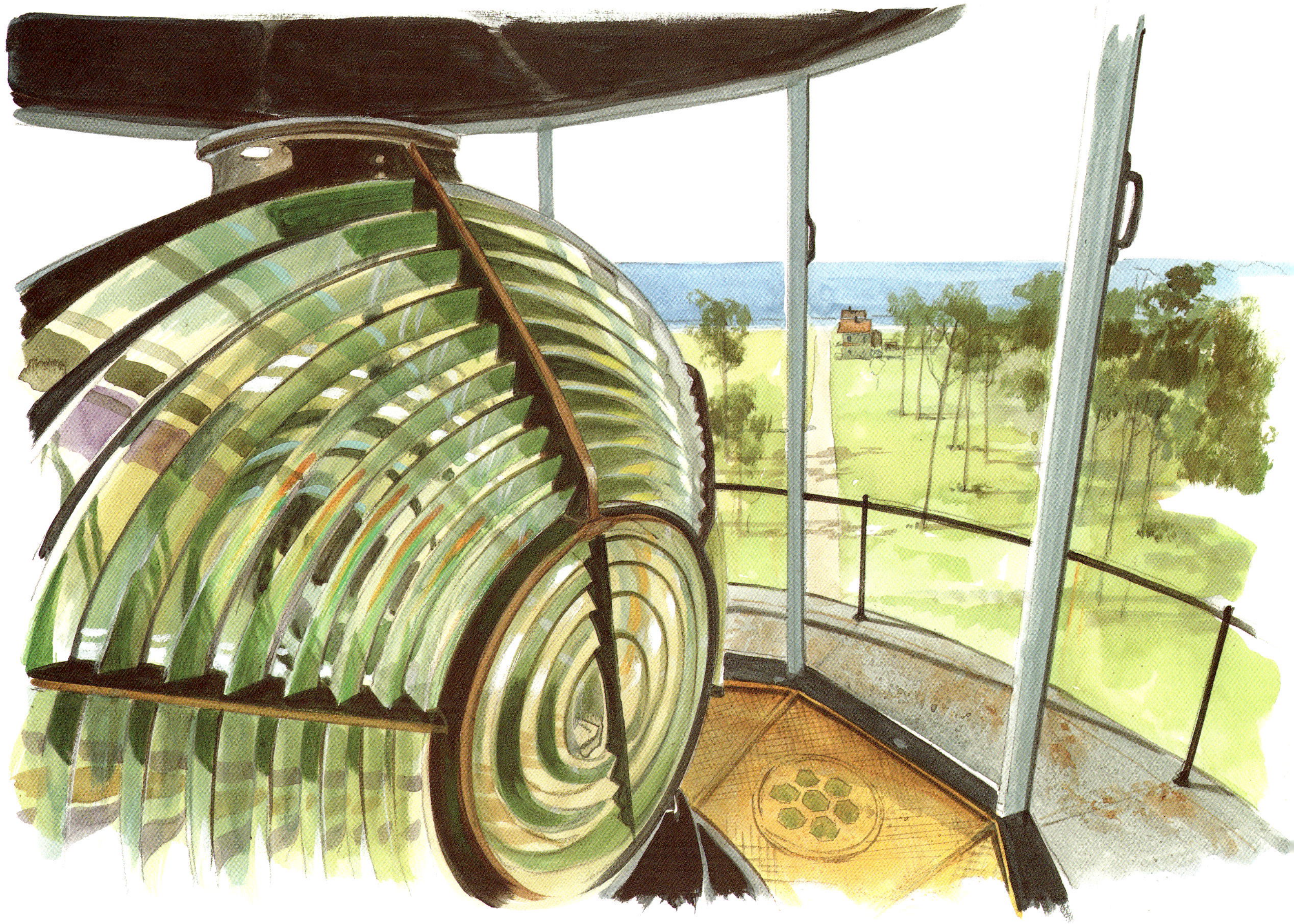

This clamshell lens would direct a powerful flash far out to sea. It was a further development from the more traditional Fresnel lens.

One hundred eleven years after the last lighthouse at Cape San Blas was lit, the Coast Guard placed a hood over the third-order clamshell Fresnel lens. Having weathered numerous storms, the lighthouse has not been able to weather government cutbacks, which have finally darkened the light.

I first visited Cape San Blas when I was doing my *Southern Shores* book in 1989. The keeper's house was about two hundred feet from the high tide mark at that time. When I visited again in July of 1997, the high tide mark was gnawing at the base of the keeper's house, and parts of it were beginning to crumble into the gulf. It is quite possible that it will be gone when you visit unless someone steps in to save it.

The Coast Guard is not in the business of saving historical landmarks and considers structures like these more of a liability than anything else, so it's up to a historical society or other group to preserve the lighthouse as a beloved landmark. Florida's lighthouses are some of the oldest structures still standing in our country. The keepers of these lights were our early pioneers. Hopefully the light will be turned back on to let history continue.

The Air Force is in charge of the land around the lighthouse and the two times I have visited, there have been military people willing to show me around. Although there is a fence around some of the property, you can easily view the lighthouse from just outside the fence or on the beach, which is open to everyone.

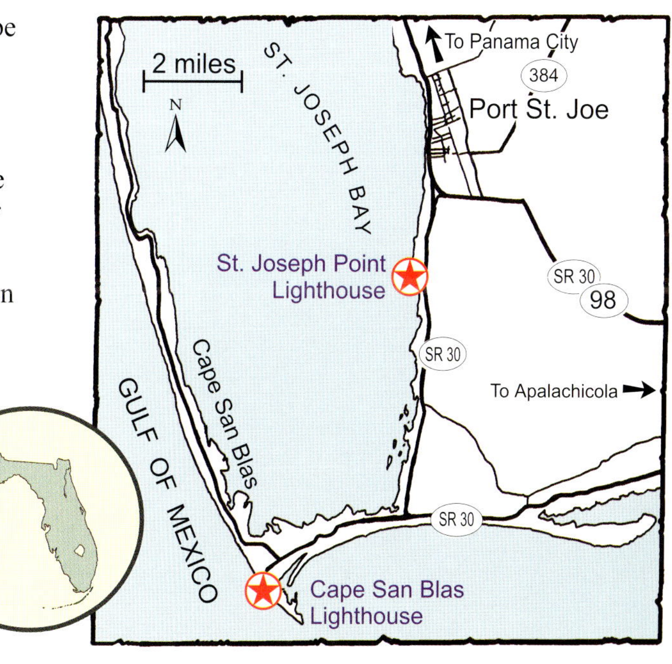

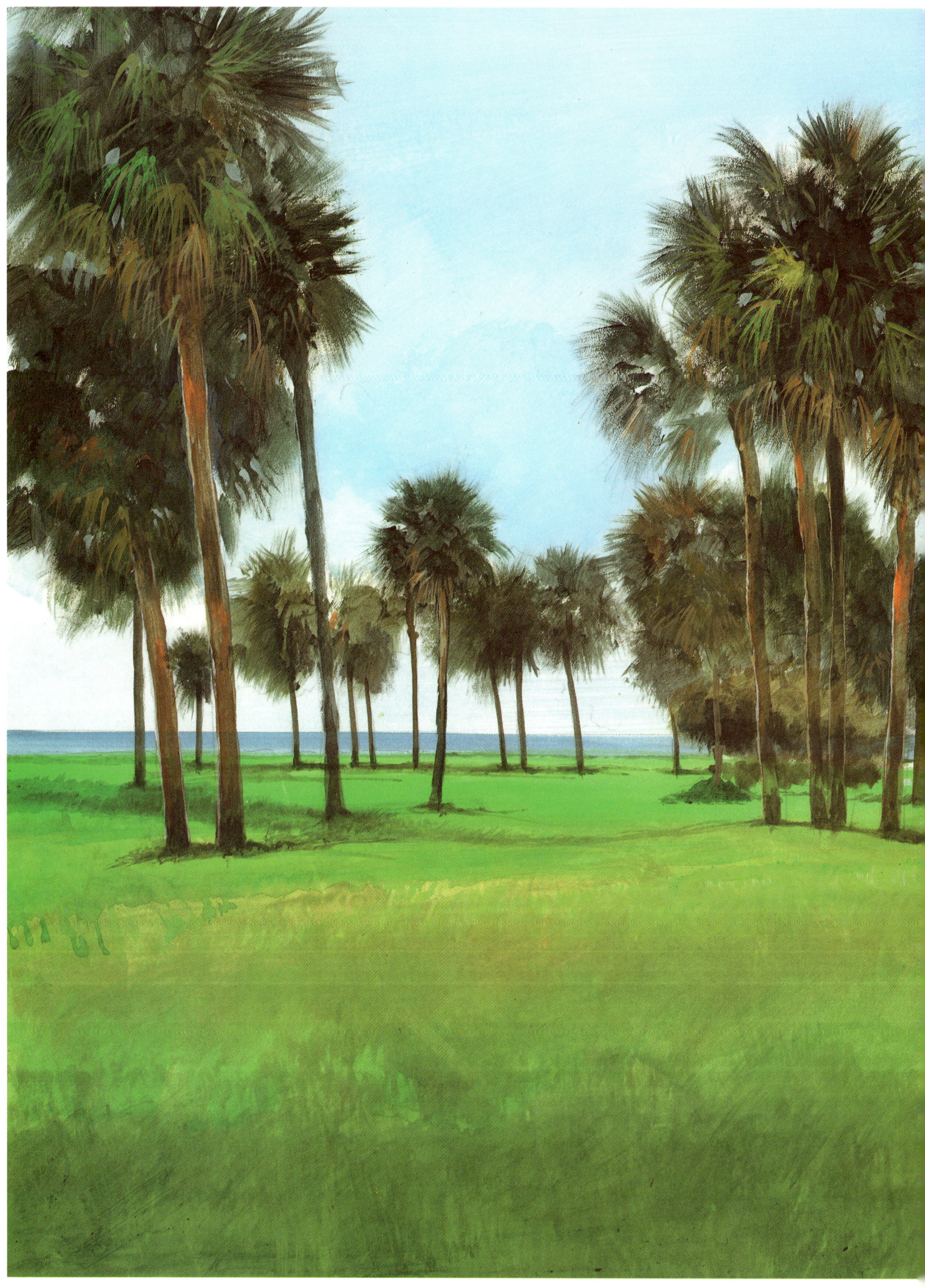

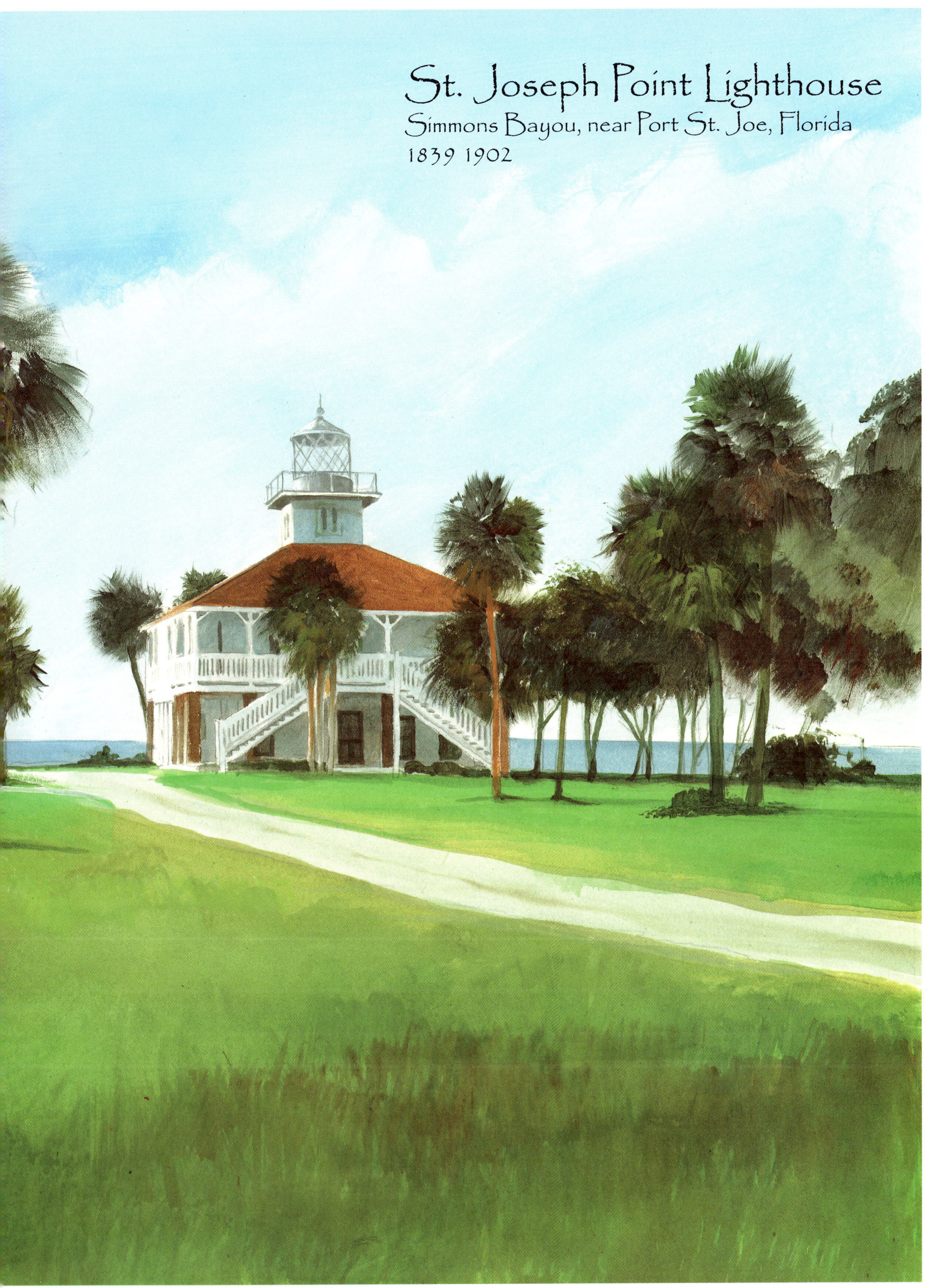
St. Joseph Point Lighthouse
Simmons Bayou, near Port St. Joe, Florida
1839 1902

During the nineteenth century, Port St. Joe, along with other towns like Apalachicola and Cedar Key, enjoyed the promise of growth from Northern investors and entrepreneurs. The population of Florida doubled between 1870 and 1890, and tourism began to be a major part of the state's economy. Although most lighthouses were built before this land boom, increased development brought even more ships to Florida's coasts, and the need for lighthouses became even more important. There were several lighthouses built at Port St. Joe. The first, located at the tip of St. Joseph Peninsula, was called the St. Joseph Bay Lighthouse and was built in 1839. Three years later, a ship pulled into port and spread yellow fever throughout the town of St. Joseph, reducing the population to zero.

If you had lived in St. Joseph at the time, here is what would have happened to you. Three to six days after the ship pulled into port, the disease would have finished incubating, and symptoms would manifest suddenly. It would start with a headache, backache, and fever. Then you would begin to have nausea and vomiting. Your temperature would return to normal for a few days, but then it would rise again. Your skin would turn yellow from an accumulation of yellow bile pigments in your body. Then you would begin to bleed from the nose and to vomit blood (It was called "black vomit."). Your kidneys, liver, and heart would begin to fail, and you would die between the fourth and eighth day after your symptoms began. If by some miracle you survived (and some people did elsewhere), your convalescence would be quick. The jaundice would persist, but you would be immune to yellow fever for the rest of your life.

A hurricane followed the yellow fever epidemic and destroyed most of the buildings in town. In 1842, the lighthouse was shut down because the town was completely abandoned. The St. Joseph Bay Lighthouse stood until 1851, when it was heavily damaged by another hurricane. Remnants of it remained and served as a daymark for some time, and the foundation could still be seen up until World War II.

From time to time, there was talk about re-establishing the lighthouse mainly for fishing vessels, many of which sank in the bay. Just after the turn of the twentieth century, in 1902, a new lighthouse was built. Unlike most lighthouses of the time, the St. Joseph Point Lighthouse allowed the keeper and his family to live in the same building as the light. Originally the lighthouse sat above the ground on brick pillars, leaving room for supplies and a large cistern below. Later, this area was walled in to make rooms.

Even though the thought of it today seems a little strange, during World War II, German ships roamed the waters right off the gulf coast. The Coast Guard used the

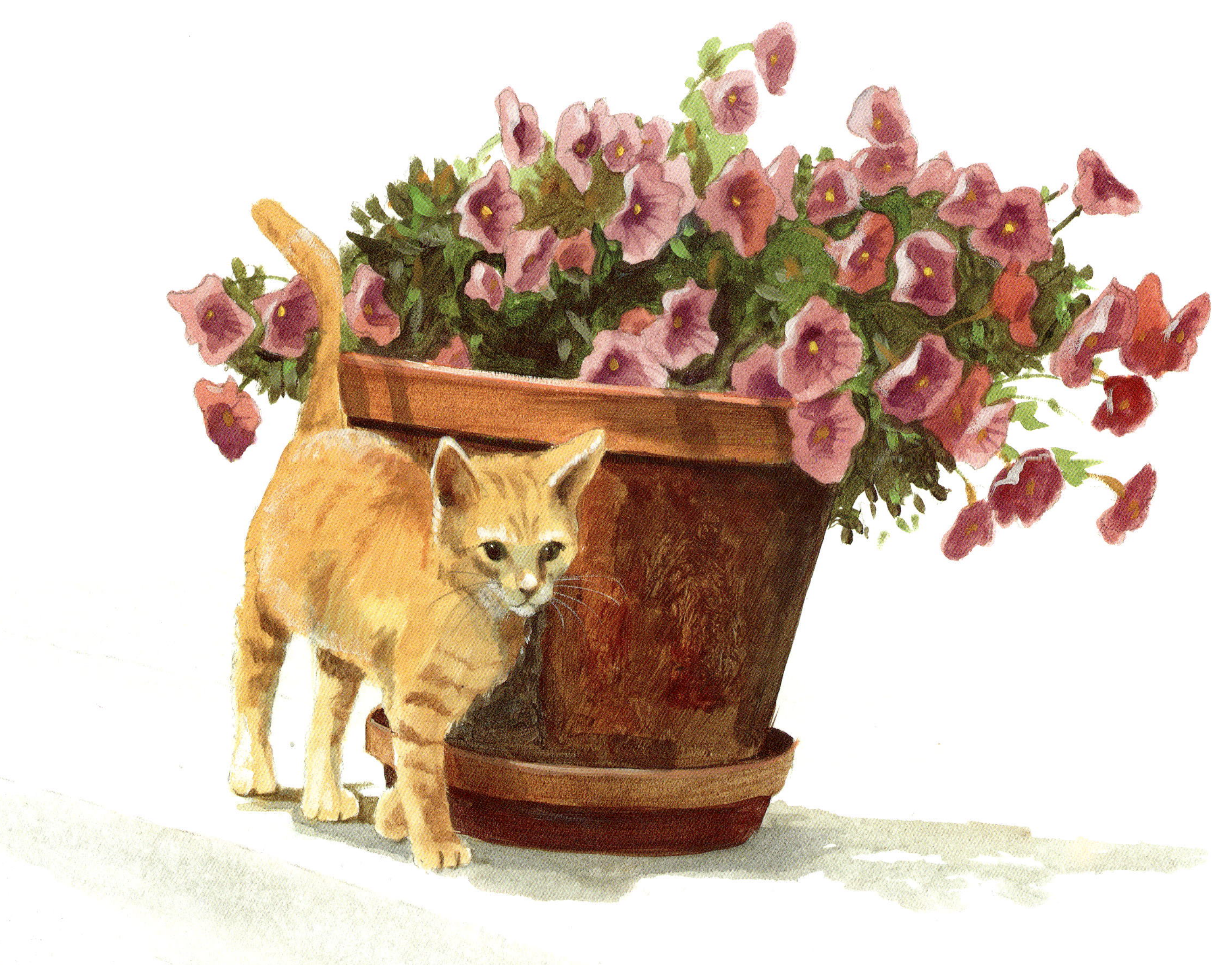

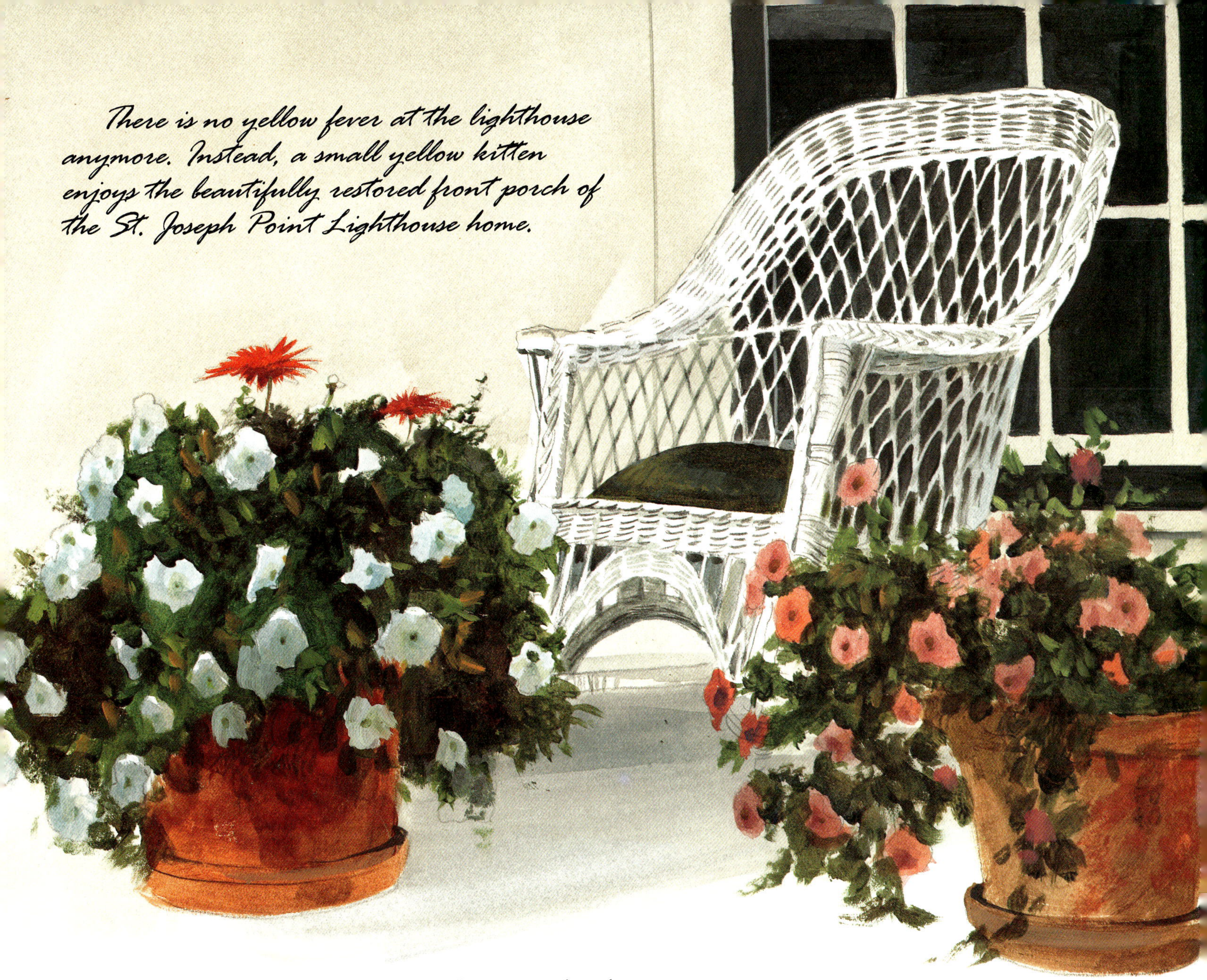

There is no yellow fever at the lighthouse anymore. Instead, a small yellow kitten enjoys the beautifully restored front porch of the St. Joseph Point Lighthouse home.

lighthouse as a base while patrolling the coast for enemy spies who tried to come ashore in rubber rafts.

The lighthouse was unmanned again in 1951. It was bought as surplus for three hundred dollars and was moved three miles inland to a small farm, where it was used as a residence and was later made into a barn. During the move, a crane inadequate for the job dropped the lantern room, totally destroying it. Then in 1979, Danny Raffield, a resident of Port St. Joe, bought the old lighthouse and moved it once again thirteen miles to its present location. He then lovingly restored it and converted it into a home, even duplicating the pattern in the wooden walls according to original plans. Much of the woodwork had been torn apart with a crowbar by someone who thought there might be money buried behind the planks. Finely grained, forty-foot-long wooden beams cut from two-hundred-foot-tall trees remain part of the house's structure. For several years, Danny also worked on reproducing the lantern room. It now crowns the lighthouse and brings the entire structure back to its long-awaited original beauty.

This is the only privately owned lighthouse in the entire state. Because it's a private residence, it's not open to the public, but it can easily be seen from the street. It's located at County Road 30 next to Pressnell's Fish Camp, just south of the intersection of Highway 98, south of Port St. Joe.

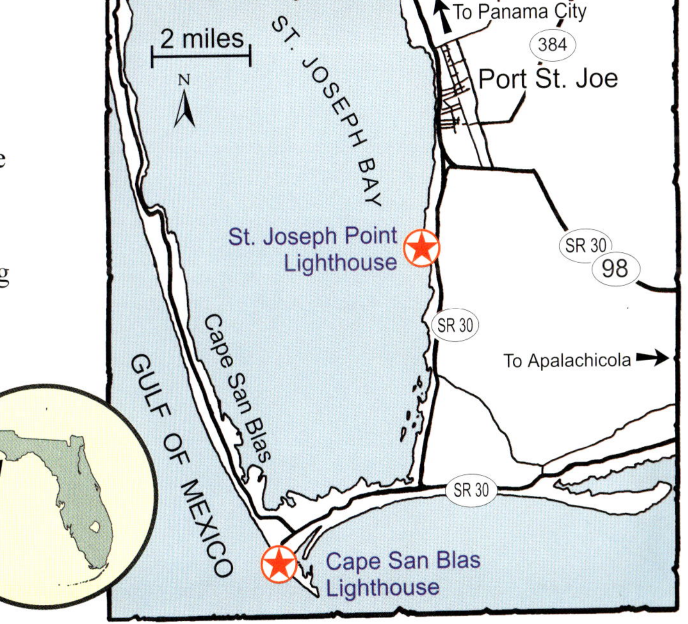

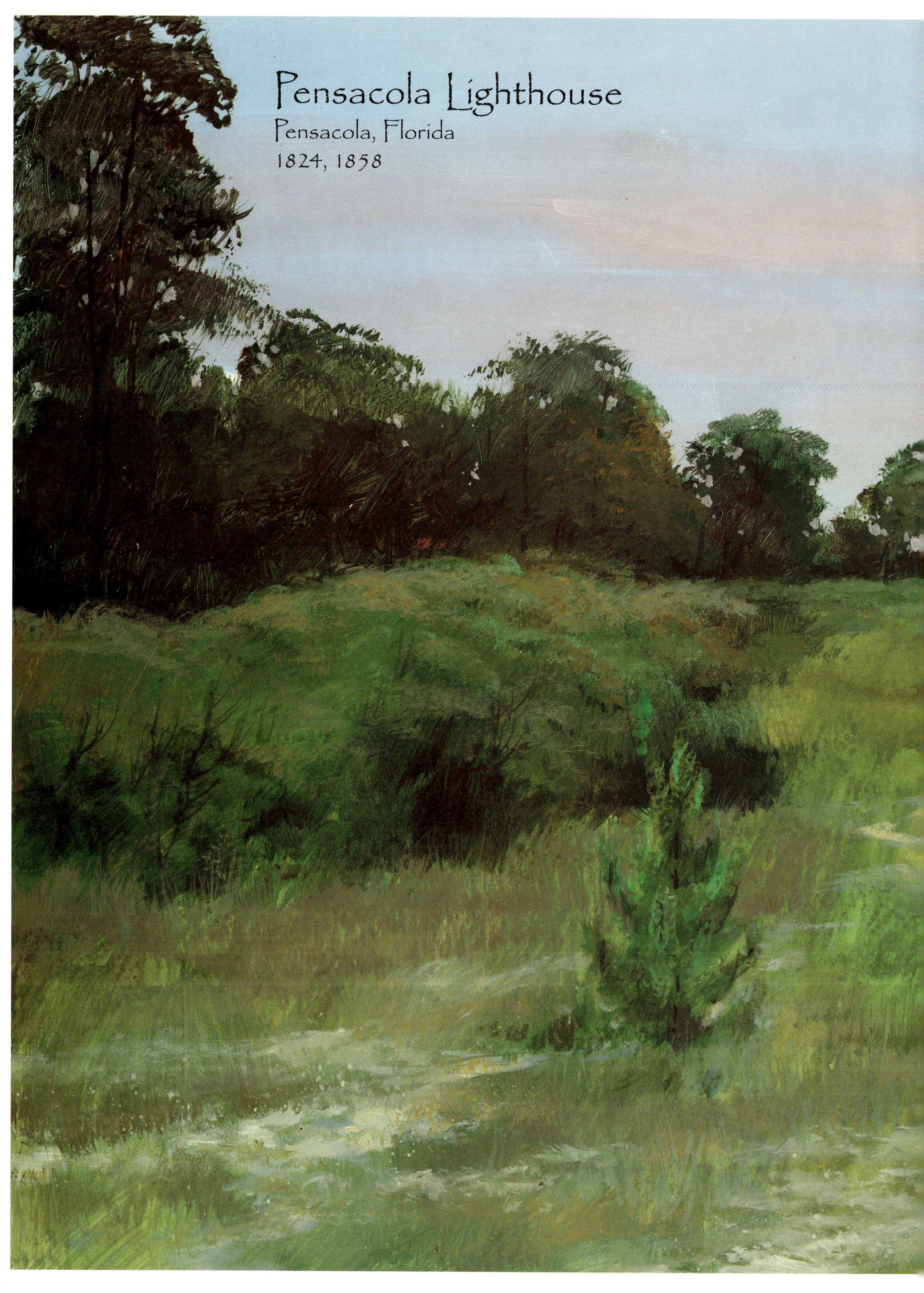

Pensacola Lighthouse

Pensacola, Florida

1824, 1858

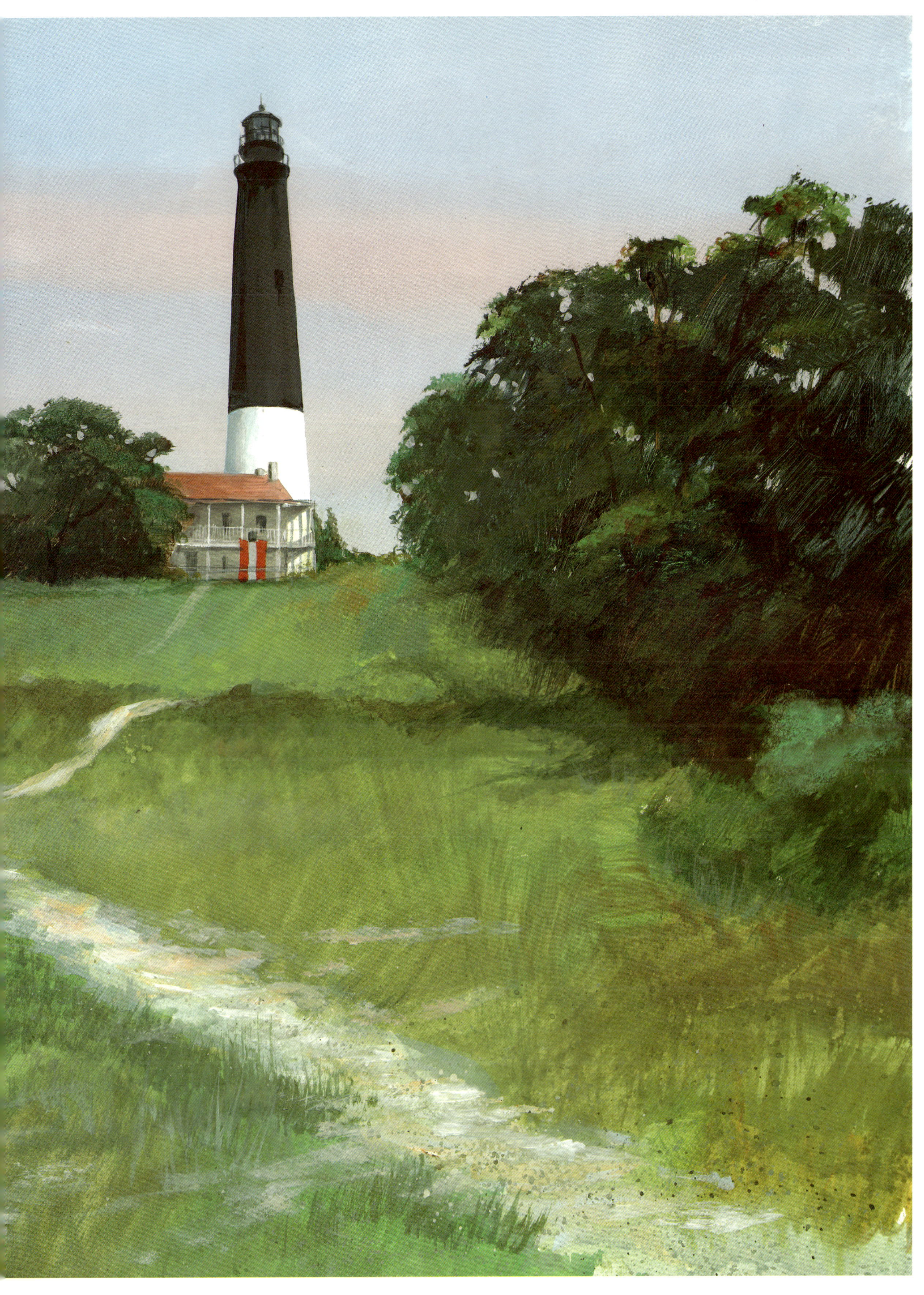

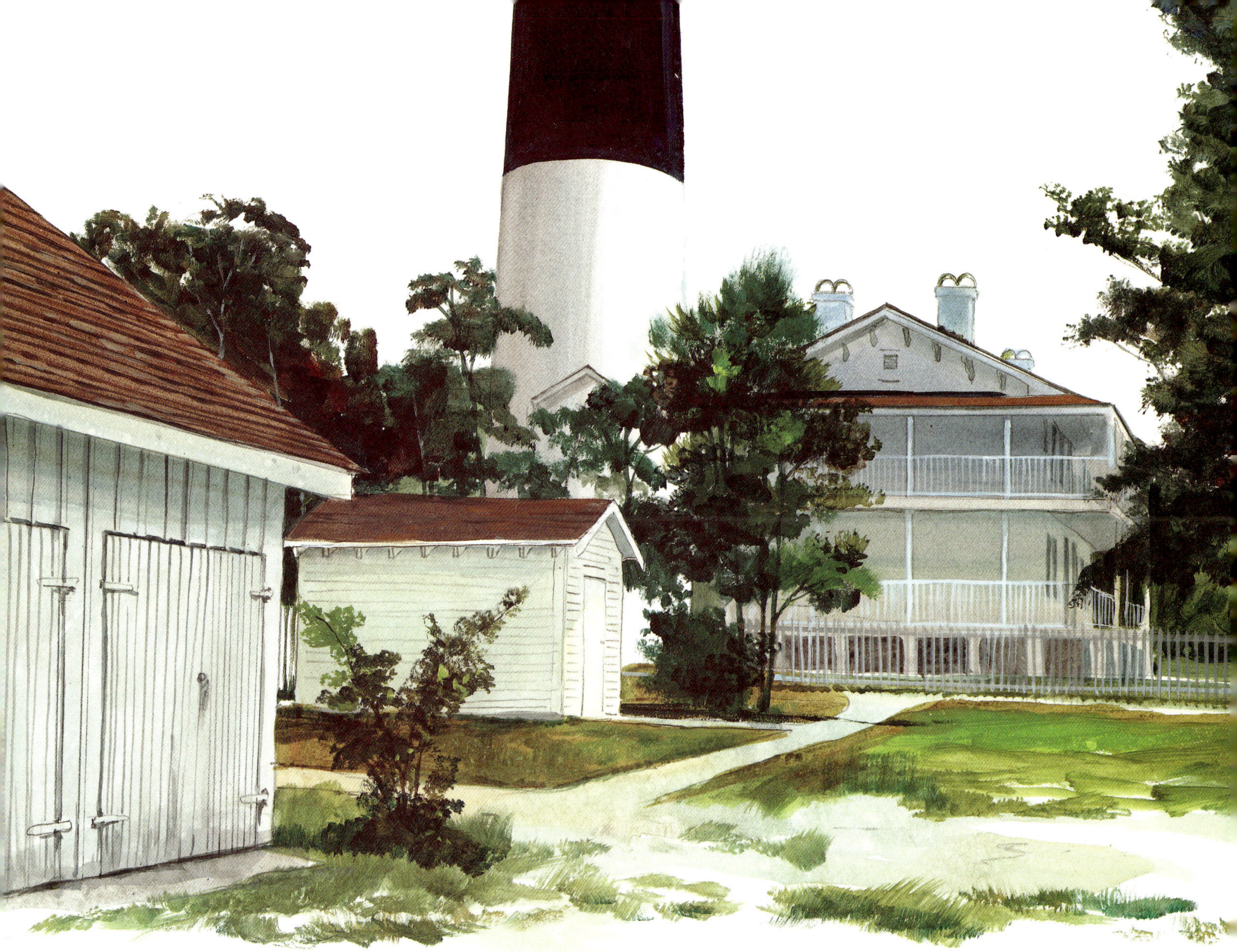

As Florida was beginning to grow, Pensacola, the state's second oldest city, began to emerge as a major port. However, it was hard to find for mariners who were not familiar with the area. Ships could pass right by without realizing the port was there. In 1823, only two years after Florida was purchased from Spain, a lightship arrived in Pensacola Bay, marking the entrance to the port. That same year Congress appropriated money for a lighthouse since lightships had very weak lights and were unreliable during storms. A year later, the new lighthouse was lit. It stood thirty feet tall, but since it sat on a bluff, the actual height was seventy-five feet above sea level. It was lit with ten individual whale oil lamps. Problems and criticism followed. Tall trees prevented mariners from seeing the lighthouse by day from many angles along the coast, and the lighthouse was so similar to the one near Mobile Point in Alabama that mariners sometimes confused the two. The clockwork mechanism that rotated the lights deteriorated to the point where the keepers would have to turn it by hand all night. The lens also proved to be insufficient because of inferior glass. The glass was eventually replaced, but overall the lighthouse remained inadequate.

Many keepers' houses were quite small, but this one at Pensacola looks more like a plantation home. I think this was about as good as it got for a lighthouse keeper back in the mid 1800s.

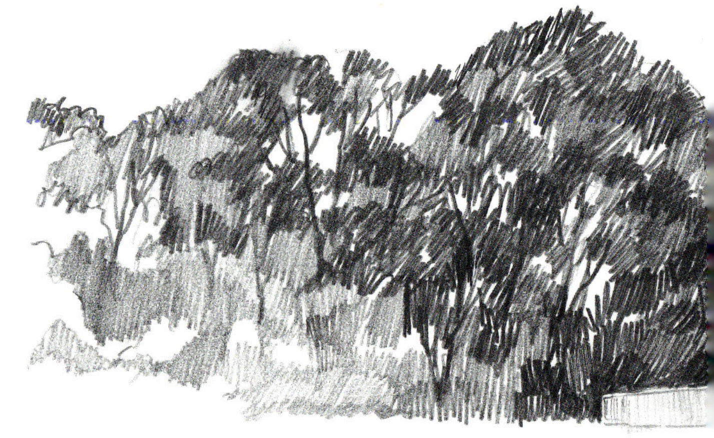

A taller lighthouse was needed. In 1851, Congress began looking into the problem, but it took eight years until a new one was built. It was almost 160 feet tall and had a first-order Fresnel lens, the largest of its type, which could be seen 22 miles away. This new lighthouse was located about half a mile west of the original light.

By 1861, the country was at war. Union soldiers stationed near the lighthouse at Fort Barrancas moved to Fort Pickens just across the bay for more security because they feared an attack by Confederate forces. Those fears became a reality when Confederate troops seized the lighthouse and other property on the mainland. The lighthouse proved to be an excellent outpost for spying on Union troops at Fort Pickens.

The light was extinguished and the lens dismantled and moved for safekeeping. An artillery battle between Union forces at Fort Pickens and Confederate forces on the mainland took place, but there was no damage to the lighthouse. On May 9, 1862, the Confederates evacuated Pensacola, destroying as much as they could before they left. Pensacola was once again in the hands of the Union. Fortunately, the lighthouse was left intact. A year later, the lighthouse was once again lit but with a smaller and dimmer fourth-order lens. It was decided to keep the more powerful first-order lens in safekeeping until the war ended.

By 1870, cracks had begun to appear in the tower. Repairs were made, along with renovations to the keeper's house, and the first-order lens was reinstalled. Once again the lighthouse was in fine condition, and for the next seventy years, everything remained about the same. Then in 1938, electricity was installed, and indoor plumbing replaced the outhouse and cistern. A year later, the Coast Guard was put in charge of lighthouses and of civilian employees of the U.S. Lighthouse Service. From that point on, all new keepers were required to enlist in the Coast Guard. Those civilians already working as keepers were given the choice to join the Coast Guard or to remain civilians. The keeper of the Pensacola light chose to keep his nonmilitary status. He remained keeper until 1953; in the mid 1960s, the lighthouse was automated.

The only railings on the spiral staircase are those attached to the brick walls—there are none towards the center—making this by far the most frightening spiral staircase in a Florida lighthouse. To add to this, there are no landings the entire way up. One slip towards the inside of the staircase, where the steps are only a few inches wide, could mean a long, disastrous fall.

When the Navy built an airstrip nearby, there was talk of tearing down the lighthouse, but historic interest kept it standing. Ads were placed in local newspapers, soliciting bids to tear down the keeper's house since it was no longer needed, but no bids were submitted, giving preservationists time to save it.

The lighthouse is open to the public only on special occasions, but you can visit the grounds anytime for a good look. The Naval Air Museum located a few blocks from the lighthouse rivals the Air and Space Museum in Washington, DC, for its quality. Admission is free—that alone is worth a trip to Pensacola. Fort Pickens, across the bay from the lighthouse, is a twenty-seven mile drive of about an hour by car and is also open to the public. Fort Barrancas is also near the lighthouse and is open to the public.

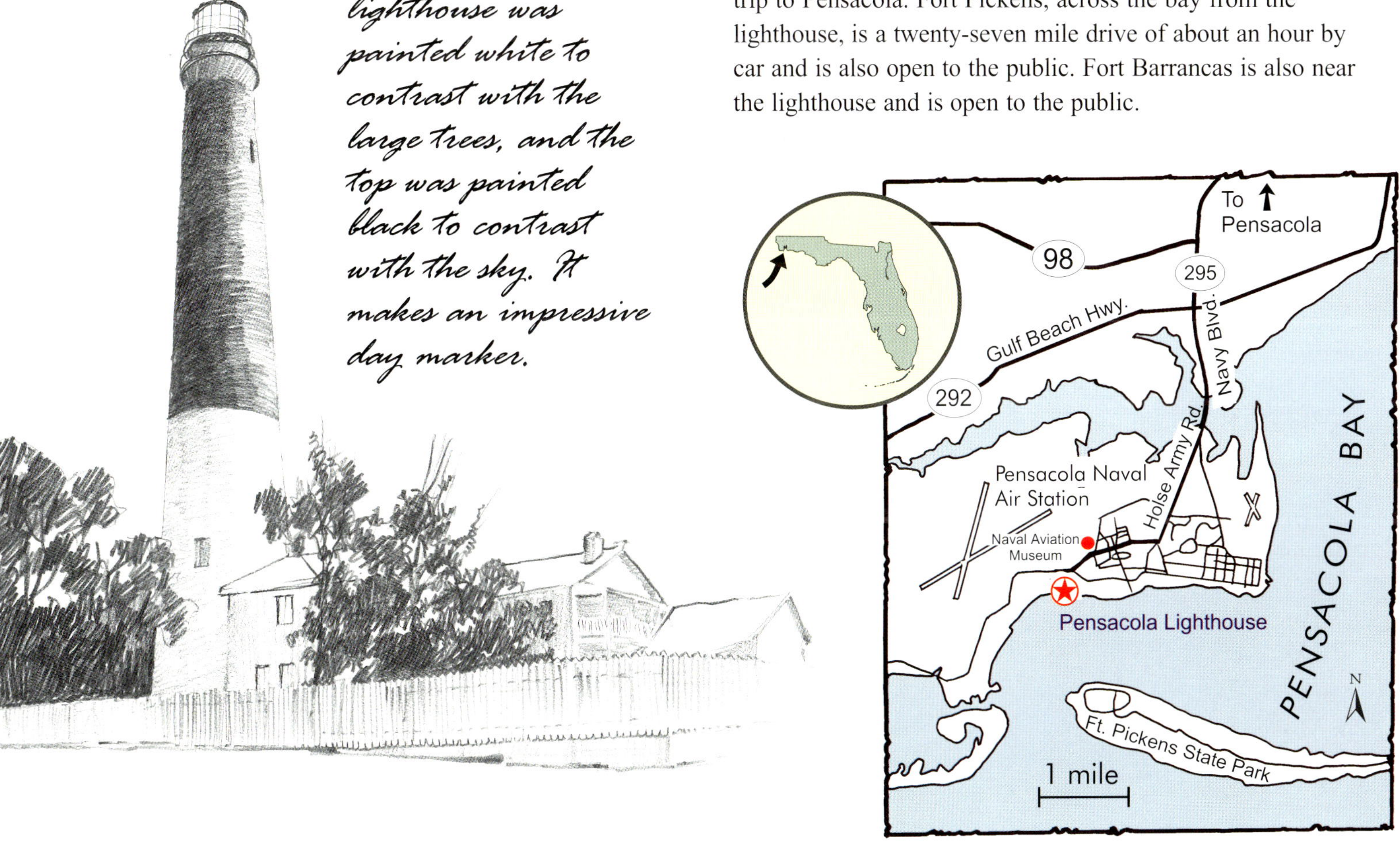

The base of the lighthouse was painted white to contrast with the large trees, and the top was painted black to contrast with the sky. It makes an impressive day marker.

Lighthouses that Aren't

There are thirty officially recognized lighthouses still in Florida. They were built by the government specifically to aid in the navigation of ships. The romantic nature of lighthouses and of the sea has great power to absorb one's imagination. Some "lighthouses" have been built just for the love of these structures and others for the tourist dollar.

The Faro Blanco Lighthouse was built in 1950. Located in Marathon in the Florida Keys, it was built specifically to serve as an attractive addition to the Faro Blanco Marine Resort. The upper two levels can be rented for overnight stays, and there's a gift shop at the base of the tower serving people on the many large yachts that visit the area.

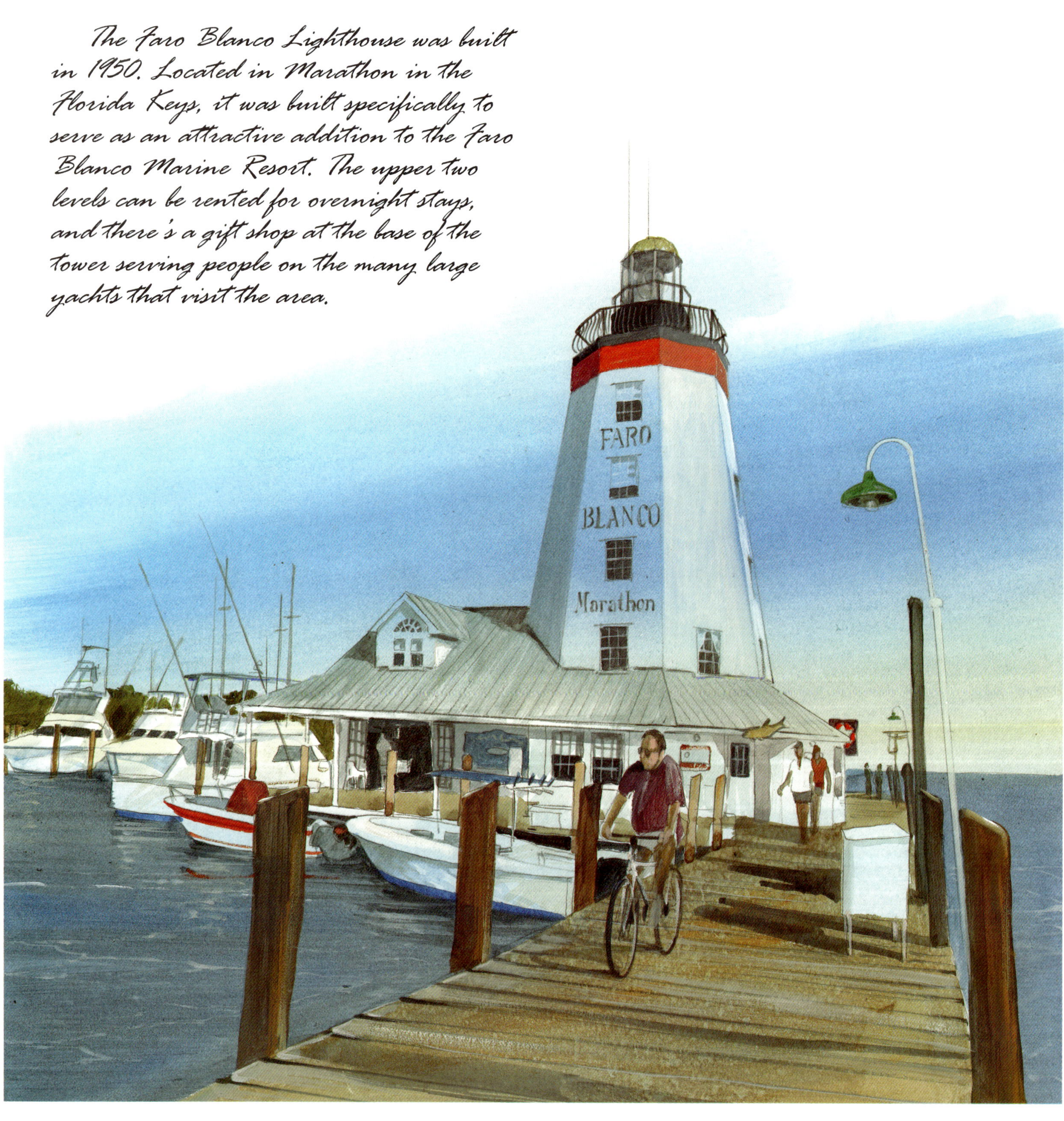

Boca Chita Key, at the southern end of Biscayne Bay, was a favorite playground for the very rich in the 1930s. At one time, industrialist Mark Honeywell privately owned the twenty-nine-acre island. Details are sketchy, but he supposedly built the lighthouse to guide his guests and himself to the island. There is a story that the Coast Guard ordered the light shut down shortly after it was lit because it was not registered or approved. However, nothing in the lantern room suggests that a light was ever installed there. The lighthouse is built of Miami oolitic limestone, which has been used as a building material since the mid-nineteenth century. The design of the lighthouse followed the style of the day. As the Art Deco period that was so popular in Miami ended, the Streamline Moderne style began to appear. Everything from railroad locomotives to toasters to the Boca Chita Lighthouse reflected the streamline look.

Today the island is part of the Biscayne National Park. Although the Visitors Center at Homestead has a glass-bottom boat and a snorkeling boat that take guests out to the reef, these boats don't go to Boca Chita. The only way to get there is with your own boat. It's nine miles offshore, and the bay can get rough, so use caution.

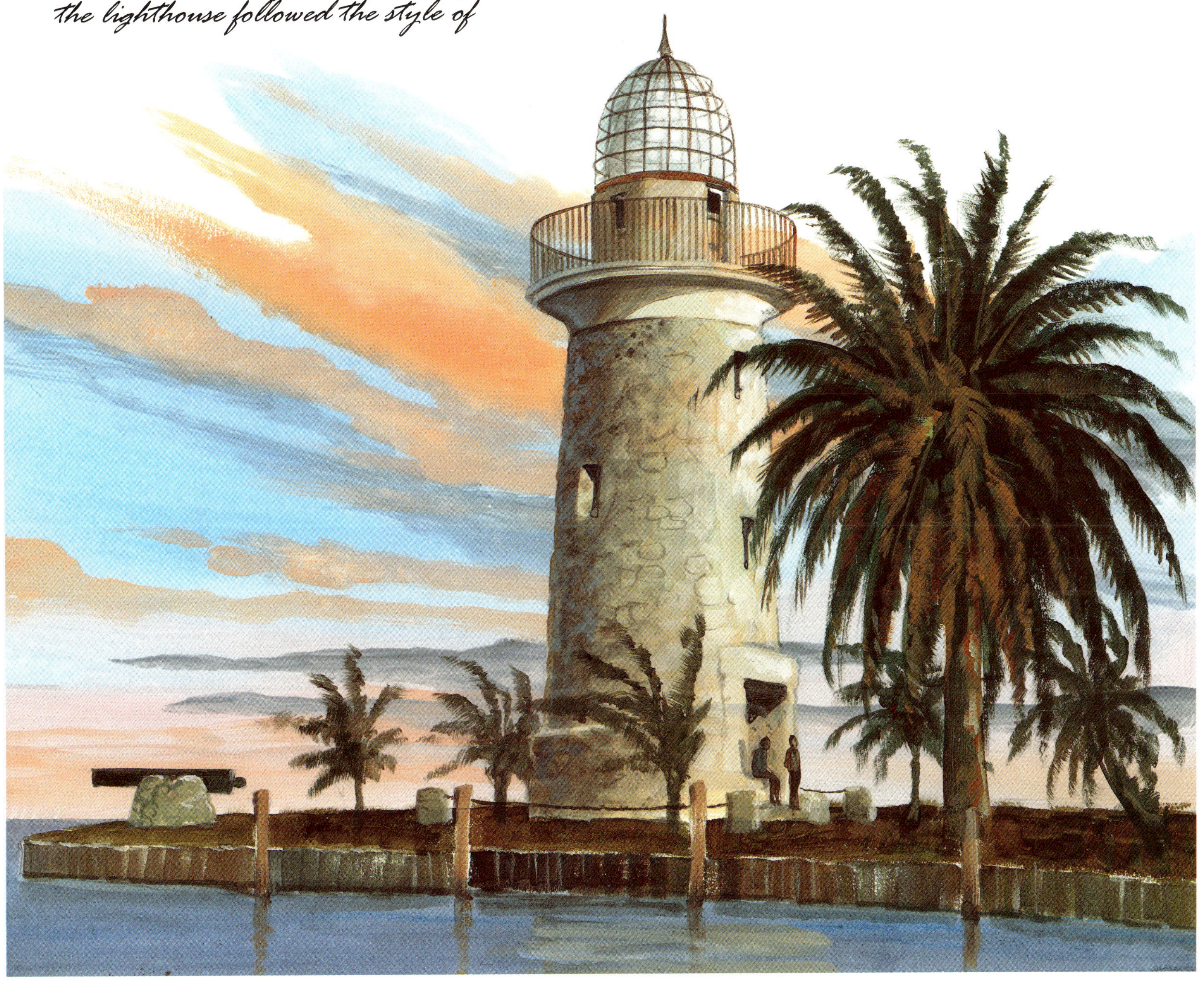

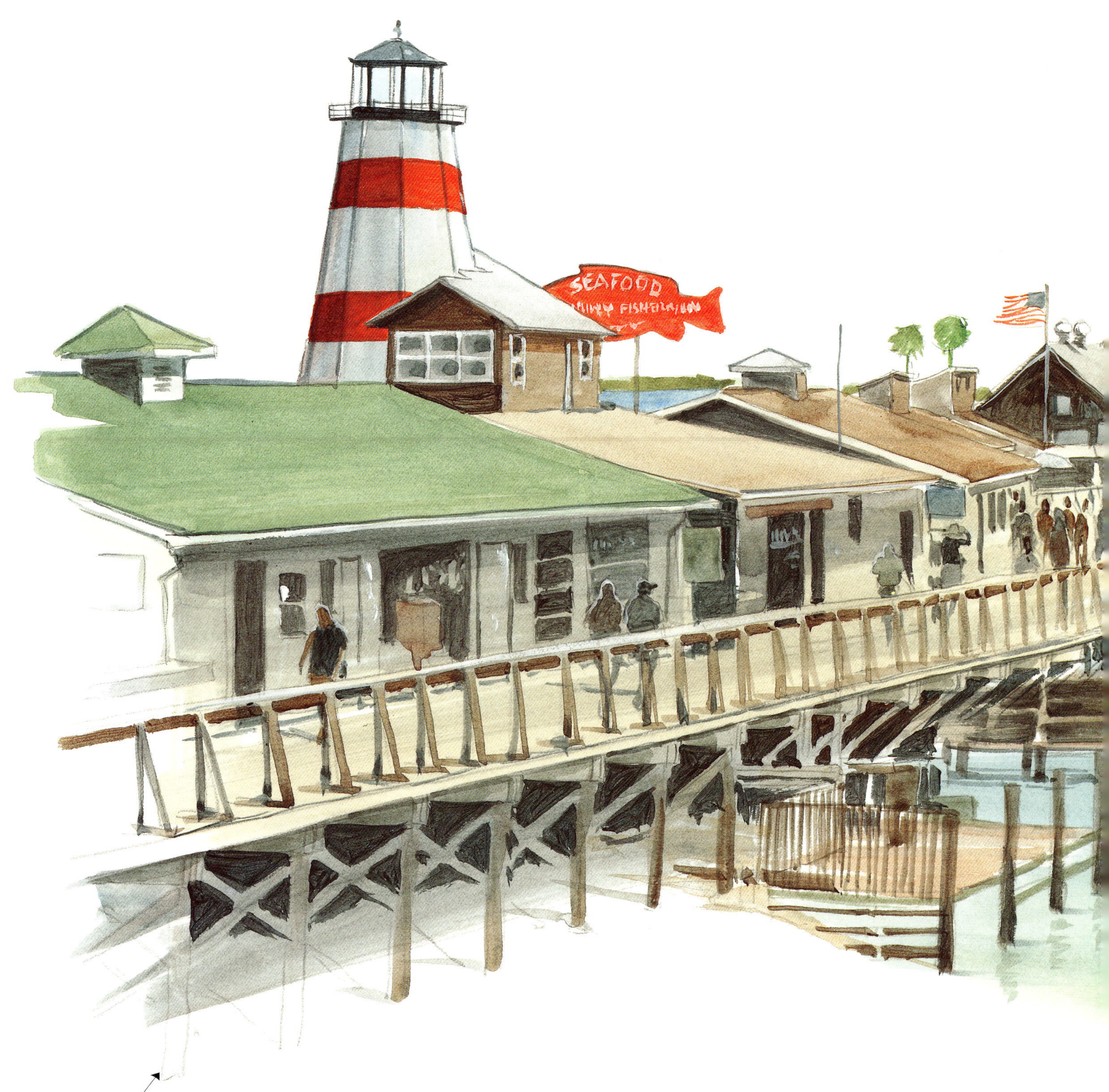

The rustic character at Johns Pass Village, near St. Petersburg Beach, makes for a fun afternoon's visit. With its boardwalk, seafood restaurants, and shops, even the pelicans have become friendly enough to sometimes touch. There is always something going on here. The lighthouse that acts as the centerpiece of this shopping area of more than forty shops is strictly decorative and adds charm to the place. Running a lighthouse was once a serious, life-or-death business. Unfortunately, lighthouses like this one sometimes make real lighthouses seem a decorative curiosity. In the end, though, even a decorative lighthouse serves some of the same purposes as a real lighthouse: commerce, free trade, and getting goods into the hands of the people who want them.

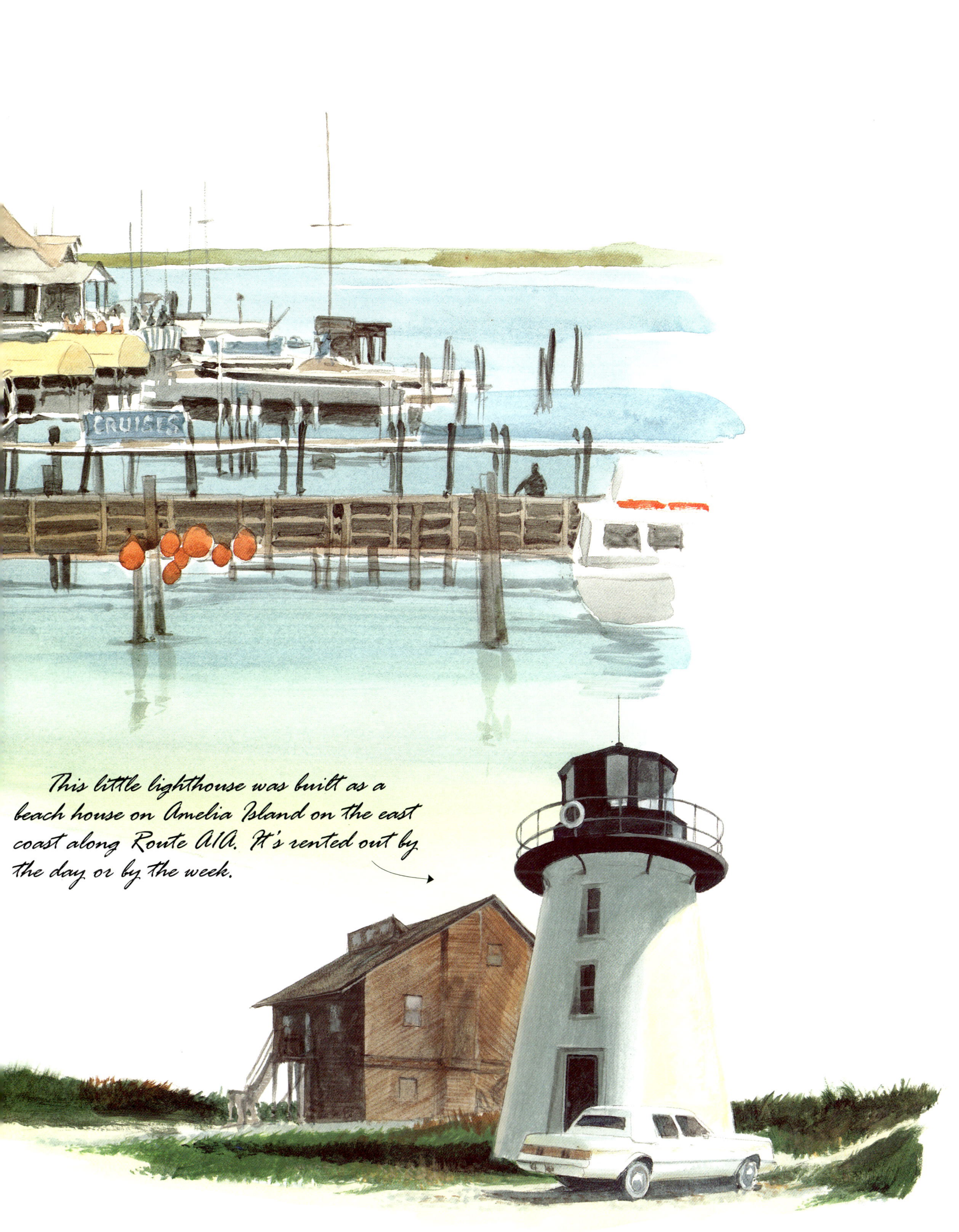

This little lighthouse was built as a beach house on Amelia Island on the east coast along Route A1A. It's rented out by the day or by the week.

Index

See table of contents for main lighthouse entries.

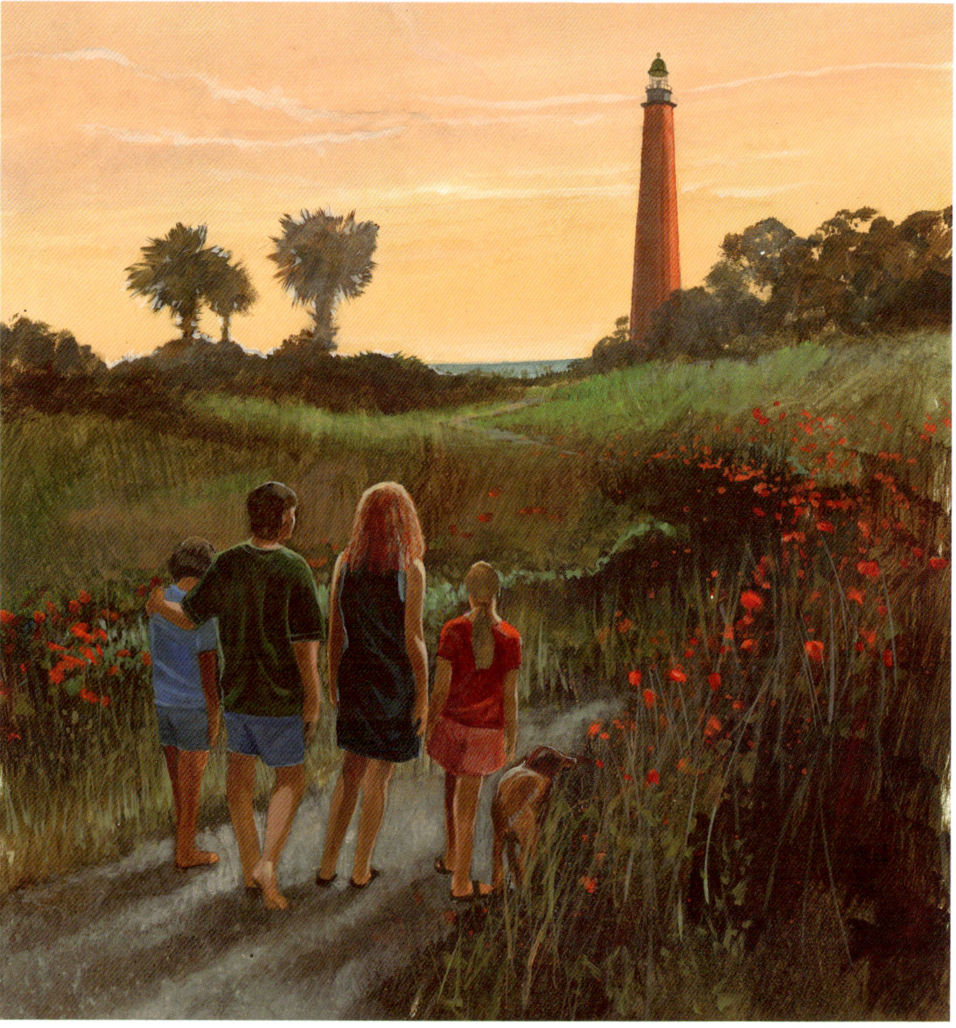

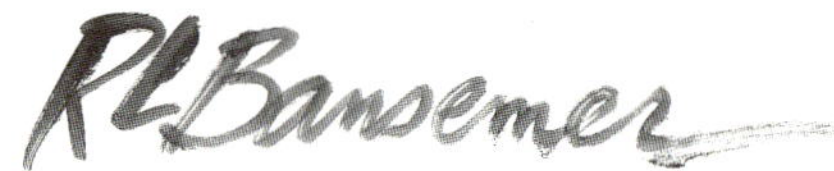

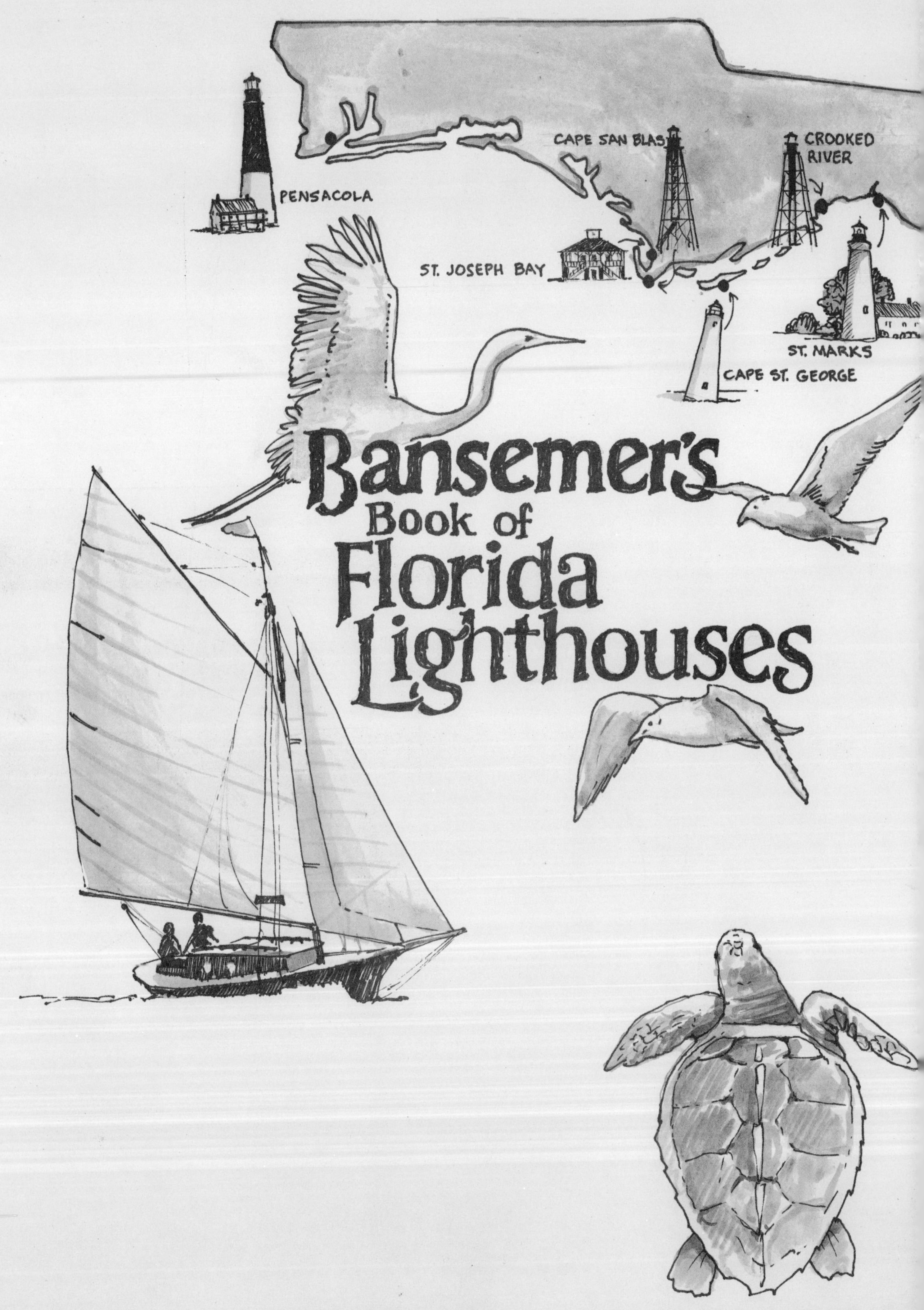
PENSACOLA
CAPE SAN BLAS
CROOKED RIVER
ST. JOSEPH BAY
ST. MARKS
CAPE ST. GEORGE
Bansemer's Book of Florida Lighthouses